Pirates of the High Cs

Opera Bootlegging in the 20th Century

Revised 2024 Performance-Linked Edition

Nicholas E. Limansky

YBK Publishers, Inc.
New York

Pirates of the High Cs: Opera Bootlegging in the 20th Century, Performance-Linked Edition

Copyright © 2024 by Nicholas E. Limansky

All rights reserved including
the right of reproduction
in whole or in part in any form.

YBK Publishers, Inc.
39 Crosby Street
New York, NY 10013
www.ybkpublishers.com

ISBN: 978-1-936411-70-2

Manufactured in the United States of America for distribution in North and South America or in the United Kingdom or Australia when distributed elsewhere.

For more information, visit
www.ybkpublishers.com

CONTENTS

Introduction   v

Pirates of the High Cs: Bootlegging Early Live Opera Recordings   1

The Two Pirate Queens: Magda Olivero (1910–2014); Leyla Gencer (1928–2008)   106

And Then There Was Leonie Rysanek, Our Runner-up Queen (1926–1998)   136

Maria Callas—Recommended Live Recordings (from Liner Notes E-Zine, December, 2023)   162

Eight Commercially Neglected (But Fortunately Pirated) U.S. Sopranos of the 1980s   178

What Does a Novice Opera Pirate Do When Not Pirating?   191

The Effect of the Richter CD-Roms and Looking Forward   201

Astrafiamante: Roberta Peters, Last Member of a Great Tradition   217

DEDICATION

This book is dedicated to all those who will discover the joys of collecting live operatic performances in the years to come.

But specifically to:
Dr. Dennis Keene, a fine musician and a lover of voices,
Russ Hornbeck, a comrade in arms, and
Ron Pollard, a great friend and an excellent teacher of piracy.

And, of course, to my wife, Gale Limansky, who had to give up much shelf space to indulge me in my collecting.

This book is also dedicated to the memory of:
Ralph Ferrandina and Ed Rosen.

INTRODUCTION

This book is about my love affair with live opera recordings and how I was involved with opera pirating in New York City during the 1970s and '80s. Although opera and concert pirating occurred mostly during just a forty-year period between 1960 and 2000, it is a history that should be preserved. It is a story that involved and affected many musicians at that time. Interest in contraband operatic recordings, which was great during that forty-year period, has faded in recent years due to the vast and simple availability of the great amounts of recorded music now easily found using the technological advances in the methods of recording and file retention. It is the right time to create a road map of that period and the recordings that were created during that time.

The term "opera piracy" is related to the term "bootlegging," a slang usage that came into being during the prohibition period in America in the 1920s and '30s. Bootlegging refers to rum-running, the illegal business of smuggling and transporting alcoholic beverages that was then forbidden by law.

Given an interest in classical music recordings one soon becomes familiar with the names of commercial opera recordings produced on LP or CD by such companies as Decca (London), Philips, DGG, BMG (RCA), and EMI (Angel). During the period between 1960 and 2000 another important line of opera recordings sprang up, produced on such lesser-known labels as Penzance, BJR, MRF, FWR, UORC, Melodram, Orfeo, MYTO, Standing Room Only, Bella Voce, Gala, and Golden Age of Opera.

Ironically, the income from commercial *popular* music recordings helps fund the efforts of the classical divisions of these mega companies. Similarly, compared to popular music bootlegging, the illegal pirating of operatic performances was a minor business.

The first instances of live opera pirating occurred during the early twentieth century at the Metropolitan Opera House in New York City. Lionel Mapleson, the then-librarian of the opera company, decided to make amateur cylinder recordings of stage performances. During 1901 through 1903, he placed recording equipment in the flies and the prompter's box. At the time this was considered neither bootlegging nor piracy because copyright laws did not pertain to live performances.

The first widespread live-performance pirating appeared almost concurrently with the availability of commercial LP recordings.

> The first real bootleg era was the 1950s and 1960s when jazz aficionados recorded live performances by many of the jazz greats. These were freely on sale in Greenwich Village but were ignored by the industry who considered them too esoteric to be profitable. The first rock bootleg was issued in 1969...
>
> (*Bootlegging: Romanticism and Copyright in the Music Industry*, page 114, Lee Marshall)

Popular music bootlegging is a huge business. Opera pirating, although not inconsequential, produces nowhere near the revenue of its popular music sister because it reaches a much smaller audience. Pirating, as it occurred in its earliest form, has been mitigated recently as there are now royalty agreements among the various producers and artists governing the very wide and freely available distribution that is provided by such organizations as Spotify, Pandora, and Apple.

The main difference between popular and classical music pirating is that to legitimize the release of pirated popular music one would need the legal permission of averagely four to ten people (the performing musicians). For opera and symphonic work, one needs legal permission (or labor union release) not only from each of the soloists and the conductor, but also the entire chorus, and all of the orchestra members as well.

Opera pirating has many fans and collectors, some of whom become obsessive in their collecting. Producing a pirated operatic recording becomes expensive only when the producer decides to include a complete libretto, notes on the opera, or photo booklets. This is why most pirate releases are little more than unaccompanied discs enclosed in paper or cardboard sleeves. The less expensive the recording, the more an avid collector will collect.

Things are considerably different now from when I first discovered live opera recording in the late 1960s. Operatic pirating originally referred to performances that had been taped in-house rather than being taped from radio broadcasts. Since the 1970s, American copyright law has allowed taping of radio broadcasts for personal use. However, profit from the sale of such broadcast recordings is not legal. I feel it is important to examine the growth and popularity of this genre of recording that occurred in the 1970s and '80s when it was of great importance to collectors and, especially, to musicians as well.

In the 1960s and '70s commercial recordings were purchased in record stores found in every city and town. Pirate recordings were bought from private sellers, mailing lists, or a few stores in bigger cities that were willing to carry contraband in their back rooms or under the counter. The Internet has gradually changed the landscape of collecting pirate recordings. Blogs, MP3 uploads, and YouTube make collecting live performances much simpler and the number of performances available is vast. Although web sites that offer live opera performances constantly surface and quickly disappear, replacements pop up with regularity. By the time this book is published many of the Internet sites mentioned will already be gone and replaced. I find it fascinating (and equally rewarding, amusing, and annoying) that many of my most treasured pirated opera performances that I searched tirelessly to find in the 1970s are now easily heard on YouTube.

During the forty year hey-day of amateur operatic piracy, pirate recordings were viewed by most singers as both an important form of publicity as well as a possible means to further one's career. Even though they gained no income, most singers were quite willing to look aside when it came to the illegal distribution of their work. One exception was soprano Jessye Norman who filed a lawsuit against a pirater in the 1980s. (I believe it was Mr. Tape.) Despite the legality issue, it is not surprising that during the mid 1980s it was common practice for music agents to send pirated live performance tapes of their singer-clients to opera companies to help secure a contract. Large-scale opera piracy on CDs continued until about 2013.

While this book is a somewhat hodge-podge collection of material that is heavily autobiographical, it also seeks to be a solid work that chronicles the allure and drawbacks of opera piracy, its musical and artistic importance, its questionable ethics, and its historical impact on the world of opera during that era. It describes many recordings and the vocal attributes (and detractions) of numerous famed singers. Parts of it come from articles I've written that have appeared on my website, divalegacy.com, and the e-zine, *parterre box*.

Most of this book is about my own small corner in the world of opera piracy in New York City; a chronicle of my experiences working with an opera pirate in the 1980s and my own pirating exploits that, ironically, coincided with my work as a professional chorister and soloist in New York City. It is about my naiveté, as well as both good and bad decisions made during that time. It is about the gradual growth of my obsession with live opera performances and the reasoning underlying my collecting and my own pirating.

[*Publisher Note:* First published in 2020, this revised edition contains discussions from that time and earlier. Where updating to 2024, or adding information that has occurred since 2020 is useful, it has simply been changed or added. When further clarification is useful, or called for, you will find an author's note in square brackets to denote the current information.]

When this book was written, YouTube was just beginning to become known as a serious audio and video repository of operatic music and, as a part of the overall, an archive of historical operatic singers. YouTube has grown to become a remarkably diverse hub for some of the most important operatic performances of the past and present century.

Performances are being added to YouTube daily. An example of this is the surprising and unusual addition to the YouTube archives in February, 2024 of a Köln radio broadcast of the English soprano, Gwen Catley singing the aria, "Steal Me Sweet Thief" from Menotti's *The Old Maid and the Thief*. The work was originally a radio opera that Menotti revised into a work suitable for stage production (1941). This rare, exquisite performance is a true treasure not only of Gwen Catley's legacy, but also of the annals of opera. It stands proudly next to the excellent recordings by Judith Blegen (1970) and Dawn Upshaw (1990). In this simple aria, Menotti captures the passionate yearning of love and Gwen Catley's poingnant, sadly sweet delivery haunts one long after it is over. I am grateful to "Songbirdwatcher" for uploading this performance.

Menotti–Steal Me Sweet Thief (*The Old Maid and the Thief*) —Köln, 1954
https://www.youtube.com/watch?v=S2KUrQhj0Tw

Many of the links are to static pages, meaning that they are audio-only pages, while there are more and more video clips, and even full operas, being added that can be both heard and seen. This revised edition, an updated and expanded, as well as, electronic edition of the first edition that was available in print only, is an exciting upgrade. The reader can now hear, and sometimes see and hear, what the text discusses. This edition includes links to entries in YouTube that are available to the opera fan/reader/listener that you can simply click and they will appear on your screen as you read on in the book. Pertinent links are placed immediately adjacent to their discussion. The links can be used on any electronic device that will enable you to see and hear the performances discussed by the author. The use of the links is only for informative and educational purposes.

Nicholas E. Limansky
May, 2024

To the Performance-Linked Print Edition Reader:

We can quickly and easily get you set up to listen to and view the performances found on the Internet links printed in this book.

Simply send an email to ybkpublishers@gmail.com, inserting the code OPERA PIRATES into the subject line. We will send you a PDF by return email to be put onto any of your smart devices such as the MacBook, your PC computer (desktop or laptop), Fire tablet, Kindles that support Internet connection with audio or video, or any other type of smart"device onto which PDFs can be loaded, *including your smartphone*!

You should then be able to simply double-click your smart device on the PDF link that will be attached to the email we send to you.

The PDF contains live links that, when clicked, will connect you to the Internet to let you listen to and see the subject material that is being discussed in the book.

The Internet is flexible and fluid, changing from moment to moment. It is inevitable that sometimes links will get broken—that, occasionally, a link will not open when it is clicked on. Because these links are not created by us, they can be withdrawn by their creators at any time. We will comb the links from time to time to keep them up to date by deleting or replacing broken links. If you would like to report a broken link, please tell us the final several characters (six or eight, say) of the broken link in an email to ybkpublishers@gmail.com and we will see to its quick repair.

There will be occasions when clicking on a link fails to make the connection. In such cases, try copying the link to your clipboard and pasting it into the browser.

PIRATES OF THE HIGH CS
BOOTLEGGING EARLY
LIVE OPERA RECORDINGS

Parallel to the growth of the 78 r.p.m. disk were the beginnings of recording live performances. The first live recordings were made at the Metropolitan Opera House in New York City by Lionel Mapleson (1865–1937). Mapleson was the librarian at the opera house and making these recordings was his hobby. Although he never sold his recordings nor made any profit from them, in many circles he is still referred to as the "Father of Bootlegging." Between 1900 and 1903 he made more than one hundred cylinders. These one-to two-minute disks were recorded with a Bettini cylinder recorder and reproducer. Primitive amateur recordings, they were recorded from the prompter's box on the stage, or forty feet up in the flies of the Met. Because of the combination of the antiquated recording process and the wearing down of the grooves from repeated hearings, most Mapleson cylinders are now difficult to listen to. They are, however, quite informative about the size of voices and the tempi taken during performances during that era. So why did making these recordings end in 1903? One belief is that it was a combination of accidents involving recording apparatus falling to the stage and a planned expansion of the stage for upcoming performances of *Parsifal* in the summer of 1903.

The making of the Mapelson cylinders was very casual. Mapleson would set up his recording mechanism and, during a performance, insert a blank cylinder to make recordings while the performance was taking place. It may seem incredible to us today, given all our orchestral, vocal, and stage-worker unions, but at that time there were no objections to his doing this. No one anticipated the commercial possibilities that could arise from such an endeavor. Luckily for us today, many of the singers that Mapleson caught mid-song are singers who recorded little or not at all—Jean and Edouard De Reszke, Milka Ternina, Lillian Nordica, Albert Alvarez, as well as such popular singers as Dame Nellie Melba, Emma Calvé, Johanna Gadski, Emma Eames, Louise Homer, Marcel Journet, Pol Plançon, and many others. Of course, because the discs were so short they would often cut off before the end of an aria or a scene—truly fragments.

The pirating of commercial recordings, was, however, always an issue:

> Record piracy—the unauthorized copying and selling of sound recordings—is a problem as old as the recording industry itself. Charges of cylinder piracy first surfaced in the early 1890s and became increasingly common as the decade progressed. Legal recourse was limited; sound recordings were not protected under copyright law at the time, and would not be for many more decades.
>
> Pirating the early wax cylinders was simplicity in itself, requiring only a couple of phonographs, an inexpensive recording head, a cylinder to copy, and some blanks upon which to copy it. Disc records were not immune to piracy, either, although the process was more complicated. The earliest discs sold for use with the new Zonophone machines used masters that were electroplated from Berliner pressings, with the Berliner name and patent notice buffed out.

(Allan Sutton, Black Swan Carusos and Other Pirate Tales, 1898–1951, Mainspring, 12/1/17)

While there were no copyright laws at the time governing such recordings, in a few years it would become an issue. In 1908 the Supreme Court ruled (in White-Smith Music Publishing Co. v. Apollo Co.) that mechanical reproduction of sound recordings, both by humans like Mapleson and player piano recordings, could not be copyrighted. This led to the Copyright Act of 1909.

Similar in circumstance to the Mapleson cylinders, but having better sound, were the disks recorded by Hermann May at the Vienna Staatsoper from 1933 to 1943. The main difference was that most of the singers captured by May made commercial recordings at the time with very good sound. But, like Mapleson's, most of May's disks end mid-phrase and before climaxes. Such recordings are suitable only as reference material for historians and the curious, because they are so short.

In the 1990s, Koch Schwann released 24 two-CD volumes of the Vienna discs, an important reference. Despite the frustrating brevity of many of the selections, there are some surprises—such as performances conducted by Richard Strauss and others in repertoire that one might not expect to be represented. Koch Schwann presented these volumes well on CD with photographs of the participants, good biographical information, and technical background material.

With the advent of electrical recording in mid-1925, live "from the stage" documentation became a more interesting reality. One of the first opera companies to take commercial advantage of this was London's Royal Opera House at Covent Garden in a joint venture with HMV. During the spring and summer of 1926 and 1928, HMV recorded excerpts from various performances directly from that famous stage. These included excerpts from a May 31, 1926 performance of Boito's *Mefistofele* with Feodor Chaliapin. Nine sides were recorded (four were published). There was also *La bohème* with Margaret Sheridan and Angelo Minghetti. (Nine sides were recorded, but none were issued on 78 rpm. The finales of acts II and IV—totaling about eight minutes—were issued on EMI RLS 742.)

Another important event recorded that year was an oddity—the formal *Farewell Concert of Dame Nellie Melba* on June 9, 1926.

Next were ten sides from an *Otello* with the famous tenor Giovanni Zenatello. Only seven survive, totalling 30 minutes. Pearl CD released them on CD (Pearl GEM0203).

Verdi—*Otello* (exc)—London, June 17, 1926
https://www.youtube.com/watch?v=bH0q7ZS6reM

Two years later Covent Garden recorded major excerpts from Gounod's *Faust* with Joseph Hislop and Feodor Chaliapin (released on Pearl GEM0203), as well as Mussorgsky's *Boris Godunov,* also with the bass, Feodor Chaliapin. These last excerpts remain, arguably, the most famous of the early live recordings.

Mussorgsky—*Boris Godunov* (exc)—London, July 3, 1928
https://www.youtube.com/watch?v=AF63wzJ80fI&t=3800s

Aside from Chaliapin's 1928 *Boris Godunov* excerpts, the Melba Farewell is perhaps the most important of all of the Covent Garden recordings. These eleven disks provide an entirely different perspective on Melba's voice especially when compared to her earlier studio recordings which do little to explain why she was so renowned and revered. From the studio acoustic recordings, one gets the impression of a remarkable technician, but an often inelegant, staid artist of little phrase tapering or creative subtlety. Ironically, along with her contemporary, Enrico Caruso, Melba was one of the most important figures in modern operatic history. It was these two singers' immense popularity and the subsequent selling of their recordings that helped to solidify the recording process as a serious medium for the making (and preservation) of operatic music and not merely as a toy for the rich. For that reason, it is all the more frustrating to listen to Nellie Melba's commercial legacy. Because of the "new" electric recording process, these Covent Garden discs were able to provide better glimpses into the real quality of her voice and the reasons for her immense popularity; primarily, it was the intrinsic timbre of her instrument. No one else had the Melba "sound." Despite that she was sixty-five years old (and occasionally short-breathed), a modern-day listener gets to experience the distinctive quality of her voice: frontally placed, pure and yet brilliant, with an exquisite, silvery, fiery shimmer -especially in the upper middle register. Anyone wanting to understand Melba's appeal has only to hear the "Donde lieta" (from *La bohème*) during her 1926 farewell. (All eleven selections were released on Naxos CD# 8.110780.)

Puccini—Donde lieta (*La bohème*)—Melba Farewell Concert -London, June 9, 1926
https://www.youtube.com/watch?v=735ENkIrPMI

HMV and Covent Garden did not record again until 1936, when some Verdi and Wagner were recorded. Covent Garden continued sporadically to record through May of 1939. During the Second World War, however, the opera house closed; not reopening until 1947.

This type of live recording differs however from what most people think of when they hear the word "live," "pirate," or "bootleg." Those early live recordings from Covent Garden were recorded professionally by commercial recording companies sanctioned by the artists, and done in agreement with the musicians and the opera house. Ironically, by opening this door, commercial record companies spawned the work of the recording pirates who, throughout the decades, have existed side by side.

There has been much litigation against pirating. Famous was the case of The Metropolitan Opera against Wagner-Nichols. This suit concerned the illegal taping of broadcast performances sent over the American Broadcasting Company radio stations that were under exclusive contract with Columbia. During the 1949–1950 season, Wagner-Nichols produced eighteen LPs of these broadcasts in five months. The Metropolitan Opera took them to court to prevent further releases.

Across the genre divide there was the famous case against Joseph Krug who was tried in federal court in 1954 for taping and releasing radio performances of bandleader Glenn Miller. Krug was required to pay royalties to Miller's widow and publisher.

Things began to change around July, 1969.

> This was when a new record album by folk-rock musician, Bob Dylan appeared in stores. Called *Great White Wonder*, it was a two-record collection of previously unreleased Dylan recordings from 1961, 1967 and 1969. The album signaled a new trend in the recording industry, but neither Dylan nor his exclusive record company Columbia, had a hand in its release or reaped any of its undoubtedly considerable profits…"*Great White Wonder* is the first documented bootleg of the rock era…(it) showed that it was possible, even desirable, for music fans to include private tapes and concerts into their own collection and, thus, in their assessment of an artist's work." (*Strange Fixation: Bootleg Sound Recordings Enjoy the Benefits of Improved Technology*, David Schwartz, Indiana University School of Law, Federal Communications Law Journal: Vol, 47, Issue 3, Article 6, 1995)

The Amendment of the Copyright Law

The pirating of performances is a big business, although when viewed comparatively with the revenue of such mega labels as SONY, EMI, and others, it may seem less so. That said, the copyrighting of artistic works is serious. Changes in the law had a profound effect on pirating. Embodying this change was the McClellan bill. It was intended as

> ...an anti-piracy measure, with only limited revelance to the bootleggers.
> Nothing in Public Law 93-140 prohibited home recording from broadcasts, tapes or records as long as the recording was used privately, with no intention of capitalizing commercially from it. Indeed, 'performance piracy' and 'personal piracy' were not even specifically addressed in the Amendment. (*Bootlegs, The Rise and Fall of the Secret Recording Industry*, Clinton Heylin, Omnibus Press, London, 2010)

Even more complicated were the many amendments to the copyright act that happened over the ensuing decades:

> By extending copyright protection to sound recordings, the federal government greatly preempted state and equitable rights in the area. Following the first federal protection in 1972, remedies for copyright infringement of sound recordings fixed after January 1, 1978, now lie exclusively in the federal courts provided those infringements fall within the scope of 17 U.S.C. § 106. (*Strange Fixation: Bootleg Sound Recordings Enjoy the Benefits of Improved Technology*, David Schwartz, Indiana University School of Law, Federal Communications Law Journal: Vol, 47, Issue 3, Article 6, 1995)

Although sound recordings were eventually protected in 1976, it does not explain the lack of protection for pre-1972 recordings.

The act continued to be amended throughout the 1990s and continues to alter as technology changes. Schwartz also states that, at that time, 1995, the professional bootlegging center of the world was in Western Europe.

For a more comprehensive look at the complicated issues of copyright laws and their infringement, read Bootlegs, The Rise and Fall of the Secret Recording Industry, by Clinton Heylin, Omnibus Press, 2010.

The Metropolitan Opera Broadcast as a Serious Endeavor

Begun in 1931, the network-sponsored Metropolitan Opera Saturday matinee broadcasts remain the longest-running, continuous classical music program in radio history. Its actual beginnings, however, stretch even farther back.

The first broadcast from the Metropolitan Opera happened in 1910 when radio pioneer, Lee DeForest transmitted (only partially successfully) acts II and III of *Tosca* on January 12, 1910, and selections from Pagliacci with Enrico Caruso on January 13, 1910. The signal reached as far as Newark, New Jersey.

It wasn't until Friday, December 25, 1931 that a complete operatic performance was relayed—Humperdinck's Hansel und Gretel. This was to begin a new series of broadcasts created to help grow the Metropolitan Opera audience during the great depression. Generally, only acts from operas were offered. Hänsel und Gretel and Das Rheingold (early in 1932) were the only operas presented in their entirety. The 1933–34 season signaled the beginning of the broadcasts of complete Metropolitan Opera performances. Although there were a few exceptions, broadcasts settled into the Saturday matinee spot. (One exception was the opening night of the "new" Met at Lincoln Center, that featured a broadcast of Samuel Barber's *Antony and Cleopatra* on Friday evening, September 16, 1966.)

Originally, the broadcasts were heard on NBC and became a part of its Blue Network. In 1944 the series was taken over by the Blue Network's successor, ABC, until 1958. From 1958 until 1960 it was broadcast on CBS

With the decline in network radio due to the surging popularity of television, the Metropolitan Opera created its own independent radio network in 1960. It is now heard internationally, relayed over 300 stations in the United States and in 42 countries on five continents. The broadcasts can also be listened to via streaming audio on the Internet.

As it turned out, 1940 was a turning point in the broadcasting of Metropolitan Opera performances. That was the year that Texaco undertook sponsorship of the matinee broadcasts, It was a partnership that would last 64 years (until 2004). In addition, in 1977, PBS (Public Broadcasting Service) began to air a series of telecasts viewed by millions of people during each event. Although they were initially simulcast live, soon most telecasts were taped in the theatre, in front of audiences, but aired at a later date. In 2006, the Met introduced a program called "Metropolitan Opera: Live in HD" which introduced high-definition performances broadcast into movie theatres throughout the world.

It was during the 1940s that the broadcast season settled into twenty-week groups of broadcasts. During its eighty years of Metropolitan Opera broadcast history there have been surprisingly few human hosts. The host is an important and integral part of the listener's experience. They are the "eyes" for the listening public. The actual responsibility is quite simple. He or she introduces the opera that will be sung that afternoon and its cast; they provide background information on the composition and performing tradition, as well as their personal observations about the music and the singers. Initially this commentary was treated casually, almost as if one were sitting with friends in a living room. By the 1940s, however, the format became more formalized. Fewer personal observations were allowed and a style of presentation appeared. In 2006, a commentator joined the announcer.

Milton Cross presided over these broadcasts beginning with the 1931 inaugural matinee broadcast until his death in 1975 (forty-three seasons). Peter Allen took over that year until the 2003–2004 season (twenty-nine years). Margaret Juntwait led the program from 2004 until her untimely death at the age of fifty-eight in 2015 (ten years). Since the 2015–2016 season, Mary Jo Heath has been its host.

The Metropolitan Opera broadcasts (and other recorded in-house performances) are an outstandingly rich heritage. They occupy a special, separate, section in my personal library—a library within a library. Especially prized are the recordings that contain original broadcast commentary by Milton Cross (1897–1975) and/or original intermission features. The performances that exist with his commentary are some of the most evocative of all surviving Metropolitan Opera broadcasts. For generations of listeners he truly was "Mr. Opera."

> His distinctive voice conveyed the excitement of live performances 'from the stage of the Metropolitan Opera House in New York City' for generations of radio listeners. Initially, he broadcast

from a seat in Box 44 at the old Metropolitan Opera House at Broadway and 40th Street. In 1966, he introduced the radio audience to the Met's new home at Lincoln Center as he hosted a special broadcast of the opening night performance from a modern radio booth in the new house. (*Wikipedia*)

Milton Cross was at first a tenor at the Westinghouse studio of WJZ, a major New York City broadcasting station at that time. He then branched out into announcing. When WJZ was absorbed by the National Broadcasting Company in 1926, he continued among their roster of announcers.

His Metropolitan assignment was the logical outcome of Cross's broadcasts of the Chicago Opera. (Ibid)

For me, nostalgic appeal factors heavily into my favoring of such documents. I remember listening to Milton Cross (and that distinctive voice) during many Saturday afternoons in my youth. Hearing his voice again after so many years has great nostalgic appeal. Cross was a colorful character. His careful, distinct, pronunciation of opera titles and singer's names was often humorous as well as endearing. He often described costumes and sets, mentioning facts and statistics about the singers as they took their bows. This helped the listener to become more familiar with the singers, their repertoire, and their performing schedules. During a time period that was not as politically correct as now, he would often comment spontaneously on the performance and the singers. Cross was like a proud uncle of the afternoon's singers; his obvious affection for the art of singing came across clearly.

Another highlight of the Metropolitan Opera broadcasts were the intermission features that were placed after the first and second acts of the opera. This helped to fill in the time between acts that was required to change scenery and costumes. A number of additional intermission features were developed and offered as operatic entertainment.

These (included) discussions of the opera being performed, roundtables, quizzes, interviews with various current and retired opera performers, and information on notable behind-the-scenes Met staff members. Since 2006, the lead singers of the day's opera have also been interviewed live as they leave the stage. Starting in December 2009, a new feature called *Talking Opera* explains various terminology used in the opera world. (*Wikipedia*)

The most popular of the intermission features was the Opera Quiz. For twenty minutes a panel of experts was quizzed with questions and musical examples submitted by radio listeners. This segment was at first called the "Opera Question Forum," debuting on December 7, 1940. Eventually it became known as the "Opera Quiz." A number of personalities played host, including Milton Cross, but in 1943 Olin Downes became the main host of this intermission, remaining so until 1948. Sigmund Spaeth, Boris Goldovsky, Deems Taylor, and Jay Harrison were sometime hosts during the decades until 1958, when Edward Downes, Olin's son, took over until 1996. After Edward's death, hosting of the Opera Quiz has been done by various guests. In the era when the broadcasts were sponsored by Texaco, listeners whose questions were used on the Quiz received a generous gift package of current opera recordings and, often, a portable radio.

Aside from the Opera Quiz, another popular intermission feature was the randomly scheduled "Singer's Roundtable" during which prominent current singers would talk about their craft—sometimes with seriousness and sometimes with humor. A number of these intermissions can now be found on YouTube.

There was also "Opera News on the Air," educational intermissions that featured guest commentators who would discuss the opera being performed that day and offer musical examples. Boris Goldovsky, a producer and lecturer popular at the time hosted many of these lectures from 1946 to the mid–1980s. There were others as well—in the 1930s, it was Marcia Davenport, novelist and daughter of the famous soprano, Alma Gluck; then-author George Jellinek (who had his own radio show); historian and libretto translator, William Weaver; the playwright Terrence McNally; and the classics scholar, Father Owen Lee.

Although originally conceived as a time-filler, the intermission features became immensely popular with listeners, helping to flesh out the Saturday afternoon opera entertainment that usually aired from 2:00 pm to about 5:00 pm.

As inconceivable as this may seem, it wasn't until 2005 that the Metropolitan Opera Company began systematically to compile these broadcasts to preserve and document their archives. This was mainly fostered through the help of private collectors, various "pirates," and veteran broadcast enthusiasts.

On December 16, 2005, Daniel J. Watkins reported in The New York Times:

> The house is pressing forward with a project to preserve, and in many cases locate, nearly 1,400 recordings of its Saturday broadcasts. Met officials said they have completed 403 preservations, with 868 still to go, spending about $1.4 million in an open-ended project that is predicted to cost more than $4 million....

As Mr. Watkins noted, although commendable, these treasures are off limits to the public. "...if you are a singer, musician or conductor at the Met, you are free to listen to them there. Few do, said Ed Beaty, the Met audio engineer in charge of the project." (ibid)

As if to seek to remedy that situation, in 1974 the Metropolitan Opera decided to release one remastered archival recording a year. These sets were made available to benefactors who contributed at least $125.

Unwittingly emphasizing the Metropolitan Opera's neglect of their aural history, Watkins explained that because the Met did not maintain archival copies of the broadcasts until 1950, a most difficult issue was to locate copies of broadcasts. Some were found as radio airchecks; others were obtained from singers who had arranged for private recordings; and of course, there were the pirates!

> Met employees have even picked up bootleg recordings in Europe and turned them over, said Ellen Godfrey, the Met's radio network producer...This is so unsystematic,' Mr. Tuggle said, adding of the early years, 'It's sort of a miracle that anything survived.' (David J. Watkins, *The New York Times*, December 16, 2005)

Another difficult part of the process had to do with the preservation of the original material. Many of the originals were on tape or even older 16-inch discs. These had to be copied onto analog tapes and then digitized. The seriousness of this situation was realized when a tape from the 1980s was accessed from the archives and was found to be decomposing.

> The alarm was rung, Mr. Beaty said, about 10 years ago when he pulled a tape from the late 1980's. The substance that binds the oxide compound, which captures the sound, to the tape had broken down, making the tape sticky and almost impossible to play. It emerged that a whole generation of tapes, from the late 80's to the mid-90's, was breaking down—a problem not limited to the Met. Many of those performances were conducted by the music director, James Levine... (ibid)

For more detail about the early beginnings of the Metropolitan Opera broadcasts, and for analyses of many of them, the reader should refer to Paul Jackson's invaluable set of three books:
Saturday Afternoons at the Old Met: The Metropolitan Opera Broadcasts, 1931–1950
Sign-Off for the Old Met: The Metropolitan Opera Broadcasts, 1950–1966
Start-Up At The New Met: The Metropolitan Opera Broadcasts 1966–1976

The amount of research and detail that Jackson undertook to produce these remarkable books makes them mandatory reading for anyone interested in the Metropolitan Opera broadcasts or the singers who took part in them. As he notes in the introduction to the series, the importance of these early broadcasts is considerable:

> The examination of the first nineteen broadcast seasons holds the most interest as a historical study. Over two hundred performances are preserved, in whole or in part. Before the advent of the long-playing LP record (about 1950) few Metropolitan artists recorded many or any of their roles in toto. Frequently not even a single aria of a seldom-performed role make it to commercial discs, so the broadcasts often represent the only documentation of the singers' conceptions. *Saturday Afternoons at the Old Met: The Metropolitan Opera Broadcasts, 1931-1950 (Introduction)*

It wasn't until December 3, 1932, that excerpts (about eight minutes) from Strauss' *Elektra* were preserved with Gertrude Kappel and Göta Ljungberg. Until 1936, the number of preserved complete broadcasts is spotty. Generally, however, after 1936, most seasons are well represented.

Strauss—*Elektra* (exc)—Metropolitan Opera broadcast, December 3, 1932
https://www.youtube.com/watch?v=8WYHs-3ORHg&t=11s

Although since 1910 there have been more than 2,500 broadcasts, only about 1,400 survive. In addition to those surviving broadcasts, there are hundreds of performances that were captured in-house by pirates (the earliest dating from the 1960s).

One of the earliest existing broadcasts (or substantial excerpts from a broadcast) from the Metropolitan Opera are snippets from Wagner's *Tristan und Isolde* (with Frida Leider, Lauritz Melchior and Friedrich Schorr)—from March 3, 1933 (about 33 minutes) and March 11, 1933 (about 90 minutes). Although these have rather dim sound, they exist on CD.

Wagner—*Tristan und Isolde* Excerpts—Metropolitan Opera, March 11, 1933
https://www.youtube.com/watch?v=UB7iuH2bjnA&t=8s

Excerpts from *Don Giovanni* (January, 1934) also exist—again in dismal sound, with Ezio Pinza and Rosa Ponselle. The first acceptably sounding broadcast (and the first to be preserved in its entirety) is the February 10, 1934 broadcast of the world stage premier of Hanson's Merry Mount with Lawrence Tibbett, Gladys Swarthout; conducted by Tullio Serafin.

Hanson—*The Merry Mount*—Metropolitan Opera Premiere, February 10, 1934
https://www.youtube.com/watch?v=LtAoks2A-Jo&t=4s

The next reasonably well-preserved broadcast was the March 10th broadcast of Pagliacci with Giovanni Martinelli, Queena Mario, and Lawrence Tibbett.

Leoncavallo—*Pagliacci*—Metropolitan Opera—March 10, 1934
https://www.youtube.com/watch?v=CM3eCCfypyg

During the next year (1935), La Traviata, *Roméo et Juliette*, act I of *Die Walküre*, *Simon Boccanegra*, *Tristan und Isolde*, Lohengrin, and *Rigoletto* were all preserved.

Until the development of magnetic tape, broadcasts were preserved by radio affiliates on acetate discs for testing purposes, or were requested by artists wanting to study their work. It may be that, save for the vanity of singers, we might not have many of these existing precious aural documents.

For example, about five days before Lucrezia Bori was to sing in the broadcast of the Deems Taylor opera, Peter Ibbetson, she received a letter from the Speak-O-Phone Studios. They wanted to be sure that Ms. Bori knew that they had made very successful recordings for Nino Martini and Edie Norena as well as for many other Met artists. Wouldn't she, too, for a very reasonable rate, want them to record the entire opera (or at least her part)?

Taylor—*Peter Ibbetson*—Metropolitan Opera broadcast March 17, 1934
https://www.youtube.com/watch?v=Gbcf-uYAtk8

This probably explains the fragmentary selections that one often finds from the earliest years of the Met broadcasts.

Because there were no copyright laws in effect at that time concerning operatic performances (as long as the given work was in the public domain) and since the recordings were for "private use," these recordings posed no problems.

It is in selling these privately made recordings that one enters into problems of legality. This is because the artists received no benefit from the sale of their work. It became even more complicated when, with the introduction of tape, it became possible to record from the audience in an opera house. It was at this time that the opera "pirate" was born. These pirates became quite ingenious at secreting small portable reel-to-reel recorders into an opera house. After Philips introduced the first consumer cassette recorder in 1963, it became easy to record in concert halls and opera houses. One of the first pirated performances to be recorded in-house via a tape machine was a Maria Callas concert in the Royal Albert Hall in London on September 23, 1959. Only the sleepwalking scene from Macbeth and a few fragments of the mad scene from Il Pirata exist.

As Michael Scott (1935–2019) reminisced in Frank Hamilton's "Maria Callas Discography of Concerts and Recitals"

> I took a large, cumbersome tape recorder into the auditorium and managed to get it to work uninterruptedly in the sleepwalking scene, one of the first pirate live recordings made in Europe...

Many lovers of historical operatic voices know the name of Michael Scott who not only founded the London Opera Society in the 1960s, but was also a highly regarded critic and vocal historian. He wrote the famous two-volume set, The Record of Singing, (1977, 1979) which traces the art of singing through the acoustic and electric eras of recording. Often controversial, always thought-provoking, Scott is mandatory reading for anyone interested in the history of voice and the art of operatic recording. He also wrote critically acclaimed biographies of Enrico Caruso (1988) and Maria Callas (1991).

Metropolitan Opera Broadcast Recordings (on LP and CD)

In the 1970s, the Metropolitan Opera Guild switched their focus from commercially made recordings (The Metropolitan Opera and the Book of the Month Club collaboration—see The Richter CD-ROMS) to authorized live recordings taken from their own archives. 1974 saw their first issue on LP: *Le nozze di Figaro* from the December 7, 1940 broadcast.

That broadcast was chosen because it was the first to be sponsored by Texaco, an American oil subsidiary of the Chevron Corporation. Their sponsorship of the broadcasts began in 1940 and continued for 64 years. In a remarkably detailed article for ARSC (Association for Recorded Sound Collections), The Metropolitan Opera Historic Broadcast Recordings, Gary A. Galo described these unusual releases. Originally, the sets were prepared in a typical LP box with a reproduction of the original program, along with artist photographs and biographies, a synopsis of the opera being presented, and a complete libretto. Each set had a round, gold seal stating "Limited Edition," and a serial number.

> The sets sold very well and the Metropolitan Opera decided to create the Historic Broadcast Recordings series with the plan to release an opera a year newly remastered and selected from their broadcast archives. In 1975, they released the January 19, 1946 broadcast of *Madama Butterfly* with Licia Albanese. Beginning with that release, and for the next seven [releases], Dario Soria served as producer. *(The Metropolitan Opera Historic Broadcast Recordings* by Gary A. Galo, ARSC Journal, Vol. 40 #2, Fall, 2009)

Those in charge of the Metropolitan Opera Historical Broadcasts recordings made sure that they were surrounded by the best people in the world for such a project.

Dario Soria was such a person. He was an important figure in the world of recorded opera:

> In 1953 (Soria) and his wife, Dorle, founded Angel Records, the American branch of E.M.I., and he was instrumental in engaging Maria Callas to head the company's roster of operatic artists. His last project was the Metropolitan Opera Historic Broadcast Collection, for which he had produced eight operas at the time of his death in 1980. (*The New York Times*, April 8, 1986, page 18)

After Dario Soria's death in 1980, his wife, Dorle Soria (1900–2002), continued to serve as a co-producer with critic and historian, David Hamilton (1835–2013).

Originally, some writings of David's had

> caught the attention of Dario Soria, President of the Metropolitan Opera Guild and Producer of the Met's Historic Broadcast series. When Soria died unexpectedly in 1980 while finishing work on MET 8, the December 14, 1940 performance of Verdi's *Un Ballo in Maschera*, David's proven expertise made him the logical choice to succeed Soria as producer of the Historic Broadcast releases, and he continued in that capacity until the series came to an end in 2008 (Soria's widow Dorle served as his co-producer until her death in 2002). He also conceived and served as programmer and annotator for the eight-volume Metropolitan Opera Guild series. *One Hundred Years of Great Artists at the Met*, released in 1985 and 1986.

Arguably the crowning achievement in David's career as a producer was *The Mapleson Cylinders*, a six-LP collection of the complete extant recordings made by Metropolitan Opera librarian Lionel Mapleson between 1900 and 1904, issued by the Rodgers and Hammerstein Archives of Recorded Sound division of the New York Public Library in 1985. Working with Executive Producer David Hall, Curator of the R&H Archives, and Tom Owen, Chief Engineer at R&H, David undertook the task of correctly identifying each cylinder recording. This included documenting the composer, title, date, cast, conductor, and the specific contents of each cylinder, as well as determining the correct playback speeds, a monumental undertaking given the barely audible nature of many of these recordings. The meticulously-produced booklet prepared by David included the specific text for each operatic excerpt, along with an English translation. In 1987 *The Mapleson Cylinders* was nominated for a Grammy in the category of Best Historical Album." (ARSC Journal, 2013, Gary A. Galo)

RCA magnanimously donated the technical and manufacturing costs of the sets. In 1986, Dorle Soria won an award for her work on issuing the 1939 broadcast of *Simon Boccanegra* for the Metropolitan Opera Historic Broadcasts.

> The packaging was in the style of the deluxe RCA Victor Soria Series releases—velvet-covered slipcase editions with an inner box that held, in addition to the records, an illustrated booklet with background on the opera's Met history, photos and biographies of the artists, plus a second booklet containing a libretto with translation. *(The Metropolitan Opera Historic Broadcast Recordings* by Gary A. Galo, ARSC Journal, Vol. 40 #2, Fall, 2009)

The 28-page booklets (12" x 12") included in the LP sets often included reminiscences written by the principal artists "[there were] more detailed historical background and biographies, and [it was] printed on heavier stock with a deluxe binding."(ibid)

First-rate productions, these booklets were tailor-made to the work being presented and were sumptuously produced with information and photos. Most sets included "recording information." The January 7, 1956 broadcast of *Tosca* (the tenth set in the series) with Renata Tebaldi, Richard Tucker, and Leonard Warren (a truly classic performance) noted:

> This performance of Tosca was originally recorded on magnetic tape from the network lines by the American Broadcasting Company. That tape, now in the Archives of the Metropolitan Opera Association, was the source of the present album. The restoration of the sound and the preparation of the master tape were the work of Tom Owen, Chief Engineer of the Rodgers and Hammerstein Archives of Recorded Sound of the New York Public Library at Lincoln Center. (from booklet in set)

In the left-hand corner of the back page is the following statement:

This presentation…like the previously issued albums of Metropolitan Opera Historic Broadcasts, is in the format of the Soria Series a mark created for RCA special editions of outstanding recordings."

It is not surprising that today, many decades from when they were originally produced, these sets are considered fine collector's items.

Once the master was created it went to John Pfieffer, Executive Producer at RCA Red Seal Artists and Repertoire. The Met released 28 of these sets until 2008, the price rising increasingly over the decades. Originally, in 1974, each set was offered as a $100.00 tax-deductible donation. In the years that followed, the requested donation was raised to $125.00 and then to $150.00. One set, The Met Centennial Collection, was offered for the hefty price of $500.00.

Eventually, the Met lowered the cost for older issues. These LP sets have been out of print for years. Although a clever gimmick at the time, because of the costly contribution requirement, the sets had limited appeal to the general public—which may account for their popularity now on such sites as eBay.

The Metropolitan Opera was able to offer these sets because they had responsibly secured legal releases from all of the surviving artists and/or their relatives. When the compact disc evolved as a primary recording medium, sets became available on CDs. The first album to appear on CD was a 1988 release of *Andrea Chenier* taken from the 1954 broadcast with Mario Del Monaco, Leonard Warren and Zinka Milanov.

Below is a list of broadcast albums that were offered by the Guild:
METROPOLITAN OPERA HISTORIC BROADCAST RECORDINGS
Checklist compiled by Gary A. Galo (2009)

_____ 153260 Mozart: *Le nozze di Figaro*—7 December 1940 (LP)
_____ MET 1 Mozart: *Le nozze di Figaro*—7 December 1940 (LP)
_____ MET 2 Puccini: *Madama Butterfly*—19 January 1946 (LP)
_____ MET 3 Wagner: *Tristan und Isolde*—8 February 1941 (LP)
_____ MET 4 Verdi: *Otello*—24 February 1940 (LP)
_____ MET 5 Strauss: *Der Rosenkavalier*—7 January 1939 (LP)
_____ MET 6 Beethoven: *Fidelio*—22 February 1941 (LP)
_____ MET 7 Bizet: *Carmen*—17 April 1937 (LP)
_____ MET 8 Verdi: *Un Ballo in Maschera*—14 December 1940 (LP)
_____ MET 9 Strauss: *Salome* and *Elektra*—19 January 1952 and 23 February 1952 (LP)
_____ MET 10 Puccini: *Tosca*—7 January 1956 (LP)
_____ MET 11 Gounod: *Roméo et Juliette*—1 February 1947 (LP)
_____ MET 12 Wagner: *Tannhäuser*—4 January 1941 (LP)
_____ MET 13 Verdi: *Simon Boccanegra*—21 January 1939 (LP)
_____ MET 14 Offenbach: *Les Contes d'Hoffmann*—3 December 1955 (LP)
_____ MET 15 Giordano: *Andrea Chénier*—4 December 1954 (CD, LP)
_____ MET 16 Puccini: *Turandot*—4 March 1961 (CD, Cassette)
_____ MET 17 Ponchielli: *La Gioconda*—16 March 1946 (CD, Cassette)
_____ MET 18 Bellini: *La Sonnambula*—30 March 1963 (CD, Cassette)
_____ MET 19 Wagner: *Die Walküre*—2 December 1944 (CD, Cassette)
_____ MET 20 Verdi: *Otello*—8 March 1958 (CD)
_____ MET 21 James Levine 25th Anniversary Collection (CD)
_____ MET 22 Puccini: *Manon Lescaut*—10 December 1949 (CD)
_____ MET 23 Strauss: *Der Rosenkavalier*—24 February 1951 (CD)
_____ MET 24 The First Texaco Season 1940–41 Highlights (CD)
_____ MET 25 Mozart: *Don Giovanni*—14 February 1959 (CD)
_____ MET 26 Wagner: *Parsifal*—20 April 1985 (CD)
_____ MET 27 Verdi: *I Vespri Siciliani* –9 March 1974 (CD)
_____ MET 100 The Met Centennial Collection, 1935–1959 (LP)" (ibid)

One of the most interesting CD releases was MET 24 (2001), an anthology of Metropolitan Opera Historic Broadcasts: The First Texaco Season 1940–41 Highlights. Like others in the series, it was available only as a "gift" from the Guild when a $150.00 donation was made. Ironically, in 2016, fifteen years later, a used copy of the set was available at Amazon for about $25.00. Some of the excerpts on the set came from broadcasts that had been released earlier in the series, but, overall, it presents an excellent perspective of the quality and diversity of the productions and the singers who had appeared during that initial Texaco-sponsored season. No fewer than fifty singers and sixteen operas are presented on the two CDs with everything protected by a hard cardboard box with an excellent 236-page booklet containing the cast rosters, texts, essays, and many unusual photographs.

On the website, Classicstoday.com, Robert Levine noted:

Dipping into this two-CD set (comprising two-and-a-half hours of music) is like going into your family's attic (or wherever they kept old stuff) and discovering a box of grandma's jewelry, some of which you remember her wearing, other pieces of which were either worn while you were away or were worn rarely. But gems they are, and with a glitter that vies with and perhaps surpasses the jewelry available today...I might add that the master recordings, using the Cedar sound restoration system, allow us to hear these performances more clearly than we probably could have 60 years ago emanating from the little speaker in our radio. This is a great history lesson, a grand opera gala, and gold that still gleams.

After that set, there were only four more releases. The most important was issue #26 released on CD in 2006, *Parsifal*, from a now legendary broadcast that took place on April 20, 1985 featuring Jon Vickers, Leonie Rysanek, Kurt Moll, Simon Estes, and conducted by James Levine. It was an important broadcast at the time and a fitting entry in the series. The excellent audio engineer was Seth Winner of Seth B. Winner Sound Studios. (Winner took over the engineering duties for the series with release #22.) The next issue, and last of the series, was #27: Verdi: *I Vespri Siciliani*, a broadcast from March 9, 1974. With Montserrat Caballe, Nicolai Gedda, and Sherrill Milnes in the cast, it was also of great importance since it represented a major revival.

In 2006 the Metropolitan Opera launched its Sirius Radio program, round-the-clock opera broadcasts containing at least three live performances a week plus newly restored Met broadcasts.

Metropolitan Opera Radio is an all-opera radio station on Sirius Satellite Radio channel 74 (previously 78) and XM Satellite Radio channel 74 (previously 79). Originally on channel 85, Met Opera Radio was shifted to channel 78 on June 24, 2008. It is also on Dish Network channel 6078. It carries live broadcasts from the Metropolitan Opera two to three times each week during the opera season. In addition, throughout the day performances are presented from among the 1,500 recorded broadcasts in the Metropolitan Opera radio broadcast archives. The channel's host and announcer for the live broadcasts is Mary Jo Heath. The producers are Ellen Keel, John Bischoff, Matthew Principe, with William Berger as writer and commentator. Jay David Saks is the audio producer.

The channel was launched (on) September 25, 2006 the opening night of the Met season. The first broadcast was a live performance of Puccini's *Madama Butterfly*, conducted by James Levine, the Met's Music Director at the time, and directed by Anthony Minghella. It starred Chilean soprano Cristina Gallardo-Domâs as Cio-Cio-San, tenor Marcello Giordani as Pinkerton, and baritone Dwayne Croft as Sharpless.

...The new channel was launched as part of new Met general manager Peter Gelb's initiative to utilize technology to make the Met's performances more accessible to a wide audience. The channel was added to the XM lineup (replacing the existing Vox channel) on November 12, 2008, as part of the merger between Sirius and XM.

Two to three live broadcasts of operas from the Met are presented each week of the Met's performing season...During the rest of the broadcast week, many of the Met's historic archived broadcast tapes are presented. These have been collected and re-mastered by the Met's sound archive department. When presented on Sirius, the original commentaries are replaced by introductions, which include short stories on principal performers and synopsis of each act, recorded by Margaret Juntwait. Of the Met's approximately 1500 archived broadcasts, Sirius's Met Opera Radio presented over 570 in its first three years...

Sirius also provides the sound transmission for the Metropolitan Opera's live high-definition video opera presentations in movie theaters world wide. The traditional Metropolitan Opera Radio Network Saturday broadcasts are also presented on Sirius's Met Opera channel. (Wikipedia)

Although a welcome radio archive, its availability is limited as one must have Sirius radio service subscription in order to hear the programs. Continuing still, however, the Saturday matinee broadcasts can be heard cost-free on many local AM and FM radio stations throughout the U.S.A.

In 2009, in honor of their 125th Anniversary, the Met released a curious two-CD set called: *The Metropolitan Opera—Celebrating 125 Years: Historic Met Performances 1937–2005*. This set is comprised of eclectic excerpts (CDs that are well-packed with music): Beverly Sills in a remarkable florid scena from Rossini's *The Siege of Corinth*; an act III Trio from *Der Rosenkavalier*; an excerpt from Corigliano's *Ghosts of Versailles*; Cleopatra's "Give me My robe" from the premiere of Samuel Barber's *Antony and Cleopatra*; the famous chorus from act III of Nabucco; and "My Elmer" from the English version of Arabella with Eleanor Steber and Hilde Gueden. There is also "In questa reggia" from *Turandot* with Birgit Nilsson, the Overture to *I Vespri Siciliani*, and scenes or arias from *Die Walküre, Il tabarro, The Rakes Progress, Siegfried, La fanciulla del West*, the death scene from *Boris Godunov* (Alexander Kipnis), *The Great Gatsby, Simon Boccanegra, Cosi fan tutte, La bohème,* the finale from Verdi's *Falstaff*, and more. It is a cornucopia of selections that highlights the diversity and breadth of repertoire of this most famous opera house. The singers range from Flagstad to Fleming. Although at first glance it might not seem a first-choice collectible—the set is rather disjointed—familiarity with the selections shows that it is actually cleverly plotted and produced. It offers an excellent range of music, styles, and singers. In a thin, attractive gate-fold format, it is an easy addition to one's library.

In 2010, the Metropolitan Opera released two huge tribute box sets: James Levine—Celebrating 40 Years at the Met—a 32-CD set and a 21-DVD set. These unusual items passed by pretty much unheralded, especially the CD box set, its unorthodox repertoire perhaps being the reason. Concentrating on the diverse productions that James Levine championed or was responsible for bringing to the Metropolitan Opera during his reign as Music Director (1976–2016), the set offers thirteen operas, including Lulu, Wozzeck, Benvenuto Cellini, Les Troyens, Moses and Aron, The Great Gatsby, and others. Although having spectacular sound and excellent production qualities, because of the general unfamiliarity of the repertoire, it can be understood why this CD set might not appeal to many potential buyers. However, the cost of each CD is under $5.00 and there is much to enjoy and learn from the set. When it was released, it was attended by criticism because no libretti were offered in the set. These days, however, libretti and background information on practically all operatic works and their composers can easily be found on the Internet.

Because his reign had been so long at the Metropolitan Opera (he made his conducting debut in a performance of *Tosca* in June of 1971), one tends to forget the many important changes that James Levine brought to the Metropolitan, including a tremendous increase in wide-ranging repertoire. This boxed set commemorates that legacy. Many, if not all of the selections in the box are available separately. Investing in the entire set, however, offers considerable savings at the aforementioned $5.00 per disc. Considering his extensive and considerable musical accomplishments, it is unfortunate that James Levine's great musical legacy was tarnished by the sexual abuse scandal that caused the maestro to be fired from the Metropolitan in March of 2018. This last is all the more unfortunate since Levine was one of the finest conductors of the last number of generations. I worked with him on a Mozart Mass in c minor suing at Avery Fischer Hall in the 1980s, and he was a rare colleague—one who treated the chorus with as much respect as the solo artists.

In 2011, during the reign of Peter Gelb as the Met's General Manager, the Metropolitan Opera entered into a temporary partnership with Sony Classical to release CD recordings of historic Met broadcasts. Although most were welcome because of their rarity, at times one questioned the reasoning behind some of the choices. In an article for The New York Times, (March 25, 2011) Anthony Tommasini noted that the main person involved in this project was Mia Bongiovanni, an assistant manager who oversees media.

> Of course, as Ms. Bongiovanni pointed out, this is a Sony venture, and Sony, which acquired BMG in 2008, will be releasing albums mostly with artists like Björling and Ms. Price who recorded, essentially, for the previous incarnations of these corporate giants: the old Columbia and RCA labels. Do not expect to see the project release broadcasts with singers in the Decca/London stable, like Joan Sutherland and Luciano Pavarotti. (*The New York Times*, 3-25-11)

These Sony sets were individual releases of broadcasts from 1940 to 1972, and included some important performances, including the first broadcast of Leontyne Price and Franco Corelli one week after their sensational 1961 debuts in Il trovatore: (Note, these YouTube clips do not necessarily originate from the Sony sets.)

Leontyne Price actual Metropolitan Opera debut
Verdi—*Il trovatore*—January 27, 1961 (Leonora's Arias)
https://www.youtube.com/watch?v=oODCrsatNPY&list=PLrrvGvy3hqRflTIcxLR2SZ_tfJg56fbdx

Franco Corelli—actual Metropolitan Opera debut
Verdi—*Il trovatore*—January 27, 1961 (Manrico's Arias)
https://www.youtube.com/watch?v=EMOwlLLcgEc&list=PLrrvGvy3hqRflTIcxLR2SZ_tfJg56fbdx&index=4

Others include:
Puccini—*Tosca*—Metropolitan Opera broadcast, 1962, with Leontyne Price and Franco Corelli
https://www.youtube.com/watch?v=cOP1VJR6Eek&t=2s

A sublime 1947 Romeo et Juliette with Bidu Sayao and Jussi Bjoerling,
Gounod—*Romeo et Juliette*—"O nuit divine" from Act II. Metropolitan Opera broadcast
https://www.youtube.com/watch?v=ztgH-TmA0DM

Lily Pons' frothy 1940 La fille du regiment
Donizetti—*Fille du regiment*—Metropolitan Opera broadcast December 28, 1940
https://www.youtube.com/watch?v=zhOBwUvuiHQ&t=116s

There are so many others.

Including a 1960 *Fidelio* with Birgit Nilsson, Jon Vickers, and Hermann Uhde,
Beethoven—*Fidelio*—Metropolitan Opera broadcast February 13, 1960 with Nilsson, Vickers
https://www.youtube.com/watch?v=ymHJszjSCLE

Then there is the famous 1962 revival of Verdi's Ernani with Leontyne Price, Carlo Bergonzi and Cornell MacNeil,

Verdi—*Ernani*—Metropolitan Opera broadcast December 1, 1962
https://www.youtube.com/watch?v=YO4Yn3X8McI

Also included is a hard-to-beat (no matter what era is being discussed) broadcast of *Die Walküre* from a now famous 1968 production with Birgit Nilsson, Leonie Rysanek, Christa Ludwig, Jon Vickers, and Thomas Stewart conducted by Berislav Klobucar. It is another of the great Met broadcasts.

In reviewing this Sony set, the BBC Magazine noted in 2011:

> [Klobucar] has a spectacular cast in this Die Walkure, with a virtually ideal pair of incestuous twins in Jon Vickers and Leonie Rysanek...Things get exciting in Act II, where Nilsson shows her determination to sing everyone else off the stage. Not a chance with the formidable Fricka of Christa Ludwig. Thomas Stewart is at his finest as Wotan, and there's a first-rate collection of Valkyries.

Wagner—*Die Walküre*—Metropolitan Opera broadcast, February 24, 1968
https://www.youtube.com/watch?v=cSVH_t2hd-s

These sets are meant to be subsidiary versions of the operas for personal libraries. To their credit, Sony offered them at budget prices—the presentation gracious, if bare, with no librettos provided. However, most who are interested in such recordings will already have other recordings of the operas (with librettos) in their collection. (Almost all librettos are available online, and most traditional opera scores are available at the IMSLP Petrucci Music Library website.)

Sony released more than twenty sets. Although primarily concentrating on the standard Italian and French repertoire, the series offered interested buyers an invaluable opportunity to hear some legendary performances for an affordable price. (Many of the operas selected reflect the original choices made by the Metropolitan Opera for their Soria LP releases)

All of the Sony sets are worth owning and getting to know intimately. As is to be expected, they have the occasional musical or vocal flubs inherent in live performances, and reflect the cuts, performing editions, and vocal practices that were prevalent during their respective eras. That said, they are accurate reflections of the humanity of artists and contain delightful historical slices of operatic musical life in New York City at that time. One of the most important was released in 2012, the broadcast of Verdi's *Un Ballo in Maschera* on December 10, 1955 (available on YouTube piece-meal). It commemorated Marian Anderson singing as Ulrica, the first black artist to perform at the Metropolitan Opera. Although she was not on the roster long (only eight performances) her presence was a milestone in the house's history.

In 2013, discarding the single-set release format, the Met began to adopt a more anthological concept, which they now seem to prefer. Sony released two impressive and important Metropolitan Opera box sets that year. In April they offered Wagner at the Met (nine operas) and in September, Verdi at the Met (ten operas). At the time this chapter was begun in 2016, the Wagner box sold on amazon.com for about $36.00. Today (2020) it sells for $125 and is listed even as high as $457. When originally released, this box set was an unbelievable bargain for those twenty-five CDs, less than $1.50 per disc; and, for that relatively small amount of money one also got important slices of Metropolitan Opera broadcast history. Most of the performances (occurring between 1936 and 1954) are indispensable to one's personal library, stemming from the glory days of the 1930s with Kirsten Flagstad and Lauritz Melchior. There are other classics, too, including a wonderful Meistersinger from 1953 with Paul Schoeffler and Victoria De Los Angeles, and a 1950 *Tannhäuser* with Astrid Varnay, Ramon Vinay and Margaret Harshaw. Although the sonics are (of course) not up to today's digital standards, there is nothing in the set that is less than listenable; most are considerably more so than that. The twenty-five CDs are packaged in mini-jackets in a lift-off box that includes a 128-page book with synopses and essays about each opera. It is an impressive and important reference that will enrich your life. Naturally, they should be considered as supplemental versions.

The Verdi box set, released in September of 2013, is slightly more expensive—about $59.00, but is more impressive in many ways. It includes some of the most famous Verdi performances given at the Metropolitan Opera during the last fifty years. (There are some piece-meal selections on YouTube. The selections that I do connect with links are not necessarily those for the Sony set.) These include Rosa Ponselle's infamous Violetta in La Traviata:

Verdi—*La Traviata*—Metropolitan Opera, 1935 with Rosa Ponselle, Fredrick Jagel, Lawrence Tibbett conducted by Ettore Panizza

https://www.youtube.com/watch?v=ilNxbcGDrEk&t=4s

A curious (and rather rare) broadcast of *Don Giovanni* comes from a 1943 Chicago broadcast from the Met on tour. The cast included Zinka Milanov (an unusual role assignment), Ezio Pinza, James Melton, Jarmila Novotna, Bidu Sayao, Salvatore Baccaloni conducted by Paul Breisach. The YouTube copy is in surprisingly good sound.

Mozart—*Don Giovanni*—Met in Chicago April 3, 1943

https://www.youtube.com/watch?v=yJ2T-gLzwzc

A critically acclaimed and now legendary 1952 revival broadcast of La forza del destino with Zinka Milanov, Richard Tucker, and Leonard Warren, conducted by Fritz Stiedry:

Verdi—*Forza del destino*—Metropolitan Opera, November, 1952

https://www.youtube.com/watch?v=N2eQIGN3YL8

There is the intensely dramatic broadcast premiere of Macbeth with Leonard Warren and Leonie Rysanek from 1959, the famous broadcast of *Un Ballo in Maschera* from 1940 with a youthful Jussi Bjoerling and Zinka Milanov, the combination of the two is incendiary.

Verdi—*Un ballo in Maschera*—Metropolitan Opera, December, 1940 with Zinka Milanov, Jussi Bjoerling, Stella Andreva, Bruna Castagna, Alexander Svéd—conducted by Ettore Panizza

https://www.youtube.com/watch?v=cY0A1dKm5q8

There is another famous 1940 broadcast of *Otello* with Giovanni Martinelli, Elisabeth Rethberg and Lawrence Tibbett, a 1950 *Simon Boccanegra* with Leonard Warren, Richard Tucker, and Astrid Varnay, a 1945 *Rigoletto* with Jussi Bjoerling, Bidu Sayao, and Leonard Warren and a curiously frustrating, intensely dramatic 1960 Nabucco with Cornell MacNeil and a miscast Leonie Rysanek as Abigaille, dynamically conducted by Thomas Schippers. To crown everything there is a sublime 1967 Aïda with Leontyne Price, Carlo Bergonzi, Robert Merrill and Grace Bumbry, conducted by Thomas Schippers. Like the Wagner box, the twenty CDs are attractively packaged in mini-jackets in a lift-off box that includes a book with synopses and essays about each opera. (YouTube has more than 250 live performances from the Metropolitan Opera.}

Not to be outdone, in December of 2013, the European label Forlane released a bare-bones box set of eight operas broadcast from the Metropolitan Opera (sixteen CDs) called "Verdi au Metropolitan Opera" This was undoubtedly released to celebrate the 200th birthday of the composer. Although packaged in simple cardboard sleeves within a clamshell box, Forlane decided upon some unusual choices—a 1955 broadcast *of La traviata* with Licia Albanese and Giacinto

Prandelli, *Il trovatore* from 1960 with Antoinetta Stella and Carlo Bergonzi, *Aïda* from 1962 with Gabriella Tucci and Franco Corelli, *Otello* from 1958 with Mario Del Monaco and Renata Tebaldi, *Rigoletto* (1959) with Leonard Warren, Roberta Peters, and Eugenio Fernandi, a fantastic *Un ballo in maschera* (1962) with Leonie Rysanek, Carlo Bergonzi, Jean Madeira, Anneliese Rothenberger, and Robert Merrril, the famous revival broadcast of *Don Carlo* (1961) with Mary Curtis-Verna, Irene Dalis, Herman Uhde, and Franco Corelli (who offers a brilliant, interpolated high C at the end of the act I duet) and more. Not only that, but Forlane sweetened the pie by filling out their CDs with additional excerpts from other Metropolitan Opera performances and broadcasts.

In November/December of 2016, the Metropolitan Opera and Warner CD teamed up to sponsor an outstanding 22-CD box set of selected broadcasts from the inaugural season (1966–1967) of the "new" Met at Lincoln Center. The operas chosen reflect the variety and excellence of that season:

Puccini—***Turandot*** (12-3-66) Birgit Nilsson, Franco Corelli, Mirella Freni, Bonaldo Giaiotti; Zubin Mehta

https://www.youtube.com/watch?v=BSRivLaGTzc&t=35s

Barber: *Antony and Cleopatra* (9-16-66) Leontyne Price, Justino Díaz, Jess Thomas; Thomas Schippers

Strauss: *Die Frau Ohne Schatten* (12-17-66) Rysanek, Ludwig, Dalis, King, Berry; Böhm;

Donizetti: *Lucia di Lammermoor* (12-31-66) Sutherland, Tucker, Colzani; Bonynge

Britten: *Peter Grimes* (2-11-67) Vickers, Amara, Evans; Davis

Verdi—***Aïda*** (2-25-67) Leontyne Price, Carlo Bergonzi, Grace Bumbry, Robert Merrill; Thomas Schippers

https://www.youtube.com/watch?v=SaRpDg2DvU0

Mozart—*Die Zauberflöte* (3-4-67) Judith Raskin, Roberta Peters, George Shirley, John Macurdy; Josef Krips

Verdi: *Otello* Act I Duet (3-11-67) James McCracken, Montserrat Caballé, Tito Gobbi—conducted by Zubin Mehta

https://www.youtube.com/watch?v=3k0jK6QbG-A

Puccini: *Madama Butterfly* (3-18-67) Scotto, Casei, Shirley, Bottcher; Molinari-Pradelli
Verdi: *Rigoletto* (4-8-67) Cornell MacNeil, Roberta Peters, Nicolai Gedda, Bonaldo Giaiotti Gardelli

There is a bonus disc of other excerpts from that season with selections from *Don Giovanni*, *La Gioconda*, Lohengrin, La bohème, *Elektra*, La traviata, Il trovatore, and *Mourning Becomes Elektra*.

The sound quality of the broadcasts is excellent and the performances are truly one of a kind. Like other similar boxed-set anthologies, this set is of immense importance not only as entertainment from the past, but also as a serious reference tool for collectors and historians. A tremendous amount of information about the singers, productions, conducting, and artistic preferences can be obtained from the CDs. Ranging from the opening night performance of Anthony and Cleopatra on September 16, 1966, to the end of that season, the set is a treasure trove of glorious singing and committed operatic performing. Some of the above performances remain my favorites including *Rigoletto* with Robert Merrill, Nicolai Gedda and Roberta Peters, Aïda with Leontyne Price and Carlo Bergonzi (also in the Sony Verdi box set) the Jon Vickers Peter Grimes and the unbeatable team of Leonie Rysanek and Christa Ludwig in Die frau ohne schatten. This boxed set is a goldmine of operatic treasures. One only hopes that the Met will eventually offer more of these anthology boxes—say "operas of Richard Strauss" or "Puccini's operas," or even a Verdi or Wagner box two!

Along the same lines, in September 2018, Sony released "Birgit Nilsson—The Great Live Recordings" a 31-CD box set with four Metropolitan Opera broadcasts including the 1965 *Salome*, a 1971 *Elektra*, a 1961 *Turandot*, and a famous 1969 *Die Walküre* conducted by Herbert von Karajan.

Taken together, among these boxed sets and the individual operas offered by Sony, there are about eighty Metropolitan Opera broadcasts in excellent sound, available to the general public in the United States at the time of this writing: a remarkable change in accessibility since 1970.

There are many, many more available from European labels and international dealers as well. Some other Metropolitan Opera broadcasts from the 1930s through the 1970s (released on European CDs) that are worth hearing and owning include the "infamous" Rosa Ponselle *Carmen* (1936 and 1937):

Bizet—*Carmen*—Metropolitan Opera, March 1936 with Rosa Ponselle, René Maison, Ezio Pinza, Hilde Burke—conducted by Louis Hasselmans

https://www.youtube.com/watch?v=VxnPl4pdPIA

The debut of the mezzo soprano, Jennie Tourel, in *Mignon* (1937) is also welcome. There is also an unsurpassed 1949 *Salome* with Ljuba Welitsch and Herbert Janssen conducted by Fritz Reiner (I listen to this at least once a year), and her reprise of the role in 1952. With her youthful, bright and clear instrument, Welitsch embodied the teenage *Salome* to perfection. This is a classic performance. The 1952 broadcast is almost as good, though the luster of her upper range had become tarnished within that short period of time.

Strauss—*Salome*—Metropolitan Opera 1949 with Ljuba Welitsch, Herbert Janssen, Frederick Jagel, Brian Sullivan—conducted by Fritz Reiner

https://www.youtube.com/watch?v=k0acaLNAT1g&t=1173s

There is a 1939 *Simon Boccanegra* with Lawrence Tibbett and Elisabeth Rethberg, and a mercurial *Gioconda* with Zinka Milanov and Giovanni Martinelli from that same year. This was one of Milanov's greatest performances;.

Verdi—*Simon Boccanegra*—*Metropolitan Opera, 1939 w*ith Leonard Warren, Elisabeth Rethberg, Ezio Pinza, Giovanni Martinelli—conducted by Ettore Panizza

https://www.youtube.com/watch?v=esG2dm2LayU

Ponchielli—*La Gioconda*—Metropolitan Opera, 1939 with Zinka Milanov, Giovanni Martinelli, Bruna Castagna, Nicola Moscona,—conducted by Ettore Panizza

Also on CD is the sweetly-sung, 1940 Lakmé with Lily Pons, (as well as a brilliant Lucia di Lammermoor from 1937 (not on YouTube at this time) and an engrossing *Rigoletto* from 1939 with Lawrence Tibbett),

Delibes—*Lakmé*—Metropolitan Opera January 6, 1940—still considered a classic of its kind.)

https://www.youtube.com/watch?v=VlyqGd37z60&t=519s

Verdi—*Rigoletto*—Metropolitan Opera March 1, 1939 (Tibbett is remarkable.)

https://www.youtube.com/watch?v=Zb1pT_iuEgc&t=4s

Giovanni Martinelli, Stella Roman, Bruna Castagna and Leonard Warren in a riveting performance of Aïda (1941)

Verdi—*Aïda*—Metropolitan Opera March 22, 1941 (Stella Roman is wonderful in this role and performance.

https://www.youtube.com/watch?v=JYosQ9BblDU

There is a dynamic, white-hot not-to-be forgotten 1956 *Tosca* with Renata Tebaldi, Richard Tucker, and Leonard Warren intensely conducted by Dimitri Mitropolous. (This is a classic performance in great sound and perfect for a wintry afternoon. Tebaldi emits a fantastic scream as she jumps from the parapet.)

Puccini—*Tosca*—Metropolitan Opera January 7,1956

https://www.youtube.com/watch?v=D6uhGbWG7KM

Moving forward a decade or two there is what many consider to be "the" *Turandot* (1961) with Birgit Nilsson, Franco Corelli, and Anna Moffo, with Leopold Stokowski conducting, (also found in the "live" Birgit Nilsson Sony box set)

Puccini—*Turandot*—Metropolitan Opera March 4, 1961

https://www.youtube.com/watch?v=6Pww5SDb0CE&t=66s

Also available is the stunning broadcast debut of Joan Sutherland in Lucia di Lammermoor from 1961.

Joan Sutherland—*Donizetti*—Mad Scene (*Lucia di Lammermoor*)—Metropolitan Opera broadcast, 1961

https://www.youtube.com/watch?v=GQ44rBDd8pc&t=963s

There is a 1959 broadcast of *Der Fliegende Holländer* with George London and Leonie Rysanek, only a few months after their legendary performances in that opera at Bayreuth (another broadcast that should be in every opera lover's personal library.)

Wagner—*Der Fliegende Holländer*—Bayreuth, 1959

https://www.youtube.com/watch?v=4juFfHrv3E0

These documents, together, prove exactly why these singers were so popular and why these recordings are so prized. Even more importantly, they illustrate the vast changes in artistic taste, vocal tradition and voices themselves that have occurred during the past decades.

There is another aspect concerning the Metropolitan Opera broadcasts that must be addressed. John Rockwell put it quite eloquently:

> The Met takes credit for helping to develop American regional opera through the broadcasts. By this argument, the Met on the radio was for decades the only, or at least the major, source of operatic entertainment for much of the country. It cultivated a taste for that art form that periodic Met tour visits couldn't slake, and eventually homegrown opera companies blossomed all over the land.

There may be some truth to that argument, but more likely the broadcasts cultivated a taste for operatic recordings…A negative aspect of the Met broadcasts, or at least a characteristic that deserves mention, is their partly deliberate, partly inadvertent emphasis on opera as music, opera as song (in a foreign language, to boot) and opera as standard repertory. In short, the perpetuation of the image of opera in America as something exotic and old and cultish and safe. Opera as music is clear: divorced from its theatrical and visual aspects, opera on the radio automatically stresses the sound of opera, as opposed to its drama or even its sense." (John Rockwell, The Met on Radio And Its Impact on American Taste, The New York Times, November 26, 1989)

A number of CD labels (mostly from Europe) offer Metropolitan Opera broadcasts. Highest on the list is Gala, a budget label from Portugal that offers excellent sound and presentation, although no libretti are included. Melodram from Italy also does not provide a libretto but offers quite a few Met broadcasts as do Naxos (their historical series), and Walhall. There are others, but those four are at the top of the list.

Many of these broadcasts provide important alternative glimpses of a singer's art differing from what is evidenced on commercial recordings. For instance, it is generally agreed in operatic circles that it is essential to own the 1956 EMI von Karajan *Der Rosenkavalier* with Elisabeth Schwarzkopf and Christa Ludwig. It is still considered one of the finest opera sets made. It is fascinating to compare Schwarzkopf's work in that recording with the live broadcast from the Metropolitan Opera almost a decade later (December, 1964) with Lisa Della Casa, Judith Raskin, and Otto Edelmann—especially for the ability to analyze the subtle differences of her interpretation. (Claque CD #GM 3010/12)

Along the same line, it is just as fascinating to compare a young Christa Ludwig as Octavian with her Marschallin, sung when she was older. (Available on a number of live sets.) Indeed, one of the most alluring things about such aural documents is the ability to compare and study a singer's growth (or consistency) in a given role. For instance, Leontyne Price made two commercial recordings of Aïda; one for Decca in 1961 with Georg Solti, and one with Erich Leinsdorf for BMG in 1970. However, because of the growth of opera piracy in the 1960s, there are also more than ten other live performances available on CD or MP3, recorded at various opera houses. This number includes no fewer than six Metropolitan Opera broadcasts (1963, 1966, 1967, 1970, 1976, and 1985) as well as additional in-house tapings and broadcasts at other international opera houses. All are of interest—especially for the pairing of Leontyne Price with singers she never recorded with. As mentioned earlier, I feel the most representative performance of Leontyne Price's Aïda is the 1967 broadcast with Carlo Bergonzi, Grace Bumbry, and Robert Merrill. The singing was wonderful that afternoon, but Price's voice was especially lambent; that afternoon she offered some of her finest pianissimi singing (especially in the last two acts).

Verdi—*Aïda*—Metropolitan Opera February 25, 1967
https://www.youtube.com/watch?v=SaRpDg2DvU0&t=6521s

Even more impressive is the case of Leonie Rysanek and Strauss' Die Frau ohne Schatten. Comparisons can be made between her first assumption of the role in Munich 1954 with Rudolf Kempe and her last performances in Vienna in 1985. Her interpretation of the Empress can be compared through at least fifteen performances including the years 1954 (commercial and live), 1960, 1964, 1966, 1968, 1970, 1971, 1976, 1977 (commercial and live), 1978, 1980, and 1985.

Strauss—*Frau ohne schatten*—Munich, August 31, 1954—Rudolf Kempe
https://www.youtube.com/watch?v=D27_A5mT3qQ
Strauss—*Frau ohne schatten*—Vienna, June 1, 1964—Herbert von Karajan
https://www.youtube.com/watch?v=SGm3FsBnPEM
Strauss—*Frau ohne schatten*—Salzburg, August 17, 1974—Karl Bohm
https://www.youtube.com/watch?v=iSnGDzV24qM
Strauss—*Frau ohne schatten*—Vienna, January 27, 1977—Karl Bohm
https://www.youtube.com/watch?v=tGYpL1hiZXM

Strauss—*Frau ohne schatten*—San Francisco, October 15, 1976—Karl Bohm
https://www.youtube.com/watch?v=ALgtLW67o6k
Strauss—*Frau ohne schatten*—Vienna, April 13, 1980—Horst Stein
https://www.youtube.com/watch?v=IRRs903uP0k
Strauss—*Frau ohne schatten* (Final of opera)—Vienna, December 6, 1984 (in-house) with Leonie Rysanek, Gwyneth Jones, James King, Walter Berry—conducted by Christoff Dohnanyi
https://www.youtube.com/watch?v=fp1DUaZ8rPQ

Even Gwyneth Jones can be heard in two surviving performances of Ägytische Helena—Vienna 1970, and Munich 1988. Both are recommended

Strauss—*Ägytische Helena*—Vienna 1970
https://www.youtube.com/watch?v=mjrycBkKvUI&t=3966s
Strauss—*Ägytische Helena*—Munich, 1988
https://www.youtube.com/watch?v=RBvSBoxRtfU

Gwyneth Jones's commercial recording on Decca is excellent—although I wish she had ended the awakening scene with an interpolated high B as she did in the performances of its revival in Vienna in 1970, now available on BMG as part of their "Vienna and Munich" series. (Inge Borkh also ended the awakening scene with a high B when she sang the aria in concert.) As an interpolation, the high B perfectly fits the music and what it expresses.

Before the Internet, one could amass such a library of broadcasts only with great effort—either by trading with others (once you figured out who and where the traders were located) or by spending an exorbitant amount of money buying them from mail order lists and individual pirates. Today, because of the Internet, MP3s, and various music blogs, the uploading and downloading of music files is easy. It is possible, with a little searching, for anyone to build a large library of many of the famous broadcasts that I have mentioned—performances that, in previous eras, most people could only dream of hearing.

Typical complaints about pirated (and even some broadcast) recordings concern sonics: less than optimum sound quality, extraneous stage noises, audible prompters, or the obvious presence of an audience. Despite these (often accurate) criticisms, there is a real sense of occasion—an electricity—found on live recordings that one misses in most studio efforts.

Compare the Testament recording of the 1951 Florence performance of *I Vespri Siciliani* (Maria Callas, Boris Christoff, Georgio Kokolios, Enzo Mascherini, conducted by Erich Kleiber) with the commercial BMG recording (Martina Arroyo, Placido Domingo, Sherrill Milnes, conducted by James Levine). The Levine recording may have better sonics, and the pairing of Milnes and Domingo is definitely a more refined partnership than Enzo Mascherini and Giorgio Kokolios, but nowhere does that BMG recording possess the spark of creativity and the palpable humanity present in the 1951 performance. (Originally, in the LP era, the Callas performance was available on the Penzance label. After the arrival of CD in the 1980s it was released by Melodram. A new version was unearthed by Elisabeth Schwarzkopf from her husband, Walter Legge's archives. In much-improved sound, it was released on Testament CD in 2008 [minus the Overture].). Mascherini, most notably, was Scarpia in the 1951 Decca recording of *Tosca* with Renata Tebaldi and Giouseppe Campora conducted by Alberto Erede.

While on the subject of Verdi's *I Vespri Siciliani*, one performance not to be missed is an exciting performance given in Barcelona in December of 1974 with Montserrat Caballe, Placido Domingo, Juan Pons, Franco Bordoni, Justino Diaz and conducted by Eve Queler. In very good, mono sound it documents one of those rare operatic evenings where everything is in place and everyone is completely committed to giving the best show they can. This has been a cult item coveted by collectors for decades—and with good reason.

Verdi—*I Vespri Siciliani*—Barcelona, December, 1974
https://www.youtube.com/watch?v=VeEhM68sb30&t=5s

Not surprisingly, during the 1960s a number of people braved taking recording machines into the opera house. One of the earliest of these is a Philadelphia performance of *Andrea Chenier* with Licia Albanese, Frank Guarerra and a 61 year-old Kurt Baum on April 6, 1961. Taped in-house, this recording is in unexpectedly clean and clean sound with much presence. The remarkable thing is that this tape has survived throughout the ensuing decades. That is fortunate, because it is a fine performance and the only example of the two main artists singing those roles.

The Author and Live Opera Recordings (Part I)

The first live opera recording I remember hearing was the death scene of *Boris Godunov* from the July, 1928 Covent Garden performance with Feodor Chaliapin. It was on an Angel LP (COLH 100) that my parents had in their eclectic record library. I remember being fascinated by the extraneous noises one heard—including Magherita Carosio crying when Boris died.

Mussorgsky—*Boris Godunov* (exc)—London, July 3, 1928—Feodor Chaliapin
https://www.youtube.com/watch?v=AF63wzJ80fI&t=3827s

The next live operatic recording that I remember is the aforementioned *I Vespri Siciliani* with Maria Callas that my friend, Landon Bowie, owned. When I was 16, we would routinely get together and trade operatic records. That album was one of my favorites to borrow. This was around 1967. I remember that the label was Penzance Records (#6)—Penzance, a clever allusion to pirating! There was no libretto or booklet in the black box with its red label, just three, red-labled LP records, in their protective paper sleeves. Despite the somewhat primitive sound quality, the performance was unlike anything I had experienced on recording up to that time. I borrowed it time and again.

Landon told me about a record store on Silverspring Road (near Baltimore), about ten miles from his house that carried that pirate set. I made a special Saturday trip to that store. It was about fifty-five minutes from my home and required multiple buses to get there. I remember that I had to ask specifically for that album and that the clerk went somewhere back in the recesses of the store to find it. To me this was all very mysterious and exciting. I bought that *I Vespri Siciliani* and carried it proudly back home on those three busses. It was my first pirate opera purchase, and although I now have it on CD, I still have a copy of that Penzance LP set. For a kid in high school, this was not a cheap purchase. If I remember correctly, the set cost me about $30.00 for that three-LP set in 1967, which is the equivalent of $229.00 today. In the mid-1960s, LPs averagely cost about $3.98 each.

Verdi—*I Vespri Siciliani*—Florence, May 26, 1951—Kleiber
https://www.youtube.com/watch?v=-jODLketXwA&t=16s

Penzance had many interesting titles including Callas's famous Armida from 1952 (#54), and Iphigenia from 1957. Penzance #1 featured the now legendary act II of a concert performance of Meyerbeer's Les Huguenots recorded at Carnegie Hall in 1969 with Beverly Sills and Tony Poncet. This was a rare revival of the opera in New York and a "golden" evening.

Meyerbeer—*Les Huguenots* (Acts 1&2)—Carnegie Hall May 14, 1969
https://www.youtube.com/watch?v=PObZ-4VDU0Q

I still have two of the original MGS LPs: highlights from a 1968 NYCO (New York City Opera) performance of Faust (#105), with Beverly Sills, Michele Molese, and Norman Treigle. A single sheet of paper came with that LP, outlining the selections and a picture of Beverly Sills.

Gounod—*Faust*—New York City Opera—October 26, 1968
https://www.youtube.com/watch?v=5gvN4yEuWxk

Also highlights from Donizetti's Lucrezia Borgia (#107) no date or place given, but it was from a 1976 NYCO performance with Beverly Sills, Henry Price, and Adib Fazah with Julius Rudel conducting. Both Penzance and MGS were barebones when it came to documentation, usually just the cast (listed on the label), no date, and no other information.

Donizetti—*Lucrezia Borgia*—Come bello (Lucrezia's entrance)—NYCO March 18, 1976
https://www.youtube.com/watch?v=XCSFB-esAn8

Another experience that sparked my growing fascination with collecting live recordings was when I attended a performance of *Lucia di Lammermoor* at Wolftrap Music Center in Vienna, Virginia starring Beverly Sills in July of 1971. It was my first live *Lucia di Lammermoor* and was being performed in an outdoor theater. I thought I would try taping the performance on cassette for fun. It was only to be for my use and made on a tiny monophonic Panasonic cassette recorder. The cast included Michele Molese (who became ill and had to be replaced by Salvatore Nuova in the last act), Richard Fredricks, Robert Hale, and Beverly Evans. The conductor was Charles Wilson. Somehow, that little mono tape recorder managed to capture a clean and clear aural document of what I heard that night. Sills was in great voice and she flung her arpeggios, trills, scales, staccati, and high Ds and E-flats to the stars that night with great beauty.

Another remarkable performance of Beverly Sills was the Semele that she sang in Caramoor, in 1969. The link is below. If you think that performance was something (and it is!), look for the Robert Shaw conducted performance a year earlier on Gala's CD Collection. That truly is "Golden Age" singing.

Handel—*Semele*—Caramoor, 1969 with Beverly Sills, Elaine Bonazzi, Carolyn Stanford, Léopold Simoneau—conducted by Julius Rudel
https://www.youtube.com/watch?v=IbhoqszMI04

Over the following years I played that Wolftrap Lucia tape so often that the magnetic particles wore off. Why? Because I had been at that performance and it therefore held strong nostalgic power, but it was also because there was an enticing electricity (and artistic honesty) captured on the tape that I found irresistible no matter how often I listened to it—truly a moment (as well as a memory) in time, captured and available to me whenever I wanted to hear it. While I lost that performance to the ravages of time and over-use, decades later I was able to get a copy of the next (and final) night of Sills's Wolftrap Lucias from a friend in New York, Ron Pollard, who had attended that night.

Although I had discovered the allure and reward of live recordings, I also enjoyed the sonic cleanliness and pseudo-perfection of studio recordings. I appreciated their artistic intention but found, more often than not, that I craved the true essence of a singer; the art that can only be experienced when a singer is in front of an audience. What did it matter if they flubbed a high note or momentarily forgot some text? That is an aspect of the human condition. Studio recordings are examples of the heights a singer aspires to. Live recordings are their reality.

Live recordings can change one's perception of an artist or, even of the music itself. Such a change happened for me with soprano Zinka Milanov (1906–1989). She and Jussi Bjoerling were among the first operatic voices that I came to know intimately from commercial recordings (the RCA Aïda and *Tosca*), but after reading some of her cruel, almost vicious remarks about her colleagues in an interview with Opera News I boycotted her recordings. I was so disappointed that I no longer wanted to hear her sing.

A few years later, I was visiting with family in Baltimore and happened to catch part of a Metropolitan Opera broadcast that featured highlights from previous, historic broadcasts from the Met. One excerpt was of the great act II duet from *Un Ballo in Maschera*. I recognized the tenor, Jussi Bjoerling. You cannot miss that wonderful, fruity timbre, but the soprano was a mystery to me. It was a voice I did not recognize. It was very solid and had an amazing high register—it was like white hot fire. She was wonderful. I waited patiently for the announcer to tell me who it was and I almost fell out of my chair—it was Zinka Milanov! Until then, I had only been familiar with her later recordings. This 1940 broadcast was both a shocker and an eye-opener. It caused me to re-evaluate my thoughts about her work. While she may have been an obnoxious human being, she was a great singer! Soon after that I began again to listen to her recordings with differently attuned ears and to collect her live recordings.

Verdi—*Un ballo in Maschera*—Metropolitan Opera December 14, 1940
https://www.youtube.com/watch?v=cY0A1dKm5q8

In respect to the possibility for change to one's "hearing" of music, I remember a Saturday afternoon on which I was typing a chapter for a predecessor to this book—it was 1977 or 1978—I had obtained a cassette of a Metropolitan Opera broadcast of *Madama Butterfly* with Renata Scotto (January 1, 1966) from a friend of mine, Curtis Ether. Curtis was a lovely man and a wonderful friend. He painted the exquisite portrait of Bidu Sayao that hangs presently in the Metropolitan Opera's lobby. That portrait was also used on a reissue of her recordings by Columbia Odyssey. Curtis died prematurely in 1997.

At that time, 1978 or so, *Madama Butterfly* was not one of my favorite operas, but I had promised Curtis that I would listen to that broadcast performance and give him my opinion of Scotto's work. I also wanted to be courteous and return the recording to him before too long. So I played it, intending to use it as background music while I typed. That was successful until Butterfly's entrance. Renata Scotto made her entrance, sang beautifully, and finished with a remarkable high D-flat (which she tapered to a tiny thread of sound). That was all I typed that day! I settled back for the afternoon to discover how a fine performance of *Madama Butterfly* (and the art of Renata Scotto) can affect one's nervous system. That performance opened my eyes to the nuance that can be brought to that role when it is performed by a first-rate interpreter.

Before I leave this section, here is a wonderful Boris Godunov from London in 1958 with Boris Christoff. Although on his two commercial recordings of this opera he sang the three roles of Boris, Pimeon and Varlaam, in this abridged performance he sings only Boris. It is a fine, early representation of his interpretation.

Mussorgsky—*Boris Godunov*– London 1958
https://www.youtube.com/watch?v=VLU7xuwi5gc

From March of 2003, comes a wonderful performance of Elgar's rarely performed The Apostles from The Huddersfield Choral Society. This is a BBC broadcast with Mary Plazas, Jean Rigby, John Dazeley, and Paul Whelan. It is beautifully conducted by Martyn Brabbins. He lets the piece breath expansively so that the chromaticism of the score is highlighted. This is a very special performance. Gale and I often sang the opening chorus during services in the 1980s and 1990s at St. Michael's Church on 99th and Amsterdam, in Manhattan. Bob Barrows, the organist and choir director at the time, was a fan of the piece.

Elgar—The Apostles—Huddersfield, March 2003
https://www.youtube.com/watch?v=5SZ0TRHdUyU&t=780s

Another is a curious performance of *Boris Godunov* from the New Orleans Opera in 1957. Boris Christoff is surrounded by Yi-Kwei Sze, a narrator as Pimen, Mary Jennings, Eddy Ruhl, Lawrence Davidson and conducted by Renato Cellini.

Mussorgsky—*Boris Godunov*—New Orleans, 1957
https://www.youtube.com/watch?v=Sw5GwlpMPSU&t=32s

The Labels

As Will Crutchfield noted in 1990:
> One bought [pirated recordings] by mail or went to a store like Rose Records in Chicago, where they were sold from a back room to which only employees and regular customers were admitted. Some "pirate" producers eventually upgraded their packaging and had booklets printed to go with the records.

But things changed significantly in the 1970's, when Italy passed a law putting any performance tape into the public domain 20 years after its first broadcast. Several Italian-based labels began packaging live opera for mainstream distribution; the emphasis was on Maria Callas above all, but also Bayreuth, certain famous conductors, rare operas in general, major singers in roles they did not record commercially, and what might be called "hot nights"—performances that, for whatever combination of reasons, caught fire and remain in the memory as something special." (Will Crutchfield, In Opera, 'Live' is Livelier, but also Riskier, The New York Times, July 15, 1990)

At that time, pirated LP recordings mostly came in plain sleeves with the most frugal presentation; for example, the releases of Eddie Smith, MGS, FWR, and Penzance Records. Penzance Records was actually a clever play on piratry, was owned and operated by Roger W. Frank, who also issued records under the name FWR, his initials in reverse. Though the packaging was more bare bones—no libretto or liner notes—Penzance had an interesting catalog, with instrumental and orchestral releases featuring the likes of Horowitz, Heifetz, Richter, and Stokowski. Penzance issued Barenboim's 1972 performance of Furtwängler's Symphonic Concerto with Zubin Mehta conducting the LAPO.

An even smaller release, a Metropolitan Opera broadcast of La traviata was released on LP as a limited edition by William Seward, a New York-based writer and record producer. Seward went on to release various boxed sets of Amelita Galli-Curci recordings, as well as a Pons 1940 Metropolitan Opera broadcast of Lakmé. Both of these came with lovely well-produced booklets with photographs.

> In *1966,* a boxed-set of *La Traviata* with Bidu Sayao signaled the beginning of a packaging revolution much like the one augmented by Dario Soria in the early 1950s with Angel Records' de luxe editions featuring complete libretti and tastefully artistic covers.

The producer of (the 1943) La Traviata and another dozen releases of singers 'no longer before the public', insisted when interviewed by Stereo Review that, 'all my albums are issued with the permission of the major artists involved, and all are autographed. I reach an agreement with the singers on the size of the edition, usually about two hundred, and they get as many free copies as they wish for their friends. I also send a free copy to the Library of Congress. The others are offered first to libraries and archives at a special institutional price not much more than actual cost, and I sell the remaining sets to collectors I know at $5 per disc or $12.50 for a three-disc set. I place a few with private dealers, but I prefer not to sell through record stores. My editions are really limited, and when they are sold out, I don't repress.' He was not the only mid-sixties classical bootlegger whose work met such exacting standards. Among the cognoscenti of classical collectors, there was clearly a demand for quality presentations. These collectors were tired of cheap pressings and poor artwork." (Bootleg, The Secret History of the Other Recording Industry by Clinton Heylin, St. Martin's Press, 1995, pg. 37)

To show how confusing this can become, the La traviata set above was only one of the versions released of this performance. Another was a three-LP set of the Met broadcast released by Historical Opera Performances Edition (HOPE) that was made in the United States.

It says clearly on the label, "Private Record Not for Sale." Different from Seward's version, no libretto or booklet came with this issue. (Not surprisingly, almost all pirated opera releases used that dodge, "Private Record Not for Sale," on their labels.)

Verdi—*La Traviata*—Metropolitan Opera April 24, 1943
https://www.youtube.com/watch?v=fnGLTSEWXMY

Edward J. Smith

Eddie Smith (1913–1984) was not the first opera pirater, but by virtue of the large number of releases he produced, he is of great importance. Smith was primarily a music critic, publicist, and journalist, but from about 1956 to 1981 he produced a huge number of live performances on LP (usually on inferior vinyl) and often of questionable sound quality. There were gross pitch inaccuracies and a remarkable disregard for correct documentation.

Smith also produced "commercial" LPs such as TAP (Top Artists Platter) Records (famous for their "20 great..." programs) and ASCO (American Stereophonic Corporation) Records that included important double LP albums of Luisa Tetrazzini, Lauritz Melchoir, and Rosa

Ponselle. I feel that, despite their shortcomings, Eddie Smith's releases served a great purpose.

Available through mail order catalogues, Smith's recordings generated tremendous interest in live performances throughout the country during the 1960s and '70s. Carrying such titles as "Golden Age of Opera" (479 releases), "Unique Opera Records Corporation, and A.N.N.A. Record Company" (73 issues), Smith released a remarkable number of LPs celebrating live operatic performances. (For more information, see my earlier book, Early 20th Century Opera Singers Their Voices and Recordings 1900–1949, YBK Publishers, 2016)

For a complete discography of Smith's releases see EJS: Discography of the Edward J. Smith Recordings "The Golden Age of Opera 1956-1971 by Calvin Shaman, William J. Collins, and Calvin M. Goodwin, Greenwood Press, 1994 (795 pages) and More EJS: Discography of the Edward J. Smith Recordings by the same authors, Greenwood Press 1999 (925 pages). These huge tomes, with fascinating footnotes, are remarkably researched and provide a glimpse into the huge number of releases that were available at one time.

Like many other historical opera aficionados, I bought many of Eddie Smith's releases as they were often the only recordings available of many works. Despite some flaws, I also bought most of his TAP records since (for me) they were a perfect starting place for increasing one's knowledge of historical singers from all over the world. It was also from his ASCO double LP of Luisa Tetrazzini that I learned about much of the rich repertoire for the coloratura soprano. But I also experienced dismay when, after time, his use of inferior vinyl became more than apparent.

BJR and MRF

During the hey-day of operatic piracy, there were a number of LP labels. but two became prominent: MRF and BJR. By the 1970s, both had become famous in pirate circles for the beautiful and artistic quality of their releases.

MRF was run by Bismarck Reine, who, by February 1977, had produced around 150 boxed sets, (including a remarkable Cherubini series). MRF stood for Mauro R. Fuggette (and Morgan Recording Federation). They primarily promoted live performances of Montserrat Caballe, Maria Callas, Leyla Gencer and Renata Scotto.

BJR primarily promoted the live recordings of Maria Callas. Both labels created beautifully constructed releases of great artistic dignity and appeal. Their booklets were often sumptuously printed on high-quality glossy paper with excellently reproduced photos, essays, and liner notes.

> As the man behind the BJR label observed, '(The bootleggers) don't compete with record companies. Callas recorded *Norma* and *Tosca* twice for Angel. Anybody who buys ours will already have both commercial versions…(Ours is) a labour of love. We work slowly and produce few albums. Quality is what we strive for, and it's often hard to achieve with some of these old tapes. We do what we can to correct fluctuations of pitch and drops in volume, but we never doctor a sour note if the singer sang it that way. We want to document what really happened. (ibid)

BJR was known for pressing their releases on extremely good vinyl and for pristine sound quality. Recordings released on LP in 1975 still sound fine more than forty years later.

You can hear many of their Callas releases (as well as many MRF releases) on YouTube.

Much of BJR's fine quality was because they owned the original transcription discs of many Callas performances. Charles Johnson and Santiago Rodriguez (the "J" and "R" of BJR) were also the owners of the label, Robin Hood Records—a kind of "budget" label off-shoot of BJR. In those releases no booklets or librettos were offered.

I met Santiago in the late 1970s when I visited him at his home on West End Avenue in Manhattan to pick up a couple of LP sets of Callas. Many standing–room patrons of the Metropolitan Opera in the 1970s remember him passing out recording lists during performances, inviting buyers back to his apartment to buy the most recent sets. After his death in 2009, his Callas collection went to Pablo D. Berruti of Divina Records. The first half of the collection was given to him directly by Santiago Rodriguez and Charles Johnson during a visit to New York in October of 2008.

Unfortunately, Santiago died the following year so Jon C. Harding of Philadelphia saw to it that the rest of the important BJR catalogue of original acetates and master tapes were safely put into Divina's hands. Thankfully, to this day, Divina Records continues to honor the legacy of BJR by releasing these important documents on CD on their website, divinarecords.com. If you are a Callas aficionado, their website is certainly worth viewing.

Covers for both MRF and BJR box sets drew the eye. They were usually in color and superbly executed with imaginative art. Most sets included booklets with full, translated libretti, performance photos and/or scholarly notes. Their efforts put to shame the more expensively produced, but often banal, commercial sets put out by EMI, Decca, and DGG.

Upon hearing a radio announcement of Maria Callas's death on September 16, 1977, I made a special after-work trip to Patelson's Music store on West 56th Street in Manhattan, to purchase one of her pirated recordings. I found a newly released 3-LP album by BJR: "Maria Callas Soprano Assoluta." It was a superbly presented "chronology of operatic scenes and arias sung from the concert stage during the great years 1949–1959." It was an outstanding release with a luxurious 11½" x 11½" 16-page booklet that had not only many photos but also an excellent an essay by Bruce J. Saxon. There were also informative descriptions of all the selections. Although now typical, this was the first set (on LP or CD) to feature Callas' historic concerts from 1952 (Rome), 1954 (San Remo), and 1956 (RAI Milan) together in one set. I still proudly own that LP set. Thanks to the generosity of Divina Records, on their Home page you can download an MP3 of this remarkable album, newly restored and remastered by Pablo Berruti in 2018. The booklet is available for download as well.

MRF and BJR LPs were expensive—in 1975 they cost between fifteen and twenty dollars per disc, but they were worth it! Pressed on high quality vinyl, they were first-rate productions and presentations. They remain important cult items that are eagerly sought by collectors during the current retro-loving period.

Both MRF and BJR included the phrase: "Private Recording" or "Private Recording Not For Sale" on each LP of every album.

Many were produced with unbelievably generous presentations. I especially remember an 8½" x 11", 36-page photo booklet in MRF's set of Callas' 1955 La traviata from Milan. It was printed on high-quality glossy paper and had stunning photographs of the soprano in costumes worn during the production. I no longer have most of those LP sets, since I now have those performances on CD, but I saved every one of those booklets.

There was also a remarkable booklet for MRF #102, the 1961 London *Medea*. The generous-sized glossy booklet of forty-eight pages was called "A Portrait of Medea" and included many photos of Maria Callas in various productions of *Medea*.

The MRF set of Callas' Il barbiere di Siviglia included a 12-page glossy booklet of photos and information as well as a bonus (on sides five and six) of a Callas/Di Stefano joint recital in London, November 26, 1973, with Ivor Newton at the piano.

The 44-page booklet for MRF #59, the 1970 performance of Rossini's Armida with Cristina Deutekom (1931-2014) was a marvel. It was the first revival of the opera since Maria Callas and Tullio Serafin unearthed the work for performance in 1952. Considering the rarity of the opera, the presentation of MRF's booklet is remarkable. Not only did it have eleven pages of photos of the cast and the production, it had a plot synopsis, a full Italian/English libretto, and an historical essay about the opera by Luigi Rognoni.

Both labels produced hundreds of releases, so it is impossible to discuss the merits of each. However, below are a few recordings from each label that I find to be of special merit. If you are interested in either LP label, I suggest checking amazon.com, eBay.com. or YouTube. Despite their age, there are some stunning treasures to be found. Many have yet to appear on CD. If you are able to play LPs, they are worth the investment.

Some excellent MRF sets include those below. When possible, I have included YouTube links—although a few of them are not to actual BJR or MRF sets. They are intended to give you an idea of the performance rather than the set being described:

MRF #18—Meyerbeer: Gli Ugonotti (*Les Huguenots*)—Milan 1962 with Franco Corelli, Giulietta Simionato, Joan Sutherland, and Giorgio Tozzi. This 1976 MRF release of La Scala's important revival is given a first-rate presentation with a 56-page booklet that includes notes by Thomas Simpson, a synopsis of the opera, a complete Italian/English libretto (also translated by Simpson), and six pages of photos of the singers in the production.

Meyerbeer—"O beau pays" *Gli Ugonotti*—(Les Huguenots)—Milan 1962
https://www.youtube.com/watch?v=H96p1XPXpC8

MRF #20—Meyerbeer: *Roberto il Diavolo*—Florence 1968 with Renata Scotto, Giorgio Merighi, and Boris Christoff. An important 20th century revival, the set includes a 60-page booklet with a generous plot synopsis, a complete Italian/English libretto (translated by Richard Arsenty) with many singer and production photos.

Meyerbeer—*Roberto il Diavolo*—Florence 1968
https://www.youtube.com/watch?v=oxvulWijmWU&t=1238s

MRF #30—Bellini: *La straniera*—Palermo 1968 with Renata Scotto and Renato Cioni. Includes a complete libretto. (This same libretto is enclosed in the Caballe *La straniera* recording on MRF (#35)

Bellini—*La straniera*—Palermo 1968
https://www.youtube.com/watch?v=htnDKg8lGvU

MRF #32—Verdi: Stiffelio—Parma 1968. This was an important revival and included such fine singers as Gastone Limarilli, Angeles Gulin, Walter Alberti, and Antonio Zerbini; conducted by Peter Maag. The 40-page booklet includes photos of the production and singers, as well as a photo of the cover of the original edition of the vocal score and the poster for the first performance. There are notes on the opera, a synopsis of the plot and a complete Intalian/English libretto.

MRF #37—Donizetti: Belisario—Venice 1969 with Leyla Gencer and Giuseppe Taddei. This is another set that is given a stunning presentation. In addition to a 48-page booklet which includes a plot synopsis, a complete Italian/English libretto and fourteen pages of photos, it also includes a seperate 8-page photo booklet.
Donizetti—Final Scene (*Belisario*)—Venice 1969
https://www.youtube.com/watch?v=Bj_oxsR7HEo
MRF #38—Rossini: L'Assedio di Corinto—Milan 1969 with Beverly Sills, Marilyn Horne and Franco Bonisolli. A legendary performance and a wonderful set. It does not include a libretto, but it does have an 8-page glossy photo booklet of the singers and the production.
Rossini—"Giusto ciel" (*L'Assedio di Cointo*)—Milan 1969
https://www.youtube.com/watch?v=t07k0FH4G7E
MRF #43—Zinka Milanov and Beniamino Gigli is a rare, single disc featuring various excerpts. There are no notes and only basic cover photos, but the selections from *Aïda* (Met 2-4-39), *Otello, Gianni Schicchi, La traviata* and others featuring the two singers are invaluable.
Verdi—*Aïda* (exc)—Metropolitan Opera 1939
https://www.youtube.com/watch?v=4B8nO-VvtkM
MRF #66—Giordano: *Andrea Chenier*—Milan 1955 with Maria Callas, Mario Del Monaco, and Aldo Protti. Always somewhat problematic in sound, MRF makes this set more attractive by including a 12-page booklet about Chenier as well as many photographs of the singers and the production given in Milan.
Giordano—Final Duet—*Andrea Chenier*—Milan 1955
https://www.youtube.com/watch?v=-jsEhvERHq0
MRF #75—Montserrat Caballe Recital—New York 1970. Although there are no inserts, the program is well represented on the back of the album. Contains almost fifty-eight minutes of music by Handel, Schubert, Bellini, Rossini, Granados (the famous *Goyescas*), Turina, and Obradors.
MRF #112—Puccini: *Fanciulla del West*—Turin 1966 with Magda Olivero, Gastone Limarilli, and Anselmo Colzani. This verismatic extravaganza is one of my all-time favorite pirate recordings for the almost unbearable dramaticism that Olivero brings to the role. Indeed, it remains my favorite performance of the opera. The set came with a 16-page booklet with the cast, an essay about the opera, and twelve pages of photos.
Puccini—*Fanciulla del West*—Turin 1966
https://www.youtube.com/watch?v=0hmHAmKLhZM
MRF #120—Mercadante: *Orazi e Curiazi*—London 1975 with Janet Price, Bonaventura Bottone, and Christian du Plessis. This 3-LP set came with a 32-page booklet that includes a synopsis of the opera, historical notes by Thomas G. Kaufman, and a complete Italian/English libretto. In addition, at the end of side six, MRF included a 1908 Fontopia 78 r.p.m. recording of "Della corna Egiata" from Petrella's *Jone* sung by Feruccio Coradetti. This was a remarkable presentation for such a rare work.
Mercadante—*Orazi e Curiazi* (exc)—London 1975
https://www.youtube.com/watch?v=xDf2pUm1rII
MRF #134—Verdi: *Il trovatore*—Philadelphia 1970 with Montserrat Caballe, Placido Domingo, Bianca Berini, and Paul Binder, conducted by Anton Guadagno. This set preserves one

of those hallowed opera performances that, over time, have become legendary. MRF sweetens the already remarkable presentation with a performance of the "Paris ending" of the work from San Francisco in 1975 with Berini, following that with a radio recital of rare Donizetti arias that Berini sang in New York City in 1975 accompanied by Judith Nitzsche. The 8-page glossy booklet has the plot of the opera and, unbelievably, the complete translations for the four Donizetti scenas.

Some excellent BJR sets include:

BJR #106—Donizetti: Poliuto—Milan 1960 with Maria Callas, Franco Corelli, and Ettore Bastianini. Long a treasured cult item, this 2-LP set includes a large, 16-page booklet with a full libretto, an essay about the work by Charles E. Johnson, and many photographs of the singers and production at La Scala.

Donizetti—*Poliuto*—Milan 1960
https://www.youtube.com/watch?v=q6ieOPWugE8&t=1102s

BJR #108—Montserrat Caballe Recital (Miguel Zinetti, pianist)—New York (late 1960s?) BJR usually documents the date and venue of their recordings but this release does not include that information. It does, however, give an English translation for each piece and an essay by Ernest Quick. The LP includes a world premiere: "L'Aucell Profeta" by Granados. At the time, none of the pieces sung on this recital were commercially recorded by Caballe. The composers include Lotti, Pergolesi, Marcello, Paisiello, Rossini, Debussy, Granados, and Rodrigo.

BJR #109—Donizetti: Anna Bolena—Milan 1957. Revered since its 1969 release for its spectacular, clean sound, this set also includes an elegant, large, 20-page booklet crammed with reviews, many photos, notes about the opera, and a complete Italian/English libretto—all by Bruce J. Saxon. This is a BJR original issue that is still sought out by collectors.

Donizetti—*Anna Bolena*—Milan 1957
https://www.youtube.com/watch?v=GG2aH3MS2kg

BJR #113—Verdi: I Lombardi—Rome 1969 with Renata Scotto and Luciano Pavarotti. The large, 16-page booklet included in this set has an essay about the opera by Henry Wisneski, a synopsis of the opera, and an Italian/English libretto. On side six, BJR provides part of a recital Renata Scotto gave in Brooklyn on October 25, 1969. The main attraction of this recital is the large Rossini Cantata "Giovanna D'Arco" given its United States premiere at Carnegie Hall by Scotto thirteen days earlier.

Verdi—"Se vano è il pregare" *I Lombardi*—Rome 1969
https://www.youtube.com/watch?v=o0MpUFMYhak

BJR #129—Cherubini: Medea—Milan 1953 with Maria Callas and Gino Penno. This is known as the "Bernstein Medea" and is one of the BJR jewels. Its 20-page booklet includes many pictures, an essay by Bruce J. Saxon about the opera and Callas, and a full Italian/English libretto (translated by Bruce Pickering in 1973).

Cherubini—*Medea*—Milan 1953
https://www.youtube.com/watch?v=HSh3FTs4sQI&t=5951s

BJR #130—Verdi: La traviata—Mexico City 1952. The 8-page brochure for BJR's edition of Callas' Mexico City *La traviata* may not contain a full libretto, but it does have an essay by Bruce J. Saxon, many photographs, and an English translation of all of the announcements made during the broadcast that evening, as well as the interview with Callas. This performance is famous for Callas' interpolation of a high E-flat at the end of the Act II ensemble. Although she sang *La traviata* many times, this was the only time she interpolated an E-flat at that point in the score.

Verdi—*La Traviata*—Mexico City 1952
https://www.youtube.com/watch?v=JZCH8oW6dAE&t=5944s

BJR #133—Donizetti: *Lucia di Lammermoor*—Berlin 1955. This LP release is still considered by Callas historians to be in the best sound of any release of the performance before or since. This beautifully produced set includes a large 8-page booklet with an insightful analysis of Callas in this production by Robert Jacobson, then-editor of Opera News. Crammed with photos, on thick glossy paper, it is as elegant as the performance.

Donizetti—*Lucia di Lammermoor*—Berlin 1955
https://www.youtube.com/watch?v=_maNJkybAwI&t=492s

BJR #141—Reyer: *Sigurd*—Paris 1974. This 4-LP set was released in 1977 and is the famous French revival of Reyer's great work. It includes such front-line French singers of the time as Guy Chauvet, Robert Massard, Andréa Guiot, Andrée Esposito, Jules Bastin, and Ernest Blanc; conducted by Manuel Rosenthal. The large 12-page booklet includes a discussion of Reyer and his music, a plot synopsis and a complete French/English libretto contributed by Eric Safran.

BJR #142—Rimsky-Korsakov: *Le Coq D'Or*—NYCO 1970 with Beverly Sills and Norman Treigle. This set was dedicated by BJR to the memory of Treigle (1927–1975). The large 8-page booklet is crammed with photos and an essay by Bruce J. Saxon about the production, the opera, and the singers.

BJR #143—Maria Callas Soprano Assoluta—Already mentioned is the 16-page glossy booklet of this 1977 3-LP set. Because of the timing of its release (near Callas's death) it has always been an important Callas pirate release. As with the Berlin *Lucia di Lammermoor* and the La Scala *Anna Bolena*, Callas historians feel that this LP release has the finest sonics of all subsequent releases of the selections. Divina Records offers a free download of all twenty selections from this remarkable album, including the sumptuous brochure. This is 142 minutes not to be missed.

Maria Callas Soprano Assoluta
http://divinarecords.com/bjr143/bjr143.html

BJR #152—Bellini: *La sonnambula*—Köln 1957 with Callas. This set includes a glossy 12-page booklet with the history of the opera, an essay by Bruce J. Saxon, an analysis of the performance, and many photographs.

Bellini—*La sonnambula*—Köln 1957
https://www.youtube.com/watch?v=CDQdQvHl304&t=3s

Both BJR (#104, the best mastering) and MRF (#21) released the famous Callas Aïda from Mexico City in 1951. This is the infamous performance in which Callas unleashed a humungous high E-flat at the end of the triumphal scene. Both sets include fine photo brochures.

Verdi—*Aïda*—Mexico City 1951
https://www.youtube.com/watch?v=1wLSF9lyTeE&t=1462s

They both also released her famous 1952 Macbeth from Milan. BJR (#117) included a four-page booklet with essay by Bruce J. Saxon, and photographs. MRF (#61) had an 8-page photo booklet and background on the opera.

Verdi—*Macbeth*—Milan 1952
https://www.youtube.com/watch?v=UUNinTk6msc&t=39s

Both companies released the 1976 revival of Bellini's Zaira, with Renata Scotto and Giorgio Casellato-Lamberti (now on MYTO CD). MRF #132 sweetened the pie of their release by including an extra LP with excerpts from Bellini's *La Sonnambula* from a 1971 performance in London, with Renata Scotto and Stuart Burrows.

Bellini—*Zaira*—Catania 1976
https://www.youtube.com/watch?v=97mIXN2rEMc

As one can surmise from the above descriptions, the booklets and bonus selections of the BJR and MRF sets greatly support and enhance the listener's enjoyment. This is especially helpful for rare works. In spite of legalities, the amount of loving care that went into the creation of these sets was a lesson in respectful and dignified presentation.

MRF documented many of Montserrat Caballe's revivals including La Straniera (Bellini), La donna del Lago (Rossini), Parisina d'Este (Donizetti), Norma (Bellini), Agnes of Hohenstaufen (Spontini), Maria Stuarda (Donizetti), Gemma di Vergy (Donizetti) as well as a number of recitals. They also featured sets of all of the early Wagner works, quite a rarity at the time. Importantly, MRF seems to have been the legacy-holder for the London-based Opera Rara and almost all of that excellent company's 1970s revivals were released by MRF.

Both BJR and MRF released unusual works on LP sets, such as Arne's Artaxerxes, Auber's Muette de Portici, Bellini's Bianca e Fernando, Zaira, Bizet's Le Docteur Miracle, Don Procopio, and Djamileh, Catalani's Loreley, Chabrier's L'Etoile, Gwendoline and Le Roi Malgre lui, Cherubini's Anacreon, Ali Baba, and Les Abencèrages, Donizetti's Parisina D'Este, Maria di Rohan, Il Castello di Kenilworth, Torquato Tasso and Rosmonda D'Inghilterra, Dukas' Ariane et Barbe-Bleu, Goldmark's Die Königin von Saba, Gounod's La reine de Saba, Hadyn's Orfeo ed Euridice, Applausus, and La Caterina, Leoncavallo's Zaza, Gli Zingari, and Edipo Re, Marschner's Hans Heiling and Der Vampyre, Massenet's Marie-Magdeleine, Griselidis, Herodiade, and Sapho, Meyerbeer's Il Crociato in Egitto, L'Etoile du Nord, Offenbach's Robinson Crusoe, Pfitzner's Das Christelflein, Ponchielli's I Lituani, Rabaud's Marouf, Respighi's Befalgor, Rossini's La Donna del Lago, Zelmira and Armida, Spontini's Fernando Cortez, Thomas' Hamlet and Mignon, Verdi's I due Foscari, Stiffelio, Aroldo, *I Vespri Siciliani*, von Schillings' Mona Lisa, Weber's Euryanthe, and Wolf-Ferrari's I gioielli della Madonna.

Most of these operas have never received a commercial studio recording.

In many cases, notes (and libretti translations) for MRF sets were written by Thomas Kaufman (1930–2010). He also provided libretti translations for Opera Rara performances that were released by MRF including Donizetti's Castello di Kenilworth, Auber's Muette de Portici, a not-to-be-missed Rosmonda d'Inghilterra, Mercadante's Orazi e Curiazi, Meyerbeer's L'Etoile du Nord, as well as commentary notes for many other sets. Kaufman was also responsible for performance chronologies of many rare operas that are used for reference today by historians. Thanks to his hard work, many obscure works of the bel canto era became approachable for a new generation of historian/writers/listeners.

One of the most exciting things about collecting live opera recordings is the discovery of a "new" work. Obviously, this would not be an opera recently premiered, but rather a work that had never before been released as a recording. One of my favorite memories is of "discovering" Mercadante's Orazi e Curiazi from MRF's box set of Opera Rara's famous 1975 London revival. (MRF #120)

In early 1976 I had bought an Eddie Smith "Unique Opera" LP (UORC 272) at Patelson's in Manhattan. It came in a white cardboard sleeve with a protective plastic sleeve, no liner notes (only what was printed on the blue label). It featured various obscure arias sung by the Welsh soprano, Janet Price. The selections had been lifted from Opera Rara performances from the early 1970s. I did not know the singer, but was intrigued by the repertoire which included some real rarities—Zoraide di Granata, Il Castello di Kennilworth, Muette de Portici, Maria Padilla and Orazi e Curiazi.

Smith noted in the November–December bulletin 'the virtues of a young British (sic) soprano named Janet Price, a supreme musician, and the possessor of a lovely lyric-coloratura soprano of exceptional quality whom I have every reason to believe is on the threshold of world fame.'…Smith was confident by 1975 that Price 'has already taken her place among the world's greatest singers." (William Shaman, William J. Collins, and Calvin M. Goodwin, More EJS: Discography of the Edward J. Smith Recordings, pg. 96)

Although the record didn't have the best sound—Smith was notorious for this problem—it was an important pirate release. Despite the occasionally murky sound, it was a wonderful record of an extraordinary soprano. At the time, Janet Price was one of the reigning divas of the London-based Opera Rara Company and specialized in the revivals of obscure works. Two of the selections that fascinated me the most came from a 1975 London broadcast performance of Mercadante's *Orazi e Curiazi*.

Price's singing of the role of Camilla in those selections so impressed me that I went looking for a complete recording of *Orazi e Curiazi*. I found the MRF set at Discophile in Greenwich Village and bought it in mid-October of 1976. It was a chance I took on a completely unknown work—based solely on two short selections I had heard on that Eddie Smith LP. It wasn't a cheap chance either, as it was three LPs and I was a struggling singer who was working temp jobs in offices at that time. It proved to be an excellent gamble. It remains one of my all-time favorite pirate recordings, and I still have that original MRF LP. Unfortunately, the performance has never been released on silver (silver, signifying a commercial CD as differentiated from an amateur-recorded CD–ROM that has a greenish tint on its face).

Gli Orazi e Curiazi was written in 1846, the same year as Verdi's Attila, and it is a remarkable, innovative work requiring a true virtuoso soprano for its lead. It also requires a gifted tenor and baritone, not to mention a chorus of the first rank. A tragedia lyrica in three acts, the libretto was written by Salvadore Cammarano. It is based on the legend of the long and bitter fued between Horatii and the Curiatii, two noble Roman families. The opera was first performed at the Teatro San Carlo, in Naples on November 10, 1846.

Camilla, the main character, has at least one major solo in each of the acts—her act I entrance aria is eleven minutes of complexity and great beauty with a vocal line encompassing high D-flat. Her tessitura (especially in ensembles) frequently sits in ledger lines. (For example, in the grand finale of act I, Camilla begins on a G at the top of the staff and rarely goes lower.) The role demands tremendous breath control and a voice that can ride easily over huge ensembles, since some of her most important work includes interjections over full chorus and orchestra. The tenor (Curiazi) is also extremely difficult with some very high tessitura singing.

Opera Rara released a commercial CD of the opera in 1995, but not with Janet Price. It was a newly recorded performance with Nelly Miricioiu. Miricioiu does a very good job, but, surprisingly, nowhere near the level of Janet Price. The versatile American soprano, Brenda Harris sang a remarkable U.S. Premiere of the work in April 2006, at the Ordway Center for the Performing Arts, in Minneapolis.

The opera is full of martial and celebratory choruses and many musical numbers that grow from individual solos or duets into massive ensembles. Through it all, Camilla's expressive florid line twines like a vine. The duet for Camilla and Curiazi (and chorus) in act I is one of those ensembles with multiple high Cs for Camilla. It is surpassed by one of my favorite moments in the opera—the huge, very difficult (at least for Camilla) finale to act I. It is a massive, stunning ensemble for soloists, chorus, and full orchestra. It surges, peaks, and then surges again with some fascinating harmonic twists, turns, and wonderful, teasing, deceptive cadencing. As Camilla, Janet Price rides over everyone with easy power and some spectacular high Bs and Cs (at least three). There is a crucial spot in this ensemble where, oddly, Miricioiu audibly tires on the 1995 recording, robbing the ensemble of the shocking impact it should have had. In addition, in act III, Camilla has a long difficult Cavatina with harp asking for two high Cs, one of them piano. The end of the opera is again Camilla's, requiring two high Cs in short succession. For the highly dramatic finish a dying Camilla (cursing Rome) rises to a final sustained high C joined by full chorus and heavy brass. It is one of the most rousing endings in Ottocento opera. The surviving broadcast recording is a fine testament not only to Opera Rara's first-rate production but also to Janet Price's willingness to undertake such a daunting role.

> I well remember the day that that score plopped through the letter-box,' she recounts. 'Because I picked it up, opened it, looked at it, and I said to my husband Adrian, 'I don't think I can do this.
>
> This is far more difficult than anything Patric (Schmid) has ever asked me to do before.'

Mercadante is so very difficult, because you have all those ensembles which climb, climb, climb to the climax, and you do it once and say, 'OH thank GOD', and then he starts ALL over again. It's tremendously sapping.' No less daunting was the exhaustingly high tessitura of the role—she recalls that a tally of the score revealed an almost inconceivable 38 high C's, a couple of high D's, and one D-flat." (An Interview with Janet Price, Opera Rara's First Diva, April 5, 2009, MusicalCriticism.com, Daniel Foley and Nicholas Limansky)

After the Opera Rara performance, Beverly Sills paid a visit to the Welsh soprano. It seems that she was considering taking on a revival of the work in New York City and wanted to find out more about the role from someone who had actually sung it. They had tea together.

> I secretly smiled and thought, well, you've paid me a tremendous compliment, really. (ibid)

In the end, though, Sills never sang Camilla; Patric Schmid (1944–2005), who co-founded Opera Rara with Englishman, Don White, was friendly with Sills. He later explained to her that the role simply was not suited to her voice.

Janet Price commented:

> There's something about that role—Mercadante could have written it for me. You know, you can get two singers who have the same tessitura, they can have the same notes, but one thing's difficult for this one, easy for the other. It's just how it happens to lie for you, and Orazi for me was just perfect. (ibid)

Asked about ornamentation, Price explained:
> [It was a] collaborative effort. Sometimes Schmid would write it, but he was equally open to what Price made up herself. Some of his demands pushed her to the edges of her capabilities. One example was the extravagant fioritura he added to an aria in Maria Padilla by Donizetti (released by BJR #135). 'Patric knew I loved to move my voice around, but he had me going up and down the octaves like crazy! He pushed me to the absolute limit, and I said to him, 'Patric, is this really going to work? Do you think I can do this? And he just looked at me and said very quietly: 'Darling, you can do it.' Well, there wasn't any answer to that. (ibid)

Mercadante—*Orazi e Curiazi* (exc)—London 1975, Janet Price
https://www.youtube.com/watch?v=xDf2pUm1rII

After my wife Gale and I moved to Manhattan in January of 1975, one of the first record stores I learned about was Discophile from my soprano friend at West Virginia University, Anna Schumate (Anna had moved to Manhattan the year before). I did not realize it at the time but it was the height of the operatic pirating movement.

As Harvey Phillips wrote in The New York Times on September 12, 1971:
> It used to be that anyone who craved a complete recording of Goldmark's Königin von Saba, Weber's Euryanthe or Respighi's Belfagor would have to go hungry. Thanks to a phenomenon known as pirated, private, unauthorized or underground recordings (the terminology changes according to the whim, pride or ire of the person referring to them), this is no longer true.

For some years now a brisk exchange, mostly centered .in New York, has existed in the reproduction and preservation of classical music performances ignored by the legitimate commercial recording industry. This has nothing to do with the multimillion-dollar bootleg enterprises that counterfeit already existing commercial records and tapes of pop music and attempt to pass them off to the dealer (who knows) and to the public (which doesn't care) as the real thing. No, this is the almost hobby—like business of perhaps a score of producers whose raison d'être is their own and their clients' consuming passion for music—especially opera. The profits, if any, are negligible.

> Stars shine in the pirated record universe just as in the counterfeit pop one. At the moment Maria Callas reigns supreme, but Montserrat Caballe, Magda Olivero and Beverly Sills, among active performers, have strong followings; most interest in singers of the past centers on Licia Albanese, Amelita Galli Curct, Lily Pons, Bidu Sayão and Jussi Bjoerling…. (Harvey Phillips, Pssst! I have a Bootlegged 'Norma' for only… *The New York Times*, September 12, 1971)

The first pirate album I bought at Discophile in early 1975, was the two-LP MRF set of Verdi's *Gerusalemme* with Leyla Gencer and Giacomo Aragall—still one of my favorite pirate recordings. It came with a full libretto, photos of the production and the artists in costume, along with essays about the opera. Before long I was making regular trips to the Village to visit Discophile. It was a tiny store hidden down dark steps on crowded 8th Street in the West Village. Originally opened in 1954 by Joseph Greenspan, when I went there in the mid 1970s, it was run by Franz Jolowicz. Franz had worked in the shop for many years and, when Greenspan died in 1975, he bought the shop from the estate. Going to Discophile was an adventure. In addition to traditionally released LP and niche recordings one could find the entire catalogue of pirates. Franz was an affable, erudite guide who was able to lead not only the seasoned collector, but also the novice (which I was) to the most interesting recordings. If you had the money, you could buy mouth-watering revivals with Maria Callas, Leyla Gencer, Joan Sutherland, Magda Olivero, Boris Christoff, Franco Corelli, Nicolai Gedda, Alfredo Kraus, and many others. At that time, pirate opera LPs were a good business and the number of releases made during those decades by various small labels was amazing. According to what I have read, Franz carried pirate releases from seven labels.

Franz was fair:
> Says Franz, owner of the Village shop: 'I believe it is a very good thing that they exist. I do not say this from the viewpoint of business. I do not sell records, but music.' Franz is a considerate dealer who bowed to the wishes of Jussi Bjoerling's widow and withdrew one of that tenor's unauthorized releases, and he will not handle the Euryanthe because a cast member has complained. 'If two pirates compete, and they duplicate, I will only handle the one with better quality.' (Harvey Phillips, Pssst! I have a Bootlegged 'Norma' for only… *The New York Times*, September 12, 1971)

Considering their own explosive demise, it is ironic that the arrogant takeover of the record market by Tower Records, Virgin Records, HMV, and other mega corporations in the major cities of the United States during the 1980s, signaled the death of small neighborhood shops like Discophile. The sacred spot that was Discophile (considered by many to be a New York musical landmark) closed its doors in July of 1985. For a while it was a dress shop. At the time of this writing, it is the 8th Street Winecellar, a bar and restaurant. During my last years in New York, I confess that I always got a sharp stab of nostalgia when I passed that location. Those megastores that pushed out the smaller, specialty shops like Discophile, are themselves gone—closed and defunct.

As you can see from the listing of operas released by MRF and BJR above, by 1976, the operatic repertoire available on pirate LP recordings surpassed that of studio commercial releases. When it came to commercial recordings, a fan at that time would be wading through a sixth or seventh Aïda or one's ninth or tenth *Tosca*. Among pirate recordings, though, one could buy Alfano's fascinating verismo epic, Risurrezione (with cult-diva, Magda Olivero), a fascinating, visceral work that has yet to see a commercial studio recording, or Mascagni's lovely and exotic Iris (also with Magda Olivero).

Opera Rara's London revivals are of great importance—especially those of Donizetti's Maria Padilla, Mercadante's Virginia as well as Meyerbeer's L'Etoile du Nord, or Pacini's Maria Tudor.

Donizetti—*Maria Padilla*—London, April 1973 with Janet Price, Margaret Elkins, Christian Du Plessis, Ian Caley—conducted by Kenneth Montgommery
https://www.youtube.com/watch?v=-d6USj-1HbU

Meyerbeer—*L'Étoile du Nord*—London, February, 1975 with Janet Price, Deborah Cook, Malcolm King—conducted by Roderick Brydon
https://www.youtube.com/watch?v=9rByojMvjHY

Those were LPs. When it came to reel-to-reel tapes, those selections were but a tiny fraction of the immense number of performances (thousands upon thousands) available from the mail-order catalogues of Mr. Tape, Ed Rosen, or Charles Handelman (the three main New York opera piraters during the 1970s and '80s).

Opera Piraters

Looking back on those years, that was a time that no longer exists. Due to the technological advances during the last few decades, the raison d'etre for opera pirating has altered and disappeared. This was a time before the Internet, Wi-Fi, and CD discs. It was the time of LP recordings and magnetic tape. In the 1970s, 78 r.p.m. records could still be found aplenty in secondhand record shops in New York's Greenwich Village, and opera recordings available in America were ruled primarily by London (Decca), Angel (EMI), Phillips, and Deutsche Grammophon.

And then there were the Pirates!

> The dedicated pirate feels that he is preserving history. Says one: 'How else can we hear what Callas and Simionato were like together? They had contracts with different companies and were therefore never able to record together.' (Harvey Phillips, Pssst! I have a Bootlegged 'Norma' for only... *The New York Times*, September 12, 1971)

There were many pirates I did not know because I was centered in Manhattan. I mainly knew of Charles Handelman, Ed Rosen, and Ralph Ferrandina, but they were hardly the only mail-order pirates in the United States. Among most of them, the theme of sharing came up often.

At the same time, one wonders why so many opera piraters suddenly appeared during this time period?

> Henry Lauterstein, a lawyer for the Metropolitan Opera, claims that very little actual pirating for commercial purposes goes on in his client's building for the simple reason that anyone with a tape recorder at home can take what he wants off the air during a Saturday afternoon broadcast. 'Why go after a few nuts who mean well and want to hear Zinka Milanov?' asks Lauterstein, but he cautions that if the Met ever makes commercial use of its tapes, any competing pirate will be prosecuted.
>
> A similar warning comes from Terry McEwen of London Records. The first one to come out with a pirated Solti 'Rheingold' from the recent Carnegie Hall concert performance will go to jail if I can help it (Franz, the owner of a record store in Greenwich Village that handles seven different pirated labels, reports that he already has several orders for Rheingold, as well as for Sills's Boston 'Norma,' although to his knowledge no such records have yet been pressed.) (ibid)

Ironically, McEwen was an ardent collector of pirated opera recordings.

As Christopher Corwin noted in his wonderful series of articles on Opera Piracy for parterre box:

> Genial Stanley Cory in Malibu always offered prompt service, while H. Lynn Fann was always wonderfully chatty and happy to answer my (surely) annoying questions. Like Fann, Bob Decker often included bonus items with his tapes. If an opera didn't fill up the entire reel, he'd happily introduce me to singers I'd never heard—beguiling snippets of Alain Vanzo's Nadir completely bewitched me, and chunks of Magda Olivero's blazing Met debut turned me into an Olivero fan for life.

Donald Kerne of San Diego became one of my heroes; after he learned of my keen interest in 17th and 18th century works, he went out of his way to beat the bushes rounding up many unusual items for me, especially lots of delicious Rameau, from his tape-collecting cronies" (Christopher Corwin, parterre box (http://parterre.com/2015/08/05/a-passel-of-pirates)

A fascinating character was Byron Hathaway, Jr from Merion, PA.

> While nearly all my tape catalogs from those days have disappeared, I still possess two. One is a guide to every Met broadcast from 1931 to 1976; before the advent of the astounding Met performance database, this little green-and-yellow booklet in tiny print was loads of fun to peruse. Byron

> Hathaway had carefully listed all the operas broadcast with complete casts along with notations about whether he had the broadcast for sale.
>
> An amateur opera singer, Hathaway also had a wide-ranging general catalog and cheap prices (an opera was around $7 if two mono works could be paired up on a single reel), so I ordered lots from him. Unfortunately searching the internet can sometimes turn up information one wished one hadn't. Looking Hathaway up recently, I was stunned to learn that he had been convicted in late 1981 of brutally murdering his estranged wife! (ibid)

I still have my own copy of Hathaway's little yellow-green book, and Corwin was right, there was nothing like the thrill of looking through that little, square book.

Then there was Alan E. Fischer in the Bronx:

> He had a superb collection impeccably listed to include all the most important information: broadcast or an in-house, stereo or mono, and best of all, a precise rating of the sound quality. (*Ibid*)

There were many others including Good Sound Associates who offered only the best-sounding performances in their catalogue; admirable, but ultimately limiting.

There were three primary opera piraters in Manhattan:

Charles Handelman became friends with many of the singers who appeared most prominently on his lists—Magda Olivero, Zinka Milanov, Samuel Ramey, Marisa Galvany, and Renata Tebaldi. I ordered from him a few times. He, too, was most generous in his sharing of information and "bonuses." He now graciously shares his immense wealth of live recordings via his website: http://handelmania.libsyn.com where he regularly offers some wonderful and informative podcasts. My favorite part of them is Charlie's discussions about the selections. His enthusiasm and his enjoyment are tangible, and as endearing as they are rare in an industry composed of cynics.

Ed Rosen (1940–2016) was problematic—in many ways a conundrum. He had one of the largest and most impressive lists of operas in the Italian and French repertoire. From my experience, however, his business ethics were questionable and he alienated many colleagues and clients by his abrasive temperament. I know for a fact that he and Ralph Ferrandina (Mr. Tape) detested each other, but I suspect this was mainly due to a strong clash of egos. Both men considered themselves to be the main opera pirater in the United States. Contrary from others in the "pirate" business throughout the United States, however, Rosen was also unpleasant to the owners of BJR and MRF Records, people who, especially in the small New York pirate world, were admired and respected for the excellent quality of their work.

Christopher Corwin's experience with Ed Rosen mirrored that of many other people I spoke with concerning Ed Rosen's business dealings:

> Back in 1975 I ordered one my first tapes from Ed Rosen, when his company—which has changed names many times over the years—was called (I think) Ed Rosen Recordings. I remember chuckling to myself during the late 1990s and 2000s when I would read on Opera-L and elsewhere people complaining about the poor customer service they were experiencing from Rosen. I had had the same experience many years earlier as that first tape only arrived many months after I ordered it. (And, of course, it was screwed up: the tape ran out before the music did.) I complained and a replacement eventually was sent. But that early experience soured me on Rosen, and like Handelman's, his list back then was far too Chenier/Gioconda for me. (Ibid)

For a time, Rosen had his own LP/CD companies, HRE Records, Legato Classics, and Standing Room Only (which released some very important pirated performances on LP and

CD). Later he founded Premiere Opera, (http://www.premiereopera.com) an online ordering source. In 2016 they instituted an important "Download Division" on the website. Despite his questionable behavior toward colleagues, Ed's passion for opera was unquestionable. His untimely death in 2016, found many friends and customers lamenting his passing. For many of them he was the King of Pirates.

Ralph Ferrandina (1948–1991) was known as "Mr. Tape." Richard Corwin remembers fondly:

> However, for my money—of which he got quite a bit, the best of all pirates was Ralph Ferrandina aka Mr. Tape. I felt my head explode when I first received his extraordinary catalog and I've saved the later edition. I had been collecting for a while already but here was an extraordinary panoply of composers and works—many, many things I'd never seen anywhere else. I became dizzy, unable to decide what to order first.
>
> Happily he was extremely professional and filled orders promptly. He was also very kind to me patiently answering all my queries about performances I coveted after having read about them in a recent issue of Opera or Opera News. Many times he found just that broadcast I wanted and then wrote me to let me know. (Ibid)

Mr. Tape

In 1980 I was a busy professional singer in New York City. I also worked part-time as an audio technician for Ralph Ferrandina—Mr. Tape—whose office was at the corner of Broadway and 68th Street. I got this job through a series of unusual events.

A little of my background is needed here. I was fortunate to go to West Virginia University under a full voice scholarship in the Applied Voice Department. In 1970 WVU had just completed the new, circular, Creative Arts Center with a professionally sized theatre, as well as smaller theaters suitable for recitals and master classes, classrooms, and many rehearsal rooms.

I studied voice with Rose Crain, the wife of the tenor Jon Crain (1919–2003), while my soon-to-be-wife, Gale, studied with Frances Yeend (1913–2008). Rose Crain and Frances Yeend had adjoining voice studios on the lower level of the Creative Arts Center. Jon Crain had his studio further down the hall while June Swarthout, another voice teacher, had hers around the bend from all three.

Yeend and Crain had come to WVU as artists in residence in 1966. Frances retired in 1978 and Jon retired in 1986. While studying at WVU we got to experience Yeend and Crain in a memorable performance of La bohème, and Frances gave a number of wonderful recitals. She was one of those remarkable natural singers whose voice stayed intact well beyond the norm. Frances was nicknamed the "Verdi Requiem Soprano" because she was so popular in that particular work. In the 1970s, when Gale was still a mezzo-soprano, Frances and Gale performed the Verdi Requiem together a number of times (after we had left WVU). Yeend was well into her 60s by this time. When Gale sang her own Verdi Requiems (as a soprano) she incorporated much of what she had learned from Frances.

While at WVU, Gale (still a mezzo at that point) was featured in a number of the operas produced during those first couple of years…Dorabella in Cosi fan tutte, (with our friend, soprano

Anna Schumate who also studied with Rose Crain as a lyric coloratura, and who had some of the most beautiful high staccati I have ever heard), *Carmen*, The Medium (also with Anna as Monica), The Magic Flute, The Rape of Lucretia as well as a concert of Copland's In the Beginning conducted by the composer. At that time there were a number of first-rate operatic voices in the voice program and the school took advantage of that in their programming. My voice was not really operatic, but I understudied some of the leads and did sing Aeneas in Purcell's Dido and Aeneas and Monastatos in The Magic Flute, as well as a number of recitals and the tenor leads in the Gilbert and Sullivan operas that were mounted by the English department of WVU.

One opera was given (studied and performed) each semester and most operas at the Creative Arts Center were double-cast. The other Monastatos was my friend John Lehman who went on to coach voice in Manhattan and write an opera, Evangeline, as well as a wonderful children's opera—Rumplestiltskin—which he wrote in 1971, while still in school. The children's opera was performed a number of times in the big theater at WVU and was a great success. I was always supportive of John's compositions; He was very talented. Knowing my penchant for high notes, when writing the end of Rumplestiltskin he inserted a clever, Donizetti-like ensemble for chorus with a solo soprano finishing on a high E-flat (at that time furnished by Mary Ellen Fisher).

I don't know what happened to that operetta. I have an ancient cassette tape of the show. It is old and flawed, but thankfully I transferred it to MP3 before the tape disintegrated completely. I have no idea what happened to the written score.

John wrote one of the most beautiful arrangements of "Autumn Leaves" I have ever heard—full of arpeggios and soft, delicate touches that broke your heart. Gale sang it on recitals for years and tenor Paul Adkins also used the arrangement many times. John also composed a song cycle of four poems that I wrote. Paul premiered the cycle in Germany in the 1980s. John Lehman was the person who introduced me to the early, 1943 recordings of Yma Sumac, a Peruvian singer whose biography I wrote some years ago (YBK Publishers, 2008).

John, too, moved to Manhattan and I would occasionally see him. By the late 1980s I hadn't seen John for some time. He was teaching and coaching from his apartment in Greenwich Village, and had written an opera, Evangeline. He was doing quite well, but I saw him only infrequently, being busy with my own hectic performing and work schedules. The last time I saw him was in 1989 when we went to see Yma Sumac at the Ballroom. (He was my guest, in thanks for introducing me to her earliest recordings—which had a profound impact on my book on Yma Sumac.) After that we lost touch and although I have periodically searched the Internet for him since then, it has been in vain.

Back to Mr. Tape! While finishing my bachelor of music degree I had ordered one of Mr. Tape's mail order catalogues. That was in 1973. I already had a few LP sets of live recordings in my collection—Callas's and Cristina Deutekom's Armida, as well as Callas's *I Vespri Siciliani*, Macbeth and the wonderful Ljuba Welitsch *Salome* broadcast from the Met in 1949.

Strauss—***Salome***—Metropolitan Opera broadcast March 12, 1949
https://www.youtube.com/watch?v=k0acaLNAT1g

In 1973, Gale and I had just been married. We had inherited a Sony reel-to-reel player from her family, opening many new possibilities for me when it came to collecting live opera performances.

I had seen an advertisement for "Mr. Tape" in a magazine and I wrote for a list of what he had. When it came on September 15, 1973, I was amazed. It was huge—pages and pages of information and listings—and very informative—not only what performances were available but also the sound qualities of the reel-to-reel tapes and what made the performances special. I found Mr. Tape's comments very illuminating and they certainly fanned my interest. I remember going through those pages very carefully—practically drooling at the things he offered. I could have had $100,000, and that still would not have been sufficient for all the performances that intrigued me. For instance, on the first page of his *Tosca* listing he listed sixty-one performances of that work representing more than forty different sopranos.

I had read reviews in various opera magazines of many of the performances that Ralph listed in his catalogue while other performances were simply part of operatic lore. As I was newly married and had limited funds (while completing my degree I worked nights in the file room of the emergency facilities of the University Medical Center), it took me weeks to carefully sift through and mark the many listings, thus paring down my wants to a list of three selections.

One could buy reel-to-reel tapes in various formats: stereo (four-track) which had one opera per reel and two-track, meaning that you could pair two operas on a single tape, one per track. There were also "half" selections that fit onto one side of the reel (usually highlights of operas, or recitals—and, sometimes, shorter concerts). So, one could order four selections (recitals) and have them put onto a single reel. (Or, as I had planned, three selections, the most economical way to order.)

Much of the enjoyment of Mr. Tape's catalogue came from reading his comments on various performances. For instance, when I first looked through the catalogue in 1973, I noticed this:

> Lucia—Ft. Worth, Texas 11/20/62—Pons (farewell Perf.), Domingo (American debut), Rayson, Hecht, McMurray—Kruger. An historical performance...with Lily Pons singing her farewell performance in excellent voice, hitting all the notes and the American debut of a very young Placido Domingo. (1973 catalogue, Mr. Tape)

Sometimes his exuberance got the best of him:

> L'Assedio di Corinto (Rossini)—La Scala 4/14/69—Sills (debut), Horne, Diaz, Bonisolli, Faiani, Paul, DePalma, Washington—Schippers. No opera collector should be without this tape. This is the legendary performance which starred Beverly Sills in her La Scala debut and Marilyn Horne as a perfect match. The day after this opera was performed every major newspaper in the world printed the fantastic reviews on Sills and Horne. The sound of this tape is excellent. A perf. no one should be without. Believe me!! (1973 catalogue, Mr. Tape)

I decided on highlights from the 1949 Naples Nabucco with Maria Callas, paired with highlights from Leyla Gencer's December 13, 1957 Trieste performance of *Lucia di Lammermoor*, and a complete recording of the famous (and historic) performance of *Lucia di Lammermoor* at Fort Worth (1962) with Lily Pons and Placido Domingo. That equaled one full reel—using both "mono" tracks on both sides.

When I got my package, I was surprised and thrilled to find that, because I was a new customer and had recently been married, "Mr. Tape" had decided to give me a "wedding present" of the whole performance of the Nabucco with Callas.

This was in the summer of 1974. That fall a friend of mine gave me a (reel-to-reel) tape of the infamous February, 1969 Metropolitan Opera broadcast of *Lucia di Lammermoor* with Anna

Moffo (who was ill), Nicolai Gedda, and Renato Bruson (his Met debut) and conducted by Carlo Franci (also his debut). Despite the performance's serious faults—mainly Moffo's unorthodox, wayward singing of an overtly psychotic Lucia—I loved that performance. Nicolai Gedda and Renato Bruson were wonderful. The entire performance had an electricity that was mesmerizing. I was becoming seriously hooked on live performances. Given my cassette of Sill's Wolftrap Lucia, the various LPs, and now some reels, I was on my way to becoming a true collector!

By December of 1974, I had finished musically digesting the reel-to-reels tapes from Mr Tape and had graduated from West Virginia University. Gale and I moved to New York City on January 1, 1975, immediately upon our graduation, eager to pursue our singing careers. A good friend of ours, and Gale's accompanist at WVU, Lawrence Skrobacs (1949–1987), had moved there a year or two before and urged us to come to the city. He was beginning to have a major career as a well-respected accompanist in Manhattan working with such fine artists as soprano Barbara Hendricks. Later, before his untimely death at the age of 38, he had worked extensively with Montserrat Caballe, Samuel Ramey, Kathleen Battle, Katia Ricciarelli, Roberta Peters, Shirley Verrett, James McCracken, Ashley Putnam, Marvis Martin, Rockwell Blake, Yvonne Kenny, John Aler, and others.

Larry knew of, and had met Ralph Ferrandina (Mr. Tape) socially. When he found out that I was an avid fan of live recordings and that I had even ordered a few items from Mr. Tape, he put us in touch with each other. That was in late 1979, just as Ralph's pirating business was really taking off and he found that he could not handle everything on his own. He needed part-time administrative and technical help. I interviewed for the job of audio technician.

I met Ralph at his office on 68th and Broadway in Manhattan. We hit it off, and he hired me. When we had finished the interview, I reminded Ralph about my first order from him a few years earlier and thanked him for his kindness.

Ralph's catalogue was vast, having more than 9,000 reel-to-reel tapes in an office/studio apartment. These included complete opera performances, recitals, concerts, and hundreds of unique collections of single artists that had been carefully crafted by creative collectors throughout the United States and Europe. I later realized that Ralph was not the only person who had such a huge library of performances. Aside from other opera pirates in the area, there were many private collectors throughout the United States who had almost as much material. That was how Ralph acquired the tapes for his business. He traded.

He had contacts in many of the bigger cities throughout the world. Traders would send lists of the items they had to offer and, in turn, requested things they wanted from Ralph. They traded back and forth. Some of the more obscure performances I have in my own collection originate from Ralph's traders.

One trader was a Harwinton, Connecticut collector, John Borrego, having since then died, who had a prodigious tape collection. The difference between John and Ralph was that John did not sell any of his collection. He only traded. His specialty was putting together amazing single-artist collections that were drawn from many sources. He also had some extremely rare items—some that I have not seen since.

Another excellent trader (and source) was George Kremenesky, who lived in Ballwin, Missouri and had one of the most comprehensive collections I have ever seen. The arrival in the mail of one of his lists of offerings was always a day of celebration.

For a while, after Mr. Tape closed, I continued to trade privately with John and George.

Around 1988, I also began to trade with a collector in Barcelona, Jose Puigjaner, who, for a number of seasons, went to specific performances at the Liceu, Barcelona's opera house, to tape performances for me: full runs of Grace Bumbry in *La Gioconda*, Dame Joan Sutherland's final performances as *Lucia di Lammermoor*, Edita Gruberova in Roberto Devereux, and others. He had a wonderful collection, was a very nice man, and he made excellent recordings. He would write to me to let me know the performances for which he had tickets and I would write back to tell him which I wanted. Due to the vagaries of life, we lost touch during the 1990s, but I treasure the tapes he made for me.

During the opera season, tapes came daily to Ralph's office from contacts in Vienna, Barcelona, Munich, Paris, London, Florence, England, and individual traders in the United States who had their own contacts in cities throughout the world. They supplied not only live broadcasts but also priceless in-house performances from most of the major opera houses in the world. One German trader's specialty was in-house performances from the Vienna Staatsoper—some of them priceless. I began to comprehend that, while opera pirating was a small world, it involved an amazing and complex network of contacts. If an important performance happened somewhere, you could bet that someone had it covered and it would appear on someone's list not long thereafter—and soon after that, it would be at Mr. Tape's office.

Ralph published an elegant 248-page catalog of his collection. It was called "The Vanguard of Live Operatic Recordings" listing the items that he had available for customers. It was classy, organized, and a remarkable repository of information. On the cover page Ralph wrote a revealing preface that highlighted his great love of live performances and the art of singing:

> Think of the possibility of reliving the legendary 1961 performance of Bellini's Beatrice di Tenda, which introduced Joan Sutherland to New York and presented Marilyn Horne in her first bel canto vehicle. By simply 'listening in' you can feel the frenzy that gripped an astonished audience when these two divas began one of the century's great musical partnerships.

Most importantly, these tape recordings offer us a glimpse into great performing styles no longer extant. They allow us to examine the actual tradition of operatic performance through the decades, with a view of how that tradition has grown, changed and developed…"

After emphasizing the wealth of recordings available and the huge diversity of the repertoire, Ralph concluded:

> The performances themselves are available to the public for free; no price tag can be attached to history. We charge only for the blank tape used as well as the labor we put into the production of our tapes."

The Mr. Tape catalog was divided into sections

Pages	Type of Performance
(1-172)	Operas
(172-220)	Recitals and Concerts
(220-228)	Joint Concerts and Recitals
(228-242)	Galas, Anthologies and Collections
(242-245)	Musicals
(246)	Special Judy Garland section.

The selections were laid out in alphabetical format, then listed by the box number (where the master tape could be found in the office), place, date, cast, and conductor.

For instance:

Donizetti—Anna Bolena

314 La Scala 1957—Callas, Simionato, Raimondi, Rossi-Lemini—Gavazzeni

New monthly additions to the catalogue were handled by releasing addendi that appeared regularly and mailed to all current customers.

Despite the ensuing decades, a devastating fire at our home, and various personal moves, I managed to keep one of those catalogues. I was surprised to find, when cleaning out my closet for a recent move to Pennsylvania, that I had kept my original lists from Mr. Tape with the original cost sheets. The cost for purchases from all of the main piraters in New York were similar, although they could become complicated. Here for example is the breakdown in 1973 for Mr. Tape.

The cost of each opera, no matter what length, is $10.00 (2-track recorder owners see below). Some tapes are $7.00 and these are noted next to the tapes which they apply to. Postage and packaging are included for all U.S. Customers.

Special: With every 3 tapes purchased at one time, one may pick a 4th tape from the catalogue free. Buy 6 and pick 2 for free, etc. This offer is always in effect and applies to all U.S., Canadian and overseas customers.

2 track mono tape recorder owners: Since only one opera can fit on each reel using the 2-track setting (2 operas can fit if a 4-track stereo recorder is used) more tape must be used for the second opera. Thus one opera will cost $10.00, 2 for $22.00, 3 for $34.00, 4th for free. Please follow accordingly when ordering larger quantities."

Canadian and Overseas customers paid a few dollars more per tape to cover shipping.

In December, 1974 the cost had increased to $12.00 an opera and in mid-1976 Mr. Tape increased the cost to $15.00 per opera.

In 1976 Mr. Tape offered the option of buying on cassette: one opera was $26.00; two operas were $52.00; three operas were $78.00 (with a fourth opera for free.) The cassette section of the business did quite well.

In April, 1976 Mr. Tape's collection numbered well over two thousand items.

All this was sweetened by a regular fall and spring special offer where, for $25.00, Mr. Tape would promote a special compilation tape "Offering a broad range of performances at the lowest possible cost. (Suitable only for 4 track stereo tape recorders.)"

In 1974 one of the specials included a number of Maria Callas's recitals from her final tour.

In 1976 the spring "special tape" included:

A complete *Frau one Schatten* from Stockholm 12-13-75 with Siv Wennberg as the Empress, Birgit Nilsson (her first Dyer's Wife), Walter Berry, Matti Kastu, and Barbro Ericsson, conducted by Berislav Klobucar

Verdi *Macbeth*—Milan 12-13-75 with Shirley Verrett (her first Lady Macbeth), Piero Cappuccilli, Nicolai Ghiaurov, Franco Tagliavini, conducted by Claudio Abbado

Major Highlights of Domingo's first *Otello*—Hamburg 9-22-75 with Katia Ricciarelli and Sherrill Milnes, conducted by James Levine (Hamburg debut)

Excerpts from *Fidelio*—Mannheim 11-2-75 with Birgit Nilsson, conducted by Hanz Wallat

Scenes from *Anna Bolena*—Dallas 11-12-75 with Renata Scotto, (her first Anna), Tatiana Troyanos, Ezio Fagello, Umberto Grilli, conducted by Fernando Previtali

A comparison of the cost of tapes from the three main piraters in New York was interesting.
Charles Handelman
In August of 1980, he noted that costs had to rise a fraction—the first time he had raised prices in over five years:

Most complete operas, shows, full-length recitals, potpourri (approximately anything over one hour) is $14.00 per reel, longer works, $18.00."

Ed Rosen
Ed Rosen was a bit more complicated. In September of 1973, the cost breakdown for an opera was:

tape—$5.00 plus $2.85 for tape cost—$7.85

for Scotch low noise—$5.00 plus $4.15 tape cost—$9.15

Packing and shipping added another $.35 for fourth-class rate,

Longer operas such as Wagner usually cost about $10.35 and are recorded on tensile mylar 2400' tape."

It is fascinating that many years after his office had closed and Ralph had died, someone took the time to scan and upload to the Internet a PDF of the entire Mr. Tape catalogue. It is now considered a valuable historical reference resource, a check-list of live operatic recordings catalogued to the time of its publication (c. 1985).

A Pirate's Day

On a typical day there were three of us in the office: Ralph, his administrative assistant, and me. The office was an unlived-in studio apartment set up for business. Ralph had a personal apartment down the hall from that office. I saw the inside of his personal apartment only once during the five or six years I worked with him.

Ralph oversaw everything. I usually worked three days a week, but sometimes more, depending on the number of orders there were to fill, the number of tapes we had gotten in that needed to be pitched and catalogued, the blurbs that needed to be written, or the maintenance work needed on the machines.

My primary duties were to select performances from the various traders' lists when they came in, review my selections with Ralph, and, since I was a trained musician with an extensive knowledge of opera scores, pitch new tapes (standardize their speed) that came in from traders. I often used a score of the work and/or a pitch pipe that I kept on hand, keeping in mind the difference between American and European tuning of orchestras. (European orchestras tended to tune a bit higher than United States orchestras.) The reel-to-reel machines were primarily Panasonic that had adjustable pitch controls on the machines. Once the correct pitch-center was decided, a written note would be made on the master box so that when copies were made the pitch would be manually adjusted (by me) to reflect the pitch alteration. Then I made customer copies.

When Ralph began to release LP recordings (and later CDs) under the label "Legendary Recordings," I would occasionally write liner notes for them and help choose selections.

When I got to the office in the morning, I checked the mail for customer orders, pulled the necessary master reels, gathered up the reels of tape needed for copying (1200-, 1800-, or 2400-feet reels—dependent on the time needed to fit the selections). I then planned which machines to use to make copies, threaded the tapes into the machines, mounted the masters, xeroxed the slips of paper that listed the correct tracking for the customer boxes, and made the copies (while monitoring them for quality). When they were done, I packed the tapes and began the cycle all over again.

It could get complicated. Because if I was often working on a number of single orders at the same time, I had to keep track of where in the office they were being taped so that I could put them together correctly when completed. Usually, I managed three or four cycles a day. Everything was recorded "double-time," so a three-hour opera would take about an hour and a half to process. (The purchasers would play them back at normal speed.) Wagner operas usually took about two hours to record at the fast speed. This meant that if I was doing operas of regular length and Wagner as well, I had to be very careful about monitoring. Generally, I worked eight-hour days (often without lunch—because I forgot to eat). It was very physical work. Once I began recording, I rarely sat down because the machines had to be constantly monitored. Mentally, I had a system. After I had set-up all the machines, but before I started them, I would calmly double-check the tracking on all the machines against the tracking on the slip of paper I had put into the customer's box. Then I would stop, take a moment to center myself, and start all the machines, one after another, at the same time.

There were twenty-six reel-to-reel tape recorders and ten double-cassette decks at Mr. Tape. Most of the time they were all working simultaneously. I was also responsible for maintenance (cleaning) of the tracking heads, rollers, and tape paths of all the reel-to-reel and cassette recorders. I did this after each recording cycle. All these operations made the job quite frenetic.

Because all copies (both reel-to-reel and cassette) were made at double speed I quickly became accustomed to hearing Aïda double time in one ear and *Tosca* in the other. As I grew comfortable with this schizophrenic way of listening, I learned how to stop each opera independently from the other for clean cassette-side breaks. Generally, reels ran until the end of the side. Cassettes had to be carefully monitored because their sides were generally forty-three minutes as against ninety minutes for reel-to-reel tapes, so they had to be checked around the twenty-minute mark when done double-time. I also learned that one can often recognize a singer's voice (even at double time) due to peculiar mannerisms they acquire during the course of their career. It was a hectic job, but I loved it!

At first Ralph and I butted heads when he tried to teach me the correct way to track the tape decks for recording. Ralph was very impatient and an awful teacher. Whatever the reason, I could not get the method of reel-to-reel tracking into my head. It made no sense to me. I thought about it. I drew diagrams. I treated the issues as if they were homework, but nothing seemed to help. Finally, I reached out to someone I knew who was familiar with reel-to-reel machines in the hope that he might do a better job of explaining this to me than Ralph and, when he did, it made complete sense.

My confusion centered on the issue of the accurate connecting of the plug from the output of one player (the one playing the master tape) into a corresponding plug on another player making the copy, even though it might be a different track from the master recording. For example, there might be a *Tosca* on track A of the master tape, but you already have something set up on the copy machine to be copied onto track A of the copying machine. In such a case, the cable from track A of the original machine had to be plugged into the track B plug of the machine doing the copying.

That is all simple enough, but it gets complicated when you are dealing with a master tape that has two performances of *Tosca* (on both tracks A and B) with the same or, perhaps, different singers. In such cases one had to be very careful to make sure that the correct *Tosca* (with the correct cast) was selected and plugged into the machine doing the copying. Another complication was that a customer would often decide that they wanted a mono version of a stereo opera on one track or they might want a mono opera made into fake stereo. All this had to be worked into the schematics of recording. I found that for me the best way to handle this potential chaos was to plot and memorize all my tracking. By that I mean I would review the purchaser's order and pair the operas in the best order that I could. I might pair two *Tosca*s together or a *Tosca* and an *Otello*. Or, if both operas featured the same famous artist, I would pair them together. It depended on what the customer ordered and what I felt would work best for their ease in listening as well as keeping the selections apart in my head. It might seem to be a lot of trouble about nothing, but I loved that part of the job. I still remember my joy when I got my first package of tapes and saw "what was where." So, in the office I imagined myself as the customer receiving the package of tapes. Naturally, what I had tracked on the machines had to match what I had included on the customer slip of paper inside their box.

Despite my rocky beginnings I became very proficient and skillful at tracking, and adept at managing the recordings. Ralph once confided to me that visitors to the office were fascinated by my rushing about from one tape machine to another, sticking my headphones into the machines, listening, adjusting, quickly moving on to the next, keeping track of the volume and the tapes being recorded. As mentioned, it was easiest to memorize which operas were going to which machine and for which customer order. Because I was a professional singer, memorizing was no problem—it was a way of life.

I loved that job! I remember going to work the day that Hurricane Gloria hit New York City in September 1985. At the time, I lived on West 95th Street near Central Park West. Despite the almost impossible weather, no way was I going to miss work! (Actually, neither the administrator nor Ralph showed up that day. It was just me!) I remember watching the torrential wind and rain hitting the windows of the office as I went about doing my work. Although I wound up having to leave early that afternoon, for a while I was as happy as could be working on orders.

I was intrigued by the diversity of the customers who purchased from Mr. Tape (Their names and addresses were kept on index cards in a file cabinet near the row of front windows of the office that faced Broadway). This list included not only regular opera lovers and well-known New York critics, musicologists, teachers, conductors and vocal coaches, but also such international artists as Leonie Rysanek, Gwyneth Jones, Grace Bumbry, Teresa Stratas, Samuel Ramey, Dietrich Fischer-Dieskau, and many others.

Ralph knew many singers personally and they often brought their own tapes to the office. I remember Teresa Stratas, Grace Bumbry, and Virginia Zeani stopping by to bring tapes to Ralph that they wanted to ensure were made available to the public. Often Samuel Ramey, Catherine Malfitano, Stephanie Sundine, and other New York City Opera artists stopped by, sometimes just to chat. I found it fascinating that so many famous singers were approving of Ralph's business.

In fact, most big-name singers approve heartily of this practice. Every time Callas returned to New York, just about the first thing she'd do was call up her pirate friends to ask, 'What are you bringing out next?' Caballe has been equally enthusiastic, saying that while she approves of most of her commercial records and hopes people will buy them, only the non-commercial ones showing her in actual performances give a true idea of how she sings.

The grapevine has it that Norman herself has been picking up *sub rosa* recordings of her performances as well…. (Jessye and the pirates, by Bill Zakariasen, New York Daily News, March 27, 1984)

One day in the early 1980s, Virginia Zeani came to New York for a visit and brought with her a shoebox of cassette tapes from which I was to make masters. It included performances of Contes d'Hofmann, Werther, *Manon Lescaut*, and others.

I also remember one day a tape was brought to the office. It was of the New York recital debut of an English soprano who was being sponsored by the Wagner Society of New York. She sang arias from Clemenza di Tito, Semiramide and *La Gioconda* as well as songs by Quilter, Barber and Bridge. Her name was Jane Eaglen and the date of that recital was June 18, 1984. (She eventually made her Metropolitan Opera debut January 1996 as Donna Anna in *Don Giovanni*.)

A very special moment for me occurred in late 1983 when Ralph's Munich contact sent a reel-to-reel stereo broadcast of a massive gala concert given on Octoeber 16, 1983 by Edita Gruberova (1946–2021), conducted by Lamberto Gardelli. Between orchestral pieces by Gluck, Verdi, Strauss and Bellini, Gruberova sang arias from Lucio Sillo, Ariadne auf Naxos (the original 1912 version), Glauce's Aria from Cherubini's Medea, "Ah non credea" from *La Sonnambula*, and the Mad Scene from Lucia di Lammeroor. It was a remarkable concert and is now rightly considered a cult item. Fortunately, it can be seen on YouTube and, since its upload in 2013, it has been viewed over 17,000 times.

Edita Gruberova—Gala Concert—Munich October 16 1983
https://www.youtube.com/watch?v=hXwtAaJyniA&t=2s

While in Munich for the concert—which featured as its centerpiece the 1912, early version of Zerbinetta's aria from Strauss' Ariadne auf Naxos—Gruberova went into the studio and recorded the scena as part of a new recital album, "Famous Opera Arias" (Orfeo C 101, 841). On both the concert and recording, Gruberova provided an extraordinary tribute to the solidity of her technique, going so far as to offer a diminuendo on the sustained high F-sharp, while playing lightly with the music and text in an appropriately brilliant and amusing manner.

When it comes to longevity, Gruberova seems to be setting records. Having made her operatic debut in 1968 in Il barbiere di Siviglia, she retired from the operatic stage in March, 2019, fifty-one years later. The seventy-one year-old soprano must hold the world's record for keeping the role of Zerbinetta (in Ariadne auf Naxos) in her active repertoire. Most sopranos would be proud to be able to sing Strauss' high-flying coquette for just five years. Gruberova sang Zerbinetta for thirty-six years—her last performance of the role being in 2009.

According to the Gruberova fan site:

She has sung this role many times ever since (in Vienna, Munich, Bonn, Zurich, Geneva, Salzburg, Barcelona, Milano, New York, Washington, Tokyo, Yokohama, Mannheim). Most recently on 6-Dec-2009 in Vienna when she announced to the audience that this had been her last Zerbinetta. She has sung the role more than 200 times, exactly 100 out of these in Vienna. (http://www.gruberova.com/index.htm)

Zerbinetta was her favorite role and remains her finest portrayal—her idiosyncratic vocal method and Slavic manner of sliding into high notes, correctly translating into the style and character of Zerbinetta. From the first time she sang the role she quickly set a new standard for what audiences now expect from this role and aria.

One of the reasons for Gruberova's success with this role was her extraordinary initial preparation. During her early years, in the 1960s, while under contract to the Vienna Staatsoper, she worked on Zerbinetta every day—although she had no engagements to sing Zerbinetta. By 1973, when she first sang the role, it had been completely integrated into her voice and technique. Such painstaking patience and preparation paid off by placing her interpretation in a class all of its own.

Undoubtedly, the most memorable day at Mr Tape's office was in December of 1985, when Gwyneth Jones' husband personally brought us cassette tapes of a performance of Strauss's *Die Frau ohne Schatten* that his wife had sung a few weeks earlier in Zurich (on November 24, 1985). He had personally taped the performance. Originally, Jones was to have sung the role of the Frau. Agnes Habereder, who was scheduled to sing the Empress, had suddenly developed laryngitis on the day of the performance and the management could not find another singer for that difficult role on such short notice.

In a Guinness book of records-like accomplishment, Jones agreed, with six hours notice, to sing not only the Frau but to sight-read the role of the Empress as well! Although she had never sung the role, she had sung in many productions of the opera and was familiar with the music of the Empress. It was an unorthodox solution, but, encouraged by the opera house's management and her husband, Jones agreed to the proposal. She sang the Empress' music behind a darkened scrim while an actress acted out the role on stage. The surviving tape proves that it was not only a successful evening, it was a stellar one. To sing the role of the Empress is an accomplishment in itself, but to also sing the Frau in the same performance is remarkable! I will never forget the thrill I felt when Jones's husband put those cassettes into my hands to make masters. I had read about the performance in Tim Page's article in The New York Times, but I could not believe that I actually held that same performance in my hands. Needless to say, once I made the master for Mr. Tape, I made one for myself as well. It remains one of the most prized performances in my personal collection. Of the many experiences I had in that office, that was, by far, a high point. Thankfully, this important performance is now available on YouTube.

Strauss—***Die Frau ohne Schatten***—Zurich November 24, 1985
https://www.youtube.com/watch?v=bYAArNv8J8Q&t=6331s

Another high point was when I came across a small unidentified tape in a pile of odds and ends.

It is the only reel that I still have from the office of Mr. Tape. It is a small box with a 5-inch reel of tape in it. "American Recording Tape" was the brand and the spine had green sticky-tape on it with a red label-maker title, "Gala Performance 3/16/68." That was all the information. There was no sheet inside explaining where the performance took place or what the program was. The box had simply been tossed onto a pile of junk.

I was intrigued. I figured that it was probably a Met gala performance, but this was before the Internet where I could quickly have checked The Metropolitan Opera Annals, so I had to do a lengthier exploration on my own.

I checked the Mr. Tape catalogue and realized that Ralph had never added it to his public collection. I saw it on no other list either. When I asked about the little box, Ralph dismissed it, saying that it was not good enough for "The Collection." I pressed him on it and he simply said impatiently that it was a Met Gala he had attended years ago.

After listening to it I calculated that Ralph must have taped it himself. He was one of the few people I knew who would dare to take a reel-to-reel recorder into the Met—especially at that time.

It was not hard to guess why he held the recording back. Although special, definitely listenable and enjoyable, there were many imperfections. It was not a broadcast but rather was recorded in-house. It must have been early in Ralph's taping history, while he was still learning how to remain quiet and not move around when recording in-house, so there are movement noises and occasional chatter. (I remember listening to an even earlier audio tape—the "First Ladies of Opera"—a telecast in January of 1966. Ralph had obviously taped it from the TV in his home with a hand-held microphone. (He was about seventeen years old at the time.) At one point, frustrated because of all the noise in the house interfering with his attempt to tape, he screamed, "SHUT UP!" (Oddly, that selection *was* in the catalogue, Ralph perhaps forgetting this major flaw.)

I decided to listen to the entire mystery Gala tape and figure out the program. I took it home to work on its mysteries. It took me a long time, but when I was done it was worth it. It is a wonderful, remarkable concert that reads like a who's-who of international opera stars. The unusual thing about this Met Gala was that it highlighted music that the performing artists had never sung at the Met! It turns out that it was a benefit sponsored by the Metropolitan Opera Guild for the Benevolent and Retirement Funds.

Among these treasures are:

Cornel MacNeil—Rossini—"Largo al factotum" (*Barber of Seville*)
Teresa Stratas—Tchaikovsky—the Letter Scene (*Eugene Onegin*)
Roberta Peters—Meyerbeer—"Shadow Song" (*Dinorah*)
Joan Sutherland- Meyerbeer—"O beau pays" (*Les Huguenots*)
 and the Finale from Gounod's *Faust* w/George Shirley and John Macurdy.
Jan Peerce—Cilea—"È la solita storia" *L'Arlesiana*
Franco Corelli—Italian folk Songs,
Sherrill Milnes—Leoncavallo—Prologue from *Pagliacci*
Leontyne Price—Charpentier—Depuis le jour" (*Louise*)
Nicolai Gedda—Tchaikovsky—Gherman's Aria (*Pique Dame*)
Robert Merrill—Thomas—"Drinking Song" (*Hamlet*)
Carlo Bergonzi—Meyerbeer—"O Paradiso" (*L'Africaine*)
Ezio Flagello.—Verdi—"O tu Palermo" (*I Vespri Siciliani*)
Richard Tucker—Leoncavallo—"Vesti la giubba" (*Pagliacci*)
Richard Tucker—Halevey—"Rachel quand du Seigeur" (*La Juive*)
Leonie Rysanek- Lehar—"Einer wird kommen" (*Zarewitsch*)
Renata Tebaldi—Rossini "Regata Veneziana" (Rossini)

There were more—the program lasted over an hour and-a-half. Taken as a whole the program was one of the most satisfying of its type that I had ever heard. Imagine my surprise when I happened across this remarkable gala on YouTube.

Metropolitan Opera Gala—March 16, 1968
https://www.youtube.com/watch?v=BIm6Gh2uD18&t=485s
Another great Metropolitan Opera Gala that was recently uploaded to YouTube (December 2023) is the April 22, 1972 Gala honoring Sir Rudolph Bing. At one time excerpts from this long (over three hours) Gala were released on DGG. But many excellent performances had to be cut due to space issues. Here you can hear the entire—almost 4 hour gala in excellent sound. Again, another wonderful upload from "Noack Somewhere." Artists included Roberta Peters, Robert Merrill, Teresa Stratas, Dorothy Kirsten, Thomas Stewart, Paul Plishka, Anna Moffo, Martina Arroyo, Joan Sutherland, Luciano Pavortti, Gail Robinson, Cornell MacNeil, Montserrat Caballe, Placido Domingo, Richard Tucker, Leontyne Price, Leonie Rysanek, Jon Vickers, Birgit Nilsson and many others. Truly a cornucopia of great artists and performances—a remarkable tribute to Sir Bing.**Metropolitan Opera Gala**—March 16, 1968
Metropolitan Opera Gala—April 22, 1972
https://www.youtube.com/watch?v=xFB_y9W4Kgg&t=1125s

A Diversion: Carnegie Hall and the history of More Pirate Recordings

(Almost all of the performances mentioned in this section are available on tape or CD—some on YouTube)

Since its inauguration in May of 1891, Carnegie Hall has stood as the apex of artistic achievement and a career goal for most classical music performers.

I never have had the pleasure of doing solo work at Carnegie Hall—all my appearances at that hall were within the arena of choral work. I sang there in various productions for about twelve years (1980–1992), at about the same time while I was working at Mr. Tape. Singing in the chorus allowed me to do much more observing than might have been possible otherwise.

In checking through my files, the first time I sang at Carnegie Hall was for Boris Christoff's New York Farewell concert on March 24, 1980. I had begun doing professional choral work in New York City the year before and I had sung a number of times in Avery Fisher Hall (now David Geffen Hall), but not Carnegie Hall, so I was excited about finally being on that stage.

I don't remember a lot about Boris Christoff. He was kept rather insulated from the chorus when he was not on stage, but I do remember an imposing (and colorful) personality that included a mesmerizing stage presence even without the aid of costumes or scenery (especially in the Boris Godunov death scene). He was at the end of a long and illustrious career and this concert truly was what one would call "legendary." Ed Rosen went to that concert to tape the performance, which included arias from Macbeth and Don Carlo—releasing them as a CD compilation of Christoff on Legato Classics (Boris Christoff Live Recordings 1953–1980—LCD-197). It was an important pirated release at the time.

Since my being at Carnegie Hall revolved around choral work, most of my strongest memories are of concert opera performances with Eve Queler (1931–). One of the first was Verdi's I due Foscari that Eve resuscitated on November 1, 1981. For decades she was known for digging up and dusting off neglected works and (for the most part) presenting them in their best light. I remember I due Foscari vividly because of the cover cast soprano. (Cover singers are hired to learn roles with the understanding that if the major artist becomes ill, they will step in at the scheduled performance. Usually, they are given a performance of their own as well. This gives the orchestra and conductor a chance to run through the piece as a unit, to get a feeling for timing and pacing.)

The cover Lucrezia was a young American soprano, Susan Dunn. It was her first professional job and there was a wonderful, open friendliness about her that was as appealing as it is rare in the operatic world. Rather than keep to herself, she welcomed the company of solo artists and choral members alike. She was as genuinely excited about this, her first "job," as we were about hearing her glorious instrument. I remember well that her voice was magnificent. It had one of the richest middle registers I had heard in a soprano—even if the top seemed a bit short. (There are many high Cs throughout the difficult role of Lucrezia and they seemed to be Dunn's comfortable limit.) I harbored the suspicion that she might, in actuality, be a mezzo-soprano. Whatever she was, she was the real thing. For her age (early 20s), her voice was huge and beautiful. (We performed the opera with the cover cast somewhere on Long Island.) Dunn sang the hell out of the role with full, rich sound and a thrilling intensity. She never got a review of her performance, at least not one that I saw. For a few years she and her voice prospered—she being hailed as the new American spinto. I was very saddened to learn that the trajectory of her career would be cut short because of vocal problems—she was one of America's treasures and it appeared that she would amplify that position had she been able to continue.

Verdi—*I due Foscari*—Carnegie Hall (in-house)—1981 with Renato Bruson, Maria Castro-Alberty (not Dunn).

https://www.youtube.com/watch?v=3T4TwujqZv0

In the 1980s when there was ample government funding of the performing arts, there were a number of "composer festivals" at Carnegie Hall that used professional choruses, each festival featuring three or four works. I enjoyed singing in each and learned much about the "stars" from watching them work. The 1982–83 season saw a Rossini Festival that was obviously meant to highlight the art of Columbia artist, mezzo-soprano, Marilyn Horne. It included a revival of Semiramide (January 10, 1983), a work that was then unfamiliar to New York audiences. June Anderson replaced an ailing Montserrat Caballe and stunned New York listeners with the purity of the high Es that she sprinkled liberally throughout her showpiece, "Bel raggio." Marilyn Horne was a dynamic and exciting Arsace, delivering her arias with remarkable flexibility, style, and singing with Anderson with great sensitivity in their two big duets. At the other end of the range, bass Samuel Ramey tickled just about everyone's fancy as the mad Assur.

Rossini—**"Bel raggio"** *Semiramide*—Carnegie Hall. January 10, 1983—June Anderson—Henry Lewis

https://www.youtube.com/watch?v=5MzUp9WGjuU

Another work produced during that festival was Tancredi (May 28, 1983), a performance specifically mounted for Marilyn Horne. I remember it mainly because of her graciousness as an artist. While being vociferously applauded for a bravura act II aria (accompanied by the men's chorus) Horne turned around with her back to the audience and applauded us, mouthing "Thank you!" Many artists choose to forget how important a chorus's contribution can be to the success of their work, but not Horne. In that generosity, she included us in her applause.

Rossini—*Tancredi* Act II Duet—Carnegie Hall, May 28, 1983—Marilyn Horne & Leila Cuberli.

https://www.youtube.com/watch?v=dEMCxo8nu74

Another in the series was a Donna del Lago featuring Frederica von Stade (who was amazingly flexible) Rockwell Blake, and Marilyn Horne. Donal Henahan felt that Horne stole the show:

> It was Miss Horne who stirred up the audience to the fiercest pitch of approval, not only with her solo flights in such numbers as "Mura felici" but with her high-flying heroics in the ensembles, which her superbly powerful and flexible mezzo voice dominated thrillingly. (*The New York Times*, 11/15/82)

Rossini—*Donna del Lago*—Carnegie Hall, (in-house)1982
https://www.youtube.com/watch?v=qF6vVOjxpCM

As sometimes happens, each of the three Rossini operas performed during that Matthew Epstein-sponsored series lost its original European leading lady and had American replacements. Agnes Baltsa bowed out of Donna del Lago and was succeeded by Federica von Stade; Montserrat Caballe cancelled Semiramide and June Anderson took over, and Lella Cuberli took over for Ileana Cotrubas as Amenaide in Tancredi.

The next year (in March, 1984) there was a rare concert revival of Donizetti's Dom Sebastian (Queler) with Richard Leech, Klara Takacs, and Lajos Miller. I recently heard a tape of the performance (which was quite wonderful) and was flabbergasted to realize that I had sung in the chorus and don't remember a note of the music!

Donizetti—*Dom Sebastiano*—Carnegie Hall, 1984—Richard Leech, Klara Takas, Lajos Miller
https://www.youtube.com/watch?v=wnpHV2LGj40

That year there was also an Eve Queler *William Tell* (separate from and not part of the other Rossini Festival) to highlight the beautiful singing of Piero Cappuccilli. He sang like a god at Carnegie Hall. This opera also had a cover cast performance that included fledgling stars, Chris Merritt and Aprile Millo (November 20, 1984). Although considered artistic lightweights, as so often happens, singers in the cover cast were often superior to the artists who sang at Carnegie Hall. Stefka Estatieva (Carnegie Hall) was perfectly acceptable as Mathilde, and is generally a fine singer. Aprile Millo, however, had that certain spark one missed in the other soprano. During rehearsals Millo was definitely accessible to one and all but proved to be a complicated woman of many facets. Chris Merritt, who sang his heart out at Lehmann College in the Bronx, was elegance personified. Franco Bonisolli who sang Arnold at Carnegie Hall, was not. Although he was gifted with a remarkable top register that he enjoyed exploiting, he was a posturing embarrassment.

Rossini—"Ah se privo di speme è l'amore" *Guglielmo Tell*—Aprile Millo/Chris Merritt November 20, 1984
https://www.youtube.com/watch?v=T6CbUQ2eFCc

Also in 1984, there was a wonderful "French Opera Comique Festival" also sponsored by Columbia Artists Management which included a lovely performance of Massenet's Cherubin with Frederica von Stade, Ashley Putnam, Valerie Masterson, Lorraine Nubar, and Sam Ramey.

Massenet—*Cherubin*—Canegie Hall, 1984
https://www.youtube.com/watch?v=wsu5sCZ9jtA

There was also Thomas's Mignon, again with Frederica von Stade as a delicious Mignon,

Gianna Rolandi as a crystalline, bravura Philine, and Barry McCauley as a lyrical Wilhelm, Kenneth Montgomery conducted.

On April 2, 1984, Donald Henahan reported in The New York Times:

> Mignon is actually a contest between the two female characters, who represent opposite temperaments and human qualities. Philine, the unscrupulous temptress, naturally has the most brilliant music to sing and Miss Rolandi took full advantage of that. Slipping into the role as if it were tailored for her, she flounced around in the best prima donna manner and threw the house into a frenzy with her dazzling "Je suis Titania," whose high E-flat was fired off with appropriate theatricality. Philine is a dizzy lady and Miss Rolandi provided dizzying coloratura all evening to match the character. Hers was no canary's tweeting, either, but full-toned, richly colored singing.
>
> Against Philine's pyrotechnics, Mignon can put only gentleness and pathos. Miss von Stade, who is a virtuoso manipulator of these qualities, offered the utmost contrast to her rival in both temperament and voice. She took "Connais-tu le Pays" at an almost funereal tempo, which lent the aria a certain lifelessness in spite of Miss von Stade's sensitive and sonorous treatment of the text. But she knew what she was doing. As the opera progressed, her Mignon gradually conquered by the power of a purer love, not to mention the discovery in the final scene that she is the long lost daughter of a rich old gentleman named Lothario. Actually, it would be possible to play Mignon as a girl of considerably more spunk (she is not above wishing down lightning on Philine at one point), but Miss von Stade's sad and languid portrayal did set out the opera's moral and emotional contrasts effectively.

Thomas—"Je suis Titania" *Mignon*—Carnegie Hall, 1984—Montgommery
https://www.youtube.com/watch?v=PSChVNapcAw

A now famous performance of Handel's *Semele* (the original, 1744 version), was conducted by John Nelson on February 23, 1985. It was part of the Handel series that year. Because of my schedule I was not able to sing in the chorus. It was one of the few works I regretted not being able to sing. But I did manage to tape it. Most of my friends sang in it and the performance was truly magic: Kathleen Battle, Sylvia McNair, Marilyn Horne, Jeffrey Gall, Rockwell Blake, and Samuel Ramey all conducted by John Nelson. Although chorus members generally do not care about having a copy of performances they were in, this Semele was one of the few exceptions. When they heard that I had a copy of the performance, everyone wanted one. Critics judged it a spectacular performance. Sponsored by Columbia Artists Management with ornamentation by Randolph Mickelson, it was one of those rare nights at Carnegie Hall where everything pulled together in the right way.

Handel—*Semele*—Carnegie Hall, 1985 Kathleen Battle, Marylin Horne, Samuel Ramey, Rockwell Blake—John Nelson
https://www.youtube.com/watch?v=FIzmBDzon_E

Two months later saw a rare revival of Lalo's *Le Roi D'Ys* (April 14, 1985), another Eve Queler extravaganza (that had some lovely choral work) with Barbara Hendricks, Alan Titus, Tiberi Raffanti, and Cleopatra Ciurca. This is a wonderful work (with an especially exquisite overture) and This was a lovely performance, especially from the Corsican tenor, Raffanti, who had a sweet voice and manner and did an excellent job with the opera's most famous number, the "Aubade." Cleopatra Ciurca rarely sang in the United States. but she gave a wonderfully nuanced portrait of Margared. It was also nice to see and hear the sweet crystalline soprano of Barbara Hendricks, whom Gale and I had met years earlier when Barbara was working with Larry Skrobacs. By the time of the Lalo performance Barbara rarely sang in New York, having settled in Paris. When she first went to France in the late 1970s, we became custodians of her piano, which was moved into our apartment.

Eve Queler first hired Gale to cover Gabriela Benackova in Smetana's Libuse (March 13, 1986). Gale sang the American premiere on March 8, in the cover performance at Lehman College. (Benackova, who was singing the Carnegie Hall performance, fondly called Gale "Little Libuse") Gale loved singing the role of Libuse and it seemed tailor-made for her voice. So much so, that the other Czech singers in the cast all agreed she should come to Czechoslovakia to sing Libuse, their National Opera. Gale's performance was so successful that Eve hired her to sing Imelda in Verdi's Battaglia di Legnano with Aprile Millo (January 12, 1987). The real purpose of her "assignment" however, was to cover Millo's vocal line during ensembles so that Aprile could rest up for climactic high notes. It was so successful, that no one was aware. Eve then hired Gale to cover Linda Kelm as the Foreign Princess in Dvorak's Rusalka in May of 1987.

One of my favorite moments from that production was a personal one—and one which I actually managed to tape. Gale sang the Foreign Princess during a Carnegie Hall rehearsal because Linda Kelm had an emergency and could not attend. The Act II ending (when the Foreign Princess curses the Prince) is especially dramatic with a number of high notes. Gale's vehemence was such that the orchestra applauded her singing.

An opera-chorus job with Eve Queler was always an adventure, but I especially remember what was probably the last time I sang at Carnegie Hall (April 5, 1992). Ironically, it was again I due Foscari, the first opera I sang at that hall in 1981! This time, however, there were some interesting differences. First there was the narcissistic Vladimir Chernov singing the Doge. Oh, he sang well, don't get me wrong, it was just that during rehearsals he seemed more concerned with his hair and its styling than his interpretation or his singing. The chorus took bets on the number of times he would toss his hair in each act. I also remember that during I due Foscari the artistic question came up as to whether Martile Rowland, the Lucrezia, should offer one of her (fabulous) high E-flats at the end of the opera. (She tried it during one of the rehearsals to great applause.) It was decided, however, that it would not be appropriate because it would detract from Chernov's final scene. Martile should have done it anyway.

Verdi—"Più non vive l'innocente" *I Due Foscari*—Carnegie Hall, 1992
https://www.youtube.com/watch?v=2UgXJMmPgEk

Martile burst into New York's awareness when she stepped in to replace Mara Zampieri in Eve Queler's resuscitation of Roberto Devereux (January 9, 1991). Eve rewarded Martile with a number of excellent productions that underlined her strengths. The fact that Martile seemed born to sing the dramatic coloratura repertoire was merely icing on the vocal cake. She reigned supreme in Eve's branch of this repertoire for almost a decade and was a fascinating singer. Even more important, she was a considerate colleague and a nice, modest person. That is not meant to suggest that she had no temperament. Similar to Marisa Galvany in the 1970s, Martile gloried in the exploitation of her high register, throwing in top Ds and Es whenever she could. Although purists clucked their tongues, audiences were thrilled and certainly got their money's worth.

Donizetti—*Roberto Devereux* (abr)—Carnegie Hall 1991
https://www.youtube.com/watch?v=FJJ9qOwPxv8

Martile went on to sing at the Met, although they did not seem to know what to do with her. She only sang four performances with them: two Acts of I puritani, when she stepped in for an ailing colleague, one performance of La bohème in the Parks and two performances of *Lucia di Lammermoor*.

In March of 1994 she sang a memorable revival of Donizetti's Caterina Cornaro with a suave-voiced Renato Bruson for Eve Queler.

Donizetti *Caterina Cornaro* —Carnegie Hall 1994
https://www.youtube.com/watch?v=hWr5sk_wNrY

Recitals? Countless recitals. I remember Anna Russell's farewell recital at Carnegie Hall (April 15, 1984) even though I didn't take part in it. I sure laughed enough—especially during her infamous analysis of Wagner's Ring Cycle (and, yes, I taped it).

Gale had met Anna Russell (1911–2006) years before. Having moved to Manhattan in January of 1975, in March of 1978, Gale returned to Morgantown, West Virginia to sing two performances of the mezzo part in the Verdi Requiem with Frances Yeend, Jon Crain, and George Osborne, conducted by Donald Portnoy. One was given at the Creative Arts Center at the University on March 18th. It was recorded and released on LP by Mark Recording Company. There was to be a second performance in Charleston a few days later, so Gale stayed on with Frances and her husband, James Benner.

Meanwhile, Anna Russell had come to WVU to give a concert (unfortunately on the same night as the Charleston Verdi Requiem). Frances and Anna were old friends, so Frances invited Anna and her accompanist to her home for dinner the night before both their concerts. Gale remembers much laughter and warmth from Anna Russell who regaled them with bits from her show, and bantered back and forth diva-style with Frances.

Years later, I was contacted by Australian conductor Brian Castles-Onion who was a friend of Anna Russell's. She was looking for a tape of a performance she had done in Canada of Fille du regiment where she entertained, as only she could, as the Duchess of Crackenthorpe. Brian knew I was a serious collector of live performances, so he got in touch with me to see if I had that particular performance. I did, and gladly sent a copy to Anna, who very kindly sent an autographed photo to me and Gale (whom Anna remembered after all those years!).

I taped a couple of other recitals at Carnegie. Surreptitious taping there was not easy. There were too many people squashed together higher up in the house where I had to sit for the best recording. I managed to capture the exquisite Alfredo Kraus (October 7, 1990), who proved that good technique and sensible role choices do contribute to a singer's longevity.

Alfred Kraus Recital—Carnegie Hall 1990
https://www.youtube.com/watch?v=5adRpXPCzm4

About a month later, I taped a young and darkly handsome Dimitri Hvorovstovsky in his New York recital debut on November 4, 1990. That was the beginning of a love affair he had with New York City that lasted until his death in 2017.

There were some real eye-openers. One was an outstanding recital given by Roberta Peters and Lawrence Skrobacs (January 17, 1985). Peters was the kind of singer who never avoided programming full, difficult recitals. That night her rock-solid technique shocked an audience that remembered her operatic debut at the Metropolitan Opera thirty-five years earlier. There were the many wonderful PDQ Bach extravaganzas, the Renee Fleming Bel Canto excursions with Eve Queler (La straniera, Armida, Lucrezia Borgia), a Strauss festival in the 1990s, and much more.

Bellini—*La straniera*—Carnegie Hall 1993
https://www.youtube.com/watch?v=P2bk6kg98oI
Donizetti—**"Era desso"** *Lucrezia Borgia*—Carnegie Hall 2000
https://www.youtube.com/watch?v=sPojAITg1Mk

At one time, Renee Fleming was also in a cover cast for Eve Queler—singing Amina in *La Sonnambula* at Pace University in February of 1991. Fortunately, the performance was taped since Fleming was a lovely Amina. She even offered a lovely diminuendo on the high E flat between the verses of the final "Ah non giunge." Even after only five years into her professional career (she made her debut in Salzburg in 1986) she was showing that she was maturing into a major artist.

Bellini—*La sonnambula*—Pace University, NY 1991
https://www.youtube.com/watch?v=48auHPFKc_I

Fleming's coloratura skills were not a surprise to those that had followed the singer. She had sung a Maria Padilla in Omaha that displayed not only her florid skills, but also her great range. The opera was preceded by a concert Fleming gave of bel canto works of Donizetti, Rossini and Bellini.

Donizetti—*Maria Padilla*—Omaha, September, 1990
https://www.youtube.com/watch?v=gigsX4klW7I

One of the most memorable events (even if bitter-sweet) was the re-opening of Carnegie Hall after its extensive renovation. Musicians were very concerned that the acoustics not be tampered with and specialists were hired to deal with that issue. Renovations began May 18, 1986 and stretched over twenty-eight weeks. I sang in the re-opening on December 15, 1986 and anyone who sang in the hall before the renovation knows exactly what I am going to say. The cosmetic changes were beautiful and very necessary. However, one noticed that a high crispness had been lost from the hall's acoustics after the renovation. The chorus noticed it during rehearsals when the hall was empty, but it was especially noticeable when the hall was full of people. To be honest though, the differences were minimal and what mattered more importantly was that we had our Carnegie Hall back.

I like to think that perhaps somewhere in the ether of that hall, the sound of my voice is blended with those of all of the other artists that have raised their voices in song throughout the decades—and that makes me proud.

Ron Pollard

Shortly after I began to work at Mr. Tape, I met Ron Pollard, an acquaintance of Ralph's. Ralph thought that the two of us should meet since we both had such a love of live opera performances, coloraturas, and especially Roberta Peters. That must have been around 1981. Both Ron and I were collectors. Ron not only collected recordings of live performances, he went to performances and taped them.

As explained earlier, pirating during the 1970s to 1990s was an underground activity that was complicated. Having gotten a taste of being a pirate myself at Wolftrap in 1971, I thought I would try my hand at more sophisticated pirating. To be fair, there was something else that played into that decision. My love of collecting live performances.

There were a number of things that needed deciding upon before I began. Even then, there were many different types of portable cassette recorders and microphones to choose from. I settled on a Sony-Pro Walkman which cost about $120.00 at the time. This was not a small amount of money for a struggling singer. However, if you want to create something of value you must have a decent machine. Next, one had to select the type and length of cassette tape to use for taping. The aim was to get an act per side—to avoid having to turn the tape during music. In some cases (mainly Wagner) this simply could not be avoided.

Ron taught me the art of theater taping and the many things that one had to take into consideration to obtain a good archival tape. This included explaining about various operas that could be problematic when taping, the timing of acts, and the best way to change a cassette tape, if you had to, during a performance. Before going to a performance, I would have the tape deck set up to record, and the first cassette inserted. I used the Sony-Pro with a $120.00 mike that I had bought specifically for pirating. (Yes, the microphone cost as much as the recorder.) I preferred to use high chrome Maxell or TDK tapes; and at times, depending on the importance of the performance, I would even use metal tapes, but they were costly.

I carried a small, thin-mesh black vinyl bag over my shoulder with the cassette recorder inside with the volume pre-set. When I got to my seat, I would put the bag on my lap, making sure that the mike was easily reached by my hands. Once the chandeliers began to ascend (one of my favorite moments at the Met) and the house got dark, I would take the mike out, press the record button on the recorder, and gently hold the mike out over the balcony—making sure that I did not move around in my seat. That was crucial. Movement draws attention. Generally, because it was so dark up in the area of the study desks, and because the microphone was dark in color, no one could tell I had a microphone in my hand.

I usually sat high-up in the house, next to the study (or score) desks on either side of the auditorium since they were single seats. These seats are for musicians who want to follow the opera with a score that they would bring for that purpose. There is a lot of wood up there that reflects the sound beautifully. Most of the time no one sat next to me at the study desk (only behind me) making the taping process a little less stressful. Although the view could be restricted, the sound was spectacular. It was easy to monitor the recording because the thin mesh of the bag let me see the LED lights during recording. I would keep my hand loosely in the bag in case I needed to adjust the recording volume. I remember one night when both Ron Pollard and I were at the Met to tape a performance. He pointed out other people throughout the audience who were also taping. Usually, I preferred to sit house left; Ron preferred house right.

I was almost caught only once during a 1990 performance of Die Entführung aus dem Serail with Mariella Devia. During that performance I was seated house right. I was jittery and my squirming around must have looked suspicious, thereby alerting the woman behind me. (I didn't dare look back.) I could sense her getting up to go back to talk to the usher. Sure enough, he came and stood behind me to see if I was up to something. He never said a word; just stood quietly behind me. I sensed what was happening, so I remained very still. I didn't dare take out the microphone. I just sat there. Once the music began and I hadn't made any odd moves, the usher left. By that time, I had lost my desire to tape the performance. I was so rattled that I left during the intermission. If I had been caught, they would definitely have confiscated my tape and, possibly, the recorder.

In the end it turned out fine. I got a copy of that performance from Ron, who was also there that night. I recorded other performances of the run with Mariella Devia so I was able to study her consistency throughout that run of Constanzas. I certainly learned a lesson about being circumspect and subtle when taping! None of the tapes I made were ever sold. They were only used for my personal, analytical reference. Occasionally, an artist would contact me and I would gladly make them a copy. For free. For me, as a singer and a vocal historian, one of the important things was to come to understand how operatic singers worked within a production and to note their vocal consistency during a run of performances. I continue to refer to those tapes when I write about a singer. They are my reality check showing me exactly what a singer did well and not so well.

I generally did not tape recitals, unless I felt them to be really important. One such special event that I taped was the U.S. debut of the Norwegian pop singing duo, Dollie de Luxe during the "Serious Fun!" series at Alice Tully Hall. Their performance was on July 25, 1987. The two high-voiced sopranos, Benedicte Adrian (lead vocal) and Ingrid Bjornov—keyboard and vocal—debuted in 1980, and from 1984 called themselves Dollie de Luxe. Surrounded by a traditional rock band, their specialty was to combine popular music with classical operatic arias. Although not a new concept, their voice types enabled an unusual slant on such merging.

> In 1985 they scored a Top 20 hit in France with their single 'Queen of the Night/Satisfaction.' Their musical *Which Witch* premiered at Bergen International Festival in 1987. The musical was staged at a West End theatre in London in 1992, with 76 performances. In 1995 they toured with the musical *Henriette og hennes siste ekte menn*, and also released the album *Prinsessens utvalgte* with selections from the musical. They were Norway's Eurovision Song Contest contestants in 1984.
> (Wikipedia)

Between 1980 and 1999, they recorded a number of albums, some of which went silver and gold. Although immensely popular in Europe, they never managed to conquer the United States.

I taped their debut at Alice Tully Hall while sitting with some singer friends. We thought it a brilliant night. Dollie de Luxe began with selections from their Rock Opera: Which Witch that had premiered earlier that year. The second half of the show displayed a skillful merging of various popular Beatles and Rolling Stones songs with arias. Although I found the concert clever and great fun, most of the New York audience did not know what to make of these strange singers and by the intermission many people had left the concert hall. Despite the degree of sophistication of New York music audiences, they just did not get what the group was attempting to do.

Although I do not entirely agree with him, Bernard Holland of the New York Times brought up some interesting points in his review for The New York Times on Monday, July 27, 1987:

> ...Dollie De Luxe is well-meaning; not totally without talent but, I'm afraid, terribly naive. One wonders at Lincoln Center's decision-making process in bringing it to this festival. Saturday's audience divided itself between the bemused and the amused, with smatterings of enthusiasm as well. It

was treated first to excerpts from "Which Witch"—a quasi-opera on witch-hunting in 16th-century Heidelberg...

'Rock vs. Opera' followed, in which Miss Adrian's coloratura soprano agonized over the Queen of the Night aria as the Stones were being evoked as accompaniment. Then there were Bizet and the Beatles and so on. It was an embarrassing evening, but one that raises points worth thinking about. Mixing rock and Mozart, first of all, is not a desecration, nor is it necessarily tasteless. Here it seemed simply a waste of time.

No matter what has been said about that performance, my tape (in excellent sound) remains one of my treasures.

Their infamous CD "Rock vs Opera" is now a hard-to-find cult item and the 1993 London performance of their Rock Opera, Which Witch, released on CD in 1997, commands exorbitant prices at amazon.com.

Earlier that year, at the end of January, I taped another landmark recital, the New York recital debut of soprano Mariella Devia, accompanied by Eve Queler. (Devia made her operatic debut in 1973 and sang her final operatic stage performance in May of 2018 as Norma, a 45-year career on stage. Although she continues to concertize as of this writing.) Through selections by Cimarosa, Pergolesi, Rossini, Donizetti, and Bellini, she gave listeners their money's worth. My tape of this made the rounds with collectors and I suspect it is the source for perhaps all of the existing copies.

Mariella Devia Recital—New York Debut, 1987
https://www.youtube.com/watch?v=NXz2Fik3p58

Two years later, in November of 1989, I taped another recital in Alice Tully Hall, the New York recital debut of Slovak soprano, Edita Gruberova. By this time she had been singing at the Metropolitan Opera for a decade. She offered songs by Brahms, Dvorak, Mendelssohn, and Strauss, as well as the mad scene from Hamlet (as an encore). That tape, too, has made the rounds.

In November of 1990 I taped a Roberta Peters recital honoring the fortieth anniversary of her career, and ten years later, in November of 2000, I taped the Alice Tully Hall recital honoring her 50th. (I came out of my own retirement from pirating to document that evening.)

Back to the 1980s. While I was working at Mr. Tape and had started to grow my own considerable library of reel-to-reel tapes, Ron and I began trading tapes. We continued to trade (at first reel-to-reels, then cassettes, then CDs) until around 2006—when both of us had life changes and became too busy. We are still in touch. Before I moved to Pennsylvania in 2019, we often met for coffee at Starbucks, to talk and catch up.

For about twenty years we provided each other with numerous precious performances. One of the things we continue to do is look for "new" bell songs from Lakmé, our favorite aria. Qualifying as a new version might not be one recorded this year, but perhaps a recently unearthed recording from 1905. Over the years we have discovered many obscure and satisfying performances. I now have a ridiculously large collection of more than six hundred commercial and live recordings of the bell song dating between 1903 and 2023. (Most of the "new" versions are obtained from videos uploaded to YouTube.) It may be a bit excessive, but I love them all.

It was from Ron that I got some of my most prized New York City Opera and Metropolitan Opera in-house performances. It was also from Ron that I first learned about Gianna Rolandi, Ashley Putnam, Beverly Hoch, and many others. His library of live opera and concert performances from around the world is truly staggering, and his generosity in sharing them with me during the 1980s was something I will never forget. (In many instances, if Ron liked a specific singer, he would travel wherever necessary to hear (and usually tape) them. I often benefitted from those trips.)

When I first met Ron he was a fan and friend of Roberta Peters. During the following years he befriended a number of high sopranos including Gianna Rolandi, Faith Esham, Beverly Hoch, Ruth Ann Swenson, and, for a period of time he even worked as personal assistant for Martina Arroyo.

Ron remembers how his love for high sopranos began:

> When I was in 6th grade, my music teacher, Mr Herman Hollingsworth, gave me a 45 rpm of a singer he thought I'd enjoy. It was Lily Pons and the record was excerpts from *Lakmé*. (it is still my favorite opera and aria today.) (Private email)

Also interested in musical theatre, Ron joined a local group and during the first year, among other works, they performed Herbert's Naughty Marietta.

> Anyone who could sing the 'Italian Street Song' was OK by me! One night while watching Ed Sullivan, a petite soprano sang the 'Italian Street Song.' Luckily, I had my tape recorder hooked up to the TV and recorded it. She also sang another song with Al Hirt on the trumpet. I was amazed at the agility and fluidity of her voice. About a week later, in a local record store, I ran across an album by the soprano on the Ed Sullivan Show. I bought it, played it, and was hooked. The album was the complete *Lucia di Lammermoor* and the soprano was Roberta Peters. (Incidentally, the song she sang with Al Hirt was the Shadow Song from *Dinorah* with trumpet obbligato!)
>
> Later Ms.Peters and I became friends. I will always be grateful to her and her wonderful voice and personality (with a special thanks to Lily Pons too!)" (private email)

I share here a casual interview I had with Ron in 2016.

Nick: When did you start live taping? When did you stop? (Or haven't you?)

Ron: I started taping as early as 1967 at a concert with Roberta Peters in Tampa, Florida. The first complete opera that I taped was on a reel-to-reel portable recorder in 1970, and was *Rigoletto* with San Carlo Opera (Tampa Florida). I used a reel-to-reel recorder even after coming to New York City in 1978. I only switched to cassette when I could no longer get the recorder fixed.

I have never stopped taping. I HATE the compressed sound of SIRIUS broadcasts...it misses the overtones of the house and makes everyone's voice sound the same size (which we know they are not).

Nick: Were you ever caught taping?

Ron: I've been caught several times...you smile and say...sorry...and life goes on.

Nick: Was taping in the Met and other places more difficult after 9/11?

Ron: Not really, they never really check the bags—and by that time I had switched to mini disc which was much easier to hide.

Nick: What are some of the most treasured performances you taped?

Ron: Anything with Roberta Peters/Anna Moffo/Mary Costa. These were the three ladies who helped open the door to the opera world for me and I will always be grateful to them. I have seen many wonderful performances through the years...and many mediocre ones too. A lot of the Florida performances were very memorable...as it was the first time I had seen these operas. La fanciulla del West with Neblett/Domingo/Colzani in Miami was a stand-out...as was a Ruth Welting Contes d'Hoffmann and *Lucia di Lammermoor*. One of my tapes—a *Tosca* with Anna Moffo has gone around the world.

Nick: Do you still listen to the tapes you made? I know that a few years ago, you got rid of some.

Ron: If I was interested in a performance or a singer, I would transfer it to CD; if not…and it was something I would probably never listen to again…out it went. I still listen to tapes I made of Gianna Rolandi, Faith Esham, Ashley Putnam, Beverly Hoch, Ruth Ann Swenson…all my "divas."

Nick: You knew a lot of the people who were pirating back in the 1980s. On any given night, how many would you say were taping?

Ron: Depending on the performance or the singers…at least three people were taping at the Met or NYCO.

Nick: What is your philosophy about the difference between "taping" back in the 1980s and now?

Ron: I think that most of those performances in the 1980s and 1990s were memorable though we didn't know it at the time. Today, one performance tends to sound like another and most singers are either mediocre or just blah. The only favorites I have at present are Jonas Kaufmann and Sarah Coburn. I like several others…but wouldn't go out of my way to hear them. (Private email, September, 2016)

Ron was able to attend many performances, but because of my work and performing schedules, I did not get to as many as I would have liked. I had to be careful about buying tickets in advance because I never knew if I might be singing that night. I was often called for a gig at the last moment and ended up not being able to use a ticket that I had already purchased.

The performances that I did attend, I taped. That included Leonie Rysanek's twenty-fifth anniversary gala at the Met in February, 1984, where she sang act I of *Die Walküre* and act II of *Parsifal* with Peter Hofmann and Franz Mazura. I later learned that at least four people were there taping that night.

One situation was unusual. I was hired to sing in the chorus of William Tell that Eve Queler had mounted (in Italian) in concert at Carnegie Hall. One of the requirements of that job was to sing a cover cast performance at Lehman Center. As mentioned before, a cover cast performance gives the conductor and orchestra an opportunity to work through the entire opera at one time. It also gave the chorus a chance to get a better idea of where they fit into the production. It also gave the cover cast a chance to perform. That particular cover cast included Chris Merritt as Arnold and a young Aprile Millo as Matilde. It was November of 1984, a month before Aprile made an early, surprise Metropolitan Opera debut, replacing an ailing soprano in Verdi's *Simon Boccanegra*. Millo was very "new" and even shared a lunch with some of the chorus members during a rehearsal at Lehman College.

During the dress rehearsal with the cover cast, Millo decided to take an interpolated, final high E in the grand act II duet with Chris Merritt. It was an uncommonly beautiful and brilliant note and I immediately thought that it needed to get taped. Unfortunately, I couldn't do it since I was going to be on stage. So I called Ron. He bought a ticket at the last minute, came to the performance, and taped it. Just as Anna Moffo's *Tosca* and some other performances that circulate through operatic circles today, it is Ron's tape that preserved that performance that so many people enjoy!

Rossini—"Ah se privo" Aprile Millo with Chris Merritt (Guglielmo Tell)—Carnegie Hall 1984

https://www.youtube.com/watch?v=T6CbUQ2eFCc

One moment that I was not able to preserve was a Town Hall rehearsal of Pacini's Saffo when, once again, I sang in the chorus. The concert performance, in February, 1982, was put on by Opera Rediviva. It was their debut, the brainchild of Richard Kapp, who led the Philharmonia Virtuosi, a chamber ensemble, and who was involved with the production of various offbeat operas. Although mounted for the soprano who sang Saffo (whose name escapes me), the most well-known singers in the cast were baritone Louis Quilico (1925–2000) and dramatic mezzo-soprano, Bianca Berini (1928–2004). During a final rehearsal, Berini was joking around and took a (very good) final high E-flat at the end of her big act II aria. The chorus, conductor, and other singers, laughed aloud while applauding her bravery (and the note's remarkable success). During the actual concert some days later, however, Berini decided not repeat that stunt (although she could obviously have done so.)

I occasionally brought my Sony Pro tape recorder to rehearsals. One such time was the dress rehearsal of Anna Bolena that Dame Joan Sutherland sang at Avery Fisher Hall in November of 1985. Having not been hired for the chorus for that gig, I taped the rehearsal from the audience.

Probably my most interesting memento is the dress rehearsal for Janacek's House of the Dead, the famous March, 1983 concert-production at Avery Fisher Hall with Richard Cassily, John Cheek, and Philip Creech with Rafael Kubelik conducting. During that rehearsal I actually taped while onstage.

At first, during piano rehearsals at St Batholomew's Church on Park Avenue, I hated the score of House of the Dead. I thought it was hideous and I felt the rehearsals to be a real chore. When the chorus got together with the orchestra in Avery Fisher Hall, it was a different story. The opera sounded completely different with the colors of the orchestral instruments and Janacek's novel scoring. It was glorious! I was completely taken by the huge differences that Janacek's brilliant orchestral scoring had created. I became so enamored that I determined that I wanted a memento of at least the dress rehearsal. I brazenly took my Sony-Pro onstage to my seat at the top of the choral bleachers and taped the dress rehearsal. The result and sound quality of the recording of that rehearsal is not the greatest, but it was simply for my own enjoyment anyway. We did three or four performances and I loved each one. WQXR broadcast a performance and I eventually got a copy of that. It remains one of my favorite operas.

Janacek—From the House of the Dead—March, 1983, New York Philharmonic broadcast with Richard Cassily, John Cheek, Jon Fredrick West, and Philip Creech with Rafael Kubelik conducting

https://www.youtube.com/watch?v=YBP0P89fiDw

Although I could not tape as many times as I wanted to during the years when I did record, I was able to tape Joan Sutherland's 1983 Fille du Regiment with Alfredo Kraus, her 1987 Il trovatore with Luciano Pavarotti, Edita Gruberova's *Lucia di Lammermoor* (the full run) and Lucia Aliberti' Lucia di Lammermoor (1988) (full run), I puritani with Gruberova (1991, full run), as well as all of the *Elektra*s by Hildegard Behrens and Gwyneth Jones (1992–1994).

I also recorded complete (or almost complete) runs of Sam Ramey in Bluebeard's Castle (1989), *Otello* with Domingo (1987), Leonie Rysanek in Lohengrin (1986) and Jenufa (1992),

Mariella Devia in *Lucia di Lammermoor* (1989) and Entführung aus dem Serail (1991), as well as many single performances of other operas like Joan Sutherland's final *Lucia di Lammermoor* at the Metropolitan in 1982, Domingo in *La Gioconda* in 1982, Alfredo Kraus and Frederica von Stade in Werther (1988), Shirley Verrett's only Lady Macbeth (Macbeth) at the Metropolitan Opera (1988)—that was a remarkable evening—and Olivia Stapp's only *Elektra* at that house (December, 1984)—also remarkable.

From these tapes I learned much about the singers, their performance practices, and how they dealt with the stress of a consecutive string of performances or the pressures of an important, one-time-only performance.

For example, the soprano Deborah Voigt sang Chrysothemis in Behrens's performances of *Elektra* in 1994. It was early in Voigt's career—she had only come to the Met a year or two before. Chrysothemis is a difficult role with many exposed high notes and places in the score where the singer can run into vocal or rhythmical problems dealing with the huge orchestration. I found it fascinating to watch Voigt grow in the role. During the first performance problems appeared. By the second performance, those had been corrected. New, different phrase problems appeared in the second performance, but by the third, they, too, were fixed. The potentially nerve-wracking thing about performing is that you can rehearse all you want, but in the midst of the actual performance anything can throw you off or distract you—a particle of dust in the throat—whatever! My point is that Voigt was clearly paying attention to what she was doing during her performances and was aware of the problems that needed to be worked on. Different from many other singers who leave these issues to fix themselves, she obviously went home and, between performances, took stock of what had gone on in the last performance—working on the problems until they were fixed. By the final performance of her first run of Chrysothemis she had that role down pat and offered a seamless performance to listeners. That is the way of a real musician.

To be honest, I have never been enamored with Voigt's voice, but I have tremendous respect for her art and work ethic, as well as the degree of seriousness with which she obviously approaches her work. Another thing I learned from those *Elektra* performances was that Hildegard Behrens was vocally and emotionally impenetrable on stage. No matter what problems occurred during a performance, she kept going. During her first performance of *Elektra* at the Met (March of 1992) there were a number of cracked high notes and unsupported chest tones. Some of them were grotesque. Undeterred, Behrens simply made adjustments for the vocal mishaps as she went, and corrected the mis-alignment of the chest voice, incorporating all into the fabric of her interpretation. She did, however, cancel the remaining performances of *Elektra* that season.

Another example is Jessye Norman (1945–2019). I have never been a fan of her voice either, mainly because her vibrato inherently oscillated on the lower side of the pitch. That said, I have tremendous respect for her as an artist and as a person. As members of the New York Choral Artists, Gale and I sang with her in a special concert given at Avery Fisher Hall—Musicians Against Nuclear Arms on October 24, 1983. Kathleen Battle, the violinist Itzhak Perlman, and actor Paul Newman took part. (Gale shocked our less outgoing singing associates by simply walking up and talking casually to Paul Newman and later, Jessye Norman.) Zubin Mehta conducted. What an artist Jessye Norman was! There was not a dry eye in the theater when she finished Mahler's Ruckert song, "Ich bin der Welt abhanden gekommen." It was one of the most moving experiences in my musical life. She stopped time with her exquisite singing.

In my experience, only one other singer has managed this with her voice; that was Marilyn Horne during her "Great American Songbook" concert given at Avery Fisher Hall in December of 1983. In a group of Stephen Foster songs, she stopped time with her other-wordly singing.

To this day I consult almost all of those taped performances (like Ron, I have transferred many of them to CD or to MP3s). I learn from them all—and I treasure each.

Without my realizing it, my love of live operatic performances gradually transformed me into a vocal historian. I was interested in being able to examine and musically dissect live performances to learn what they could tell me about the technical reserves and vocal consistency of the artists. This also clarified much about their training and practice habits. Some singers were amazingly consistent—like Leonie Rysanek. Her Ortrude and Kundry (aside from a differently accented syllable or phrase) rarely changed. Each performance was as fiery as the last. Or, Placido Domingo. Some might question his commitment to various operas, but he is such a fine musician that he has managed to continue singing and make valuable artistic contributions for almost sixty years. So have Birgit Nilsson, Joan Sutherland, Alfredo Kraus, Luciano Pavarotti, and a host of others. There are many reasons why these singers were so famous, but the most important is their consistency as performers.

In the case of Gwyneth Jones, one has a perfect example of a singer who needed to be heard in large spaces. I taped all four of her *Elektra* performances at the Metropolitan Opera in April of 1994. She first sang the role in Cologne eleven years earlier in December of 1983, and thereafter sang the role quite often. At the age of 57, and in the Indian summer of her career, she gave four spectacular performances of the role—the first as good as the last. I sat in "peanut-heaven" next to the study desks, yet her voice was so huge that it seemed as if she was singing right next to me. Never have I heard such huge-voiced, beautiful high B-flats and Cs. Not only that, but her voice and her phrasing were completely responsive to her demands. Despite the expected Jones "mannerisms," these were truly magical performances. Leonie Rysanek singing Klytemnestra opposite Jones's *Elektra* was a special gift for listeners. Their confrontation scene was the stuff of legends. Actually, the success and vocal stature of Jones' *Elektra* should not be surprising. In a 2014 interview at the Royal Opera (found on YouTube) she remarked that *Elektra* was her favorite role, "but I waited twenty years to sing it."

Royal Opera Interview with Gwenyth Jones
https://www.youtube.com/watch?v=ncUBH7wO_fw

During the late 1990s, Ron became disillusioned with the wayward casting of many of the operas in New York. As a consequence, his taping slowly decreased and he now rarely tapes, preferring to get to know the many recordings already in his collection. I completely understand this because I, too, came to feel the same way.

I tired of the effort and stress required to record everything I went to. It became a chore, an unnecessary pressure that I documented each performance I attended. I was starting to not enjoy the performances—I was too preoccupied with the taping.

The End of Mr. Tape

Mr. Tape never became a huge business because of copyright laws. What Ralph Ferrandina did was illegal and the ramifications of that made the business complex. While the 1970 U.S. copyright acts allow for the recording of broadcasts for private use (taping inside an opera house has always been forbidden), by selling those performances and profiting from their sale, Ralph was breaking copyright law. Internationally, this becomes even more complicated because American copyright laws differ from those in Europe.

Did it bother me that I was involved in a business so "gray" in terms of legality? Especially since I was a professional singer, and a member of AGMA (American Guild of Musical Artists)? Not really, but I should explain.

Ethically, I admit there were times that I felt a slight twinge as I entered the office, but I always overcame that as I performed my job. There were a number of reasons why. One was that, regardless of the legal issues, like Ralph, I believed in what we were doing. I believed then—as I do now—that live recordings are an invaluable documentation of singers and their performing practices during the 20th and 21st centuries. They represent an artist's truth.

Like Ralph, I felt that this should be accessible to everyone. I cannot stress enough that another, important factor was that so many of the artists featured in our catalogue regularly visited the office to bring us new performances of theirs to add to our catalogue. It was a very accepting atmosphere in which to be working despite the reality of the laws.

Also, because I was young, I found it exciting to work in such an unusual (if naughty) environment. Because of my musical interests, working there was a dream come true. Access to these great performances sweetened the pie for me intellectually and I was able to separately compartmentalize my life in the Mr. Tape office with my life as a professional singer.

Much of my ease came from Ralph's attitude toward his business. I realize now, way after the fact, that there was a surprising naiveté in the man (or maybe it was a lack of arrogance). No matter, Ralph had a true, deep love and genuine respect for the art of singing.

Despite the apparent illegality, from everything Ralph said to me, I am sure that he believed that he was not only preserving and promoting something important, but that he was helping to safeguard the past, and the art of operatic tradition even as it was being created by its interpreters.

I got to meet many famous singers who brought their tapes to Ralph. He was a personal friend of many first-rank singers in New York, singers who applauded and appreciated his ability to get their work out to the public. During those times one either sang at a theatre, or on a radio broadcast, or on the occasional telecast. There was no YouTube, or the cloud, or sending people a link to see or hear your work. Unless you made commercial recordings, or could be found on mail-order pirate lists, opera-goers did not know your name or your work. This encouraging and accepting atmosphere was what I worked in, so legal concerns rarely entered my thinking.

Because of Ralph's sincere attitude I never felt furtive while working at Mr. Tape; neither was there anything sleazy about the work I did, nor the surroundings I was in. It was a first-class operation and I was proud of what we did because all who were involved cared deeply about the quality of what was being produced. I believed in the importance of making those invaluable performances not otherwise available to anyone before, easily accessible to all who wanted to hear and to learn from them. I felt I was an important, if only part-time, custodian of many great treasures of vocal art. A priceless library that, whether right or wrong, I felt all had a right to hear. What was interesting was that in the 1980s most singers I had contact with, both famous and not so famous, agreed with me, and felt that this was ultimately beneficial to their careers.

I do not regret a single moment of my time at Mr. Tape. But, of course, being a lover of operatic singing, tradition, and repertoire, the perks of working at that office were great. During those years, I had a finger on the pulse of every major operatic performance happening around the world and I was able to build my own extensive library; a library I consider invaluable in my work to this day. For that I am profoundly grateful. I was given a rare opportunity to learn about obscure works and experience their revivals and I often knew about singers who would become famous long before they became known.

On November 3, 1986, Mr.Tape was closed down by the FBI. This was not because of opera pirating specifically, but because of American Ballet videos, an operation in the office that I knew nothing about. Although I worked there at least three days a week, I dealt only with operas and audio and was never involved with video orders or the duplicating of ballet videos. Ralph took care of those himself.

Ironically, I would have been in the office that day, but I had taken the day off to rehearse for a concert I was participating in that night—the fiftieth anniversary gala of The American Guild of Musical Artists (AGMA) hosted by Beverly Sills. It was a major musical event held at the New York State Theater in Lincoln Center. All proceeds were donated to benefit the AGMA Relief Fund.

It was an amazing program! Conducted by Julius Rudel, many current and former opera singers took part including Gale's voice teacher from WVU, Frances Yeend. (Bill Zakariasen of the *Daily News* noted that Yeend "was apparently 70 but [sounded] marvelous"). Also singing were Robert Merrill, Paul Plishka, Samuel Ramey, Renata Scotto, James McCracken, and John Alexander. The most memorable moment for me was when Lucine Amara took center stage and sang a strikingly ferocious "In questa reggia" from *Turandot*. (And, yes, I taped some of that concert.)

Gale and I sang in the chorus for a segment of Alvin Ailey's Revelations. We sang the same selections that we would later perform at the gala opening of the New Jersey Performing Arts Center (NJPAC) on October 18, 1997.

I will never forget returning to the office the day after the AGMA Gala. I had a question for Marcello, Ralph's new administrative assistant, and was eager to get to the office, despite the previous late night. I knew nothing about the FBI sting and unlocked the door as I did every morning to go to my desk to begin work.

I was stunned. There was nothing there! The entire place was empty. Nothing! The tape machines were gone, as were all the double-cassette recorders. All the reels of tape and tape boxes had been taken from the many shelves. What remained looked ransacked. I felt like I had fallen into the Twilight Zone. At first I thought we had been robbed. I walked around the office staring, silent, looking around while trying to figure out what had happened.

Then I thought Ralph must have suddenly decided to move without telling me. I began to become pissed off, but I realized that that was ridiculous. It was the most surreal moment of my life. Confused, I spent some more time looking around and finally left in a daze, locking up the office.

It was only later in the day that I learned what had happened—that the FBI had staged a sting by purchasing some American Ballet videos. When they came to the office for a third or fourth purchase, they had arrested Ralph and Marcello and took everything with them and shut the office down.

On November 22, 1986, Billboard reported:
> Two men were arrested here Nov. 3 on charges of making illegal videotapes drawn from the Public Broadcasting Service's Live from the Met series. Arrested and charged with copyright infringemnent and mail fraud were Ralph Ferrandina and Marcello Jara.
>
> Federal law enforcement authorites also seized 6,833 audio master recordings and 859 video master tapes that were allegedly used as part of an illegal manufacturing business operating under the name of Mr. Tape, located here at 155 W. 68th Street. Ferrandina and Jara were charged with manufacturing and distributing pirate videotapes of copyright PBS broadcasts of Live From the Met, a series that present ballet and opera performances at New York's Metropolitan Opera House...If convicted, Ferrandina and Jara could receive the maximum penalty of $250,000 and five years in jail.

When I heard the news, I was horrified and felt especially bad for Marcello who had only recently been hired as Ralph's administrator. During the years I worked with Ralph, he had lost at least three administrative assistants. Ralph was not easy to work with in some respects. Marcello knew little, if anything, about the illegality of the work he was doing. Neither Ralph nor Marcello went to jail. If I remember correctly, Marcello was released immediately and not charged. He was traumatized, but went on with his life. Ralph, I believe, paid a hefty fine, but spent no time in jail. I've heard a number of rumors about what happened to his personal collection, but never found out for sure. By that time, I had moved on.

As far as I know, nothing like that happened to the other piraters in the New York area. I think Ralph was chosen as having the most high profile. Attractive, engaging, and full of positive energy, Ralph drew much attention to himself. He had an affluent Manhattan address and office location. He had relationships with many famous singers, agents, and managers. Other piraters tended to remain in the background while Ralph flaunted his notoriety.

I later got to talk with Ralph, who had become a broken man. His regularly genial and positive attitude was gone. I managed to stay in touch with him over a year or so. Soon after the raid he became ill, and a few years later, he died. The last time I saw him was in the hospital, a short time before his death. I would have liked to have been more present during his last months, but my mother had died, and shortly after that Gale's and my good friend from WVU, Larry Skrobacs, died of AIDS. Gale, I, and other friends from WVU had taken daily care of Larry during the last months of his life.

I was emotionally drained from all that, and felt I couldn't handle much more. Because of cuts in monies appropriated for the Endowment for the Arts during President Regan's administration, by 1988 a lot of opportunities for freelance singers had dried up and I was forced to take a regular job to make ends meet. Gale had sung many of the same choral gigs, but in the mid-1980s began to concentrate on her solo career. I got a job as a receptionist for an interior design firm, Cioppa-Rosen on thirty-fourth street (across from the Empire State Building); they were good people and willing to teach me office etiquette. I eventually became their office manager. That job and my church job and occasional professional choral work occupied my life into the'90s.

At the end of Ralph's life, his main support, aside from his family, came from soprano Teresa Stratas who, I understand, stood by him and helped to care for him until the end. Always a remarkable woman and artist, she demonstrated a level of compassion that one rarely encounters.

Live Opera Recording and Me (Part II)

It was around 1980 that commercial recording companies discovered that releasing live recordings was a viable alternative to making them in a studio. The reasons are less artistically motivated than you might think. Recording an opera during a run of performances is considerably cheaper and easier to manage than locating and renting a separate space in which to schedule and conduct rehearsal and recording times with the many participants having multiple calendar events around which one must maneuver.

The live recordings released during the following decades by such labels as Sony, BMG, EMI, Philips and Decca differ from pirate recordings in that signed copyright releases are secured from all of the participants thus permitting the resulting recording to be legally distributed and sold. Also, the end product is the result of the careful patching together of rehearsals and performances into a unified, carefully recorded and sound-engineered whole. Rarely is a performance released "as it was."

I remember living in New York in the early 1980s spending more than $60.00 for a set of CDs of the legendary 1952 Bayreuth performance of *Tristan und Isolde* with Marta Mödl and Ramon Vinay (his debut), conducted by Herbert von Karajan (on Hunt CDs). During the 1990s, however, many of the most-prized pirate recordings of a decade earlier became available for sale at Tower Records in Manhattan and other record outlets such as Virgin Records and HMV. This was because many of these performances originated in Europe, not the United States, so U.S. copyright laws did not apply.

You can buy that same Tristan performance now on Opera D'Oro CD (having very good sound) for about $15.00. Or you can hear it for free on YouTube.

Wagner—*Tristan und Isolde*—Bayreuth July 23, 1952—Herbert von Karajan
https://www.youtube.com/watch?v=Rof8FfcMWjE

Those mega-sized record stores are now gone, replaced by Internet "stores" such as amazon.com and barnesandnoble.com along with specialty websites such as eBay.com. The reverse copyright concerns were true in Europe where the most sought-after pirate recordings originated from the Metropolitan Opera. This international copyright line was sometimes crossed by crafty store managers.

While welcome, this shift in availability created an unfortunate paradox.

For the novice opera-record buyer in the 1950s there were only a handful of complete recordings of Aïda on LP from which to choose from. You could buy sets with Maria Callas (Angel), Renata Tebaldi (Decca), Caterina Mancini (Cetra), Maria Caniglia (RCA), or Zinka Milanov (RCA). Today, with the uniting of live (whether live-legit or live-pirated) and commercial releases, the novice listener can choose from more than thirty versions of Aïda. On one hand, this offers the seasoned listener the ability to choose among a wide variety of artists and to make valuable artistic comparisons (sometimes even between a singer's studio and stage work). On the other hand, it can be extremely intimidating and overwhelming for the novice. How does one select a representative recording of an opera if one doesn't know the singers' work?

The Internet now provides us many opportunities to sample both operas and singers (on YouTube), thus narrowing the confusion. If nothing else, one can choose by the sound of music that one likes, or by the qualities of a singer's voice. Earlier (between 1980 and 2000), if a walk-in customer at a record store didn't know which recording to buy, there almost always was a knowledgeable sales clerk in the store who could guide them. That no longer exists, so prospective consumers must do their own Internet research for information, reviews, music samples, or they can rely on word-of-mouth.

As most people who buy recordings prefer to buy a live version of their favorite opera (such as Aïda, *Tosca*, or *Madama Butterfly*), many find that live recordings have great allure. Often, live recordings are the only accounts of a work that can be found. In 1999, Dynamic CD released Giordano's fascinating final opera, Il re. Recorded at the Martina Franca Festival revival in 1998, the CD is an invaluable opportunity to listen to and study such seldom-staged works. (Since that time a few other recordings of Il Re have surfaced.) In the case of Il re, the reasons why it is so rarely revived are not difficult to understand. The lead female role, Rosalina, is the most bizarre verismo role ever written. Her music is a cross between *Tosca* and Zerbinetta. Patrizia Ciofi proves that the role is not only singable but it is also one of great beauty. She not only encompasses the dramatic, verismatic outbursts, but is able to easily articulate the runs, staccati, and melismatic passages that appear throughout the role, capping the difficult, florid central scene with a respectable high E!

Giordano—*Il Re*—Martina Franca, 1998

https://www.youtube.com/watch?v=-F-_cs0_nxs&t=367s

Rarities

There are many excellent rarities. Many of them appeared on the fascinating, if flawed, LP releases of Eddie Smith and his Unique Opera Recordings. Some are incredibly rare. One of the most interesting (and one I have never seen anywhere else) was an Opera Rara concert—the twenty-fifth jubilee of Queen Elizabeth II—a magnificent gala held in London on August 7, 1977. Scenes and arias were presented from *Maria Stuarda, Roberto Devereux, Anna Bolena, Rosmonda D'Inghilterra, L'Assedio di Calais, Il Castello di Kenilworth,* and *Alfredo il Grande*, with such fine singers as Yvonne Kenny, John Tomlinson, Janet Price, Christian du Plessis, Marilyn Hill Smith, Maurice Arthur, Eiddwyn Harry, Graham Clark, Milla Andrew, John Brecknock, and Della Jones all conducted by Alun Francis. It was an excellent program, but of all the selections, it was mezzo-soprano Della Jones who stole the show with her incredible singing of the seven-minute aria, "Che potrei dirti" from Donizetti's obscure *Alfredo il Grande*. Such superb cantilena and fluid, virtuostic singing has rarely been heard in any era. Complex roulades, difficult intervallic jumps, and the pinging forth of staccati high B-flats were all framed within dynamic bel canto singing. I bought my copy of Eddie Smith's two-record LP set at Patelson's the year of the concert, but it lasted only a few years before the inferior vinyl began to disintegrate. I transferred it to CD (and then to MP3) and I am glad that I did. I listen to the Della Jones selection at least twice a year. Fortunately, in January of 2023, jovi1715 uploaded that London Gala performance to YouTube so that all can enjoy Della Jones' legendary singing.

Donizetti—"Che potrei dirti" (*Alfredo il Grande*)—Della Jones London Gala August 7, 1977

https://www.youtube.com/watch?v=WSVYLvOwROY

Donizetti—"Che potrei dirti" (*Alfredo il Grande*)— Della Jones Opera Rara commercial recording
https://www.youtube.com/watch?v=E_bLSwEcL54

There are too many wonderful performances now on CD for me to go into detail here, but I do have some favorites. There is a fascinating 1957, Italian-sung performance of Menotti's The Medium (part of a three-CD Gala release) with Gianna Pederzini and Graziella Sciutti, conducted by Nicola Rescigno. There is Nielsen's Saul and David, a 1972 Copenhagen broadcast in English with Boris Christoff, Elisabeth Soderstrom, and Kim Borg (Opera D'Oro), Catalani's Loreley from a 1968 Milan performance with Elena Suliotis, and Piero Cappuccilli (originally on BJR LPs, now Living Stage CD), and Meyerbeer's L'étoile du nord—given a bravura performance by Elisabeth Futral and the Wexford Opera (Marco Polo). Occasionally one can still find LP copies of the important Opera Rara London revival of L'Etoile du Nord from February 25, 1975 with Janet Price and Deborah Cook. Or you can hear it on YouTube.

Meyerbeer—L'Etoile du Nord —London, 1975
https://www.youtube.com/watch?v=9rByojMvjHY

Most everyone is familiar with Humperdinck's Hänsel und Gretel, but how many know about his Königskinder, from a 1952 Cologne performance with Dietrich Fischer-Dieskau and Peter Anders?

Humperdinck—*Königskinder*—Cologne 1952
https://www.youtube.com/watch?v=x85jpxcFZ2Y

There is also Rubenstein's The Demon from the Wexford Festival (Marco Polo), as well as a 1971 Milan radio revival with Virginia Zeani and Nicola Rossi-Lemeni on MYTO,

Rubenstein—*The Demon*—Milan 1971
https://www.youtube.com/watch?v=kh9jvvHQ0w8

There is a 1974 Munich revival of Marschner's Der Vampyr with Arlene Auger and Anna Tomowa-Sintow (Opera D'Oro). There is also a 1960 Venice performance (BellaVoce) of Handel's Alcina with Rescigno conducting and with Clifford Grant—Conducted by Richard Bonynge That night, the Venice audience received a rare encore of Handel's "Let the Bright Seraphim" from his Samson—brilliantly sung by Sutherland with an interpolated high D of remarkable radiance and fire. It was after these Venice performances that Sutherland was dubbed "La Stupenda."

Handel—*Alcina* (Act I)—Venice February 1960
https://www.youtube.com/watch?v=7zj5cKc0yA0

An Opera Rara London performance not to be missed:
Pacini—*Maria, regina d'Inghilterra*—London, 1983 with Penelope Walker, Marilyn Hill Smith, Keith Lewis—conducted by David Parry
https://www.youtube.com/watch?v=bjJ4ub3ZgP0

Then there is Mascagni's Parisina, Isabeau, Piccolo Marat, and Giordano's rarely revived Il Re and Siberia, or even Handel's Semele—a 1968 performance conducted by Robert Shaw, with a radiant Beverly Sills and Seth McCoy that, to this day, rivals all commercial efforts.

An important revival was Massenet's *Esclarmonde*. The 1974 San Francisco Premiere with Dame Joan Sutherland, Huguette Tourangeau, Giacomo Aragall, conducted by Richard Bonynge. I saw this exotic production when it came to the Metropolitan Opera in 1976. Unfortunately, at that time I was not taping, otherwise I would definitely have captured the entire run of performances.

Massenet—*Esclarmonde*—San Francisco Premiere 1974
https://www.youtube.com/watch?v=CZo3Xh6MDyI&t=1966s

Another take on Esclarmonde's difficult "Esprit de l'air" from Act I of *Esclarmonde* is Angela Meade's thrilling singing on the 2014 Richard Tucker Gala with Jennifer Johnson Cano—conducted by Emmanuel Villaume.

https://www.youtube.com/watch?v=XDK7Q1rlARA

Some rarities from the Dynamic label include the (1856) French version of Il trovatore, the early versions of Verdi's Macbeth, and *Simon Boccanegra* as well as some true rarities: Massenet's Roma from Martina Franca (1999) and Le Roi de Lahore from Venice in 2006, Donizetti's Pia de Tolomei—again from Venice 2005, and Pietro il grande from Valle d'Itria in 2004. The casts are all young singers—some quite good (like Patrizia Ciofi—who has carved out quite an exceptional career for herself during the last decades) while some are just so-so. For the most part, the opportunity to hear such rare works makes up for any artistic compromises one might have to make.

Then there are the bel canto revivals including: Rossini's *Ciro in Babilonia*, a 1988 Chiabrera performance with the versatile Daniela Dessi and Ernesto Palacio (Agora). Donizetti's *Castello di Kennilworth* (Fonit Cetra) and *Adelia* (BMG) both with Mariella Devia.

Donizetti—*Castello di Kenilworth*—RAI Milan 1989
https://www.youtube.com/watch?v=o31ZROAaXek

Renata Scotto is most moving in the famous 1968 Palermo revival of Bellini's La straniera (Melodram) with a dynamite final scene capped by a long, high D-flat. (Opera Rara has since released a commercial recording of this interesting work starring Patrizia Ciofi.)

Bellini—*La straniera*—Palermo 1968
https://www.youtube.com/watch?v=htnDKg8lGvU&t=13s

Cristina Deutekom is remarkably brilliant, if quirky, in the 1970 Venice revival of Rossini's Armida—the first after Maria Callas's 1952 performances. (Later revivals included those with June Anderson, Katia Ricciarelli, Nelly Miricioiu, Cecilia Gasdia, Renee Fleming, and Jessica Pratt.) This Venice performance is a must-have for the collector and admirer of Deutekom for a number of reasons. One is the sensitive and dynamic conducting of Carlo Franci—an underrated conductor of the 1970s. There is also excellent work from the three tenors of this production (Pietro Bottazzo, Ottavio Garaventa, and Edoardo Gimenez). And then there is the vocal wizardry of the Dutch soprano, Cristina Deutekom (1931–2014). Hers was an odd voice, but distinctive and memorable. Her disjointed, rather than smooth, fioriture, or "cluckeratura" sounds unworldly enough to underline the magical powers of the title role. Throughout the performance she displays her prodigious breath control, remarkable pianissimi (up to high D) and fearless abandon on high. Her dramatic intensity and sweet singing of high pianissimi is as startling as is the dramaticism of her final scene. Her voice had a tinge of coolness that, remarkably, disappeared when she spun a high pianissimo. Those notes always had a surprisingly warm, almost lush, quality to them. The long, complicated final scene is a wonder of changing moods and furious declamation and abandon. The final (interpolated) high E-flat is a remarkably long note providing a staggering finish to the opera. Deutekom sang the role again with great success in Bregenz in 1973

She once confessed that Armida was one of the most daunting operas she had ever undertaken.

> Let me tell you a secret! The first time I did it was in Venice…I thought I couldn't do it…Because it is so difficult. (*A Conversation with Bruce Duffie*, http://www.bruceduffie.com/deutekom.html)

There are two, different performances of that 1970 Venice production circulating on CD. One is on the label, Memories—a broadcast originally released on CD in the 1980s, and another, an in-house performance, that is on Mondo Musica released in 1998. Both are recommended to fans of this artist.

Rossini—*Armida* Venice 1970 (Mondo Musica CD)
https://www.youtube.com/watch?v=vqzg0lNpOzg

Rossini— *Armida* Final Scene Venice 1970—Memories CD
(Deutekom jumps a measure early to the final high E flat)
https://www.youtube.com/watch?v=sYdwv2xFe70

The Bregenz revival of 1973 with Deutekom has been available on tape for decades, but has yet to be transferred to CD or to appear complete on YouTube.

The final Scene however is available—conducted by Carlo Franci. It provides some fascinating comparative listening between the other performances.

Many New Yorkers remember the exceptional 1970 Carnegie Hall concert performance of Donizetti's Fille du Regiment (two years before the more famous Sutherland Met revival) with Beverly Sills, Grayson Hirst, Fernando Corena, Muriel Costa-Greenspon, conducted by Roland Gagnon. In the annals of operatic revivals, this performance has rightly become legendary. Originally released on LP by FWR (or Penzance Records) it was released by Legato CD with excellent liner notes by James Jorden of parterre box. It is not only a tribute to Beverly Sills' remarkable musicianship and exquisite coloratura but also to a great un-sung hero, Roland Gagnon, who composed virtually all of Sills's cadenzas and ornaments during her NYCO prime. Sills (in phenomenal voice) dominates the performance, addings top Ds and E flats throughout the performance, She even threw in an excellent final high E at the end of the Lesson Scene. All evening, she demonstrated an expressive style of florid singing that harkened back to the earlier eras of virtuosi.

Donizetti—*Fille du regiment*—Carnegie Hall, 1970
https://www.youtube.com/watch?v=XTDo5snoytw

There is an exciting (and rare) pairing of Renata Scotto and Boris Christoff in a 1968 Italian-sung revival of Meyerbeer's Robert le Diable (MYTO). Mentioned earlier, this was the first performance of the work in the twentieth century. Although somewhat abridged, the opera is given a strong, flavorful performance. During act II, Scotto offers florid singing of the first order in the "La trompette guerrière" and caps the final with a brilliant high C. In the act II duet with Robert, Scotto treats the audience to a spectacular penultimate high E. Not only that, but her "Robert, toi que j'aime" in act IV is a model of elegant, bel canto singing. Christoff is suitably menacing as Bertram and his summoning of the Nuns' ghosts in act II is mesmerizing.

Meyerbeer—*Roberto il Diavolo*—Florence 1968
https://www.youtube.com/watch?v=oxvulWijmWU&t=1205s

There are two important revivals of Meyerbeer's Les Huguenots—one is an historic Italian performance from Milan, 1962 with Franco Corelli and Dame Joan Sutherland, (originally released on a fine MRF LP set) and a 1971 Vienna concert-abridged performance with Nicolai Gedda, Rita Shane, Enriquetta Tarres, Jeanette Scovotti, and Justino Diaz (originally released on LP by BJR but now on MYTO). Aside from Gedda's remarkably suave singing and beautiful high notes as Raul, the Vienna concert performance is notable for Rita Shane's dynamic high note interpolations (up to F-sharp) and Scovotti's, pert and crystalline Urbain. It is another must-have for any library. At the time of this writing, bits and pieces of this performance can be found onYouTube.

The now legendary La Scala revival of Les Huguenots (sung in Italian) from June 7, 1962 (Gala CD, at budget price) has been a collector's item for almost sixty years and would not be out of place in any library. There are two performances from this run circulating: this one from June 7 and an earlier performance from May 29th. It has a starry cast consisting of Franco Corelli, Joan Sutherland, Giulietta Simionato, Fiorenza Cossotto, Giorgio Tozzi, and Nicolai Ghiaurov (on a number of labels, but the best is Gala). This is an often rough-and-tumble performance short on French elegance, but heavy on dramatic urgency. Despite its lack of representative French atmosphere, it is one of the most highly prized of pirate recordings because of its cast and their dedication to bringing Meyerbeer's music to life. Vocally, Corelli is magnificent, full of virile, masculine ardor while Simionato does a remarkable job with her unlikely assignment as Valentine. Sutherland is beyond reproach in the coloratura fireworks of her great act II scena, and although her role is not the largest, she makes sure you do not forget her contributions. There is undeniable excitement. Typical of the time, Meyerbeer's score is hacked to bits. If budgetary constraints are an issue for you, however, or if you admire Joan Sutherland, Franco Corelli, or Giulietta Simionato, start with the Gala set, and then branch out from there.

Meyerbeer—*Gli Ugonotti*—Milan 1962
https://www.youtube.com/watch?v=4p61KIO12zs

Undoubtedly, the classic recording of this opera is the 1969 recording conducted by Richard Bonynge on Decca/London with Joan Sutherland reprising her La Scala role seven years later. The set is marred only by a weak Raoul—Anastasios Verenios—who was ill at the time. The most startling moment in the recording comes at the end of the act I finale when Urbain, sung by the contralto-voiced, bizarre-timbred Huguette Tourangeau, lets rip with a magnificent, sustained high D that must have infuriated sopranos on two continents. (This, by the way, was no trick. In a concert performance at Royal Albert Hall, preceding the recording, she duplicated the feat. She also offered a number of notes in altissimo in her one commercial Aria album for Decca. Such high flights were not natural for her however, and were short-lived.)

Meyerbeer—*Les Huguenots*—Finale of Act I Decca Commercial 1968—Huguet Tourangeau
https://www.youtube.com/watch?v=cvCqoVGrC5k

Verdi—"Ah! Sgombro" *Oberto*—Decca Recital: Arias from Forgotten Operas
https://www.youtube.com/watch?v=ccq6ZlSLzcY

Joan Sutherland gives another demonstration of why she was renowned as a superb technician. Her Marguerite de Valois is a wonder from beginning to the end. Although a smaller role, she makes every moment count and her famous act II aria, "O beau pays" is a lesson in fine singing and bravura. I think that this recording is one of Martina Arroyo's most inspired and lushly sung efforts. The characterization is sympathetic and the many high notes, especially Cs, ring easily and with great beauty. And, for diva watchers, there is the unexpected pleasure of hearing a young Arlene Auger popping out coloratura and high notes as a gypsy in act III. (Another baby diva who appears on this recording is Kiri Te Kanawa as a Maid of Honor.)

Another important revival recording released on commercial CD was the RCA import set of a 1998 Rome performance of Mascagni's Iris with Daniella Dessi (1957–2016) and Jose Cura. Conducted by Gianluigi Gelmetti, this is an exquisite performance. Gelmetti shines in the many orchestral interludes—promoting the exoticism and beauty of the score.

Daniela Dessi's sculpting of Iris's gentle phrases is pure magic. Iris suits her voice and temperament perfectly. She is up against some stiff competition including Clara Petrella, but especially Magda Olivero who made the role her own during the 1960s and '70s. With an obvious love for the role and its musical idiom Dessi gives a poignant performance of great dignity. Paying special attention to Mascagni's dynamics and the many difficult chromatic twists of the vocal line, she is artistically poised yet intensely dramatic. By artistically shading her voice and its timbre and offering countless accentuations and vocal hues, she gives as complete a portrait of this sweet innocent as you will ever hear. During her career, Dessì sang many wonderful and varied performances of Monteverdi, Rossini, Donizetti, Giordano, Puccini, Bellini, and Verdi. This Iris is one of her finest.

Mascagni—*Iris*—Rome 1998
https://www.youtube.com/watch?v=xU9LfMFwil4

Mascagni—*Iris*—Amsterdam 1963 (The legendary Magda Olivero performance).
https://www.youtube.com/watch?v=FjTyf7E-5tY

There are many performances of the basic repertoire that are outstanding. These include a Christmas Day, 1978 Munich Cavalleria rusticana with an ardent Leonie Rysanek and Placido Domingo (on Orfeo CD). This was a cornerstone opera in Rysanek's gradual move into a lower tessitura. At this time only the duet has been uploaded.

Mascagni—"Ah lo vedi" *Cavalleria Rusticana*—Munich, 1978
https://www.youtube.com/watch?v=C2jnh5-kFG4

There is an eloquently-sung *Lucia di Lammermoor* from Florence (1996) with Mariella Devia, Jose Bros, and Roberto Frontali conducted by Zubin Mehta (Fone). There is another *Lucia di Lammermoor* from Rome with Mariella Devia and Alfredo Kraus from September,1990 when the opera is performed in the original, higher keys with Devia offering some glorious high E-flats and Fs. Aside from the beauty of her voice in this music there was also the imaginative cadenza that she uses in the middle of the Mad Scene.

Donizetti—*Lucia di Lammermoor*—Rome 1990
https://www.youtube.com/watch?v=yrfC6dH343A

There is also a unique *Don Giovanni* from Vienna in 1963 with Leontyne Price, Eberhard Waechter, Hilde Gueden, Fritz Wunderlich, Walter Berry (Gala).

Mozart—***Don Giovanni***—Vienna 1963
https://www.youtube.com/watch?v=4bCqJrniVlE

Many performances provide surprises.

One is an intensely sung (idiosyncratically rearranged by von Karajan) performance of Die Frau ohne Schatten from Vienna in 1964 (DGG) with Leonie Rysanek as an unforgettable Empress, Christa Ludwig (one of the greatest Fraus of all time), Jess Thomas as a virile, dominant Emperor, Walter Berry as a darkly-tinged Barak, and Grace Hoffmann (malevolently wonderful as the parasitic Nurse, her Act II finale with its climactic high Bb is one of the best), Lucia Popp and Fritz Wunderlich are in supporting roles—vocally this set documents one of the finest performances given during the 1960s. This should be in all personal libraries.

Strauss—***Die Frau ohne Schatten***—Vienna 1964
https://www.youtube.com/watch?v=SGm3FsBnPEM&t=5s

Although not in the best sound (yet definitely listenable) is a surprisingly cohesive performance of *Madama Butterfly* with a young Regina Resnik as Cio-Cio San. One often forgets that she began her career as a soprano. This is a true curiosity and certainly worth investigating. Charles Kullman brings a charm to everything he sings.

Puccini—***Madama Butterfly***—Metropoltian Opera broadcast February 8, 1947
https://www.youtube.com/watch?v=R5WWLXyXNcE

There is a frantic (almost undisciplined), but surprisingly satisfying 1949 performance of *Un Ballo in Maschera* from Edinburgh with Ljuba Welitsch, Mirto Picchi, Paolo Silveri, and Alda Noni, conducted by Vittorio Gui (On Stage).

Verdi—***Un ballo in Maschera***—Edinburgh, 1949
https://www.youtube.com/watch?v=tazKT30Rl-g

Verdi—***Un ballo in Maschera*** Another *Un ballo in Maschera* that should be heard is the Metropolitan Opera broadcast from December of 1955 in excellent sound on the Sony Met Series. The cast included Jan Peerce, Zinka Milanov, Roberta Peters Robert Merrill and, most importantly, Marian Anderson as Ulrica. Anderson was the first black singer to perform at the Metropolitan Opera and this was her broadcast debut. The conductor was Dimitri Mitropoulos.
https://www.youtube.com/watch?v=ccXwDR2fT-w&t=29s

A unexpected treat is Milanov's last *Tosca* with the Met. This was during their tour when they appeared in Atlanta on May 4, 1963. Richard Tucker, Anselmo Colzani and others from the Met supported her Tosca. For a recording made during the "early" days of pirating, the performance is in surprisingly clear sound and is very enjoyable.

Puccini—***Tosca***—Met in Atlanta, May 4, 1963
https://www.youtube.com/watch?v=LHIYdwQT2xs&t=26s

One of the first of Peter Grimes broadcasts from the Metropolitan Opera is definitely one to hear. In decent sound for the time period, it has a sensitively-sung Peter by Brian Sullivan. Sullivan made his Metropolitan Opera debut with this role and among his other achievements, he was the first American-born singer to sing Lohengrin at Bayreuth in his generation. Assisting him is a cast of great voice-actors—Polyna Stoska, Lawrence Tibbett, Jean Madeira, Jerome

Hines, Paula Lechner, conducted by Emil Cooper. This is one of those performances that one is grateful exists. Below that link is one to the now famous broadcast of Lohengrin from the Metropolitan Opera in 1953 also with Sullivan.

Wagner—*Lohengrin*—Metropolitan Opera broadcast, 1953 with Brian Sullivan, Eleanor Steber, Margaret Harshaw, Sigurd Björling, conducted by Fritz Siedry
https://www.youtube.com/watch?v=YFxD8GyORwk

Surprisingly, a number of Metropolitan Opera performances featuring Renata Tebaldi have recently surfaced. These 1960-1970s in-house performances are of great importance since they help fill out a vocal portrait of one of the most important Italian divas of the 20th century. Most of these previously hidden gems seem to come from the library of "Noak Somewhere", who has kindly uploaded them. Many are in very good sound. Especially considering the fact that they were done in-house before the advent of cassette tapes. Some are listed below, but there are many others.

Giordano—*Andrea Chenier*—Metropolitan Opera performance December 15, 1970 with Renata Tebaldi, Richard Tucker, Anselmo Colzani, Judith Forst—conducted by Fausto Cleva.
https://www.youtube.com/watch?v=aUNUmD0S0Cc&t=29s

Puccini—*Fanciulla del West*—Rome, 1961 with renata Tebaldi, Daniele Barioni, Giangiacomo Guelfi conducted by Arturo Basile
https://www.youtube.com/watch?v=HI1OFIsy7ZQ

Puccini—*Fanciulla del West*—Metropolitan Opera performance February 21, 1970 with Renata Tebaldi, Sandor Konya, Anselmo Colzani conducted by Fausto Cleva—in great sound.
https://www.youtube.com/watch?v=em9Ot7mLJyY&t=2193s

Puccini—*Fanciulla del West*—Metropolitan Opera performance February 25, 1970 with Renata Tebaldi, Sandor Konya, Anselmo Colzani conducted by Fausto Cleva
https://www.youtube.com/watch?v=M_OMLteBwzk&t=375s

Puccini—*Tosca*—Metropolitan Opera performance, March 22, 1964 with Renata Tebaldi, Franco Corelli, Tito Gobbi, Justino Diaz, Fernando Corena—conducted by Fausto Cleva
https://www.youtube.com/watch?v=PCkeF80Y-BA

Puccini—*La bohème*—Metropolitan Opera performance, December 14, 1965 with Renata Tebladi, Franco Corelli, Anneliese Rothenberger, Frank Guarrera, Jerome Hines—conducted by Fausto Cleva
https://www.youtube.com/watch?v=AYA2NPKYoo8

Moving on to another revered opera house, there is also an outstanding 1955 Bayreuth performance of Die Götterdämmerung with a young Birgit Nilsson surrounded by Leonie Rysanek, Bernd Aldenhoff, Herman Uhde, Gottlob Frick, Herta Topper, and Marianne Schech, conducted by Hans Knappertsbusch (Orfeo).

Wagner—*Die Götterdämmerung*—Bayreuth 1955
https://www.youtube.com/watch?v=8xTWHq3KtDo

Also top of the list sits a very special performance of Macbeth with Christa Ludwig's singularly evil Lady Macbeth paired with Sherrill Milnes's effective, virile Macbeth from Vienna 1971 (Opera D'Oro). For those interested, Ludwig does not take a high Db in the Sleepwalking Scene, but offers a huge Db at the end of Act I. One of the highlights is her Act III duet with Milnes.

Verdi—*Macbeth*—Vienna 1970
https://www.youtube.com/watch?v=uXvWKnLb39s

This last can now be compared to a stunning 1950 Berlin Macbeth with Marta Mödl and Josef Metternich (MYTO). This was a revival that took place two years before Maria Callas's more celebrated performances at La Scala. Even though it is sung in a German translation, in this opera's performance annals this was a important revival.

Without a model and from her own fertile imagination, Marta Mödl creates a riveting, constantly shifting portrait of the power-mad, psychotic queen that is frighteningly realistic. Her short-breathed, suffocated, even labored singing (at other times a hinderance), serves here to illuminate the wondrous imagination behind the palate of colors she conjures. Like other unique artists (Maria Callas, Magda Olivero, Leyla Gencer, Hildegard Behrens, and Gwyneth Jones), you either like Mödl or you don't. Although her voice was bottled-up and technically flawed, her performances always had flashes of artistic genius, not to mention an alluring frisson of danger and the unexpected. Josef Metternich also gives a fine portrayal of Macbeth's disintegration. By the banquet scene and the appearance of the apparition, he sounds completely unhinged; subjugated by the cruel nagging of Mödl's Lady Macbeth. Alternating between beautiful legato and craggy sprechstimme he deftly delineates Macbeth's guilt and demoralization. His final aria is magnificent and crowned with a tremendous, interpolated high A-flat.

By itself, Mödl's harrowing rendition of the sleepwalking scene, is worth the cost of the set. It is the culmination of a carefully crafted portrait. Callas's famous version (1958, EMI recital) is a study in elegant madness done in shades and by degrees. Mödl, however, chose to explore the other end of the spectrum. She provides a tortuous (and disturbingly real) interpretation of psychotic dementia. Her first utterance, "Dieser flecken!" is startling and listeners familiar with her commercial version (available on Preiser CD) will be surprised by the differences. No high D-flat appears at the end—even though it is written in the score. (Mödl sings the bastardized mezzo-soprano version that was traditionally used in Germany at that time.) But, one does not miss the high note after the emotional impact of her performance.

Verdi—*Macbeth*—Berlin 1950
https://www.youtube.com/watch?v=GuimFn6m_uM

While discussing Macbeth, there is the splendid Orfeo recording of a 1964 Salzburg performance of Macbeth featuring the beautifully sung, haunted Macbeth of Dietrich Fischer Dieskau with a ferocious Grace Bumbry as his Lady, conducted by Wolfgang Sawallisch.

Verdi—*Macbeth*—Salzburg 1964
https://www.youtube.com/watch?v=j_HiETLKqO0

And yet an even more explosive reading from Barcelona in 1975, with Guillermo Sarabia, Marisa Galvany, Mario Rinaudo and Pedro LaVirgen, conducted by Giuseppe Ruisi. Both Sarabia and Galvany are completely committed to their respective roles and do much to make their personal stamps on Verdi's music. Galvany is in exceptional voice, even interpolating a sustained high Eb at the end of the dramatic Banquet Scene. She also interpolated that high note in Frankfurt appearances of this role in 1976 and in Cincinnati, in 1978.

Verdi—*Macbeth*—Barcelona 1975
https://www.youtube.com/watch?v=P0E1nO2sdkc&t=2573s

And yet another Macbeth—this time from the Metropolitan Opera. April, 1964. This is the only surviving tape of Birgit Nilsson singing Lady Macbeth at the Metropolitan Opera. The in-house tape documents her last (of three) appearances in the role at that house. In December of 2023, "Noack Somewhere" uploaded a copy of the performance that is in much better sound than ever before. This is a performance to treasure. Nilsson delivers a great Lady Macbeth, partnered with the wonderful Cornell MacNeil. Carlo Bergonzi, Giorgio Tozzi and Franco Ghitti round out the top-notch cast. Great moments for Nilsson include an excellent interpolated high Db at the end of Act I, a dark and sinister "La luce langue," a fleet "Brindisi," the Act III duet with Macbeth where Nilsson hurls out a huge, penultimate high C at the end, and a vivid Sleepwalking scene. At the end of that scene Nilsson emits a ghostly straight-tone high Db that haunts one's memory long after it is heard. The only other live performance of Macbeth with Birgit Nilsson that I have found, dates from Vienna in late 1970 with Kostas Paskalis as Macbeth, conducted by Berislav Klobucar (also now on YouTube).

Verdi—*Macbeth*—Metropolitan Opera performance, April 24, 1964
https://www.youtube.com/watch?v=wmWZ1fOs3N0&t=6287s

So Many treasures! Live recordings often offer the only chance to hear artists in roles for which they were famous but never commercially recorded, or singing with colleagues in casts not possible to duplicate in a recording studio due to conflicting alliances with recording companies. During the 1960s, Richard Strauss's *Elektra* was performed all over the world by three women who became closely identified with their roles—Birgit Nilsson, Leonie Rysanek, and Regina Resnik. Although Nilsson and Resnik recorded the work together on Decca, it is only on pirate recordings that you can hear the trio intact. Tapes preserve a December, 1966 Metropolitan Opera broadcast, and both Legato and Orfeo CD have released a 1965 Vienna broadcast performance starring all three singers. This was an immensely satisfying performance. With a cast that also included Wolfgang Windgassen, Eberhard Waechter, Gandula Janowitz, and Dancia Mastilovic (soon to become a formidable *Elektra* herself), conducted by Karl Böhm, the Vienna performance is a piece of operatic legend. There is also a Montreal performance from 1967 with the trio. (It is available in the boxed set: Birgit Nilsson-The Great Live Performances, released by Sony in September of 2018.) All three performances demonstrate what the fuss was about.

Strauss—*Elektra*—Vienna 1965
https://www.youtube.com/watch?v=flrwAtBuICU

The 1966 broadcast of *Elektra* with the trio of Nilsson, Rysanek and Resnik caused a stir when first heard. All three outdid themselves in vocal realism in interpreting their roles that afternoon. There are so many spots in this broadcast that stand out. The nightmarish confrontation between Nilsson and Resnik even manages to surpass the wonderful commercial version on Decca. Nilsson's opening monologue is a marvel of singing and drama with secure top notes and subtle nuance. "Was bluten muss?" with its impossibly high tessitura is handled with uncommon ease by Nilsson and her finish on the exultant high Bb is something to hear. While Resnik's call for "mehr lichter" and her following laughter makes one's skin crawl. The ensemble after Aegisth's death is pure Staussian ecstasy with Rysanek soaring over the singers. It shows her complete understanding of Straussian structure in such a piece. The following (final) duet between the two sisters has rarely been done better. Despite occasional sonic overload, this is a performance that you should definitely hear. And savor.

Strauss—*Elektra*—Metropolitan Opera performance December 10, 1966
https://www.youtube.com/watch?v=ndsqOdx9O-4

Another great Nilsson Strauss broadcast from the Metropolitan Opera is the now legendary *Salome* from March 13, 1965. The cast included Walter Cassel, Karl Leibl, Irene Dalis, George Shirley—all conducted by Karl Böhm. This is not only in the "live" Birgit Nilsson box set from Sony but also on YouTube. This is one of the great Saturday afternoon broadcasts with all the singers giving their all and providing listeners with a consummate listening experience. Nilsson may never have sounded like a petulant teenage *Salome*, but she was a force of nature and her *Salome* is one of the best.

Strauss—*Salome*—Metropolitan Opera broadcast, March 13, 1965
https://www.youtube.com/watch?v=iNXWBrUTNxc&t=1639s

There are many Birgit Nilsson performances on YouTube—and surprisingly there are a lot of broadcasts from the Met. These are especially important since she appeared there during her "glory years." All of them are worth hearing. But two are especially good. They are a *Fidelio* from 1966 with James King, Mary-Ellen Pracht, Geraint Evans, Sherrill Milnes, conducted by Karl Böhm, and a February 13, 1960 broadcast with Jon Vickers, Laurel Hurley, Hermann Uhde, and Oscar Czerwenka—again conducted by Karl Böhm.

Beethoven—*Fidelio*—Metropolitan Opera broadcast, January, 22, 1966
https://www.youtube.com/watch?v=1cF3b3smZTo&t=101s

Beethoven—*Fidelio*—Metropolitan Opera broadcast February 13, 1960
https://www.youtube.com/watch?v=b3MVFkcUHbM

Two performances of Lakmé provide famous pairings that happened on stage, but not in the studio: Ruth Welting and Alfredo Kraus in Dallas (1980, Ornamenti) and Mariella Devia and Nicolai Gedda at Carnegie Hall (1981, Legato). Or, how about a 1960 New York concert of Les Troyens with Regina Resnik, Eleanor Steber, Richard Cassilly, and Martial Singher (VAI), or Grace Bumbry paired with an explosive Magda Olivero in an Italian-sung, curiously verismatic revival of Janacek's Jenufa.

Delibes—*Lakmé*-Dallas, 1980
https://www.youtube.com/watch?v=_yh9CKl5UHw&t=4941s

Delibes—*Lakmé*—Carnegie Hall, 1981
https://www.youtube.com/watch?v=8NJHzxpKxDg

Berlioz—*Les Troyens*—Carnegie Hall, 1960
https://www.youtube.com/watch?v=Ql_V9Ldu1E8

Janacek—*Jenufa*—Milan, 1974
https://www.youtube.com/watch?v=e2DbmjtyyAU

There are many performances that are one of a kind -a hilarious, not to be missed 1965 New York revival of Dittersdorf's Arcifanfano with Eleanor Steber, Patricia Brooks, and the musical satirist, Anna Russell (VAI, but not yet on YouTube.) And the NYCO performance of Le Coq D'Or with Beverly Sills and Norman Treigle, once on BJR LP, now on a Gala CD

Rimsky-Korsakov—Hymn to the Sun plus 2 excerpts (Coq D'Or)—NYCO, 1971
https://www.youtube.com/watch?v=Rq4OKFkCk4w&t=2s

For a real treat there is the famous—and now considered legendary—1954 Florence revival of La fanciulla del West with a white-hot Eleanor Steber, heroic Mario Del Monaco and superbly villainous Jack Rance of Giangiacomo Guelfi. This performance of Fanciulla was one of Steber's greatest achievements. Her Minnie is full of etched nuance that makes the character unforgettable. Conducted by Mitropoulos, this is one of those performances that will haunt you long after first heard. Her singing of the "bible scene" in Act I is worth the cost of the CD set. Now easily heard on YouTube it should be heard by anyone interested in this opera or in Steber. The CD set belongs in every opera-lover's library. (MYTO),

Puccini—*Fanciulla del West*—Florence, 1954
https://www.youtube.com/watch?v=iGnkcfu8_SQ

There is one other live *Fanciulla* with Steber. This was fortunately taped by a pirate in-house at the Metropolitan Opera. It was Steber's last *Fanciulla* and her last appearance at the Metropolitan Opera. Including such fine singers as Franco Corelli (Act I) Gaetano Bardini (Acts 2&3), Anselmo Colzani, conducted by Jan Behr. Both the tape and performance are not without flaws, but considering the importance of Steber in the operatic annals of Fanciulla, it is of great importance. Fortunately, Noack Somewhere uploaded this performance mid-January of 2024.

Puccini—*Fanciulla del West*—Metropolitan Opera, January 17, 1966
https://www.youtube.com/watch?v=ACAFcXjTTcw&t=44s

There is a fascinating, surprisingly reflective, Italian-sung 1962 performance of Die Meistersinger with Giuseppe Taddei, Boris Christoff, Renato Capecchi, Luigi Infantino, and Bruna Rizzoli (Datum). This is one of those performances that tends to slip through the cracks of opera collections—yet it shouldn't.

Wagner—*Die Meistersinger*—RAI, 1962
https://www.youtube.com/watch?v=Ru2l1Wl-co4

There is an unorthodox yet outrageously exciting *Don Giovanni* from the 1950 Salzburg Festival with Tito Gobbi, Ljuba Welitsch, Elisabeth Schwarzkopf, Erich Kunz, and Anton Dermota (EMI Salzburg Festspiel Documents). Unfortunately, at the time of this writing, only a few snippets from this performance are on YouTube.

I have to confess that of all the Meistersingers I have heard, one of my all-time favorites is the 1955 Bayreuth performance with Paul Schöffler, Imgard Seefried, Erich Kunz, Eberhard Waechter, Gottlob Frick, Hans Beier and conducted by Fritz Reiner. One of the features that I most enjoy about this recording is being able to hear the complex winding of instrumental solos over the chorus during the Prelude. This is an exquisite moment in the opera that is so often not head. For once their beautiful chromatic twists and turns are clearly miked. So often these passages are lost in a theater's acoustics or on recordings. This is a memorable performance and Reiner's conducting is superb. All of this does not take into account Schöffler's towering, justly famed portrait of the cobbler, Hans Sachs.

Wagner—*Die Meistersinger*—Bayreuth, 1955
https://www.youtube.com/watch?v=NHiEfp3WG7A

There is also the famous 1969 Vienna revival of Smetana's Dalibor with the rare chance to hear the Rysanek sisters, Leonie and Lotte, singing together on the same stage with Ludvico Spiess and Eberhard Waechter, and the (also 1969) legendary La Scala performance of florid specialists Beverly Sills and Marilyn Horne in Rossini's L'assedio di Corinto (originally on MRF LPs, now on Opera D'Oro CD).

Rossini—"Giusto ciel in tal periglio" (L'Assedio di Corinto)—Milan 1969
https://www.youtube.com/watch?v=t07k0FH4G7E

Continuing, there are Monserrat Caballe, Kurt Moll, Renee Kollo, and Jeanette Scovotti in a 1973 RAI performance of Strauss' Arabella (Bella Voce), or a 1976 German-sung performance of Dvorak's Rusalka from Switzerland with a poignant Teresa Stratas with Gwendolyn Killebrew, and Sir Willard White (Bella Voce), or the landmark 1956 Munich revival of Die Ägyptische Helena with Leonie Rysanek, Anneliese Kupper, Hermann Uhde, conducted by Joseph Keilberth (Orfeo), an outstanding document. Or a real sleeper—*Tosca* from Los Angeles, 1974, with Birgit Nilsson, Jose Carreras, Richard Fredricks, and Samuel Ramey (Legato).

Strauss—*Die Ägyptische Helena*—Munich, 1956
https://www.youtube.com/watch?v=p49ZPr_7LeE&t=21s

Puccini—*Tosca*—Los Angeles, 1974
https://www.youtube.com/watch?v=__3oDosBnZA

Long a favorite with collectors and singers, and for good reason, is a phenomenal performance of La forza del destino from San Carlo in 1958, with a star-studded cast including Renata Tebaldi, Franco Corelli, Ettore Bastianini, Boris Christoff, Oralia Dominguez, and Renato Capecchi (GOP). (There is also a video of this performance.) This was one of those magic nights where everyone was at the top of their game, offering an unforgettable, cohesive performance.

Verdi—*La forza del destino*—Naples, 1958
https://www.youtube.com/watch?v=263OritqcDc

There is a dangerously passionate revival of Verdi's Nabucco from Milan in 1966-67 with Giangiacomo Guelfi and twenty-three year old Elena Suliotis (1943–2004) making her debut at that house as an almost combustible Abigaille. They are surrounded by such singers as Gianni Raimondi, Nicolai Ghiaurov and Gloria Lane, conducted by Gianandrea Gavazzeni. This is a wonderful performance that packs a huge punch. It is a superb representation of this early Verdi opera. Guelfi is one of the great Nabuccos and his interpretation is one to be savored time and again. Vocally abandoned, almost reckless, Suliotis' singing belies her age and is exactly what the difficult role demands. High C's (at least six) are secure and beautiful, coloratura is dramatically defined, but always musically interpreted (even though she does not have a trill), her liberally used chest register is clean and clear and she has a malevolent growl that is not easily forgotten. Her grand scena that opens act II is one of the best you can hear. Along with Leonie Rysanek, Suliotis' final line of the act II finale ("Ma del popolo di Belo") is arguably one of the most exciting Verdian finales captured on tape (available on Opera D'Oro). Suliotis' career was not a long one. Due to health issues she had to retire in 1974 at the age of 31- a time when most sopranos are reaching their vocal maturity. Fortunately, over 50 performances of her work were captured by pirates—including no less than eleven performances of Nabucco, eight of Norma, and four of Anna Bolena (some of which are on YouTube). Her repertoire embraced, Bellini, Donizetti, Puccini, Verdi, Mascagni, and Zandonai. Although one laments the trajectory of her short career, thanks to industrious pirates, we can be grateful that so many fine examples of her artistry exist at all.

Verdi—*Nabucco*—Milan 1966-67 with Elena Suliotis, Giangiacomo Guelfi—Gianandrea Gavazzeni
https://www.youtube.com/watch?v=qqeyQFy37X0

Bellini—*Norma*—Tokyo, 1971

Another fascinating performance with Suliotis on YouTube is a Norma from Tokyo in August of 1971. It is in excellent sound with Gianfranco Cecchele, Fiorenza Cossotto and Ivo Vince—conducted by Gianandrea Gavazzeni. Like most of her performances, Suliotis proves to be a vocal force of nature—she even interpolates a penultimate high D in the trio at the end of Act I. Elsewhere in the opera she puts her personal stamp on many phrases.

https://www.youtube.com/watch?v=fwjuI8nOQ0w&list=RDfwjuI8nOQ0w&start_radio=1

There is also the dark, haunting *Elektra* from August, 1957, Salzburg with Inge Borkh, Lisa della Casa, Jean Madeira with Marilyn Horne as one of the five serving maids. This is an extraordinary performance. Inge Borkh had a rather "shrewish" voice but was a consummate vocal actress and her *Elektra* is among the best you can hear. The surprising cast choice in Lisa Della Casa as Chrysothemis works well—her sweet timbre contrasting well with Borkh. Jean Madeira is one of the most underrated vocal actresses of the era in which she sang. She is one of the best Klytemnestras on record. Her painter's palate of vocal colors embodies to perfection the conflicting moods of the guilt—haunted queen. The confrontation scene between Borkh and Madiera has to be heard to be believed so potent is their singing. As if sensing this artistic connection between the two singers, Dimitri Mitropoulos gives them space to enact their scene with uncommon sensitivity and dramatic impact. Madeira's line "Ich habe keine gute nächte" with its indrawn gasp of breath alone speaks volumes. Madeira's relating of her nightmares makes one's skin crawl with horror. In the annals of this opera, this performance remains one of its greatest. The excellent sonics are mere icing on the cake.

Strauss—*Elektra*—Salzburg, 1957 with Inge Borkh, Jean Madeira, Lisa Della Casa—Dimitri Mitropoulos.

https://www.youtube.com/watch?v=7Ngj2TfQmuA

The career of the 1950s Wagnerian specialist, Astrid Varnay is well documented. Varnay was the daughter of the once famous Swedish-born coloratura Maria Javor. Varnay's Wagner documents are many and all are worth investigating. Interestingly, for a soprano of her artistic stature, she made few commercial recordings. There are, however, at least seven complete live Ring Cycles with her as Brünnhilde that have been released (mostly on CD) across the years (1952, 1953, 1955, 1956, 1958, 1959, etc.) With Marta Mödl, Varnay co-owned the role of Brünnhilde during the 1950s.

Varnay can be heard in a number of other live opera performances—*Simon Boccanegra*, Macbeth, Aïda, Il trovatore, *Fidelio*, Lohengrin (Elsa and Ortrude), *Tannhäuser* (at least two from Metropolitan Opera broadcasts: 1954, 1955), *Parsifal*, *Tristan und Isolde*, Der Fliegende Holländer, *Salome*, *Der Rosenkavalier*, Die Frau ohne Schatten (Die Amme), and *Elektra* (at least four performances, all with fascinating differences). Varnay's Germanic "whine" might not be to everyone's taste but her musicianship is impeccable, her vocal stamina extraordinary, and her individuality enviable. When her top register began to shrink, she simply moved from *Elektra* to Klytemnestra and from *Salome* to Herodias. She was one of the great artists singing during the 1950s to 1980s.

Verdi—*Simon Boccangra*—Metropolitan Opera, 1950

https://www.youtube.com/watch?v=vk3ww-d1n1k

Verdi—*Macbeth*—Florence, 1951
https://www.youtube.com/watch?v=52i658xJWCM
Wagner—*Tristan und Isolde*—Metropolitan Opera, 1955
https://www.youtube.com/watch?v=WLwo5aU_yIw
Wagner—*Parsifal*—Bayreuth, 1966
https://www.youtube.com/watch?v=-FJhDd9K-Vg
Wagner—*Der fliegende Hollander*—Bayreuth, 1955
https://www.youtube.com/watch?v=FEOkmmluMW0
Wagner—*Lohengrin*—Metropolitan Opera, 1950
https://www.youtube.com/watch?v=YBrfqSlDRw4
Strauss—*Die Frau ohne Schatten*—Munich, 1966
https://www.youtube.com/watch?v=Romj3gi-32o

Perversely fascinating (but surprisingly beautiful) is a 1969 Manon from Milan with Mirella Freni and Luciano Pavarotti in which the two leads perform Massenet as though it was Puccini (Opera D'Oro).

Massenet—*Manon*—Milan, 1969
https://www.youtube.com/watch?v=RA3o922woZE

Contrasting that is a delicious 1965 Salzburg performance of Mozart's Die Entführung aus dem Serail with the sweetly crystalline Anneliese Rothenberger, Reri Grist, Fritz Wunderlich, Gerhard Unger, and Fernando Corena, conducted by Mehta (Orfeo).

Mozart—*Die Entführung aus dem Serail*—Salzburg, 1965
https://www.youtube.com/watch?v=gu70ARSVG3Q

There is a moving, Italian-sung performance (1958) of Massenet's Don Quichote with Boris Christoff and Teresa Berganza (Opera D'Oro). Another once-in-a-lifetime performances is a 1962 Salzburg Il trovatore (Gala) with Leontyne Price, Franco Corelli, Ettore Bastianini, and Giulietta Simionato, conducted by Herbert von Karajan—spectacular singing, excellent recording, and an unforgettable evening of listening, all for about $10.00. I cannot emphasize enough, that all the recordings I have mentioned above are but a tiny fraction of the many, many recordings available.

There are so many others—depending on your preferences. Below are some more of my favorites.

Massenet—Don Quichotte—Paris video 2000, with Samuel Ramey in one of his great roles as a moving beautifully sung Don, with Jean-Philippe Lafont and *Carmen* Oprisanu, beautifully conducted by James Conlon.

Massenet—*Don Quichotte*—Paris 2000
https://www.youtube.com/watch?v=mCXku5PoyK8&t=10s

Donizetti—*Lucia di Lammermoor*—Rome, 1990—Mariella Devia, Alfredo Kraus, Roberto Serville, Aurio Tomicich—conducted sensitively by Franco Mannino. A remarkable performance that many do not know about. The score was sung in all the original keys and all the singers give first-rate performances. Kraus is sublime in the final scene and Devia shines on high with a generous sprinkling of high Eb, E, and Fs.

https://www.youtube.com/watch?v=yrfC6dH343A&t=7624s

Bellini—*Beatrice di Tenda*—Naples, September 2023 with Jessica Pratt, Chiara Polese,

Matthew Polenzani, Andrzej Filonczyk—Giacomo Sagripanti. Pratt pulls out all the stops singing some novel ornamentation and offering all of Joan Sutherland's original high note interpolations from Milan in 1962 (no mean feat). The rest of the cast is just as good each having their own memorable moments. This was kindly uploaded to YouTube by Australian conductor, Brian Castles-Onion.

https://www.youtube.com/watch?v=TPxrke321Mg

Verdi—*Aïda*—Metropolitan Opera, 1952—Zinka Milanov, Mario Del Monaco, Leonard Warren, Nell Rankin, Jerome Hines—Fausto Cleva—A wonderful performance with intense singing from all the cast.

https://www.youtube.com/watch?v=zmcWCzFVL-I

Puccini—*Tosca* (abr)– Metropolitan Opera performance April 4, 1956 with Zinka Milanov, Jussi Bjorling, Walter Cassell conducted by Dimitri Mitropoulos. This is rare item for the mid 1950s with surprisingly clear sound—probably from house speakers. A rare opportunity to hear the two main protagonists in their roles before they recorded them for RCA.

https://www.youtube.com/watch?v=wqc-3Ppubz8

Puccini—*Tosca*—Metropolitan Opera performance, November 20, 1961 with Zinka Milanov, Giuseppe Zampieri, George London—conducted by Kurt Adler—a wonderful performance taped, it seems, from the prompters box or the house speaker system.

https://www.youtube.com/watch?v=vqPhBwvbNLo

Strauss—*Salome*—Carnegie Hall, (Chicago Symphony)—December 1974—Birgit Nilsson, Norman Bailey, Ragnar Ulfung, Ruth Hesse—Georg Solti conducting. Great sound and a white-hot performance.

https://www.youtube.com/watch?v=O8T4be5d08M

Verdi—*Il Corsaro*—Dortmund, June 2011—Elena Mosuc, Maria Guleghina, Zvetan Michailov, Sebastian Catana—Carlo Montanaro—A lovely performance with Guleghina pulling out all the vocal stops in her difficult role of Gulnara. Elena Mosuc is a good foil for Guleghina.

https://www.youtube.com/watch?v=4XeK5_o4TIM

There are at least 2 Don Carlos that remain cult classics to this day—mainly for the extraordinary sustained final high B as sung by Montserrat Caballe. In the case of the Metropolitan Opera broadcast, 16 seconds!

Verdi—*Don Carlo*—Verona, August 2, 1969—Montserrat Caballe, Placido Domingo, Piero Cappuccilli, Fiorenza Cossotto—Eliahu Inbal—Wonderful work by all involved.

https://www.youtube.com/watch?v=0Jtkxi5qKZA

Verdi—*Don Carlo*—Metropolitan Opera broadcast April, 1972—with Montserrat Caballe, Franco Corelli, Grace Bumbry, Sherill Milnes, Cesare Siepi—conducted by Francesco Molinari-Pradelli

There is also an exceptional Il trovatore from Florence in December, 1968 with Montserrat Caballe, Richard Tucker, Franca Mattiucci, Mario Zanasi—conducted by Thomas Schippers. Caballe sings an exquisite "D'amor sull ali rosee" in Act IV and Tucker is in fine voice as Manrico.

https://www.youtube.com/watch?v=PShz2ZUPvjI

Berg—*Lulu*—Paris 1979 (film)—Teresa Stratas, Yvonne Minton, Franz Mazura, Kenneth Riegel, Hanna Schwarz, Toni Blakenheim, Robert Tear—Pierre Boulex. The historic and harrowing performance with a star-studded cast. Not easily forgotten.

https://www.youtube.com/watch?v=L4Cjm_wa6VI

Berg—*Lulu*—Vienna, 1968—Anja Silja, Marta Modl, Hans Hotter, Waldemar Kmentt, William Blankenship—Karl Böhm—A different take on this great work with another very famous interpreter of the lead role.
https://www.youtube.com/watch?v=GY2Tt9BMVrU

Braunfels—*Die Vögel*—Strassbourg, 2022—Marie-Ève Munger, Tuomas Katajala, Cody Quattlebaum, Josef Wagner, Christoph Pohl—conducted by Aziz Shokhakimov. A beautiful, Straussian score with a spectacular coloratura role of the Nightingale. It is a free adaptation based on "The Birds" a Greek comedy by Aristophanes. The work premiered in Vienna in 1920, with Maria Ivogün as the Nightingale, her husband Karl Erb, as Good Hope and conducted by Bruno Walter. In the last couple of decades, the work has seen a number of revivals. The first was in Karlsruhe in 1971 with Elana Carcaleanu. This link leading to the most recent. If the roles are filled with appropriate singers, the work has a magical quality.
https://www.youtube.com/watch?v=iK62tO0jMMw

Handel—*Semele*—Caramoor, June, 1969—Beverly Sills, Elaine Bonzaai, Léopold Simoneau, John Ferrante, Michael Devlin—Julius Rudel. When it comes to Baroque ornamentation (supplied by Roland Gagnon) many criticized Sills for using over-elaboratre fioriture. No matter what, you will rarely hear such beautiful coloratura singing. Sills originally sang Semele in Cleveland in December of 1967. Reportedly, she was ill at the time, but the existing tapes (not on YouTube) show a performance even more spectacular than this from Caramoor. The Cleveland performance is on Gala's Beverly Sills collection.

Handel—*Semele*—Caramoor, June, 1969
https://www.youtube.com/watch?v=IbhoqszMI04

Another Semele that should be heard by more people is the St. Petersburg production (video) of the opera from February, 2022 with a remarkable Semele sung by Holly Flack, Ryan Belongie, Sara Couden, Stephanie Jabre, Kyle Tomlin, and conducted by Mark Sforzini. Flack offers some startling, inventive and high ornamentation to the role including flights up to at least the A above high C. One high F in "Myself I shall adore" prompts an immediate audience response. Another excellent singer in this cast is Sara Couden who sings Queen Juno. Using a modern staging this is certainly worth seeing.

Handel—*Semele*—St. Petersburg, February 2022
https://www.youtube.com/watch?v=wCjkjQtr8lo&t=847s

Another Holly Flack gem can be found on YouTube—the reprise of "Tornami a Vagheggiar" from Handel's Alcina. Flack's colorful ornamentation with much staccato work, takes her to a sustained Bb above high C.

Handel—"Tornami a Vagheggiar" *Alcina*—Fargo-Moorhead Opera, 2018—conducted by Clinton Smith.
https://www.youtube.com/watch?v=xfQ2VVNWLy8

Stravinsky—*The Rake's Progress* (World Premier) Venice. 1951—Robert Rounseville, Elisabeth Schwarzkopf, Otokar Kraus, Jennie Tourel—Igor Stravinsky—One of the most important operas of the 20th century fortunately conducted by its creator and recorded at its Venice premiere. Sung in its original English with a wonderful cast including the great mezzo-soprano, Jennie Tourel. Schwarzkopf sings a beautiful Anne—her great scene, "No Word from Tom" and the last act lullaby are both outstanding.

Stravinsky—*The Rake's Progress* (World Premier) Venice. 1951
https://www.youtube.com/watch?v=RynuAq_GBHQ

Halevy—La Juive (excerpts)—RCA 1974—One of the great "highlight" albums of the 1970s with Richard Tucker, Martina Arroyo, Anna Moffo, Bonaldo Giaiotti—Antonio de Almeida. Unfortunately, Arroyo doesn't get her great aria "Il v avenir" but Moffo does get the rarely recorded Bolero from Act III (which she elects to finish on a splendid high E).

Halevy—*La Juive* (excerpts)—RCA 1974
https://www.youtube.com/watch?v=H8vw7xhopk4

Meyerbeer—*Les Huguenots* (Acts 1 and 2)—Carnegie Hall 1969—Beverly Sills, Tony Poncet, Justino Diaz, Kay Creed—Reynald Giovaninetti
https://www.youtube.com/watch?v=PObZ-4VDU0Q&t=2856s

Meyerbeer—*Les Huguenots* (Conclusion)—Carnegie Hall 1969—Beverly Sills, Tony Poncet, Justino Diaz, Kay Creed—Reynald Giovaninetti
https://www.youtube.com/watch?v=_v-YxuHD36k&t=6s

Donizetti—*Lucia di Lammermoor*—London, 1959—The historic performance that catapulted Joan Sutherland into international notoriety. With Joao Gibin, John Shaw, Joseph Rouleau—Tullio Serafin
https://www.youtube.com/watch?v=9ZNBfXi4CqQ

Donizetti—*Lucia di Lammermoor*—Edinburgh, August 1961—Another early performance of Covent Garden on tour in Edinburgh. This caught Sutherland in especially fine voice.
https://www.youtube.com/watch?v=Yz6H_zuRNxE&t=258s

Massenet—*Thaïs*—Amsterdam, 1995—Nelly Miricioiu, John Bröcheler, Guus Hoekman, Neil Jekins, Elena Vink—One of the great concert revivals of this opera during the 1990s. A long coveted tape.
https://www.youtube.com/watch?v=rMn62iTvXAg

Donizetti—*Lucia di Lammermoor*—Metropolitan Opera performance, June, 1970, This is now a cult favorite. Dame joan Sutherland, Placido Domingo, Mario Sereni, John Macurdy—Richard Bonynge (I am pretty sure that this is one of Ralph Ferrandina's tapes—I recognize his screaming after the Mad Scene.
https://www.youtube.com/watch?v=NBK9StmHJFg&t=4s

Janacek—*Jenufa*—Salzburg, July, 2001—Hildegard Behrens, Karita Mattila, Jerry Hadley, David Kuebler, June Card—John Eliot-Gardiner
https://www.youtube.com/watch?v=iMFAOiXDmuo

Verdi—*Nabucco* (excerpts)—San Francisco, 1982—Olivia Staff, Matteo Manuguerra, Paul Plishka, Gordon Greer—Kurt Herbaert Adler—great high D
https://www.youtube.com/watch?v=W6IoEIIckM8

Strauss—*Die Ägyptische Helena*—Vienna, 1970—Gwyneth Jones, Mimi Coertse, Jess Thomas, Peter Glossop, Edita Gruberova—Josef Krips—An important revival with Jones in spectacular voice. She even interpolates a final high B at the end of the Awakening scene in the opeing of Act II (as did Inge Borkh).
https://www.youtube.com/watch?v=mjrycBkKvUI&t=201s

Giordano—*Andrea Chenier*—Metropolitan Opera broadcast, March 26, 1960 with Richard Tucker, Renata Tebaldi, Ettore Bastianini conducted by Fausto Cleva. This performance, in excellent sound, is a white-hot rendition of this great verismo work. Tebaldi and Tucker are at their freshest.

Giordano—*Andrea Chenier*—Metropolitan Opera broadcast, March 26, 1960
https://www.youtube.com/watch?v=tfWKU6DjGN4

Puccini—*Tosca*—Metropolitan Opera, December, 1981—Carol Neblett, Jose Carreras, Sherrill Milnes, Russel Christopher—Giuseppe Patane—A wonderful performance.
https://www.youtube.com/watch?v=PsBVgqKqlD8&t=3s

Puccini—*Tosca*—London 1964—Maria Callas, Renato Cioni, Tito Gobbi, Eric Garrett—Carlo Felice Cillario, In excellent sound and one of my favorite of the Callas *Tosca*. She may not have liked the role but it drew the best from her. Great vocal acting from everyone in the cast. The ending is particularly harrowing.
https://www.youtube.com/watch?v=A2XYaxdyf7o&t=1446s

Verdi—*Nabucco*—Chicago broadcast—May, 1997—Alexandru Agache, Maria Guleghina, Samuel Ramey, Patrick Denniston—Bruno Bartoletti
https://www.youtube.com/watch?v=hZ5UUyRorvA

Massenet—*Roi de Lahore*—Vancouver, 1977—Joan Sutherland, Huguette Tourangeau, Cornelius Opthof, Spiro Malas—Richard Bonynge—A true Massenet rarity meant to showcase Dame Joan Sutherland. Huguette Tourangeau, however, almost steals the show by her singing of the exquisite aria for Kaled in Act II. Tourangeau always had an odd, idiosyncratic voice, and here her unique timbre perfectly suits Massenet's exotic music.
https://www.youtube.com/watch?v=LgypuMfXYUw&t=1s

Bellini—*I Capuletti e I Montecchi*—Milan, 1967—A remarkable performance with both Giacomo Aragall and a young Luciano Pavarotti put against a mighty Renata Scotto eager to show her high Ebs and Es.

Bellini—"Tace il fragor…Se ogni speme" *I Capuletti e I Montecchi*—Milan, 1967
https://www.youtube.com/watch?v=qyOJiy4W3DE

Bellini—"Morte io temo" *I Capuletti e I Montecchi*—Renata Scotto—Milan, 1967
https://www.youtube.com/watch?v=0JbY9BOz4U4

Strauss—*Ariadne auf Naxos*—Chicago, 1981—Leonie Rysanek, Ruth Welting, Trudeliese Schmidt, Willam Johns—Marek Janowski. A remarkable performance of this difficult work.
https://www.youtube.com/watch?v=xhFRGsqxuwE

Donizetti—*Anna Bolena*—New York, 1966—Elena Suliotis, Placido Domingo, Marilyn Horne—Henry Lewis—A fascinating performance despite some questionable cuts. Suliotis proves why she was such a popular singer and vocal dynamo despite running to grief on the final notes of the role.
https://www.youtube.com/watch?v=cdLRmTQh9_Y

Wagner—*Die Götterdämmerung*—Metropolitan Opera, 1962—one of the important revivals of the work at the Met with a stellar cast including Birgit Nilssom. Gladys Kutcha, Hans Hopf, Gottlob Frick, Norman Mittleman, Irene Dalis—all under the direction of Erich Leinsdorf. This performance has one of the great performances of the "Dawn Duet" one can hear.
https://www.youtube.com/watch?v=poyuiJnqlXg

Mascagni—*Cavalleria rusticana*—Metropolitan Opera Performance—November 5, 1974—with Grace Bumbry, Franco Tagliavini, Anselmo Colzani—conducted by John Nelson. This is a true curiosity and worth investigating, Thanks should go to nir0bateman for uploading this video. Originally it was a performance of the double-bill of Pagliacci and Cavalleria rusticana that was meant to be Telecast, but never was. There are a few technical glitches during the tape, but whether they are from when it was originally recorded or later, is not clear. It is unfortunate since it is a wonderful performance. I have heard Bumbry in a number of performances of Cavalleria—Santuzza suited her voice and temperament very well, and of them all this is one of the best. Cavalleria rusticana is a dramatically tight work with no wasted space or notes, and Santuzza is one of the great characters in opera. This performance has a rousing Easter Hymn with the chorus, with the trademark Bumbry "thrust" to a final high B, and a dramatically vivid, "Voi lo sapete." The famous confrontation-duet with Turiddu (Tagliavini) is a dramatic highlight of the opera. The moment of Santuzza hurling her curse at Turiddu raises goosebumps. Franco Tagliavini is excellent in the Brindisi and his farewell to Mama Lucia and Bumbry finishes the opera with a remarkable high C. Do yourself a favor and watch this.

https://www.youtube.com/watch?v=uo5dSgSVn08&t=1s

At one point I had two thousand reel-to-reel tapes of opera, concert, and recital performances as well as thousands of cassettes. Space problems caused me to donate almost everything to a collector who I trusted would make sure they were made available and got out to people. Although I seriously mourned the loss of my collection, because of technological changes requiring no space at all through the Internet, MP3s, and other computer file formats, within a few years I regained nine tenths of what I had donated.

Pirate Opera CD Labels

There are excellent budget labels available such as Gala and Opera D'Oro, each offering generally excellent sound.

Gala has been in existence since about 2000. Over the decades it has shown itself to be an invaluable resource of valuable recorded live operatic performances having excellent sound. Most performances are important revivals or famous broadcasts of the Metropolitan Opera or other international houses. Attractively packaged with booklets of notes, and almost always with excellent bonus music to fill up the CDs, they are budget-priced and irresistible. From Alfano to Zandonai, I have found their releases to be fascinating and worth collecting.

Opera d'Oro is more bare bones in their presentation than Gala and do not offer additional music filler on CDs, but some of their selections are quite rare and many are important classics.

There are the more expensive labels of Melodram (Italy) and MYTO (at one time the premiere label of pirate recordings), Dynamic (Martina Franca Festival), BellaVoce, Marco Polo (Wexford Festival), Arcadia (formerly Hunt), Voce della Luna, Arlecchino, Grand Tier, On Stage, Nuova Era, Walhall, Eclipse, The Fourties, Mondo Musica (Teatro La Fenice), Legato Classics, Music and Arts, G.O.P and VAI (New Orleans series), along with live releases now offered on major labels such as BMG (Munich and Vienna series), EMI (Salzburg, La Scala, and the Callas "live" library), and Sony (Opera Orchestra of New York).

parterre box

Before we discuss online stores at which to purchase live opera, there is a website that I would like to point out: parterre box (parterre.com). Sites that offer free opera downloads are rare.

Most sites are subscription-based. But there is one—parterre box—an opera e-zine that offers a free downloadable live opera each Thursday.

This website is the brainchild of music critic James Jorden (1954-2023) who created the site as an Internet spot for accurate information and tart gossip about operatic happenings in New York and elsewhere. Over the years, parterre box has developed into the central place where one can go to read eloquent reviews of opera performances, fascinating articles, and witty banter about opera singers.

> James Jorden (who writes under the names La Cieca and Our Own JJ) is the founder and editor of parterre box. During his twenty-year year career as an opera critic, he has written for the New York Times, Opera, Gay City News, Opera Now, Musical America and the New York Post. (parterre box website)

Originally, parterre box was a type-written publication that Jorden wrote, duplicated, and distributed himself from 1993 to 2001. (PDFs of the original forty-eight issues are available in the archives on the site.) Bitingly humorous and remarkably accurate in its reviews and gossip, I still have my original copies. I even wrote a few singer appreciations for parterre box under the nom de plume, Leila de Lakmé.

Jorden was quite far-sighted in deciding to create his website. Among the first innovative things he instituted was a section called, "Unnatural Acts of Opera." This is a podcast hosted by "La Cieca" of individual opera acts offered sequentially. A wonderful segment, it presents classic pirated opera performances, including famous bel canto revivals of the 1960s. It can be downloaded directly to your computer or found on downloading services such as iTunes and other aggregators. It is an excellent repository for many classic pirated opera performances.

After Christopher Corwin wrote a successful series of five articles for parterre box called "chris and the pirates" about his experiences with pirated opera recordings, Jorden suggested he head up a segment called Trove Thursday. It features opera performances for which Christopher also prepares an introductory page. His first offering was published on September 10, 2015—Les Troyens, a live performance from London's Covent Garden, October 7, 1972 sung in English. The cast included Janet Baker, Jon Vickers, Josephine Veasey, and Robert Kerns, conducted by Colin Davis. The unusual thing about this is that each selection is individually downloadable. It is going strong over four years later.

Christopher, (who came to New York in 1990) was thrilled with the idea. As he explained to me:

> (James) offered to host the project and gave me the technical parameters necessary for me to submit the audio files to him. At the time there was another podcast on parterre but you couldn't download its content so James proposed that Trove Thursday would be downloadable and I was happy about that. The other podcaster and I also had very different tastes and interests so there was almost never any clash. James named the series as well. (Private email, June 2018)

Christopher explained that a file used for the Trove Thursday program needed to be in a specific format and that took some time to accomplish along with editing out announcements. Writing the accompanying text varied greatly, depending on the time needed to conceive of and write it.

Christopher's operatic tastes are quite eclectic, although he admits to a special fondness for seventeenth- and eighteenth-century works. When asked about his choices of performances, he said:

> I choose the weekly installments based primarily on what interests or excites me. Occasionally I will post things because I believe there might be interest from readers outside of my own enthusiasms. I sometimes try to post works that will be coming up at the Met or at other local or even international venues. I've always had eclectic tastes and I think Trove Thursday reflects that...well beyond the usual *Aida-Boheme-Carmen* favorites. (ibid)

When I asked Christopher about differences he noticed between "then" and "now" piracy, he said that he was surprised that Trove Thursday was still so popular after three years.

> Although, as I mention in chris and the pirates, the catalogs listing reel-to-reel pirates were widely advertised, I suspect it was a fairly tiny group that actively bought or traded these items. Eventually the advent of CDs and changes in copyright laws allowed for more and more of this material to be more widely had. The invention of the internet AND digitization and most importantly YouTube has meant that lots of this material has now become easily available to its largest public ever. I think it remains a specialized taste—those who require optimum sound quality and studio polish will not be happy with much of this stuff. (ibid)

For more about Christopher Corwin's story, I refer the reader to his articles "chris and the pirates" begun on August 3, 2015, on parterre.com.

Within his Trove Thursday segment of the parterre box website, you will find more than two hundred downloads of such diverse works as Rimsky-Korsakov's May Night and Tsar's Bride, Dvorak's Spector's Bride, Cherubini's Medea (from a rare 1955 performance in New York with Eileen Farrell and a young James McCracken), Massenet's Cendrillon, Mercadante's Virginia, Handel's Teseo, Monteverdi's L'Incoronazione di Poppea, Britten's Death in Venice, Weber's Euryanthe, Vivaldi's Montezuma, Hasse's Olimpiade, Cimarosa's Il Marito Disperato and many, many more. Corwin's contributions to parterre box enables one to easily build a considerable and impressive library of live recordings. A most generous gift from both Chris and James. At the time of this writing, after seven years of uploading performances, Corwin has decided to limit his opera uploads to an occasional treat.

As a sign of the differing times, Christopher, who once eagerly awaited the arrival of parcels of live-opera reel-to-reel tapes from the piraters, now shares his love of live opera with an audience of visitors who come to the parterre box website. One can only guess at the number of people he has managed to touch with his own bounty.

Online Stores

Forty years ago, the possibility of going online to obtain pirated live opera performances could not have been imagined. Times have changed as have laws and priorities. For collectors and those interested, it is a dream come true. For the novice collector of live performances, a drawback to live recordings on the smaller CD labels is that most releases have tiny pressings and do not include a libretto. Most do include a synopsis of the opera's action, and libretti can be easily found online.

> Unique is Guild
> (https://www.guildmusic.com/)
> and Immortal Performances
> (http://www.immortalperformances.org/),

interconnected through one man, Richard Caniell. They offer both silver disc and CD-Rom types of CD. As mentioned earlier, a silver (or regular CD) is commercially produced while a CD-Rom has a greenish tint and is technically "home-made." The Guild label is a commercial venture established in 1967 on LPs. It now enjoys a world-wide reputation for quality. Their vast catalogue includes premiere recordings of unjustly neglected music, beside performances from gifted young musicians and recordings of organ and choral music. The Guild Historical series is a segment of the label and features lovingly restored legendary operatic recordings and broadcast performances.

They are most famous for The Dream Ring Cycle released between 2002 and 2003 consisting of 1930s Metropolitan Opera broadcasts of Wagner's Ring Cycle cobbled together to create dreamcasting for that time. This seemingly impossible project was the brainchild of Richard Caniell. This remarkable set of discs was released by Guild (on silver CD). In 2013, Immortal Performances released the set completely remastered.

No small feat, the amount of careful splicing and pitching of all four of the Ring operas took tremendous patience by Caniell.

Immortal Performances, a Canadian-based, federally chartered, non-profit archive, has a huge number of historic broadcasts gathered over a more-than-fifty-year period. The archive was created in 1980 to provide music lovers with copies of historic broadcasts. They began as a mail-order subscription society with an exceptional list of reel-to-reel offerings with spectacular documentation and individual analysis of sound quality. Very often Richard Caniel would write essays on the performances that proved to be very interesting reading.

Very appealing was a very large spiral-bound book, The Metropolitan Opera Broadcasts, a forerunner of Paul Jackson's Saturday Afternoons at the Old Met (but not by Jackson). I joined the society around 1990 and got a few tapes from them. They were just as excellent as advertised. I still have the remarkable brochures and leaflets that came with joining the society.

Their first forty-eight albums were released by Naxos, followed with fifty-three albums by Guild Music. Both companies originally formed their historical label series in order to release Immortal Performances' restorations.

Their history takes us full circle to the problems of piracy that have plagued the industry since the beginning of recordings.

In order to gain membership, applicants signed a contract agreeing not to sell, lend, or transfer any of the broadcasts received, nor allow their publication on LP or CD. Regrettably, over a hundred and fifty of Mr. Caniell's major restorations were obtained by Eklipse and Walhall CDs, the owner of which was Robert Horneman, who, allegedly, posed as a music student, obtained the tapes and then issued them on CD. (They were premieres in the CD format, but the CD company used an inferior form of Cedar, a noise suppression computer program).

Eventually, Horneman sold the Eklipse/Walhall catalogue to Gebhardt in Germany. They distributed some of them, but not all. Archipel has also begun issuing the Eklipse/Walhall holdings composed largely of IPRMS restorations.

> Although we wrote to the major music critics and magazines about Horneman's conversion of our restorations, the Society lacked the funds to sue Horneman / Eklipse / Walhall, and so our work became disseminated by other labels (MYTO, et al) as well. This brought about our decision to end availability of our holdings, as these CD issues greatly reduced our membership.

These circumstances led John Ardoin, music critic and famed biographer of the art of Maria Callas, to intercede. He introduced our work to Jonathan Wearn, a record producer based in London, England. As it turned out, Mr. Wearn, a very well known and highly regarded record producer, shared with us a dedication to preserving the original sonics of our broadcast holdings and became instrumental in bringing about our relationship with Guild Music. Shortly after our association with Mr. Wearn, he introduced our holdings to Naxos, entering into an agreement whereby Naxos would create a Historical Series built around our work. During the years 1997 to 1999 some 47 albums of our material (Operatic and Toscanini broadcasts) were issued. Many of these releases proved highly unsatisfactory. Our producer, Mr. Wearn, filed suit against Naxos in London High Court on his and our behalf. This suit is now in preliminary proceedings.

After a two-year withdrawal from the field, and after careful consideration, Immortal Performances allied itself to Guild Music Ltd., choosing this Swiss company based upon its devotion to design excellence in presentation. This fledgling endeavor was greatly aided by Dr. Irwin Elkins (Omega Opera), one of the true pioneers in broadcast preservations, Keith Hardwick, EMI Chief Sound Engineer emeritus, Bill Youngren, music critic, Nathan Brown and others. The National Library of Canada gave its permission to issue broadcast recordings from their Jobin collection. The late Robert Hupka has given written permission to use his famous photos of Toscanini in Guild booklets. Mr. Wearn, now a long-standing friend as well, continued as producer of the Guild Historical series…" (Immortal Performances website)

Following an amicable separation from Guild, Immortal Performances continued to devote their efforts on accurate restorations.

> In 2009 we began to issue, on our own label, the albums presented on this site, with many more to come. We believe we can deliver a dedication to quality that will eventually make itself known to music-lovers who have collected our releases under the Naxos and Guild labels. Our new series of albums delivers to an interested public a treasurable wealth of great singing and conducting presented in the best sonics possible. (ibid)

There are a number of online stores where one can buy live opera performances.

Celestial Audio

(http://www.celestialaudio.com.au.)

has hundreds of opera performances and the covers of their sets are especially attractive, showing a lot of thought in their execution. The only drawback is that it is a CD-Rom (Compact Disc Read-Only Memory) not silver, commercially pressed CD. All online stores for live opera are CD-Rom. One should immediately save the music on one's computer to avoid the loss of the performance when the CDR goes blind. I have had personal experience with such losses.

The main drawback of Celestial Audio for U.S. customers is cost. Typically, a two-CD set including shipping and handling from Australia will cost $75.00. They also offer a mastering service for LPs and cassettes. I have ordered a few things from them and all have been nicely presented and tracked.

The largest online store for live opera in the United States is Premiere Opera founded by Ed Rosen. It can be found at

http://www.premiereopera.com.

They are probably the largest repository of live performances on CD and DVD, about

25,000 performances and growing. A plus for this site is that digital downloads are also available. They have an excellent website that is easy to navigate and has a good search engine. They frequently have sales with considerable savings. Premiere Opera's CDs are barebones. I found them to be quick to fill an order and the performances I got were well-tracked and in good sound.

They are one of the few places (House of Opera is another) that offer a selection of the wonderful MP3 and CD-ROMS of the audio encyclopedia of Mike Richter (1939–2013), a remarkable resource of operatic history. (See the chapter on The Richter CD-ROMS) Mike Richter's work was of great importance not only to fans of opera and live performances, but to historians. Premiere Opera offers twenty-four of these precious, historical releases. If you are not familiar with his CD ROMs, I urge you to check them out.

Similar in structure and size as Premiere Opera is House of Opera (run by Ed Rosen's cousin). Its website can be found at
http://www.operapassion.com.

They, too, offer MP3s, CDs, and DVDs (as well as Mike Richter's CD-ROMs). Different from most other sites of its type, they have an interesting disclaimer—although it might put off some people, I find it rather refreshing (part of the below obviously refers to DVDs):

> The recordings are sent to you in paper sleeves with no tray card or inserts, just the raw discs with printed labels. These recordings are of nonprofessional quality that are in the public domain. The quality of these old opera recordings is not very good and they are meant for collectors and educational purposes only. Most of them are 30 or 40 years old, so they might be blurry, colors faded, and not sound very good, but they might not be available elsewhere. Please note that most of our recordings do not have tracks, they have 1 long track per disc. (House of Opera web site)

One of the best online live-opera stores is Opera Depot (https://operadepot.com). They provide a full track and cast listing with their sets. Their website is one of the better ones since it includes not only an honestly presented description of the performance (its good and bad points) but abbreviated sound samples that are invaluable for the prospective buyer. Their prices are quite reasonable. They regularly offer free opera downloads from their library; sometimes it is a complete opera, and sometimes a compilation of an artist's work. Andrew Whitfield, who runs Opera Depot, worked for Ed Rosen for two years in New York City, before he opened Opera Depot in 2007. Since then, he has amassed over 1,000 titles, some of them quite unusual.

Whitfield lives in San Francisco and is a respected conductor and chorus master at Opera San José, founded by Metropolitan Opera mezzo-soprano, Irene Dalis (1925-2014). Importantly, he notes on the website that: "all our CDs are created to order from a digital image of the master. This eliminates wear and tear and ensures that the CD…will be free of digital clicks and other flaws."

I have gotten many titles from Opera Depot and all have been of excellent quality. His website is easy to navigate and has a number of helpful search levels. The turn-around is quick and when you order CDs, MP3s of your selections are immediately made available for you to download to your computer. Talk about instant gratification! If you are as impatient as me, that is a tremendous bonus. Andrew has frequent theme-based sales and his work ethic is as elegant as his website.

A Pirates Nightmare—La Puma Opera Company

During the 1980s and 1990s, it was not only traditional opera performances that were in demand by the purchaser of pirate records, but also such items as the notorious New York performances of the La Puma Opera Company with their then-reigning diva, Olive Middleton, the Florence Foster Jenkins of the 1960s.

As Anne Midgette reported in The New York Times (April 9, 2006)

> ...when I present you with the recordings of Olive Middleton, you may think I've taken leave of my senses. Middleton's singing goes beyond parody. And it goes well beyond good singing. It's just plain awful.

Middleton, who died in 1974, was a British singer who had once had an actual voice and career. But by the 1960's, when she was prima donna assoluta of La Puma Opera Workshop in New York, she had hardly any voice at all. Her sound swooped and squawked in vague proximity to the pitches of the toughest roles in the repertory: *Tosca*, Aida, Sieglinde. It didn't seem to bother her, and it certainly got attention. Like Florence Foster Jenkins before her, she amassed a coterie of adoring fans who greeted her every entrance with thunderous applause and continually demanded that she learn new roles, like Bellini's Norma."

Today, Donald Collup, a former singer and now vocal documentarian, has been archiving the La Puma performances. They are available on his Web site (collup.com). Collup is known in operatic circles for his excellent documentaries Florence Foster Jenkins: A World of Her Own (2008)—now on VAI DVD and Never Before, The Life and First New York Career of Astrid Varnay (2004)

By the 1970s La Puma had disintegrated into an opera company of parody, though not by intent. Well known opera pirater, Charles Handelman, gave an informative discourse on La Puma for the Opera-L Archives (11-22-2000):

> A not-very-well- kept- secret is the fact that Mme. Josephine La Puma was the mother of that marvelous Met coach, Alberta Masiello. Mother la Puma ran an opera company in New York in the 50's, 60's and I think 70's where the singers paid her for the great pleasure of appearing upon an opera stage. Even a few of them (Andrij Dobriansky was one) ended up at the Met; however, most of the singers would not even be welcome in the living rooms of even the most die-hard opera fan, for the level was so unbelievably LOW that one might attend a performance and either walk out in disgust or utter boredom, or experience severe bladder problems and aching ribs from the hilarity on the stage.

The reigning star of this company was dear Olive Middleton, known in the 20's (1920's, I think) as Olive Townsend, and who actually did appear at Covent Garden. Olive walked with a cane, had a few teeth, and even into her 70's (80's?) had the ability to 'get through' roles like Fedora, Norma, Tosca, etc. and even took the 'Kitty Carlisle High C' in the Miserere from Trovatore...Olive became a cult figure among the cognoscenti, and even some of the big Met stars attended some of her legendary performances, usually held in a junior high school in Manhattan, or at other locations. We once met the dear lady at a Milanov Gioconda, and treated her as we treated Zinka...she just adored the attention!"

The La Puma Opera Company was casual to say the least. At one performance, Mme. La Puma announced that the Barnaba in that night's performance of *La gioconda* was ill. So, instead, they would be performing *Tristan und Isolde*.

The vocal efforts of the la Puma "singers" (who paid for the privilege) were pathetic, but their willingness to publicly exploit their lack of talent opened them up to the ridicule they often received. There are some grotesque La Puma videos on YouTube (including excerpts from *Die Walküre, Lucia di Lammermoor,* Pagliacci, *Tosca,* Aïda, *Rigoletto,* etc.) But be warned, a little goes a long way (also there is much more that exists on tape).

One of my favorite videos of this type (favorite, only because it is so disturbing) is what must have been one of the La Puma offshoot companies: Monteverdi Opera Company with a resident octanagerian diva named Francesca di Balassa. It is eight-minutes of an al fresco, piano-accompanied performance of excerpts from Adriana Lecouvreur in Lincoln Center's Damrosch Park. Despite using a mike, Di Balassa is barely audible, and when she is, she is off-pitch. Most of the time she stands like an emotionless, embalmed mummy. Colleagues on stage try desperately to encourage applause from the audience. No tenor was available so they used a male dancer dressed in a short silk kimono, with a head band, and a huge Japanese hand-fan that he twirled, swooshed, and dipped interpretively as he danced around the stage. During this time, the pianist played the tenor's music. When the opera was completed, di Balassa, stood motionless like a wax figure and eventually had to be led off the stage lovingly by her fan-dancer, whom I assume from the program was Attilio Aschai.

Groups and Workshops like the La Puma Company are a layer among the varied strata of the New York musical scene. They provide an opportunity for young (or old) singers to sing the roles they want to by straight-out paying (or subsidizing by the sale of tickets) for the privilege.

Although such organizations have their place in New York's musical world, they are less than useless when it comes to the building of a serious artistic resume. YouTube has many examples of such performances. My favorite is a concert performance of the act II finale of Aïda performed in what looks like a showroom that sells grandfather clocks using lawn furniture for the sparse audience to sit on. The ensemble sings one of the most ragged examples of the finale of the triumphal scene that you could possibly imagine. "Aida" reaches for an interpolated high E-flat that ends up a strangled, throat-splitting scream.

Streaming Live Opera

For those interested in streaming live performances, Met Opera on Demand (https://www.metopera.org/season/on-demand) is probably the best site. It is the online streaming service where one can watch and listen to more than six hundred Met performances.

> This online streaming catalog includes HD videos (from the Met's award-winning *Live in HD* series of worldwide cinema transmissions), classic telecasts (standard-definition videos that were originally broadcast live on television from 1977-2003), and radio broadcast (audio-only) performances dating back to 1935 (from the Met's long-running series of Saturday matinee radio broadcasts as well as more recent satellite radio broadcasts.)
>
> Subscribers to Met Opera on Demand enjoy unlimited access, anywhere in the world, to everything available through the service. Met Opera on Demand is now available and accessible on many of the most popular device and platforms, including: computers (desktop or laptop, directly through the Met website), tablets (iPad and Android), smartphones (iPhone and Android), and TVs (via Apple TV app, Roku Channel or Samsung Smart TV app.) (Metropolitan Opera website)

New users are offered a seven-day free trial to explore everything available on Met Opera on Demand. However, the performances available on Met Opera on Demand are not able to be downloaded—only streamed from their website and Met Opera on Demand apps.

Launched on May 8, 2015 is a similar site: "The Opera Platform," which features broadcasts from 15 opera companies in Europe

The Opera Platform is a new website which will broadcast and archive (for six months) full opera productions from some of Europe's leading opera companies, including Welsh National Opera, The Royal Opera and Teatro Real Madrid.

> The first opera to be streamed in full from The Royal Opera will be Szymanowski's Król Roger, which will be broadcast on The Opera Platform on May 16. Kasper Holten, the Royal Opera's Director of Opera said, 'This is a fantastic European-wide initiative offering opera lovers and newcomers to opera a chance to enjoy the very best that Europe has to offer for free! I am particularly thrilled that our brand new production of Król Roger is the first to be captured for this new platform for streaming opera. (Grammophone, May 2015)

The Last of the CD Pirates

I thought it might be interesting for readers to have a brief understanding of what it entails to be the producer of "good quality" pirate recordings. I reached out to WH, producers of the last pirated opera recordings on CD (many can still be found at Academy Records on 18th Street in Manhattan).

> I believe we began production in late 2006. And it was more or less an experiment to see what people would buy. The owner of Academy Records was willing to pay for the cost of pressing and to give us a stipend.
>
> To be honest, we basically learned as we went along. But all along the way, the most important thing was the aural quality of what we were offering the purchaser. We never threw something at the opera-lover in a hap-hazard way assuming that all that they were interested in was the performance.
>
> Throughout the years, many people have commented on our releases' aesthetic appearance (how they were presented) and also how good the sound was. Soprano Lucine Amara loved the two releases we did of her performances. Renata Scotto also loved what we did. Through one of her assistants, Leontyne Price told us that she, too, was appreciative. I know for a fact that James Levine kept some of our releases on his shelf in his office at the Metropolitan Opera and that he especially liked the Lulu we produced.
>
> Other piraters? MYTO continues to do good work but their sources can be suspect as well as their pitch. Gala simply does not pay as close attention to the aural aspect as they should. House of Opera can be very frustrating; poor tracking, incomplete (and sometimes incorrect) listing of venue and cast, and doing little to make the overall sound more listenable.
>
> Sometimes as I worked on performances of singers who never (or rarely) recorded commercially the thought came to me that we were actually contributing to their prestige by promoting their performances. A good case in point is Leontyne and her San Francisco Opera appearances. She rarely sang and certainly never recorded Manon Lescaut or Dialogues of the Carmelites. While the Ariadne auf Naxos and Il Tabarro she performed at San Francisco are easily to be preferred over her studio efforts.
>
> Another thing we are proud of was that different from most other pirates, whenever possible we

offered bonus selections in line with the main performance we were offering. Such things as Renata Scotto in act 2 of Parsifal, a complete recital with Alfredo Kraus, a recital featuring Judith Blegen, an interview with Anna Moffo, etc. (Private conversation, 2018)

That was in 2006. By 2018, the market for live opera recordings on CD had more or less dried up because people were able to download many of these operas from the Internet, or access them on YouTube—even if they might be of inferior sound quality. WH stopped its production of CDs.

The Overall Process

First of all you have to decide which recordings you want to issue. Consideration must be given to what repertoire and/or artists will sell and whether what you want to issue has already been released by other labels: MYTO, Melodram, Gala, Ponto, Opera D'Oro, etc. This calls for a lot of Internet research. We often consult with various well-known collectors as well.

Once you have chosen a performance, you then have to listen to the source material for the sound quality and completeness. Also, is the performance actually what it states it is? Is it an in-house performance or a broadcast? Performances may be marred by sloppy tape turn-overs, by late starts or missing bars of music, or by cutting certain sections, or even running out of tape before the work is completed. You also have to know if a performance is on pitch, or does it fluctuate and if so how to correct this. A knowledge of the score is essential.

After you have selected the performance and checked all those things, you still may need to reduce hiss or add bass, basically improving the sound to the point where you are satisfied with the result and feel it would be acceptable by potential buyers. (ibid)

Making the Master

You can't just run a tape and walk away. You have to listen carefully to the whole opera or recital, and many times everything will start fine but then something goes wrong. This could be the result of many things: mechanical issues, noise (coughing) or a talkative audience, too distant in sound, or just carelessness on the part of the person recording the performance, to name just a few. Many great performances were ruined because of these reasons and therefore were lost to posterity.

After spending hours on a performance that we suddenly realize we could not use, the last thing I want to do is start another. After all, we have lives and there are only so many hours in a day. We were a small operation and I used just one reel player to produce the rough master and then it would need to be cleaned up, the tape-joins would have to be edited and finally it would have to be properly tracked. Not to mention the work that went in to create the booklet and tray cards.

Because of this, our output was slow but, even so, we released almost 200 titles in five years.

Once the master is complete, the next step is to find a duplicating house that will accept a work order for a small run of product—usually around 100 copies of a title. This can be tedious as it is hard to find a duplicating house that understands the importance of attention to detail, to say nothing of their own ignorance (and even dislike) of opera. It is also at this point that artwork is decided on.

The booklet with the track listings is also important and takes a lot of work. We issued performances in Italian, German, French and Russian, and sometimes Spanish. A knowledge of the languages helps make sure the spelling is correct and the right accents are given. All of this is very time consuming. (ibid)

When the printing house sent a set of discs for proofing, they needed to be checked to make sure that the labeling and spelling on the disks was correct, and that the disc number matched what was on the CD. In addition, the booklet needed to be proofed for spelling errors and to make sure the track listings were correct. This was the most time-consuming part of the process as one must listen to the opera again from start to finish while proofing everything in the package (front tray card, booklet, back tray card, and spines).

Because WH was a small operation and did not have national distribution, they relied on word-of-mouth sales. They usually only printed about one hundred copies of each title, and because of the small quantity produced, the cost of duplication became important. Helping to promote many of the titles were the words on the back cover: "Bonus material is included."

The aim of WH was to issue performances they felt were artistically important.

> We never did it for the money. It was more a source of pride in what we were doing—especially in offering diverse repertoire that was not usually issued by other private companies. The focus was not on just Verdi, Puccini or Wagner, but also Britten, Berlioz, Berg, Massenet, Rossini, Handel, etc. (ibid)

WH also issued commemorative boxed sets of artists who were leaders in their field who had passed away: Luciano Pavarotti, Leonie Rysanek, Birgit Nilsson, Dame Joan Sutherland, and Elisabeth Soderstrom.

> I suppose that we set the bar very high and limited what we felt was good enough for us to release. We never regretted that. As I stated before, it was never about the money but it was about serving the music and artists that we loved so others could fully enjoy our efforts as well. What I do regret is that we could not do it longer.

(Private conversation via email, 2019.)

Below are a few performances the producers were especially proud of having released:

> Britten: *Billy Budd* from San Francisco. Dale Duesing should have been better utilized by the major opera companies.
>
> Berlioz: *Les Troyens* from New York. We didn't know until we tuned in to the broadcast that Jessye Norman would be singing both roles. I am the only person I know who got the entire thing. I always made certain I had enough tape.
>
> Massenet: Cendrillon from Paris. Frederica Von Stade is perfect as Cendrillon as is Ann Murray as Prince Charming. She should have been on the SONY recording. Absolutely a splendid performance.
>
> Verdi: *Il trovatore* from New York. The stars were all lined up properly for this performance with Scotto, Pavarotti and Manuguerra.
>
> All the items we put out with Renata Tebaldi! (ibid)

Never before in the history of recording has such a wealth of live material been so easily accessible to the general consumer. Indeed, the labels Gala and Opera D'Oro (both about $4.99 per disc) now make it possible for one to build a fine, varied, and exciting library of live recordings for practically no money at all. For people interested in such cost-heavy operas as Wagner's Ring Cycle, both labels offer revered performances for about $50.00—about a third of the cost of a commercial recording of the four-opera cycle.

MP3, Cloud Storage, and the Internet

Accumulating live performances today is vastly different from when I began collecting. At that time it meant owning LPs and CDs and having a physical library and the space that it requires. Today, most people access music from the Internet and have much less in the way of material possessions. Such change is mirrored even in the lives of performers. When I was preparing for recitals in the 1980s I had to carry bulky scores to all my rehearsals. Now singers can find and download almost everything from the Petrucci Music site to a handy tablet; pianists and organists, too.

Collecting MP3, WAV or Flac files is different from collecting LPs or CDs. MP3 files can be saved to a multi-gigabyte USB stick, and then plugged into any computer, and, if the computer has iTunes, you can listen immediately. You can carry more than a hundred operas on a stick and take your library with you! It is amazing to think that one can carry thousands of opera performances on a few USB sticks (or a portable "passport"external hard drive that will hold up to 5 Terrabytes) that easily fits into a shirt pocket.

Much of this change began about twenty years ago with the availability of CD ROM and the ability to store MP3 files on them. Around that time, too, sharing blogs began to appear. It was easy to upload MP3 files to Internet share-groups such as OperaShare (once a Yahoo Group, now a Google group), Opera Tod from Argentina (recently defunct), and Operalia (also now defunct) and Afina tus odios.blogspot.com. These sites are/were tied to file hosting services (third-party subscription services). One pays a small amount to allow clicking on a link that (after passwording) takes you to another site where you can download the music.

MP3s are computer files and weigh nothing. But with this new form of portable music comes a warning. Be sure to archive! This is of paramount importance. Anyone who works on a computer knows to back up. So it should be with any music files saved on your computer. Among the easy ways to do this is to subscribe to a backup service and store them in the cloud (some offer free storage). I use "Crash Plan." No matter what happens to your computer's hard drive you will have access to your music files. They can be downloaded at any time to any computer to which you have access.

Finally, there are torrent files. These are used primarily for trafficking illegally pirated popular music. It is a somewhat complicated computer procedure that is mentioned here without going into detail. Known also as peer-to-peer, ala the Napster site of an era ago, Googling the term "torrent" will tell you more about it.

Last year, a musician friend of mine went to a Met performance of *Tristan und Isolde*. He really enjoyed the singers and the opera. When I asked him if he was going to buy a CD of the opera, he said, "Why? I don't even have a CD player."

When I looked at him in mock horror, he replied, "What? No Probem! If I want to hear it again, I can find it on YouTube." Collectors of my generation grew up with a different mindset. If I hear an opera and really like it, I want to own it—especially if it is sung by the performers that I heard. I do not want to trust that someone will eventually upload or re-upload something to YouTube. From experience, I know better.

Filesharing

The main function of such groups as OperaShare is the sharing of files, not the selling of them for financial gain. Understandably, many people want to share their live opera performances with others and through that activity some unusual treasures can appear.

I well remember a Sunday morning in 2009. I saw that a performance of Lucrezia Borgia from Munich with Edita Gruberova, Pavol Breslik and Alice Coote had been uploaded (in spectacular stereo broadcast sound). This was done by some kind soul in Europe who wanted to share it with other members on the OperaShare website. It had been performed the night before!

Before I knew it, the video of that night (it had be telecast) had been uploaded to YouTube.

Donizetti—*Lucrezia Borgia*—Munich 2009
https://www.youtube.com/watch?v=7bvEhMTb54A

That kind of international immediacy had been impossible before the Internet. Such availability makes it easy to amass a huge library of performances of various singers.

For instance, Placido Domingo. You can find performances as early as 1962 and as late as 2022. There are at least nine Aïdas, twelve Bohèmes, eleven Adriana Lecouvreurs, eleven *Un Ballo in Maschera*s, fifteen *Simon Boccanegra*s, fourteen Fanciullas, nine Nabuccos, seventeen Pagliaccis, fifteen *Parsifal*s, ten Samsons, fourteen Andrea Cheniers, thirteen Hoffmanns, twenty-nine Toscas, sixteen *Carmen*s, fourteen Trovatores, and forty-three *Otello*s.

In addition to more standard operatic offerings, many imaginative collectors create live aria collections of various singers that mimick the "collection" offerings of the original opera pirates from decades earlier. Collections of singers can provide a complete survey of their performing careers to the date of download. One collection I have seen has five volumes of tenor Juan Diego Florez performing various arias. Another is six volumes of selections of Franco Corelli taken from Metropolitan Opera performances; another has eight volumes of tenor Jonas Kaufmann.

There are some wonderful rarities to be found at both extremes of performance; wonderful and wretched.

There is a wonderful October 26,1980 broadcast of Arietta's Marina with Cecilia Nunez Albanese and Alfredo Kraus from Caracas, in excellent sound

Arrieta—*Marina*—Caracas October 1980
https://www.youtube.com/watch?v=0U0S-Ht5jKs

Massenet's *Werther* is another special work of the French repertoire. The 2010 Paris televised broadcast of Werther with Jonas Kaufmann, Sophie Koch, and Ludovic Tezier, conducted by Philippe Jordan will tear your heart out.

Massenet—*Werther*—Paris 2010
https://www.youtube.com/watch?v=Oqli8TTLmQg

A 1963 American Opera Society, Carnegie Hall performance of Massenet's Herodiade with Rita Gorr, Regine Crespin, Guy Chauvet, and Robert Massard is a treasure. The special thing about this performance is that both Regine Crespin and Rita Gorr took part on the now-famous Angel (EMI) LP highlights of the opera recorded the year before. The LP highlights are no longer available, but they are available on CD within a ten-CD boxed set of EMI French Opera

Highlights. (10 Opéras Français [EMI 73089] recorded from 1959 to 1968 of highlights from Gluck's Iphigénie en Tauride, Alceste; Cherubini's Medea/Médée; Rossini's Guillaume Tell; Berlioz's La Damnation de Faust; Gounod's *Roméo et Juliette*; Delibes Lakmé; Thomas's Mignon; Massenet's Hérodiade and Thaïs. A number of them feature Rita Gorr.) The Carnegie Hall Herodiade was obviously recorded in-house and, for that era, is in decent, if flawed sound. It is an exciting, idiomatic performance of great intensity and nobility. Like the LP version, Rita Gorr proved to be a force of nature as the title lead. The opportunity to compare the extracts on Angel with an actual live performance was a treat for me and it remains one of the prized performances in my library.

Massenet—*Herodiade*—Commercial Excerpts from 1963 Angel LP—Regine Crespin, Rita Gorr, Albert Lance, Michel Dens.

https://www.youtube.com/watch?v=EGzMoJqU-14&t=1084s

Massenet—*Herodiade*—Carnegie Hall, 1963—Regine Crespin, Rita Gorr, Guy Chauvet, Robert Massard, Robert Patterson—Alain Lombard—It is remarkable that this even exists. One of the great performances at that august hall. One must thank YouTube contributor, "Best Opera Moments."

https://www.youtube.com/watch?v=evVREMEgn_4

Another Rita Gorr knock-out performance is from Carnegie Hall—Massenet's verismatic opera, La Navarraise. Although short, the opera packs quite a wallop and even has a mini-mad scene at the end of the opera.

Massenet—*La Navarraise*—Carnegie Hall, 1963—Rita Gorr, George Shirley, Fernando Corena—Robert Lawrence

https://www.youtube.com/watch?v=bjyZSQp3ViE

Another Rita Gorr performance not to be missed is a Milan broadcast of Wagner's *Parsifal* in 1960 with a fascinating cast of Sandor Konya, Rita Gorr, Boris Christoff, Gustav Neidlinger, with a surprise of Montserrat Caballe singing the First Flower Maiden early in her operatic career. Conducted by André Cluytens—this is a remarkably engaging performance with excellent vocal acting from all the leads.

Wagner—*Parsifal*—Milan 1960

https://www.youtube.com/watch?v=_QpvEzROM4w

A guilty pleasure of mine is Rossini's L'Assedio di Corinto from a Metropolitan Opera performance of January 5, 1976 with Beverly Sills's alternate, Rita Shane as Pamira. Joanne Grillo, Enrico di Giuseppe, and Justino Diaz also sang, conducted by Richard Woitach. Although not a Rossini specialist, Shane gives a remarkably high-powered performance of a difficult and long role full of blazing high notes and daring ornamentation. The surviving in-house tape is in remarkable stereo sound and a great way to spend an afternoon. The whole performance is not yet on YouTube—though I am sure it will be at some point But below is a tasste.

Rossini—"Si ferrite" *L'Assedio di Corinto* (Act II)—Rita Shane—Metropolitan Opera January, 1976

https://www.youtube.com/watch?v=OMjWkLtm06g

There are tons of opera files on YouTube. They include a large playlist of BJR LP recordings. In the last few years, YouTube, has become a historical media kingdom with countless videos and soundtracks of all types of music. Many important historical opera performances from the 1960s are also available as videos—uploaded with a "static" video as its base.

Due to my long history with live performances and the instability of the various Internet sites that offer them, I am very protective of the live opera files that I own. I do all that I can to ensure that they are well protected by multiple forms of backup. They are to me the rarest of jewels; priceless.

Wanting to ensure that I do not lose any of my collection, to safeguard them I triple-back-up my opera, concert, and recital MP3 files on my MAC, stand-alone Passport drives (holding up to five terabytes of space), and with a back-up service in the cloud. I do this to ensure that if I have any problems with my computer, my library of live performances is protected, safe, and accessible in two other places.

As with acoustic recordings of an earlier period, 1900–1925 (see my earlier book, Early 20th Century Singers: the Voices and Recordings, YBK Publishers), I urge you to enrich your life and music collection with live performances. I warn you, however, that once you develop a yen for them, they will become an obsession. They are the modern singer's legacy. They reveal, without apology, a singer's humanity and spirit. Without them we would be deprived of aural documents of some of the greatest performances ever to have taken place.

THE TWO PIRATE QUEENS
MAGDA OLIVERO
(1910–2014)
LEYLA GENCER
(1928–2008)

In the heyday of opera piracy, Maria Callas reigned supreme as its Empress. Almost all of her important roles were captured by pirates and circulated through various mailing lists and pirated LPs. Different from the two ladies in this chapter, Callas was also a prodigious recorder of her art in the studio.

There were a number of fine divas during the 1950s –1970s who did not record commercially or, if they did, their recording was extremely limited. Highest on the list were two divas: Magda Olivero, the gutsy, verismatic specialist, and Leyla Gencer, the fearless Donizetti (or bel canto) specialist. Interestingly, during the course of their careers, both sopranos were independently wealthy and could pick and choose what, where, and when they performed. Also, both sopranos were champions of modern music.

Both singers illustrate why operatic pirating became so popular in the 1960s and 1970s. Olivero and Gencer are perfect examples of the "visual art" of singing. Their search for reality in their interpretations provides the listener a rare opportunity to "see with one's ears." Both were capable of making beautiful sounds in their legato singing but were also capable of making ugly, sometimes alarming sounds. Each reached an apex in vocal interpretation through unconventional yet extremely effective means that has never been equaled. The listener is assured that at some point in the opera, both sopranos will deliver both exquisite soft singing as well as almost unbearably intense dramaticism. They had the uncommon ability to take phrases and turn them into something of remarkable beauty or of unforgettable, dramatic impact. Through the illumination of their imagination, they put a personal stamp onto any music they sang. Despite these unusual abilities, both singers were largely ignored by the large commercial record companies.

Magda Olivero

Magda Olivero (1910–2014) was actually born Maria Maddalena Olivero on March 25, 1910 in Suluzzo, close to Turin. She was extremely popular in Italy and a true specialist in her particular fach. A proud woman from a good family, she did not relish the back-stabbing silliness of many of her colleagues. Early in her career (around 1932) she was given some advice.

> During preparations for *Favorita*, Ebe Stignani told Olivero, who was of retiring disposition, 'If you have to remain in this environment you'd better become a bitch'—advice Olivero didn't heed. (According to her, neither did Stignani.) (https://www.belcantosociety.org)

> ...My career was in the theater, but I never lived there. I never loved life in the theater...For me the theater was of the utmost importance. I truthfully can say that every time I stepped out onstage I gave the best of myself. I sought passionately to do better, to make things more beautiful— my voice, my interpretation. But the moment the opera was over and the lights were turned off I left the theater and resumed my life as a completely normal person.
> (*Bel Canto Society Newsletter*, Interview with Magda Olivero, Part II,
> https://www.belcantosociety.org/newsletter)

To this day, Olivero remains one of the most popular of the "pirated" sopranos. (More than 70 live performances are available of her work.)

> 'I never had a voice,' she said in 1993. 'What I had was expression, a face, a body, the truth. If one prefers the opposite, that is their right.' (*The New York Times* obituary for Magda Olivero on September 8, 2014, Margalit Fox)

Many agreed:

> Growing up, she studied piano and voice, and when she was barely out of girlhood she auditioned to sing with a Turin radio station.
>
> Hearing her audition (she sang Mi chiamano Mimì, from Puccini's La Bohème), the conductor Ugo Tansini, as was widely reported years afterward, pronounced judgment:
>
> 'She possesses neither voice, musicality nor personality. Nothing. Absolutely nothing! She should look for another profession.' (ibid)

She auditioned again and got the same criticism. But that time voice teacher Luigi Gerussi happened to be present and said that he wanted to work with Olivero.

Olivero studied hard with Gerussi, a very hard task-master, he constantly demanded that she "sustain, sustain, sustain!" Eventually, through this hard work, she evolved into the vocal magician she became famous for being. As it turns out, Gerussi was her fourth voice teacher and, remarkably, although her father failed to see the necessity of she studying voice, (he wanted her to become a pianist) he agreed to the fourth (and final) try at a voice teacher.

She made her debut in December of 1932 in a minor role of a radio production of Cattozzo's I misteri Dolorosi and, because of the initial lightness of her timbre and the extent of her vocal range—up to high F, she followed the advice of conductor Tullio Serafin and studied a number of coloratura roles (but never actually performed them) including Gilda in *Rigoletto*, *Lucia di Lammermoor*, Sophie in *Der Rosenkavalier*, and the vivacious Philine in Mignon.

The last role was promised to her by Serafin. When the contract came, however, it was for Elsa in Lohengrin, not Philine in Mignon. Rather than confront the maestro over this grotesque error, and, because of previous behavior on his part (leading her to believe that the mistake was intentional—she had rebuffed his amorous advances), Olivero decided to accept the contract. She carefully prepared the role and sang it successfully. Eventually, through systematic development, she metamorphosed into a lyric soprano. (With the great dramatic soprano Gina Cigna and Francesso Merli, she sang Liu in the first complete recording of *Turandot* for Cetra in 1938.) From there she went on to become a spinto soprano who specialized in verismo roles.

Although she claimed to be retired in 1941, from 1938 to 1953 she recorded nineteen 78 r.p.m. sides of various arias for Cetra. One of them, a 1940 "Ah fors e lui...sempre libera" from La traviata, is a remarkable testament of her ability to blend bel canto with versimo. It also displays her remarkable diaphragm support (acquired from her rigorous training with Gerussi) which remained with her until the end. The record boasts excellent coloratura work and a spectacular messa di voce (one of several) on a penultimate high C at the end of the "Ah fors e lui." The scena is concluded with an amazing, solid high E flat. Although she obviously had the facility and the range for roles in the florid repertoire, she found her temperament more suited to the abandon of verismo works. None the less, her recording of the Traviata scena remains one of the best during that decade.

Verdi—"Ah fors e lui" *La traviata*— Magda Olivero 1940 disk
https://www.youtube.com/watch?v=iepjFmUA9DQ

After appearing as Adriana in Ravenna in May of 1941, she retired from the stage. There were a number of contributing factors that led to this. One was her decision to marry business man Aldo Busch in June of 1941. The manager of a large plant it became difficult—politically-for Olivero to travel and she decided to stay with him. There was also the fact that she had had two miscarriages as well as her general dissatisfaction with the opera world at the time.

Not only that, but the pretentious personalities of many of her colleagues, Olivero decided to retire in 1941. She married Aldo Busch, the president of a large lamp company and for the next number of years sang only an occasional recital or appearances for charity events.

It was not that I had lost my love of music, but there was nothing in the world that could make me like the atmosphere of the theater…the atmosphere there (was) something I always hated."

Although she did not perform on the stage during those years of "retirement" she did occasionally sing for church concerts and charity events. The composer, Cilea, mourned the loss of his "ideal interpreter" of Adriana, and severly ill, he asked his friend, publisher Piero Ostali to ask Olivero to return to the stage in his greatest work. Olivero took 6 months to decide whether to sign the contract. Although Cilea died before the performance, Olivero returned to the role in Feburary 1951 at the theatre in Brescia. Her "poveri fiori" had to be encored.

It was the composer Francesco Cilea who urged the soprano to reconsider her self-imposed retirement and return to the operatic stage. She did, ten years later, in January 1951, as Mimi in Puccini's La bohème. By this time, she was financially independent, and was able to be more selective as to what and where she sang; and importantly—how often. Unfortunately, Cilea died before he was able to see her make a comeback singing his Adriana Lecouvreur. From 1951 until her retirement from opera in 1981, she remained an important performer on international stages. This signaled the start of a second career on the stage as quickly other offers began to pour in. Olivero never had a manager, preferring to pick and chose her own performances. It was at this time that she began to expand her repertoire to include such verismo works as Fedora and Iris. By 1957 she had added *Tosca* and Fanciulla to her repertoire. And by 1958 was singing *Manon Lescaut*.

Olivero also sang in a number of contemporary operas—during the later years of her career becoming especially known for her intense performances of Poulenc's one-woman opera—La Voix Humaine.

In 1967 she made her American debut in Dallas as Medea. Throughout the ensuing decades she occasionally strayed from her usual repertoire with appearances in such works as Werther, Cavalleria Rusticana, Jenufa (Kostelnichka), the Countess in Pique Dame.

Although she sang at La Scala, she was not a regular guest, appearing only as *Adriana,*

Francesca (1959) and *Jenufa* (1974). She seemed to prefer the more provincial houses where the politics of the opera world tended to be less annoying.

In 1975, at the instigation of mezzo-soprano Marilyn Horne, the Metropolitan Opera hired Olivero to sing three performances of Puccini's *Tosca*. The soprano was 65 years old.

Ira Siff describes the performance:

> …Although the audience was wildly demonstrative, this was no mere nostalgia event. After a few minutes to warm up and conquer nerves, Olivero's voice was astonishingly fresh, shedding decades by Act II. At the second performance, this listener was treated to the most touching, spectacularly sung Vissi d'arte of his experience. During Act III, Olivero's ascent to a spectacular, lengthy high C and plunge down two octaves into chest voice on the line Io quella lama earned her a spontaneous ovation. This old-school audience response was inspired by the artist's old-school stage deportment; it was an evening that, in the best sense, turned back the clock whenever she was onstage. Olivero's total belief in the reality of the drama prevented her performances from ever being reduced to shtick. And her prodigious technique and breath control spoke of a bygone era, but one in which she was unique among veristas, none of whom matched her vocal capabilities. (*Opera News*, September 8, 2014)

She reprised the role in 1979 while on tour with the Metropolitan Opera.

Despite her popularity with audiences, when it came to the recording studio, she made only the 78 r.p.m discs for Cetra, the recording of Lui in *Turandot* (also for Cetra), an LP of highlights from Zandonai's Francesca da Rimini with Mario Del Monaco and Nicola Rescigno (April 1969), and a complete recording of Giordano's Fedora, (May 1969) also with Mario Del Monaco and Tito Gobbi, conducted by Lamberto Gardelli.

Zandonai—***Francesca da Rimini*** (excerpts)—Decca Commercial 1969
https://www.youtube.com/watch?v=dHuifpKg0r8

Giordano—***Fedora***—Decca commercial 1969
https://www.youtube.com/watch?v=F4ashN-Ah9E

An interesting Olivero anecdote dates from the time of the recording of Fedora and the death scene of the title character. After the opera had been recorded, there was still some studio time left. The conductor, Lamberto Gardelli, asked Olivero if there was anything that she wanted to re-record.

> …I said, 'The death of Fedora, but with my eyes closed, so as not to see the mechanical apparatus in front of me, as though I were on stage.'…And so we repeated the death of Fedora, with my eyes closed, and I think you can sense this on the recording. They inserted Loris's brief phrase, which Del Monaco already had recorded. When I listen to the scene, I think young people who are prejudiced against the opera will feel such emotion that they can no longer say we can't accept this, this voice singing on and on, with all those high notes, while the character is supposed to be dying. But I succeeded in making even those high notes ethereal, even if they weren't written this way, because I had the good fortune to study with two exceptional maestros [Gerussi and Luigi Ricci]. They taught me the true technique, which enables the artist to go onstage thinking about acting rather than singing. This is something wonderful, because you feel emotions, sensations that are indescribable.' (https://www.belcantosociety.org)

This remarkable working relationship between Lamberto Gardelli and Magda Olivero describes how relationships used to be between singers and their conductors.

> Once singers could depend on their maestros, but conductors today know a lot about instruments and nothing about the voice, There is no longer a Serafin, who created more great singers than any other. What one learned from him! He would say, 'You cannot sing that high note because three notes earlier you were not supporting properly You must begin a phrase with good support and then follow it through; a high note is not an isolated thing.' Details like this guided singers and helped to create artists. Who can tell singers these things today? (John Ardoin, One of a Kind *Opera News*, 12/3/77)

The fascinating thing about Magda Olivero's voice was that it was not really attractive. It had a very fast vibrato (a type of voice that was once in fashion, but is no longer) and it had a timbre that could variously be described as throaty, edgy, hooty, hollow, raspy or hoarse. It often sounded too mature for some of the characters she portrayed. This latter may be the crux of the reason why, despite her immense popularity, she made so few commercial recordings. In the theatre, with space between her voice and an audience, this might not present an issue. At the time, however, even though various verismo operas sold out in a theatre, recording companies were less inclined to take chances on unproven repertoire for recordings.

(For instance, in 2018, there were only four commercially available recordings of Fedora:
1950—Cetra recording with Maria Caniglia and Giacinto Prandelli (the first)
1969—Olivero and Del Monaco. Decca recording
1987—Eva Marton, Jose Carreras Sony recording
2011—Angela Gheorghiu, Placido Domingo DGG recording

When it comes to an artist such as Magda Olivero, the question rises: How could someone with such an ugly voice become so successful, much less become the focal point of adoration of a huge cult following? I disliked her voice when I first heard it and wondered at her success and following. I found the answer in every live recording of this singer.

Different from most other singers, Olivero molded, shoved, and mangled her voice into countless colors and emotions in order to serve the music she sang. Although her gifts in imagination were somewhat similar to those of Maria Callas, Callas' voice could be quite beautiful. Olivero's art was extreme and brutal. Because of this she had to find the means to "make" her voice beautiful. In full-throated outbursts, Magda Olivero had a visceral allure and impact that could not be ignored. She took vocal chances and offered outrageously raw eruptions of sound. A listener's reaction was often one of disbelief that a singer could utter such sounds wondering how her voice could survive such abuse.

This last was Olivero's unique ability:

> ...to 'break a note' by unleashing a fury of sound culminating in a scream or sob originating from an unbearably intense crescendo... (Konrad Dryden, "From Another World," *The Opera Quarterly*, Volume 20 #3)

In reviewing a performance of Adriana Lecouvreur Olivero sang with Placido Domingo on November 5, 1973, Peter G. Davis (1936-2021) wrote;

> The secret of Magda Olivero's success with certain segments of the operatic public and her longevity is complex. Her voice will not appeal to those with conventional standards of vocal beauty; its reedy timbre often turns hollow and strident, although she can float a bewitching pianissimo and unfurl a full voice that is still powerful and secure. The actual sound has remained astonishingly unchanged over the years, judging from the few records she made before 1940.

After adjusting to the singular instrument, one hears an extraordinarily shrewd singer deploying some extraordinary expressive effects, all of them calculated to wrench a maximum of melodrama from the vocal lines. Her acting is also judged to a hair—occasionally studied and mannered, perhaps, but executed with an intensity and sincerity that exerts an immediate impact...

She would probably never have sung in America at all were it not for her discovery here via pirated live performances taped in Italy and the strong appeal she exercises for homosexual opera fans who have always been her most loyal and vociferous admirers in this country. In some quarters she is considered to be the operatic equivalent of Judy Garland, Marlene Dietrich and Bette Midler, although like those heroines of homosexuals her art goes well beyond mere cult worship. (*The New York Times*, November 6, 1973)

Rodolfo Celletti (1917–2004), the famous Italian musicologist, critic, and voice teacher once wrote of Magda Olivero:

> In the early part of her career, she had a enormous range and a technic which was perhaps unique among Italian sopranos of that time, An absolute mastery of breath and impeccable phonation allowed for a perfect legato as well as smorzature, diminuendos and crescendos at all pitches. These rich dynamics were at the service of an interpreter of great sensibility and imagination in terms of accentuation and phrasing and who was, moreover, an attractive and gifted actress. To this was added a thorough musical training. Olivero's way of singing and interpreting was definitely countercurrent for the time." (sic) http://401dutchdivas.nl/en/joops-favorites/magda-olivero.html

Despite the odd structure of her voice, and through her own artistic magic, she was often able to turn her voice into a thing of beauty. One has only to listen to the ending of the first scene of Act IV of Zandonai's Francesca da Rimini, especially the phrase "Tu canterai domani" to understand the magic Olivero was able to create. Olivero knew her voice inside out and, unbelievably, was able one moment to sound as if she were shredding her vocal cords through an overt guttural attack, and then, in the next moment, spin out a beautiful, suspended high pianissimo of ethereal beauty. Her art was bewildering.

Although Olivero sang with what often sounded like complete vocal abandon, everything was carefully planned. She knew exactly what she was doing. Even more important, EVERYTHING was supported securely on the breath. So even those moments when she would turn a high note into a shredded tone she did no damage to her voice. It is also important to notice when listening, that she rarely sings chest voice. She used chest voice—but more as an effect rather than as part of her vocal technique. Even at the ending of the *Mefistofele* aria which is quite low, she carefully avoids chest voice.

Her voice was a slender instrument, fastly-spun and despite her abandon, not of great size. She was an illusionist. She made you hear things that are not there—like beauty, smooth softness and delicacy. To be honest it was always a rather ugly sound. It was hollow sounding and often throaty. But what she did with it WAS beautiful. Although here in America she is often considered the height of "camp" and a "screamer" she actually was much more. She was one of the few singers of her time who could devastate with a scream and then throw out a gossamer, heavenly pianissimo. Her art was governed by musicality of the highest order and her singing always had "FACE."

To get a taste of Olivero's unique gifts listen to Act II of Resurrezione by Franco Alfano (1875–1954) a RAI Turin performance of October 22, 1971 [Gala 100-716] conducted by Elio Boncampagni. As the lead, Katiusha, Olivero offers everything from great beauty (the aria

"Dio pietoso") to unbelievable, vocal-shredding horror. It is overt, almost over the top, but great interpretive art. Importantly, it is easily visible to the listener.

Alfano—*Resurrezione*—Turin 1971
https://www.youtube.com/watch?v=NRohzd1Mn_k

The first album that I owned of Magda Olivero was an Opus LP purchased from Patelsohn's on 56th Street in Manhattan in the mid-1970s. It was a compilation LP of live performances (1963–1968) that offered a varied program of arias and/or scenes from *Adriana Lecouvreur, La bohème, Manon Lescaut, Tristan und Isolde, La traviata, Medea, Mefistofele* as well as two songs. The cover was all black with a simple, square "label" on the front with a small photo of Olivero as Adriana and a listing of the operas being featured. Surprisingly elegant, the album immediately drew my attention in the record store. I had heard about the soprano and was eager to hear her work, so I bought it. Initially I was perplexed, almost horrified. What an ugly, coarse voice, I remember thinking. But then I began to listen more closely. I listened many times.

I later heard her sing a 1966 Turin performance of La fanciulla del West on an MRF LP release (#112). This has since become my favorite live performance of that opera.

I heard my first Fanciulla in November 1979—a San Francisco Opera broadcast relayed to New York at the time. The performance featured Carol Neblett, Placido Domingo, and Benito di Bella in the cast and was conducted by Giuseppe Patane. It was an incredible performance, with both Neblett and Domingo full of vocal fire. I became so fascinated by the work that I made a trip to the Discophile record shop on 8th Street in Manhattan (on December 28, 1979 to be exact) to look for a live recording and I found the MRF set with Olivero, Gastone Limarilli and Anselmo Colzani. Over the years I have practically worn the grooves smooth. Act II is brilliant "ear" theater. I still have that original LP set. Luckily the performance is now on YouTube for all to enjoy.

Puccini—*La fanciulla del West*—Turin 1966
https://www.youtube.com/watch?v=0hmHAmKLhZM&t=2785s

Soon after that, I bought Olivero's famous 1963 Amsterdam concert performance of Mascagni's Iris (also a beautifully produced MRF set). This is a wonderful opera by Mascagni with all sorts of exotic orchestral harmonies. Olivero first sang the role in Turin in September of 1956. As fine as the 1945 broadcast is, by 1963, Iris was completely in her blood.

Mascagni—*Iris*—Turin 1956
https://www.youtube.com/watch?v=CjPHOH0w4hI

By the time I first heard the Olivero Iris, all the praise of the Olivero "magic" began to make sense. With Luigi Ottolini, Renato Capecchi and Plinio Clabassi, Olivero weaved her special vocal magic to create an Iris that is unlike anything you have ever heard. In excellent sound, her death scene amid the filth of the Japanese sewers, her cries of "perché?" is the stuff of legends.

Mascagni—*Iris*—Amsterdam 1963
https://www.youtube.com/watch?v=FjTyf7E-5tY&t=1916s

This 1963 Amsterdam Iris is one of the classic Olivero recordings. Iris was an Olivero specialty and her identification with the betrayed, naïve Iris goes beyond mere posturing. Her death scene is a good example. With simplicity she manages to capture the pathetic alienation of Iris and her sorrow, weak and dying in a squalid sewer. What I found interesting in this final scene was not only Olivero's heartbreaking singing of Iris' last lines, but the fact that her emotions and intense dedication to the music seem to spur conductor Fulvio Vernizzi and the chorus into carefully maintaining the intense mood Olivero had created. Because of this the final chorus of this concert performance blazes into a truly triumphant celebration of the mystery and glory of life.

I became obsessed with Olivero's beautifully ugly voice and snapped up everything I could find of her work. I soon learned that one thing was always true of an Olivero performance—at some point in the opera she would almost rip your heart out with a huge theatrical or vocal gesture.

Her Dallas Medea (1967) was her United States debut and the first revival since Callas' famous assumption of the role. (That same year, Gwenyth Jones recorded the role for Decca.) Originally Olivero was hesitant to sing the role because of Callas' hold on the work. She studied Medea seriously for three months before she agreed to sing the role. Her interpretation—different from Callas—proved to be just as strong and just as frighteningly potent. The next year, Leyla Gencer followed with her own unforgettable Medea in Venice.

When it comes to Olivero's Medea, Geoffrey S. Riggs notes:

> Magda Olivero's interpretation best heard 'live' from Dallas in 1967, is the most unstrung there is. This is not a plush sound. It doesn't even have the amplitude of the Callas of 1958. There are also distinct gaps in her voice in its lower half, which plays havoc with some of the legato lines. But she is an imaginative musician who knows how to phrase a Cherubini utterance well. (*The Assoluta Voice in Opera, 1797–1847*, McFarland & Company, Inc, 2003 pg. 28–29)

Reviewing the Dallas performance for Opera, in February of 1968, Martin Bernheimer wrote:

> (Medea) was a gamble taken and won by a soprano no longer young, making her overdue American debut: Magda Olivero. What a brave lady she is, to come to America at this stage in her career, in a role entirely new to her, and in a city which has retained vivid memories of Maria Callas in the same part! But no apologies are necessary, for she left a very personal stamp on the role. Anyone who knows Olivero's art will not have to be told that her characterization and acting of Medea were exceptional. But her singing was no less exceptional. What an impact that crazy, strange but wonderful voice of hers made! It is a voice like no other, utterly poignant one moment, flashing with rage and brilliance the next."

Cherubini—*Medea*—Dallas 1967
https://www.youtube.com/watch?v=yC4N-5WTMRE

The 1970 performance from Amsterdam is also of prime interest. Below is a link to the Act I duet with Mirto Picchi.

https://www.youtube.com/watch?v=TGCne5MLRxQ

Another fascinating Olivero performance was her one Charlotte in an Italian-sung, 1963 RAI Werther. Her surrounding cast included Agostino Iazzari, Nicoletta Panni and Saturno Meletti, conducted by Mario Rossi.

Massenet—*Werther*—RAI 1963
https://www.youtube.com/watch?v=Sk53cXTB5-4&t=73s

Olivero's pirated operatic recordings are now rightly considered classic performances of their kind, often displaying ferocious, gripping singing. Even after 50 years, many are cult items seriously and aggressively sought after by collectors. I would even dare to say that every collector or vocal historian should have at least four Olivero performances in their collection; Adriana Lecouvreur, Iris, Medea, and La fanciulla del West.

> The recorded legacy of Olivero's public performances provides documentation of verismo style at its most poetic. In an age as obsessed as our own with authenticity in music, such documents are of enormous interest. Yet to appreciate their impact one must accept the otherness of the aesthetic sensibility that informs them. The explicit emotionalism of Olivero's singing, which can prove disconcerting by today's standards, must be heard with the same openness of mind and heart with which one might listen to a performance on period instruments. (Stephen Hastings, Magnificent Obsession, *Opera News*, March 19, 1994)

And in reviewing a MYTO release of Zandonai's Francesca da Rimini—a legendary 1959 revival at La Scala with Olivero and Del Monaco, Robert Levine of Classics Today notes:

> As a bonus, we get the last 15 minutes of Cherubini's Medea in a 1971 performance starring Olivero. It is beyond criticism–Olivero uses a choked, raspy voice to portray Medea's perversity, and she's never afraid to shriek; in just a quarter-hour you get to know what a monster this character truly is. Again, it's subtlety free, but you won't be bored. (www.classicstoday.com)

Zandonai—*Francesca da Rimini*—Milan 1959
https://www.youtube.com/watch?v=U_Ryio4K98I&t=241s

With the advent of CD, most of her important revivals have been released. More than 50 different operatic performances and countless recitals and concerts are available. All are of interest including *Werther, Manon Lescaut, Voix Humaine* (the famous SF broadcast). Some have yet to appear on YouTube.

One of my favorites is a concert the soprano gave in Turin on July 2, 1975 in which she sang excerpts from the Massenet Manon and the Puccini *Manon Lescaut*. One would not think of her voice as being suited to Manon's music, but somehow, she makes it work. Her pianissimo work in that concert is beyond description it is so beautiful. (For those interested, these selections can be found as filler for the 1964 Amsterdam concert of *Manon Lescaut* on BellaVoce CD, 107.221) (Unfortunately, not on YouTube yet.)

Olivero was extremely popular in Amsterdam and some of her finest performances were given there. These would include concert performances of such works as Adriana Lecouvreur, Iris, and Medea, She also gave many concerts in that city, often performing entire acts of operas rather than just selected arias. This was because, in reality, Olivero was not a miniaturist. She was more effective when she had a whole scene (or Act) of an opera to sink her "vocal" teeth into.

Cilea—*Adriana Lecouvreur*—Amsterdam 1965
https://www.youtube.com/watch?v=rhycqM8O4Sw
Magda Olivero—San Jacopino Concert 1969 (with 13 selections)
https://www.youtube.com/watch?v=pL15SDLT9yc
Magda Olivero—Padova Concert 1971 (8 selections)
https://www.youtube.com/watch?v=B-rYB9Xk-rk

Because of this many of her concerts included such items as the finale of Act III of *Rigoletto* (remnants of her early studies), the final act of Zandonai's Francesca da Rimini, Act III of Fedora, Act II of *Tosca*, Act III of La traviata, Act III of Mefistofele, and Act IV of both La Wally and Adriana Lecouvreur. In addition to this type of concert, she also sang aria concerts and gave many recitals. (Many of these appeared on live recording mail-order lists shortly after they occurred.) Fans couldn't seem to get enough.

Her November 2, 1971, New York Philharmonic Hall debut was with Thomas Scherman conducting the Little Orchestra Society and included arias from *Manon Lescaut* and Adriana Lecouvreur as well as Poulenc's 1958 40-minute monodrama, La Voix Humaine, with text by Jean Cocteau based on his own play.

Writing of the 1971 concert, Alan Hughes found the Olivero experience a bit passé.

> Her traditional style, as revealed in arias from Puccini's La Bohème and Cilea's Adriana Lecouvreur, is old fashioned by contemporary standards—very impassioned, embellished with sobs, filled with rhythmic liberties and so on. When Miss Olivero was younger, she may well have been able to realize her ambitious vocal goals easily and convincingly. On this occasion, however, her success was not complete. (*The New York Times*, November 4, 1971)

Olivero also sang the Poulenc piece with the San Francisco Opera in 1979. (It is in this performance that Olivero felt she most entered into the spirit of the Cocteau text.) Olivero once said that the hardest part of performing the short one-act Poulenc opera was being able to convey to the audience what the lover is saying on the telephone. This monodrama played an important part in her repertoire during the latter part of her career.

Reviewing the San Francisco performance for Opera News (12-15-79) Stefanie Von Buchau wrote:

> Miss Olivero needed no apologies in this role. Supported by Poulenc's short-breathed style of phrasing, she was able to search out nuances and intensities with utmost subtlety and still save enough voice for the few passages of violent declamation.

About half of the October 19, 1979 broadcast was included as filler on the Gala issue of Rota's Il cappello di pagia di Firenze, a 1976 performance from Brussels with both Magda Olivero and Mariella Devia. Although it is true that Olivero interprets La Voix Humaine as a piece of verismatic glory rather than the French delicacy it is, the San Francisco performance was riveting, a devastatingly realistic performance—the ending not easily forgotten. It worked because of the sheer force of her personality and her musical and artistic conviction. She sang La Voix Humaine at a number of venues, including a remarkable performance in Dallas in 1970 (paired with a 1969 Dallas performance of Fedora on a Music and Arts CD (671)), and a Florence 1969 performance, conducted by Nicola Rescigno. Olivero left the operatic stage in 1981 with the monodrama.

Poulenc—*La Voix Humaine*—Venice 1970
https://www.youtube.com/watch?v=VIPKqmhVdXA&t=406s

There are many concerts and recitals as well. Standing Room Only CD released her December 13, 1977 Dallas Recital with selections by Hahn, Respighi, Tosti, Donaudy, as well as the Act IV aria from *Manon Lescaut*, with bonus items from I Capuletti ed I Montecchi, *Tosca*, and Manon. Her celebrated October 27, 1979 Carnegie Hall recital has been making the rounds for decades on tape and as FLAC downloads. This recital holds a special place in the voice/piano annals since the accompanist is none other than the famous concert pianist, Garrick Ohlsson.

Bella Voce offers the "famous" Amsterdam concerts of 1967, 1968, and 1972.

FanClub CD offers selections from concerts given in 1962, 1963, 1964, 1968, 1972 and later. (This CD is considered one of the most highly recommended CDs of this artist by operatic forums.)

There is an Il Mito Dell' Opera CD of a rare concert in Marsiglia, Italy on February 18, 1973 given with tenor Flaviano Labò and there are a number of CDs that offer various selections as fillers. In 1993, Verona CD released a wonderful 3-disc set of arias and scenes from her performances (some of which overlap the selections on Bella Voce). One of the aspects of the Verona release that is appealing is that most of the selections are complete acts from concerts—Act IV of *Fedora*, Act I of *La bohème*, Act II of *La traviata* and Act IV scene 2 of *Francesca da Rimini*. These chunks of operatic music allow the listener to experience Olivero in her true medium—interacting with other characters. It is in such scenes that her true artistic genius is easily heard.

CDs testify to her continued popularity and her fascinating interpretations of such varied roles as Boito's Margherita in Mefistofele, Cherubini's Medea (at least three performances), Cilea's Adriana Lecouvreur (at least four versions), Giordano's Fedora—one of her greatest roles—(at least three versions), Massenet's Werther, Puccini's *Madama Butterfly*, La bohème, La fanciulla del West (at least three versions), *Manon Lescaut* (at least three versions), *Tosca* (about six versions), and Il tabarro, Mascagni's Cavalleria rusticana, Iris (at least three versions), Rosselini's La Guerra, Janacek's Jenufa, Zandonai's Francesca da Rimini (a famous 1959 revival at La Scala with Mario Del Monaco) and Wolf Ferrari's I Quattro rusteghi. Not to be missed is an Italian-sung Mussorgsky's Mazeppa from 1954 (a unique Olivero treasure!) With her is Ettore Bastianini, Boris Christoff, Mariana Radov, and David Poleri— conducted by Jonel Perlea. Not stylistically Russian by any means but a fascinating dramatic conglomeration. Maria's final lullabye to Andrei as he dies, and she slips into profound madness is unforgettable.

Mussorgsky—*Mazeppa*—RAI 1954
https://www.youtube.com/watch?v=GcxaVrMsFvM

The infamous Jenufa at La Scala in 1974 with Grace Bumbry and Magda Olivero is an odd treat. Sung in an Italian translation, it was the first staging of the Janacek opera in Milan. The performance was originally released on LP by Legendary Recordings (#208) "Vocal Masterpieces Documented for Posterity" (Mr. Tape). The performance has always been a popular cult item, although it bears little resemblance to the original Czech opera. The translation into Italian distorts the original, spiky vocal line and the singing falls into the veristic rather than the Czech nationalistic singing style. When released on CD by MYTO, the company sweetened the pie by adding an invaluable bonus filler of more than 27 minutes of scenes from Act II of a later (in-house) performance on April 9, 1974. This allows for wonderful opportunities in comparative listening.

Janacek—*Jenufa*—Milan 74
https://www.youtube.com/watch?v=e2DbmjtyyAU&t=97s

Of her Kostelnicka in Jenufa, Aliki Andris-Michchalaros wrote in Opera News (8/74):

> (Bumbry) had fierce competition (as Jenufa): in the role of Kostelnicka after a fifteen-year absence from La Scala, Magda Olivero stole the show. From her first entrance, this formidable singing actress gave a thrilling portrayal of the dour, tormented stepmother; her voice is miraculously intact. She was singing this role for the first time, yet her command of effects (her pianissimos are incredible) and her dramatic impetus made one think she had been performing her role for years.

Certainly, the surviving broadcast finds Olivero offering an astoundingly realistic performance as Kostelinicka. Although veristic rather than Czech in its interpretation and tradition, there is a casual horror that is quite realistic and one that no other artist has managed to highlight in this character. Throughout the ensuing decades only Leonie Rysanek matched Olivero's intense desperation and distress in the role. It is a magnificent opportunity for a singing actress and Olivero seizes the opportunity by the throat and gnaws through it with demonic ease. Grace Bumbry quickly realized the role's allure:

> I said, "You know, I'm at the age now when I could sing the Kostelnicka." They asked me then which part did I want. And young as I was, I said certainly Jenufa, never thinking that the better part is really Kostelnicka. When I saw Magda (Olivero) in the first rehearsal, I said, "Grace, you made a big mistake." (Grace Bunbry—Interviewed by Joel Kasow for Operanet, 2 September, 1997)

Olivero's early 78 r.p.m. recordings made for Cetra have been collected on Preiser's Lebendige Vergangenheit series; a 2005 release (89612) that includes selections from Iris, Louise, Loreley, Resurrezione, Suor Angelica, *Manon Lescaut*, Mefistofele, Adriana Lecouvreur, La traviata, *Tosca*, Manon and others.

There are a number of Olivero video clips on YouTube—although few are actually live performances—most are dubbed. Perhaps the most charming is an Italian television appearance made sometime in the 1960s of Mascagni's delightful "Cherry Tree Duet" from L'Amico Fritz. Olivero sings with Claudio Villa who has a lovely, sweet voice. The two of them create an enchanting mood during the duet. Villa was a bit shorter in stature than Olivero and the early part of the clip is spent trying to remedy this situation by putting him on a conductor's stand so that he is taller than Olivero. This is done with lightness and sensitivity, and Villa is a good sport.

Mascagni—"Cherry Tree Duet" *L'Amico Fritz* Magda Olivero and Claudio Villa
https://www.youtube.com/watch?v=eUP9UyuD9ow

Longevity certainly is the by-word when it comes to this artist's career. She could impose a patina of girlishness to her tone when she needed it for effect, but the voice showed little change or aging in its basic timbre since the 1960s.

> My teacher always reminded me that a singer is at the service of music, not the other way round. It is a sacred responsibility, one I have always taken seriously, whether I was on the stage of La Scala or Newark. And I think I have always been repaid for remembering this. I have enjoyed great admiration and respect from my colleagues, and I have never harmed anyone. I have helped all I could if they were in difficulty on or off the stage, even to the point of creating difficulties for myself. But I have no regrets, I've given the best I could. (John Ardoin, "One of a Kind" *Opera News*, 12/3/77)

Olivero continued to perform on the stage until March of 1981 singing Poulenc's Voix Humaine and in churches until well into her 80s. In 1983, with the death of her husband, she stopped performing for a number of years.

In 1993, at the age of eighty-three, Olivero recorded excerpts (71 minutes) from Cilea's Adriana Lecouvreur for Bon Giovanni Records. The disc was considered her last will and testament concerning the role of Adriana and was recorded with piano accompaniment (Carmelina Gandolfo) in an office in Milan rather than a studio. With the assistance of tenor Alberto Cupido, and Marta Morretto (Principessa) and despite her advanced age, Olivero displayed her true mettle as a supreme verismo artist. As Lee Milazzo wrote in The American Record Guide (5/6/1994):

> The arias, indeed the contents of the entire disc (it was recorded in one take), are not a matter of notes on a page; this is life and death. Yes, the voice is sometimes hoarse, sometimes short of breath, sometimes brittle. Then the years fall away, and Olivero floats one of those incredible pianissimos—or sings an aching long line or expands to full voice—and you are left speechless. Would that sopranos half her years could do as well. And to hear her presentation of the text, her emphases and nuances, is to take a lesson in Italian opera (and life).

Also in 1993, during the Gala Lirico VII Premio Giacomo Lauri-Volpe television show, the 83 year-old soprano sang Puccini's "Sola...perduta abbandonata" from *Manon Lescaut*. She gave a remarkable performance of almost frightening intensity, with all the high notes intact, solid, and potent.

Puccini—"Sola perduta abandonata" *Manon Lescaut* 1993
https://www.youtube.com/watch?v=EyrMSDRWcw0

At the age of 86 she still managed to sing Adriana's monologue from Adriana Lecouvreur in Jan Schmidt-Garre's film Opera Fanatic. She was still making occasional singing appearances in her nineties. Reminiscing about her career, she once told Stefan Zucker:

> ….my career has always been very strange. I took it as it came. I never tried to organize my career. I never was deadly serious about it. Artistically, perhaps, yes, but as a career per se, I took it rather lightly."

On April 17, 2009, at the age of 99, Olivero sang a passage from Zandonai's Francesca da Rimini in the Palazzo Cusani Radetsky, Milan. She explained to those present that recently her dreams had been haunted by the particular phrase "Paolo dàtemi pace." (Paolo give me peace). Because of this, after many years, she felt compelled to sing. And sing she does. Olivero proved that at the age of 99 she could still mesmerize an audience with her unusual voice. After her finish, the humble smile on her face is something to behold.

Zandonai—"Paolo dàtemi pace" *Francesca da Rimini*—Maga Olivero sings at 99 years of age
https://www.youtube.com/watch?v=nZe3TKQxF0s

Magda Olivero died on September 8, 2014 at the age of 104.
Some More Magda Olivero performances on YouTube

Magda Olivero Amsterdam Concerts 1962-1972 (nineteen opera arias)
https://www.youtube.com/watch?v=NOGvNmngcRc

Puccini—*La Boheme* (abr)—Amsterdam 1968
https://www.youtube.com/watch?v=TgRPI1t8K2Q

Magda Olivero Concert—Martini and Rossi December 1968 (includes the Liebestodt from Wagner's *Tristan und Isolde*)
https://www.youtube.com/watch?v=r88NRHWu8k4

Puccini—*Tosca*—Geneva 1975 with Gianfranco Cecchele, Aldo Protti, Giorgio Giorgetti—Francesco Molinari-Pradellil
https://www.youtube.com/watch?v=BAM2tBYk4n4

(For additional biographical information and a discussion of her recordings see The Record Collector, Volume 42, #2, June 1997.)

Leyla Gencer

From the 1960s to the 1980s Leyla Gencer (1928–2008) was known as the "Queen of the Pirates." Different from Magda Olivero, Gencer never made a commercial recording of a complete opera. This is one of the reasons why her pirate legacy is of such importance.

Her very name is exotic. She was an artist of Turkish ancestry who, during the 1950s and 60s, held her own despite the presence of Maria Callas, Renata Tebaldi, Renata Scotto, Montserrat Caballe, and Magda Olivero. All of whom shared roles in her repertoire. Ironically, Gencer had a number of important credits to her name that many tend to forget. Wrongly viewed as the poor man's Callas, the Turkish soprano actually showed more artistic versatility.

There was something about that voice...something about the oddness of the mezzo-tinged middle and low registers contrasted by a pure and sweet, flute-like, high pianissimo. It was not only the voice, but also the way in which it was used. The commitment—a poised, almost noble grandeur contrasted by moments of frailty or demonic fury. Seen objectively, the soprano was very clever. She did not have the genius of Callas nor the natural endowment of Tebaldi—but she built on what she had to form an enviable career.

So why was she so popular?

Born in 1928, in Istanbul to a Polish (Catholic) mother and a well-off Turkish, Muslim father, Gencer readily accredits her Nanny for introducing her to the fine arts when young. She studied with Italian soprano Giannina Arangi-Lombardi, and, after Arangi-Lombardi's death, with Italian baritone Apollo Granforte, who was teaching in Ankara. (Although it has been reported that she studied with Elvira de Hidalgo, Gencer maintained that was not true.)

Gencer made her professional debut in 1950 at Ankara's State Theater, as Santuzza in a Turkish-language Cavalleria rusticana. The famous conductor, Tullio Serafin, heard her and offered Gencer the opportunity to make an Italian debut as Cio-Cio-San in *Madama Butterfly* at the Teatro San Carlo, conducted by Gabriele Santini (1954). In 1956, she made her U.S. debut, singing Zandonai's Francesca da Rimini in San Francisco. In 1957, Gencer made her La Scala debut as Mme. Lidoine in the world premiere of Poulenc's Dialogues des Carmélites.

Between 1957 and 1983, Gencer sang 19 roles at La Scala, including Leonora in Forza del Destino and Il trovatore, Elisabetta in Don Carlos, Aïda, Lady Macbeth, Norma, Ottavia in L'Incoronazione di Poppea, and Gluck's Alceste. The company's 1958 world premiere of Pizzetti's L'Assassinio Nella Cattedrale found Gencer performing—by the composer's request—the First Woman of Canterbury. She made her London debut during the 1962 season at Covent Garden in Don Carlo and *Don Giovanni*. Other roles include Liu in *Turandot*, *La Gioconda*, Tatiana in Eugene Onegin, La Vestale, Elvira in Ernani, Odabella in Attila, Beatrice di Tenda, Adriana Lecouvreur. Because of the similarity of some of their repertoire, and the fact that she also sang at La Scala, Gencer was often compared, unfavorably, to Maria Callas.

Although her repertoire was quite large and embraced works from Monteverdi to Pizzetti, she became primarily known for her bel canto revivals—Anna Bolena, Roberto Devereux, Maria Stuarda, Caterina Cornaro, Belisario, Lucrezia Borgia, Bellini's I puritani, and Norma, as well as roles in Verdi operas: *Macbeth, La traviata, La battaglia di Legnano, Gerusalemme, I Vespri Siciliani,* and *I due Foscari*. As she once remarked:

> My specialty… is revivals. For many years I did bel canto and Puccini, but now I've made a specialty of four Italian composers. I've launched many operas and received the Commendatore for it. I

am very proud of this because I am *not* Italian and yet I received it for reviving these operas and for reviving the international interest in these national operas. (Leyla Gencer: The Belle of Bel Canto, Robert Jacobson *After Dark* November, 1972)

Gencer retired from the stage in 1985, with Gnecco's La Prova di un'Opera Seria at La Fenice. She did, however continue to do recitals and concerts until 1992. After her retirement she sat on various juries of competitions, giving masterclasses, and serving as the jury chairwoman of Istanbul's Yapi Kredi International Leyla Gencer Voice Competition. Maestro Riccardo Muti selected Leyla Gencer to oversee La Scala's School for Young Artists in the late 1990s

During the early part of her career, she was known as a champion of modern works and sang in the world premiere of a number of operas, including works mentioned earlier by Pizzetti and Poulenc as well as Prokofiev's Fiery Angel (the Italian premiere at Spoleto) and Rocca's Monte Ivnor. During her career, she had a repertoire of about 70 roles.

Vocally, Leyla Gencer was a collection of disparate contrasts. Initially she was a lovely lyric-coloratura. In order to remain in the "vocal race" dominated by Maria Callas (in the bel canto repertoire) and Renata Tebaldi (in the verismo repertoire) Gencer took her basically sweet, light voice twisted it, shoved it, and pushed it to extremes, molding it into the instrument that she sought at that time.

There was a price to pay. Because of the pressure she put on her voice, registers segregated, and a resulting coarseness invaded her singing. She was left with an odd, unequal instrument, but one of infinite colors and capable of large volume gradations which contrasted an often wild, unfocused quality of the top register. She had a serviceable high E-flat, but she rarely strayed above high D. Considering how she pushed and pulled at her voice it is surprising that Gencer's pianissimi were so elegant.

It wasn't until 1957 that she began to branch out and embrace the more dramatic bel canto works that had become so favored by Maria Callas. By the mid-1960s, Gencer had established herself as the leading Donizetti specialist. Indeed, the aural documents of her performances of works such as Belisario, Anna Bolena, Roberto Devereux, Maria Stuarda, Caterina Cornaro, Lucrezia Borgia, are models of their kind. During an extremely fertile period of distinct soprano artists, Gencer remained a unique entity—offering listeners the (at times confusing) combination of a Greek Fury's intensity and the fragile, delicate, hauntingly sweet pianissimi of an Amelita Galli-Curci. At her best she represented the glory and frailty of humanity in opera.

Like most divas, Gencer evokes strong reactions in her listeners. One either likes or dislikes her work but rarely is unmoved. Much of this has to do with the distinct quality of her voice. When young (1950s), the voice was a soft-grained lyric coloratura voice of gentle, sweet timbre. As mentioned before, however, as she began to mature as an artist, she reshaped her voice into a more dramatic instrument. By the time of her "prime" (around 1969) this had created some incongruities within her timbre: a dark, mezzo-like lower register with a forceful chest extension contrasted by an often unwieldy top register (when sung forte) contrasted by floated pianissimi that had an attractive vulnerability to their tone and that were some of the most haunting sounds one could hear. Because of her mauling of her instrument, the tricky, upper passagio area of F & G (at the top of the staff) always gave her problems.

Some problems with the Gencer instrument were there from the beginning. Especially "iffy" was the passaggio area into her top register—the area of F and G at the top of the staff. It was always a bit suspect as to pitch. She also had a tendency, when excited and in the midst of dramatic utterances, to sing off the breath so that her tone not only curdled but also completely dissipated. Like other great artists, however, she bent her faults to her will, incorporating them into the fabric of her interpretations. She is a perfect example of both the merits and detriments of vocal compromise. By the mid 1970s, her vibrato had begun to unravel and display wide oscillations that, depending on the area of her voice, often failed to center on the correct pitch. She would often cleverly rectify this problem by suddenly pulling the voice back to pianissimo—thus removing all pressure.

Actually, this was one of her most clever effects. One can hear it in most of her performances. A good example can be found at the ending of Norma's recitative of her Act I "Casta diva." It happens on the word "mieto." Gencer thrusts up to a pianissimo high A that she endlessly suspends. It is in the approach to the high A that her secret lies. What she does is to preface the soft note with a tremendous thrust—kind of like a feint move in boxing. Because of her approach, however, the listener thinks it will a be a loud high note. Gencer, however, shocks the listener by doing the exact opposite. It is a brilliant effect that, in the hands of a creative and clever singer like Gencer, is extremely powerful and works on a number of levels: it is a brilliant interpretive device, it highlights Gencer's soft singing, it lends a certain elegance to the note itself, and, most interestingly, provides real intimacy to the phrase. The was a favorite trick of Gencer's and one she often used.

Gencer was a dynamic performer and she knew what audiences liked. She was captured in so many pirated live performances in the 1950s and 60s that she was nicknamed "The Queen of the Pirates." Her popularity in this realm was also due to the fact that she was the perfect singer for the then burgeoning arena of pirate opera recordings. For buyers her uninhibited dramaticism was, aurally, extremely satisfying and this did much to spread her popularity. Not surprisingly, Gencer's pirate "catalogue" contains some of the most vivid performances ever captured by a microphone. Fortunately, because of copyright expirations and changes, today most of these once rare recordings are easily available.

Gencer was an artist who often went over the top. By this I do not mean to imply that she could not be a singer of restraint and delicacy. Many of her performances offer classic examples of bel canto phrasing and articulate musicianship. She was, however, a creature of the stage, often erratic even during the same performance. And yet, oddly, it is that very inconsistency that draws one back to her performances time and time again. As William Ashbrook wrote of her: "[She is] a singing actress of imagination, one who pushes herself to the limits, one who prowls a stage like a wild thing confined behind bars, and that restless energy permeates what she does." Indeed the 5' 4" soprano hurled imprecations like no one else in the business.

Like Magda Olivero, Leyla Gencer was an intellectual singer. By that I mean that although her vocal and dramatic effects may seem spontaneous and immediate, they were actually very well plotted. Had they had not been, she would never have made it through performances of such dramatic works as Macbeth or Medea. And most importantly, her singing had "face" By that I mean that through her singing you could easily visualize her emotions. When it comes to listening to opera without the benefit of the stage action or costumes, this becomes of great importance. It is through such creativity that a listener becomes completely swept away by a singer's interpretation. Gencer intuitively knew the value and emotional impact of such commonplace things as the intake of breath, the length and silence of rests, initial guttural attack, and contrasting vivid, guttural vocalism with soft, elegant pianissimi. This is why so many of Gencer's live recordings remain popular—even though they too place over sixty years ago.

Her pianissimi were her most appealing feature. One often has difficulty in describing vocal sounds, but in her case it is easy: Leyla Gencer's softest high notes resemble the wispy, sweet pianissimo sounds Amelita Galli-Curci (1882–1963) made on many of her late 1920 recordings. This peculiar sound, coming from such a dramatic instrument, is as striking as it is odd, as was her peculiar way of thrusting up to such tones with force only to suddenly float and suspend them. As a mannerism, it was extremely clever for its shock effect. There was also Gencer's liberal use of glottal stroke. When it comes to the unique combination of both coarse and elegant soft singing, you can't beat Gencer.

Perhaps contributing to her preference to perform primarily on Italian stages was her dislike of travel. As she said in interviews, "Io son pigra" which means she considered herself lazy because she does not like to travel. Financially comfortable, she was in a position to pick and choose what and where she sang. It remains unfortunate that even though negotiations began with the Metropolitan as early as 1956, they eventually fizzled out and never were concluded. She did sing in concert in Manhattan, Donizetti's Caterina Cornaro, and in New Jersey, Verdi's Attila.

Gencer's rise during the 1950s and '60s paralleled the rise of pirate tape recording and specifically the ability to tape performances on portable tape recorders inside an opera house. Although never considered a particularly great stage actress, because of her "visible" manner of singing, Leyla Gencer was a perfect singer for the medium of recording. Ironically, this went largely unnoticed by the larger recording companies. (A 10" disc of arias recorded in 1956, by Cetra seems little more than an extended "test" for the artist. Another 10" disc of songs and a few arias recorded in 1974, toward the beginning of a rather long decline, did little to affix her name or reputation in the record books.) As if to compensate for that gross error, her work on stage was faithfully captured by fans and "professional" pirates and fortunately now provides us with a remarkably honest portrait of this proud diva.

Her kaleidoscopic voice lent itself extremely well to the new medium, allowing listeners to be swept away by the force of her colorful interpretations. As her reputation rose, so did the number of Gencer recordings on "pirate labels" or on tape mail-order listings. Because her studio recording activity was practically nothing, her live recordings became highly prized. More than 100 of her performances exist on tape and/or CD.

As of this writing, around 50 of her performances are on CD. Because of the nature of pirate opera recordings as a small business, releases regularly go in and out of print. Created in smaller lots than would the commercial labels, pirate CDs are often not reprinted after the first run is depleted. You will have to look hard to find her Aïda, Monte Ivnor, La Vestale, Poliuto, Attila, Lucrezia Borgia, Dialogue of the Carmelites, Beatrice di Tenda, I due Foscari, Schwanda the Bagpiper, *I puritani, Rigoletto, La forza del destino, Tosca, Adriana Lecouvreur,* and *Madama Butterfly*. Gencerians should be alert, however, because those performances will undoubtedly reappear in other editions at some point. Many are now available on YouTube.

Gencer, herself, condoned the pirated recordings made of her work. When interviewed about her lack of studio recordings, she said:

...I have never been really preoccupied with this problem, and at least there are all the pirate tapes and records. I keep quite a collection myself, supplied by my friends, and although I realize the risk that a bad performance might end up on records (we all have our bad nights!) I am still delighted that these documents of my art exist. (Susan Gould, Leyla Gencer Queen of Pirate Recordings, *High Fidelity*, September 1976, page 75)

Leyla Gencer's career can be divided into two segments: from 1954 to 1957 she pretty much sang whatever she was offered, moving from *Madama Butterfly* to Dialogues of the Carmelites, and other modern works, to Francesca da Rimini.

1957 seemed to be a turning point in her career when she was hired (at the last minute) to sing *Lucia di Lammermoor* in San Francisco in November of 1957, and the Venice revival of Verdi's I due Foscari. It is after that, that one notices her beginning to concentrate on revivals of long-unheard works by Donizetti, Bellini, and Verdi. Works such as Anna Bolena in 1958, I puritani (1961) Rigoletto (1961), La Battaglia di Legano (1963) Gerusalemme (1963), *I Vespri Siciliani* (1964), Roberto Devereux (1964), Lucrezia Borgia (1966), Maria Sutarda (1967), Medea (1968), Belisario (1969), Elisabetta Regina d'Inghilterra (1970), and Caterina Cornaro (1972), Medea in Corinto (1977).

Many Gencer performances can be found on the labels MYTO, from Italy, arguably one of the finest pirate labels in today's market, Opera D'Oro, a budget label which is rapidly vying with the Dutch label, Gala, as one of the best buys around for opera lovers.

Suggested Recordings

Bellini: *Norma:* Complete performance from *Milan, January 13, 1965* plus excerpts from performances in *Buenos Aires (7/18/64), Verona (7/24/65)* and *Naples (1/30/65)* MYTO (3 CDs)

Norma has had an interesting recording history. Although various single excerpts appeared on 78 r.p.m. disks in the early 1900s, especially the famous "Casta diva," the first complete commercial recording of Norma did not appear until 1937, when the Italian firm Cetra recorded the work with the then-famous dramatic soprano, Gina Cigna and the conductor, Vittorio Gui. Cigna also sang a Metropolitan Opera broadcast of the work that same year (available on CD). Hers is a rough-and-ready, veristic interpretation that was typical of the time.

The next complete recording was made in 1954, the famous Callas/Serafin, Angel release. It was this recording that began to alter modern perceptions about Bellini's work. In the artistic hands and voice of Maria Callas, the work was returned to the province of the dramatic coloratura. Soon there were recordings by Dame Joan Sutherland, Montserrat Caballe, Elena Suliotis, Beverly Sills, Renata Scotto, Maria Bieshu, and Edita Gruberova. Live performances captured all these singers in the role as well as even the Wagnerian specialist Gwyneth Jones. Even mezzo sopranos such as Grace Bumbry, Shirley Verrett, and Cecillia Bartoli have essayed the role. Today you can find many recordings of the work (both live and studio) on amazon.com.

Edita Gruberova's assumption of Norma exemplifies problems we face today with this opera, including some tricky grey areas. In April 2003, Gruberova (at age 57) surprised everyone by undertaking the role of Norma for three Tokyo concert performances. During the next number of years she gave other performances of the opera as well. In March, 2005 Nightingale Records released a CD of one of them. Some critics were horrified at the idea of a "Zerbinetta" and former Norina in Don Pasquale undertaking such a dramatically taxing role. When it comes to singers of longevity like Placido Domingo (his operatic debut was in 1959) and Edita Gruberova (her operatic debut was in 1968), the fact remains that their voices must be approached and evaluated as the individual gifts they are. Taking into consideration Gruberova's career choices, her role preparation, her rock-solid technique, her previous cleverness in dealing with "killer roles" (like Elisabetta in Roberto Devereux and Anna Bolena) her decision should not have surprised anyone.

One might not agree with Gruberova's interpretation or how she negotiates some of the role's more complex emotional or dramatic moments but one cannot deny the authority and individuality she brings to the role. When Cecilia Bartoli undertook the role, even more criticism came her way, although the role never became an integral part of her performance repertoire.

As with any role, there are only a handful of artists whose voices truly fit *Norma* in all the right places. During the 1960s the list was quite short, but it did include Joan Sutherland, Montserrat Caballe, and the heroine of this MYTO set, Leyla Gencer.

Bellini: *Norma:* Complete performance in Milan, January 13, 1965 plus excerpts from performances in Buenos Aires (7/18/64), Verona (7/24/65) and Naples (1/30/65). MYTO (3 CDs)

MYTO has always been a champion of Leyla Gencer's. In this recording they also provide fans with the rare opportunity to compare contrasting performances of the same opera within the same CD release.

After the "main" performance, the listener is offered about an hour-and-a-half of excerpts from three other performances. I love this kind of release because it gives you the opportunity to learn so much about a singer. One quibble, however. I realize that MYTO was trying to be organized in presenting music from these four performances, but I would have preferred a slightly different way of handling the layout. First, we are given the complete performance from Milan, January 13, 1965. This appears on CD #1 and part of CD #2. This is supplemented by selections (carried over onto CD #3) from the July 18, 1964, Teatro Colon (Buenos Aires) performance, which is followed by selections from a July 24, 1965, Verona performance and a January 30, 1965, Naples performance. What is even more confusing is that in MYTO's printed layout of the track listing, everything looks the same.

The sound is not bad in the central Milan performance, but it varies during the others. (I found the Naples performance a bit too dark for my taste. I like to be able to hear the "bite" of a singer's natural timbre.) Generally, however, the sound is quite acceptable. There are occasional glitches in the recordings, but none that detract from the performances.

As this release proves, Norma was one of Gencer's great roles and she had an excellent instinct for Bellini's music as well as a requisite inherent sense of drama which enabled her to illuminate the character's public and private emotional struggles. Although the score does not rise above high C, it was Gencer's habit to conclude the final Act I trio with an interpolated high D. At one time this was a huge deal in performances of this opera. Nowadays throwing in a penultimate high D at this spot is almost expected—even an occasional mezzo who has essayed the role, has interpolated that note. More unusual is the interpolation of a penultimate high E-flat at the end of the duet with Pollione in the last-act confrontation. Some singers who have used this interpolation include Joan Sutherland, Cristina Deutekom, Marisa Galvany, Beverly Sills, and Edita Gruberova.

In the La Scala performance, all Gencer-trademarked effects are present. I tend to think of Leyla Gencer as a "belcanto" Magda Olivero. Both singers had distinctive voices and an uncanny ability to grab high pianissimi out of thin air, spinning (or floating) them with great beauty. Both could also utter unbelievably ugly sounds to support their theatrical interpretations. Different voices, of course, but both were extremely savvy in their expressive vocalism, had strong musical temperaments, took the same kind of vocal chances, and sang with an almost animal savagery that could be aurally riveting. With both singers there are moments within their performances in which they sound as if in extremis, but don't let that fool you. Both Gencer and Olivero knew exactly what they were doing. That was their art.

A passage early in the Milan performance shows just how clever Gencer was: we covered this earlier—her thrusting up to piano sounds—a favorite trick of hers.

There are other examples of trademark-Gencer vocalism as well, including guttural, choked glottal stops, and chested, dramatic singing. There are also suspect pitches, occasional misjudgments of placement, and flat singing. The area between F at the top of the staff and high B-flat often posed a problem for this soprano in terms of keeping a loud tone focused and attractive. There are a few moments during the performance that fall short of perfection—the finish of the Norma/Adalgisa duet, "O rimembranza!" finds the singers finishing almost a half-step flat. Similar pitch problems occur during the famous "Mira o Norma" duet. (The problem may actually be with Giulietta Simionato, and would be unusual for that excellent singer.)

As one might expect, the outstanding moments of Gencer's performance include two of the most difficult: the "Qual cor tradisti" and the "Deh non volerli vittime," both from the last act. These are moments when she can (and does) offer some of her special, thrusted pianissimi. This section also finds Gencer cleverly emphasizing the different registers of her voice by digging deep into a raw chest register and then, in a split second, moving into a heady register. On the written page, that hardly sounds moving or artistic, but when experienced, it can have an overwhelming emotional impact on the listener. One such moment can be found on track 8 of CD #2 in the bridge between "Deh! con te" and "Mira o Norma." In that section there are certain sounds that Gencer makes that are peculiarly hers and that add much to the intensity of the moment. They flesh out the portrait of Norma that she carefully creates for the listener. Like similarly gifted singers such as Maria Callas, Hildegard Behrens, Marta Mödl, and Leonie Rysanek, there are certain phrases Gencer sings that are unique and become indelible in one's memory.

Most importantly, Gencer provides a character with a vivid face. When it comes to listening to opera without the benefit of stage, costumes, or other visuals, such "aural faces" become extremely important. It is through such creativity that a listener is swept away by a singer's interpretation. During a time when Callas, Sutherland, and Caballe were each placing their own stamps on this role, it is to Gencer's credit that she manages to do the same without encroaching on the interpretations of the others.

I do not mean to sound dismissive by saying this, but all of her colleagues are excellent. Prevedi offers an often suave Pollione. Giulietta Simionato and Fiorenza Cossotto, as Adalgisa, both have their moments. With them it is a matter of one's personal preference for vocal sound— whether one chooses the round, vibrant voice of Simionato or the more steely bite of Cossotto. Despite occasional pitch problems, I favor the more sympathetic timbre of Simionato. Zaccaria is a good and dependable, if wooly, Oroveso. Their contributions to the success of these performances are considerable. No less important is the leadership of Gianandrea Gavazzeni who provides strong support for one of his preferred sopranos. No matter what, however, this is Gencer's show and what a grand show it is.

Bellini—"Deh! Non volermi vittime" to end of opera *Norma*—Milan 1965
https://www.youtube.com/watch?v=zJx5mZgbMkM

Cherubini: *Medea*—Venice December 15, 1968

This Medea is one of my favorites. At least when it comes to the "theater of the ear."

Ironically, in reviewing the performance in Opera magazine in March 1969, Alessandro Comuto found much less to enjoy:

> The Turkish soprano, much appreciated for her emotional intensity and keen insight into character, now seems to be concerned entirely with the incisive, penetrating accents and burning impetuosity of Romantic phrasing. This she carries to the limits of *parlando* in recitative, whereas Cherubini's music demands a severe, absolutely cold vocal line, that is to say the complete opposite of this artist's, though she was quite effective dramatically and gave a well-integrated portrayal of the character. She was not in good voice and this may have contributed to an excessive harshness from time to time.

Generally known as "The Gencer Medea" it has been available in various pirated formats since the time of its performance. The wonderful and enterprising CD budget label, Gala (GL 100.555) has made it more accessible to the public at a budget price. Like the "Callas in Dallas" Medea (1958) and the "Olivero in Dallas" (1967) I believe that this is one of those must-own performances, especially if you are a fan of the titular artist. Different from both Callas and Olivero, Gencer did not sing the role after this production. Like the Callas and Olivero performances, Gencer's performance makes use of the Lachner recitatives. Leyla Gencer turns in a gutsy, powerhouse performance that is an unforgettable aural experience. Supported by Aldo Bottion (Giasone), Daniella Mazzucato (Glauce), Ruggero Raimondi (Creonte), and conducted by that friend of singers, Carlo Franci, this is a classic live performance.

The sound quality of the mono broadcast is very good. Gencer brings innumerable personal touches to a role that, for the most part, had been considered Maria Callas' personal property. Admittedly, much of Gencer's interpretation involves guttural growls, but, like Magda Olivero who sang the role the year before in Dallas, Gencer uses her uneven instrument with imagination and makes her vocal attributes (as well as her flaws) work to advantage in creating a vivid portrait of the conniving, vengeance-mad Medea. And, importantly for the listener, she creates a vivid aural portrait. There is a familiarity, an abandon and commitment to her singing that is rarely heard today. For that reason alone, it is worth hearing. The strength and variety of her nuance provides an unusually illuminating tapestry and, in that, a rewarding listening experience. Gencer provides more tonal beauty than either Callas or Olivero, with some truly stunning pianissimi, but she is just as dramatic. The big moments do not disappoint! Like Callas, Leyla Gencer often takes her chest voice dangerously high, lending a thrill of its own. There are many moments of fascination on this recording. For example, listen to the differing ways

Gencer sings "fuggir" during the Act I duet with Jason. Her final, desperate "fuggir" perfectly evokes shock, incredulity, and disgust—all this within a single word. The opening of act III is as harrowing as one might expect. Indeed, the entirety of act III is a frightening exhibition of pure vehemence. Gencer's use of her well-produced chest voice is almost psychotic in its delivery.

The cast is excellent, providing suitable foil to this fiery Medea, but Gencer's commitment and dynamic singing towers over the production and dwarfs the others. This performance has also been released on CD by Mondo Musica as part of the La Fenice series. Priced at about $10, however, the Gala issue is a bargain you should not miss.

Cherubini—*Medea*—Venice, 1968
https://www.youtube.com/watch?v=jU2cpz50tU8&list=RDjU2cpz50tU8&start_radio=1
Donizetti—*Belisario*—Venice, 1969

Another Gencer favorite, Antonina in Belisario. This was one of her greatest role assumptions. It was an important revival and fortunately, it is one of her best-preserved performances (now available on Mondo Musica CD). Actually, Gencer sang in two more revivals of this opera; one the next year, in 1970, in Bergamo, and one in Naples in January of 1973. In November, 2013 Opera Rara released the first commercial recording of the opera with Nicola Alaimo and Joyce El-Khoury as Antonina, conducted by Sir Mark Elder.

In his review of a DVD of this opera, David Shengold wrote:

> Donizetti's uneven but worthwhile three-act lyric tragedy—the opera that followed *Lucia di Lammermoor* (which also had Salvatore Cammarano as librettist)—was a success at its 1836 Venice premiere. The work concerns heroism and betrayal mixed with thorny family drama worthy of the House of Thebes. Set in Justinian's bellicose Byzantine Empire, *Belisario* follows in the bel canto subgenre of classically set plots with stately, noble music — a trend ushered in by *Médée* and *La Vestale*, with *Norma* perhaps its pinnacle... (*Opera News*, February 2015, Vol. 79, #8)

If you don't know this work or Gencer's contributions, you can sample its considerable merits on YouTube. It will be a pleasant surprise. A reviewer for Opera magazine at the time mentioned that Gencer was a regular participant in revivals and the reviewer's only reservation was the excessively dramatic excitement that Gencer brings to her portrayals.

Antonina's opening scene (recorded commercially by Montserrat Caballe on her Donizetti Rarities album) is arresting for its intense declamation and forceful delivery which, within moments, establishes the character. Her singing covers all; from excitingly coarse, to sweetly elegant, to virtuostic and brilliant. A vocal highlight is the way Gencer launches into the Act II finale, compellingly emphatic with its four high Cs. The final scene, one of the great works of its type, is a complex, extended scena with a double aria and a final cabaletta for the contra-heroine. Gencer delivers the goods and more. Of special note is the Galli-Curci-like high pianissimo suspended over the chorus, the smooth-flowing legato, the gutteral, dramatic accents, and a mighty, exalted finish that is capped by a stunning, very long high D (16 seconds). Taddei is a vocal powerhouse as Belisario, beautiful and rich in tone while dramatic in his accents.

In 1990, Hunt CD released the 1970 Bergamo performance with Leyla Gencer and Renato Bruson as Belisario, with Gencer's major scenes from the 1969 Venice Belisario thrown in as a bonus. Although Bruson's work in that performance is wonderful, Gencer fans prefer the 1969 Venice performance with Taddei. Mondo Musica's mono sound is excellent, clean, and clear. If you can find the Hunt release (on eBay) that is the one to get.

Donizetti—*Belisario* Final Scene—Venice, 1969
https://www.youtube.com/watch?v=Bj_oxsR7HEo

Donizetti—*Belisario* (complete)– Bergamo, 1970
https://www.youtube.com/watch?v=x1r4AqVStEg&t=20s

Donizetti: *Lucia di Lammermoor* (excerpts) 12/13/57 Trieste (Melodram)

Leyla Gencer learned the role of *Lucia di Lammermoor* in five days when she was called upon to replace an ailing Maria Callas in San Francisco in 1957. Although she had put the role on the resume that she originally gave to the administration of the San Francisco Opera, she did not, in fact, know the role (she knew only the mad scene). This "padding" of one's resume is not an uncommon practice for young singers in order to boost their repertoire and make their resume look more impressive. David E. Stevens, reviewing Gencer's performance for *Opera News* noted that "The attractive Turkish artist projected in clear, lyric tones a heroine who seemed to have a somber premonition of her fate." (*Opera News*, 1957)

Taken from a broadcast in December of 1957, this Trieste performance is a valuable document of Gencer in a role she sang only a few times in the early years of her career. Although not a Lucia in the same league as Callas or Sutherland, Gencer brings to the part her own ideas and haunting lyrical singing. Available on both Melodram and Arkadia CDs (and as filler for the MYTO issue of Donizetti's Les Martyres [1975]). This is a worthy addition to any Gencerian's library. The "Regnava nel silenzio" is quite successful with nice ornamentation as well as some surprisingly delicate staccato work. In the mad scene, Gencer uses the traditional Liebling cadenza with flute (as do most of her contemporary colleagues at the time) which promotes the heady sweetness of her high register. Despite a quick learning of the role, Gencer has a secure grasp of who the character is and what parts of her persona she wants to highlight. Those listeners familiar with Gencer's furious outbursts in such works as Pacini's Sapho, Donizetti's Belisario and Lucrezia Borgia will be surprised at the sweet and gentle manner she has with *Lucia di Lammermoor*. Overall, Gencer offers a basic, lovely, lyric interpretation of the role. Although high E-flat is the obvious limit of her top register, her delivery of them in the mad scene are excellent in this performance.

Another Gencer performance of the mad scene can be heard on a Melodram CD of highlights from the Trieste performance. It was taken from an RAI concert given in Milan during the same year. Her program for that concert also included "Senza mama" from Suor Angelica and "Martern aller arten" from Die Entführung aud dem Serail), the only recording of Gencer of this dramatically pyrotechnical music. Interestingly, the varied repertoire of the concert reflects the daring concerts given by Maria Callas a few years before.

Donizetti—*Lucia di Lammermoor*—Trieste, 1957
https://www.youtube.com/watch?v=ACYX9EURYcQ&t=1310s

Donizetti—*Lucia di Lammermoor*— Mad Scene RAI Concert, 1957
https://www.youtube.com/watch?v=O4Rukw3wsjw

The Donizetti Queens

Given the American furor in the 1970s, when Beverly Sills first sang the trio of Donizetti queens, many people do not credit that Leyla Gencer did it first—years before! Between 1958 and 1967 the Turkish diva sang all three heroines.

She once remarked with irony: "I discover the opera, Sills sings them, and Montserrat records them." Leyla Gencer can now receive full credit for her important pioneering work with these particular operas due to surviving pirate recordings. At the time of their performance, however, many found fault with the Turkish diva.

Fortunately, all three of those important revivals are now available on YouTube.

Gencer's 1964 Naples revival of Roberto Devereux did not get good reviews, but time has put a different patina on the performance. Writing of the pirated performance 20 years later, in Opera on Record Volume III, Richard Fairman noted:

> The opera was given almost complete (only a few minor cuts) and was well cast. Leyla Gencer is a regal Queen Elizabeth; she really commands the role Her voice, especially at the beginning of the evening, lacks ease and a sure centre, but by the *Norma*-like trio she has built up an imposing presence. The shadow of Callas is with us, as always. Glottal stops, covered tones and flashing of a growling chest register pay homage to her influence. (Longwood Press, 1984, page 64)

Fairman concludes that of the five performances (recordings) available at the time it is Gencer's that is to be recommended.

At one time, Gencer must have heard Beverly Sills's recording of Roberto Devereux. Without mentioning names, she condemned the lighter soprano's portrayal:

> (Roberto Devereux)…is another opera Gencer would like to record commercially, 'to show the public what were the composer's real interpretive intentions…These have nothing to do with the embellishments he did not write, nor with the exaggeration of florid vocalism that destroys the drama of the musical text.'

Donizetti—*Roberto Devereux*—Naples, 1964
https://www.youtube.com/watch?v=oIWSmKN-4FU

Maria Stuarda, Gencer's original 1967 revival was reviewed by William Weaver for Opera (autumn, 1967):

> Her performance in the Donizetti opera was again a mixture of intense acting, musical intelligence, and frequently ugly sounds. One has the feeling that her voice simply cannot meet the demands she (and Donizetti) make on it. As Mary of Scotland she looked and behaved with the suitable mixture of pride and despair, and when her voice was under control, chiefly in the quieter scenes, she had moments of real efficacy.

Donizetti—*Maria Stuarda*—Florence, 1967
https://www.youtube.com/watch?v=imq0zxlK6T0

Looking back some twenty years, Richard Fairman commented on Gencer's 1958 RAI broadcast of Anna Bolena which was given the year after Maria Callas's La Scala revival:

> In general, this is a less compelling performance. Gencer is an impressive Anna Bolena, very much in the Callas tradition even down to details of phrasing. (Gavazzeni presumably coached them both.) The attack is true and the voice has brilliance and weight; but Gencer lacks the full vocal quality of her rival, and also her depth and memorability. (*Opera on Record Volume III*, Longwood Press, 1984)

Donizetti—*Anna Bolena*—RAI, 1958
https://www.youtube.com/watch?v=6HFJNauFbnM

At this writing, Roberto Devereux (Naples, 1964) and Anna Bolena (Milan, 1958) are available (both only about $10.00 on Opera D'Oro). I am sure the Maria Stuarda (Florence, 1967, Naples, Edinburgh, 1969) and the Glyndebourne Anna Bolena (1965) will eventually become available again. Gencer's performances in any of these operas are certainly worthy of close inspection. By this time Gencer was gaining renown as a Donizetti specialist. Although in these roles I prefer the imaginative but admittedly ornate and highly individual recordings (and the live performances) of Beverly Sills and Edita Gruberova, it is only an idiosyncratic preference on my part. You should definitely listen to the Gencer performances, if only to remind yourself how well-constructed these roles are when they are sung (for the most part) come scritto. Aside from an occasional top D or so, Gencer indulges in little ornamentation or interpolations. Maria Stuarda was especially well-suited to her voice and in at least one performance Gencer is partnered by a forceful, exciting Shirley Verrett as Elisabeth. Their scenes together are worth any price.

Donizetti Addendum:

Interested Gencer fans should listen to another special Gencer performance—The *Requiem* by Donizetti from Venice, 1970. Gencer sings with Mirna Pecile, Armando Moretti and Alessandro Cassis with Gianandrea Gavazzeni leading a beautifully sculpted performance. Donizetti's requiem was a quick composition in 1835 (during frantic final rehearsals for the premiere of *Lucia di Lammermoor*), in honor of the death of his friend Vincenzo Bellini. It was not performed until 1870, years after Donizetti's death in 1848.

There is some remarkably elegant soft singing from Gencer in this performance. Generally, the soprano has little to do in the Requiem. In this performance, however, Gavazzeni gave the "Ingemisco" (originally written for the tenor) to her. She does a remarkable job, sensitively twining her soft-grained voice in between the string lines, offering perfect soft attacks and smooth legato. She crowns the finish with a spectacularly beautiful high A suspended over the orchestra.

The "Dies Irae," sung by the quartet, is a rousing, dramatic reading. (How different is Donizetti's concept of the Requiem from Verdi's, although one suspects that Verdi may have taken some hints from Donizetti's composition.) Gencer finishes the "Dies irae" with a 17-second pianissimo high G suspended over the ensemble. It is a remarkable moment.

Donizetti—*Requiem*—Venice, 1970
https://www.youtube.com/watch?v=elcwr_3SmUI&t=207s

Pacini—*Saffo*—Naples, 1967

Premiered in 1840, Saffo falls midway in Pacini's operatic compositions. This 1967 Naples performance was an important revival, and the first in the 20th century. Ironically, after this performance the work was not revived again until the 1980s when it was sung by another fascinatingly flawed singer, Adelaide Negri. Saffo received its New York concert premiere in 1982 at Town Hall (in a cast which included Louis Quilico who sang in the original 1967 revival) and Bianca Berini. In 1995 it was given in Wexford with Francesca Pedaci.

In the 1967 revival, Capuana and Gencer made a strong case for future revivals of the work. Also excellent was the young Louis Quilico, whose softly grained, beautiful voice is a definite plus. As is true with any Gencer performance, she illuminates the role from within with phrases of individual, unforgettable colorations and various vocal tricks that go toward highlighting aspects of the character. Her pianissimo was in an especially good state that evening and she gives many examples of its haunting quality. Like Montserrat Caballe, Gencer's pianissimo was a sound that hovered in an opera house's acoustics. Of special note is the extended Norma-like Act II, duet "Di quai soavi lagrime" between the two female protagonists, Saffo and Climene (Franca Mattiucci). It is followed by a rousing cabaletta, which Gencer caps with another of her wonderful high Ds. Pacini follows this with a long, white-hot, Donizettian-like ensemble that concludes the act, with Gencer at her most ferocious. After hearing it once, who could forget her desperate singing of the line: "D'altra donna...no Giammai" with its intentional shifts of register, or her furious, strangulated denunciation: "Infame altar!" The Naples audience certainly enjoyed it.

A contemporary of Bellini and Donizetti, Pacini's score is an interesting setting of the Greek poetess Saffo's story with some novel orchestral effects. Like Mercadante, Pacini often surprises the listener with his modulations and orchestration. The extended finale to the opera, "Teco dall'are pronube," with its harp accompaniment, is delicately sung by Gencer and then concluded with a rousing cabaletta-like finish in which Gencer interpolates yet another strong top D. If you don't know this work, but enjoy Donizetti and the early-Verdi period of operatic writing, you should like this opera.

Pacini—*Saffo*—Naples, 1967
https://www.youtube.com/watch?v=qdYTfMeR4u8

Rossini—*Elisabetta Regina d'Inghilterra*—Palermo 1970

One of the fun things about this opera is recognizing music that Rossini stole from himself. Although not stated, this was taped in-house and is actually the dress rehearsal of the production, not the premiere. In this recording, Sylvia Gestzy sings the secondary role of Matilde. Just before the premiere, however, Gestzy became ill and was replaced by Margherita Guglielmi.

Gencer acquits herself with honor in this, one of Rossini's most florid scores, and manages to convey a strong, realistic character as well. Indeed, the final aria is an intricate show of florid work that demonstrates Gencer's superb ability to sensitively phrase such music and invest it with meaning. One intricate sequence of pianissimi melimas is outstanding. The only drawback is the evident encroaching loosening of her top register when singing at anything close to forte. Pianissimi are still exquisite but forte high notes can be a trial. Some of this suggests that the soprano might have been having an off night. This can be especially trying if one is not familiar with her voice and its idiosyncratic faults. Gencer manages a loud, if not pretty, top D at the end of the very long act I. This is a fascinating performance and like so much of her live legacy was an important revival at the time.

Rossini—*Elisabetta regina d'Inghilterra*—Palermo, 1970
https://www.youtube.com/watch?v=ci-V0lnTs7A

Verdi—*Gerusalemme*—Venice, 1963

This performance is one of Gencer's favorites of her pirate recordings. It is also one of mine. It was the first revival of the work in the twentieth century. Gerusalemme is actually a significant 1847 revision of Verdi's 1843 I Lombardi. It was Verdi's first grand opera in French at the Paris Opera.

This version is an Italian translation of the original French. Gencer was always a favorite with Venetian audiences and this September 24, 1963, performance explains why. It is one of the most remarkable performances in the Gencer canon. In good mono broadcast sound for the time, it presents Gencer at her best. She is having an extraordinary night with her voice completely responsive to all of the dramatic demands she makes of it. She shows herself to be an imaginative, contrastive artist showing both elegance and earthy thrusts. Along with her peculiar, "thrusted" pianissimi and elegant glissandi there are glottal strokes and the rough shifting of registers—she cleverly weaves all of these into the fabric of her interpretation. The interpolated high Cs and Ds are superbly done. The act I prayer of Giselda and the act II duet with Giacomo Aragall are magnificent, containing pianissimo shadings and dramatic, glottal fortes. The "D'un padre oime! l'imagine" section of the duet (with its Aïda-like high, piano finish) is a very special moment. The following, short "Fuggiamo" duet-cabaletta is a perfect finish to the act, excitingly propulsive, with Gencer finishing on a spectacular high D. Act II has the massive, dramatic scena "Son vanni i lamenti." It is a vocal obstacle course of great difficulty. Gencer sails through it with exquisite pianissimo high notes and elegant phrasing, followed by a cabaletta of frightening ferocity capped with a magnificent, penultimate high C, which she offers at the conclusion of the opera as well. Gavazzeni leads the remarkable performance. Two years after this production, the la Fenice opera guested in Munich where they gave a performance of this work with Giacomo Aragall and Leyla Gencer reprising their roles, but with Ettore Gracis conducting. (This is available on MYTO CD.)

Verdi—*Gerusalemme*—Venice, 1963
https://www.youtube.com/watch?v=wOHpCPYu9Mo

Two excerpts from performance in Munich:
Verdi—"Elena mia!" *Gerusalemme*—La Fenice guesting in Munich, 1965
https://www.youtube.com/watch?v=MDGmKf0IE18
Verdi—"Che mi cal della vita" *Gerusalemme*—La Fenice guesting in Munich, 1965
https://www.youtube.com/watch?v=WJOYBA8NnBU

I due Foscari was an important role in Gencer's annals although she only performed it once as far as I can tell. Fortunately, the December 13, 1957 Venice performance with Tullio Serafin is available to hear on YouTube. Taking place six months after the Il trovatore below, it shows the changes beginning to happen to the Gencer instrument, a certain intractability and coarseness cleverly contrasted by an unsuspected elegance and authority of delivery that other sopranos can rarely match. Singing the score come scritto, Gencer's opening aria "Tu al cui squardo," with its gentle harp accompaniment and supportive women's chorus, is memorable for her suspended high pianissimi. There is also a riveting performance of the Gran Duet with Il Doge (admirably sung with Guelfi). During the performance, Gencer's voice is everything: shimmering, suffocated, dramatic, lyrical, sweet, and ugly. An important revival at the time, Serafin leads a taut, vivid performance.

Verdi—*I due Foscari*—Venice, 1957
https://www.youtube.com/watch?v=YC5crxfEZDw&t=1118s
Verdi—*Macbeth* Palermo, 1960

This Palermo performance was the first time Gencer essayed the famous donna. Although Mondo Musica recently released the more famous 1968 performance, I prefer this 1960 revival with the wonderful Giuseppe Taddei and Vittorio Gui's magisterial conducting. Gencer performed this role just a few times during her career, but she was famous for her interpretation. It was one of her favorites and one can hear that she is having a wonderful time. Different from the performance eight years later, her voice is more unified and her interpretation relies less on awkward shifts into registers (which quickly became her trademark) to supply drama. Instead, she concentrates on singing the role. Another difference of little consequence is that in the later, 1968 performance, Gencer eschews the written high D-flat in the sleepwalking scene.

Verdi—*Macbeth*—Palermo, 1960
https://www.youtube.com/watch?v=C0rr5UxLstE

Verdi—*Il trovatore* RAI Milan, 1957
Recorded as the soundtrack for the 1957 RAI film, Il trovatore, this recording captures the 29-year-old Gencer voice in its youth. One can hear, however, that she is already pushing her light instrument to its limits in order to match (what she perceives to be) the role's weight. There is enough of her naturally youthful sound, however, to create a sympathetic and colorful character. Her famous glottal stroke is less in evidence here than it would be later in the 1960s, but appears at some well-judged moments. In the opening "Tacea la notte placida" she surprises the listener with a beautifully floated high D-flat plucked out of the air and decides to interpolate the note again at the close of the act. Surrounded by such veterans as Ettore Bastianini, Fedora Barbieri and Mario Del Monaco, the performance is idiomatic and white hot. Gencer's finest moments come in act IV with a moving "D'amor sull' ali rosee" and a rousing "Miserere." Although Gencer never had a true trill, she makes an acceptable nod in its direction and, instead, concentrates on a sweet, lyrical, flowing line that caresses the listener's ear. There are many beautiful pianissimi, not the least being another sustained top D-flat. Once heard, one cannot forget her emotional singing of such lines as "le pene, le pene dell' mio cor" with its deliberate shifting in and out of deep chest voice.

Verdi—*Trovatore*—Milan, 1957
https://www.youtube.com/watch?v=Bv1d-QtY8Zk

Donizetti—*Poliuto*—Barcelona, 1975
Once an important revival of Maria Callas' this Barcelona performance finds Gencer in fine fettle surrounded by Amedeo Zambon, Vincente Sardinero, Ferrucio Mazzoli and conducted by Giuseppe Morelli. Gencer even treats the Barcelona audience to an (at the time) rare sustained high D at the end of Act II—and it is a very good one. There is pandemonium afterwards.

Donizetti—*Poliuto*—Barcelona, 1975
https://www.youtube.com/watch?v=DuLiVcy9ljQ

Other Gencer performances on YouTube:
Verdi—*Rigoletto*—Buenos Aires, 1961 with Cornell MacNeil, Gianni Raimondi, Giorgio Algorta—conducted by Argeo Quadri
https://www.youtube.com/watch?v=RUQm3pBv2ns

Verdi—I Vespri Siciliani—Rome, 1964—with Giangiacomo Guelfi, Gastone Limarilli, Nicola Rossi-Lemeni—conducted by Gianadrea Gavazzeni
https://www.youtube.com/watch?v=AvsIxrCPnmw

Verdi—Simon Boccanegra—Vienna, 1961 with Tito Gobbi, Rolando Panerai, Giorgio Tozzi, Giuseppe Zampieri—conducted by Gianadrea Gavazzeni
https://www.youtube.com/watch?v=PNX2pCm4Uik

Bellini—*I puritani***—**Buenos Aires, 1961 with Gianni Raimondi, Ferruccio Mazzoli, Manuel Ausensi, Mario Verazzi—conducted by Argeo Quadri
https://www.youtube.com/watch?v=IgIme57Z4DY

Rocca—*Monte Ivnor***—**Milan, 1957 with Miriam Pirazzini, Renato Gavarini, Anselmo Colzani—conducted by Armando La Rosa Parodi—an odd opera if there ever was one.
https://www.youtube.com/watch?v=EsPKoNWv_yU

Donizetti—*Lucrezia Borgia***—**Naples, 1966 with Giacomo Aragall, Anna Maria Rot Mario Petri, Giuseppe Moretti—conducted by Carlo Franci. There are no fewer than 3 different performances of this opera with Gencer on YouTube. This Naples performance was a historical revival of the work and one of Gencer's great performances. Even so, there were still a few problems. Due to her over-enthusiasm she shreds her voice on a high C during the Act I duet with Alphonso (Mario Petri) on the line: "Ti potria fa la Borgia pentir." It doesn't stop her, however, and she goes on to finish the very dramatic duet with a fine penultimate high C. (Petri almost enters but, realizing his mistake, backs away immediately). This was her first Lucrezia and like all the others, she interpolates a long high D at the end of the Prologue -when her identity has been revealed.

Donizetti—*Lucrezia Borgia***—**Naples, 1966
https://www.youtube.com/watch?v=sRU92Fv6oXg

Donizetti—*Lucrezia Borgia***—**Dallas, 1974 with Jose Carreras, Tatriana Troyanos, Matteo Manuguerra, Nicola Zaccariah—conductod by Nicola Rescigno. This in-house tape was to commemorate one of Gencer's few appearances in the United States. It was a memorable night. Gencer was in fine fettle offering all the Gencer trademark singing—includid a good high D interpolated at the end of the Prologue. The "modi, ah modi" in the final scene was haunting. Jose Carreras was full of youthful exuberance and Tatiana Troyanos gave a remarkable rendition of the Brindisi with a couple of fantastic high Cs.

Donizetti—*Lucrezia Borgia***—**Dallas 1974
https://www.youtube.com/watch?v=OwxipxuN7X0

Although late in her career, this 1979 performance of *Lucrezia Borgia* from Florence pairs her with the great Alfredo Kraus (a rarity). The end of the Prologue is still capped with one of her high Ds. The lovely "Come bello" from the Prologue is unusually smooth with some exquisite piano singing.

Donizetti—*Lucrezia Borgia***—**Florence, 1979
https://www.youtube.com/watch?v=M3td6kQv4jo

Donizetti—*Caterina Cornaro***—**New Jersey Opera, 1973 with Giuseppe Campora, Samuel Ramey, Giuseppe Taddei, James Morris—conducted by Alfredo Silipigni. This is another invaluable in-house tape of an important revival. With a cast of excellent singers, this is one to cherish. Gencer takes a bit to warm up, but delivers the goods in her typical Gencer "style." She even manages to offer one of her eonderful high Ds—this time at the end of Act I.
https://www.youtube.com/watch?v=eGkaQKdcwY0

Leyla Gencer MYTO "Solo" Volumes:
Volume 1 (1954–1957); Volume II (1957-1958); Volume III (1958–1959)

There are three volumes in the Leyla Gencer recital series on the MYTO label. The selections take the listener from the year of her Italian debut (1954) to just before her ascendancy as a Donizetti specialist. Gencer, like Callas and Olivero, was not a miniaturist, but painted in broad strokes. To get the full flavor of her art one needs to hear an entire scene. MYTO has been extremely clever in their selections. There are many wonderful tracks throughout the three discs, but I would like to mention a few surprises on volumes one and two.

Volume one has an "Un bel di" from her Italian debut in 1954, as well as selections from some unusual repertoire for this diva—Eugene Onegin, *Die Entführung aus dem Serail* (an excellent "Martern aller Arten" from a 1957 concert) as well as a creator's recording from Dialogues of the Carmelites, and an exquisite aria from Rocca's Monte Ivnor. This last is the sleeper of the album. It is an odd, exotic piece full of Moorish, chant-like inflections that is capped by a remarkably beautiful pianissimo high C.

Volume two has another creator's performance, Pizzetti's Assassinio nella Cattedrale. Perhaps the most important excerpts, however, are from Naples performances of *Suor Angelica* and *Il Tabarro*. They leave one wishing that the complete performances had been released. The Suor Angelica is especially moving. It takes the listener from a lovely "Senza mama" to the end of the opera where Gencer is incredibly moving, providing not only hefty top Cs, but also a softly spun high C that puts to shame a number of commercially recorded efforts. Conducted by Serafin, these excerpts alone are worth the price of the disc.

An excellent Leyla Gencer Collection on YouTube:
https://www.youtube.com/watch?v=7X3kVavSN1k

A much-abbreviated version of this section first appeared in parterre box #38, 199

AND THEN THERE WAS LEONIE RYSANEK
OUR RUNNER-UP QUEEN
(1926–1998)

Some singers become legendary for good reason. Leonie Rysanek was one such singer. Like Olivero and Gencer, Rysanek's live performances have been well-served by the CD medium. At least 30 are available on CD and at least 250 performances exist in private collections. Her voice, unmistakably recognizable with all its flaws and imperfections, is a trusted friend to my ears. Its weaknesses and its strengths have provided me with many unforgettable hours of listening.

She was not a perfect singer, however. There were always problems with her voice, many of which were never corrected.

When she was not fully warmed up, her middle voice was sluggish and incorrectly placed. Like molasses, it gurgled around pitches and it was often hollow-sounding and wildly erratic. However, when she finally did settle into her middle register, the result was like sinking into a soft, comfy sofa. She did not have much of a chest register, and when she used it, it was often squeezed out like paste from a tube of toothpaste.

Her sense of pitch during rising vocal lines could be as erratic as her middle register—the voice often veering off the mark and sharping—especially in the upper transition area of F# and G. She had little affinity for "little black notes" (coloratura), as surviving broadcasts of Macbeth and Nabucco prove. (Singing Nabucco was an admitted mistake on the diva's part, but the surviving documents are exciting nonetheless.) Since the beginning of her career, her voice sounded unusually mature. This didn't help when portraying youthful characters.

So, what were her good points? Firstly, she had commitment to whatever music she was singing. Although some might question whether this as an attribute, it is a quality that is lacking in many artists who sing before the public. Her voice was a beautiful, lush, rapidly spun instrument of great power and luminescence. Most remarkable was the glory of her top register, which she approached with almost reckless abandon.

She perfected a vocal effect early in her career that served her well and provided many moments of excitement for her listeners. It was the manner in which she approached many high notes. She thrust up to them with great abandon. The act of "lunging" was one of her secrets. Similar to (but not the same as) the effect used by Leyla Gencer in her piano singing. It was resourceful and suited not only the music she sang, but also her temperament.

Once the actual thrust was achieved, Rysanek let the pitch and its height do the work for her, never actually forcing or pressing on the top register. Fortunately, she had prodigious breath control to back up these effects. When you add her tendency to sharp, her singing could have an almost primal effect on listeners.

I believe that Rysanek's tendency to sharp was one of the reasons for the longevity of her instrument and career -47 years, from 1949 to 1996.

A singer will generally warm up their voice for a performance by making sure they can sing the notes necessary for the role they are singing (with perhaps one or two notes to spare). By sitting on the top side of a pitch, she stretched that pitch upward (to where high B-flats came closer to B natural and high C veered closer to C-sharp), Rysanek kept her voice and range constantly "oiled." I'm not saying that she consciously "stretched" her voice; it seemed an idiosyncratic result of combining the physiological structure of her voice and its vibrato, with her particular manner of singing. But it may have been one of the reasons why she was able to keep the high and very difficult role of the Empress in Die Frau ohne Schatten in her repertoire for thirty years! It might also explain why she retained so much of the lush sheen of her top register. This same sharping and resulting longevity can also be heard in the work of Placido Domingo and Birgit Nilsson.

This inadvertent stretching of the voice is similar to a trick that some singers use when they find themselves having trouble with an aria. When experiencing a problem sustaining an aria's tessitura (the general area in which notes lie), singers will practice the aria a half-step up from where it was originally written in order to encourage their voice (and muscles) to stretch into a higher tessitura. There is a pattern to this process. First the music is sung in the higher key once or twice and then left alone for a day or so. The singer then returns to sing the music again in the higher key and again leaves the music alone for a day or so; and so on. This is repeated until the singer finds the music more comfortable in their voice. When the voice begins finally to stretch into the new area, the singer returns to the original key. Almost without fail, they find that the original key is no longer difficult. Rysanek's method of vocal production was similar to this.

As Ralph V. Lucano noted in a review of a CD of Rysanek in Fanfare (1995), "…[Her voice] was too big for the microphones, and its ability to expand in the upper range like a mushroom cloud had to be witnessed to be believed..."

The Career

Leonie Rysanek was born in Vienna in 1926. Her mother was Austrian; her father a stonecutter of Czech descent who later became a chauffeur. During her youth and the war years, Leonie worked in a munitions factory. She wanted to be an actress, but her oldest brother encouraged her to take singing more seriously. She entered the Vienna Academy at sixteen, where she studied with Alfred Jerger, and later with Rudolf Grossmann, a baritone, who, in 1950, became her first husband. They were later divorced. In 1968 she married Ernst-Ludwig Gausmann, a journalist. They remained married until her death nearly thirty years later.

Rysanek made her concert debut in 1948. Her opera debut came a year later at the age of twenty-three in Innsbruck as Agathe in Weber's Der Freischütz. She sang her final performance, as Klytämnestra in *Elektra*, at the Salzburg Festival in August 1996 when she was 70.

> In 1951, the Bayreuth Festival reopened and the new leader Wieland Wagner asked her to sing Sieglinde (in *Die Walküre*). He was convinced that her unique, young and beautiful voice, combined with her rare acting abilities, would create a sensation. She became a star overnight, and the role of Sieglinde followed her for the rest of her career. (Wikipedia)

Wagner—*Die Walküre* (exc) Act 3 complete—Bayreuth August, 1951
https://www.youtube.com/watch?v=6AfFW49iGIc

Strauss—*Der Liebe der Danae*—London, 1953
Another early performance featuring Leonie Rysanek is the historic broadcast from Covent Garden, September 1953, with Ferdinand Frantz, Howard Vandenburg, August Seider, Kathe Nentwig, conducted by Kurt Eichhorn.
https://www.youtube.com/watch?v=xBFBkgR8lGQ

Rysanek joined the Saarbrücken Opera in 1950 for a three-year period, singing Arabella, Donna Anna (*Don Giovanni*), Senta (*Der Fliegende Holländer*), Leonora (La forza del destino) and Sieglinde in *Die Walküre*. She returned to Bayreuth in 1958 as Elsa in Lohengrin, in 1964 as Elisabeth in *Tannhäuser*, and in 1982 as Kundry in *Parsifal*.

She sang all over the world, but was especially loved in Munich and Vienna where she made her debut in 1954 as Aïda at the Vienna Staatsoper. She sang there until 1992 in more than 500 performances. Her last appearance was as Kabanicha in *Kátja Kabanová*. Rysanek received many honors during the course of her career, but perhaps the most appropriate one was the title: Kammersänger—a German honorific reserved for distinguished singers of opera and classical music.

The records of the Vienna Sataatsoper show some interesting statistics. Rysanek's most often performed role was the Marschallin in *Der Rosenkavalier* (61 performances) *Tosca*—53 performances. Sieglinde in *Die Walküre* came next with 46 and Chrysothemis in *Elektra* with 45. *Salome* had 38 performances and Die Frau ohne Schatten 35.

She was also a favored singer at the Metropolitan Opera in New York. Rysanek made her United States debut with the San Francisco opera in 1956 as Senta in Der Fliegende Holländer. For the next four years San Francisco heard her as Sieglinde, Aïda, *Turandot*, Amelia in *Un Ballo in Maschera*, Leonora in La forza del destino, Elisabeth in *Tannhäuser*, and Lady Macbeth in Macbeth, the role in which she made an "unscheduled" debut at the Metropolitan in 1959, by replacing Maria Callas in the Verdi opera.

Rysanek made her New York debut on March 26, 1958, at Carnegie Hall in a concert performance of Verdi's Macbeth with the Little Orchestra Society conducted by Thomas Scherman. William Chapman was Macbeth, Donald Gramm was Banquo, and John McCollum was an excellent Macduff. The performance was truncated in that there was no act III duet for Macbeth and his Lady, and no final aria for Macbeth. Rysanek was in fine fettle, her voice soaring into Carnegie Hall with power and great energy. She offered a superb high D-flat not only in the sleepwalking scene, but also at the finish of act I. The performance, having been broadcast, has survived with pretty good sound quality for the era. It is now a revered cult item. Luckily, YouTuber "Best Opera Moments" uploaded it so that all could enjoy.

Verdi—*Macbeth*—Carnegie Hall, 1958
https://www.youtube.com/watch?v=zE8eETKMrW4

While much has been made of the Callas/Bing/Rysanek/Macbeth story, the truth is that Rysanek had already been hired by the Metropolitan Opera and was scheduled to make her debut in Aïda. When Bing fired Callas from Macbeth, he approached Rysanek about taking over. Since she had already received notoriety in the New York press for singing Lady Macbeth in the March, 1958 Carnegie Hall concert with the Little Orchestra Society, she was an obvious choice.

Although the February 1959 Metropolitan Opera broadcast is not yet on YouTube (it is on CD), the January 1960 broadcast is available.

Verdi—*Macbeth*—Metropolitan Opera, January 1960 with Leonard Warren, Daniele Barioni, Jerome Hines, William Olvis, Teresa Stratas (21 years old)—conducted by Erick Leinsdorf.
https://www.youtube.com/watch?v=rDjWfG7fPUQ

Another Macbeth is now on YouTube. It was Rysanek's last Met broadcast of the opera. In the March 1962 performance, she is with Anselmo Colzani, Carlo Bergonzi, George Shirley, Giorgio Tozzi and conducted by Joseph Rosenstock.
https://www.youtube.com/watch?v=rRPC9mKz2uo

In the hands of a great singing-actress such as Leonie Rysanek, Lady Macbeth's music becomes doubly potent and exciting. Miss Rysanek did not have the complete ease in her upper register that she had two seasons ago (she barely tipped the D-Flat in the Sleepwalking Scene), but otherwise this is still one of the memorable vocal and dramatic characterizations of this decade. She has sharpened her portrayal of the Sleepwalking Scene to a rare point of dramatic excellence. As she sang "Andiam Macbetto," she seemed to be actually pulling an invisible and frightened Macbeth from the scene of their crime." (John Ardoin, Musical America, review of a performance earlier in the run.)

Despite making an early debut at Covent Garden (1953) Rysanek rarely sang there, (only Chrysothemis in *Elektra*, Sieglinde in *Die Walküre*, *Tosca*, and the Marschallin in *Der Rosenkavalier*).

She made her true Metropolitan Opera debut in February, 1959 as Lady Macbeth. She sang 299 performances of 24 roles in 38 years while there. She performed her farewell to the Met on January 2, 1996 as the Countess in Tchaikovsky's Pique Dame. Her affection for the audiences of the Metropolitan Opera was mirrored in that audience's love for the Viennese soprano.

Writing of her final performance (Pique Dame) at the Metropolitan Opera, Mike Silverman reported in the Associated Press:

> The applause on Tuesday was just as heartfelt, but tinged with sadness. Rysanek felt it too, giving way to tears the first few times she came out, dressed in a red ball gown and grayish-white wig, to stand beside conductor Valery Gergiev and fellow cast members Maria Guleghina, Gegam Grigorian, Dmitri Hvorostovksy and Nikolai Putilin.
>
> Finally, she shushed the audience and spoke briefly: 'It's very difficult for me ... I'd rather sing than talk. Thank you for 37 heavenly years. I love you, and God bless you.'
>
> The performance marked Rysanek's farewell to opera in America... Her last operatic appearance anywhere will be at the Salzburg Festival next August as Klytemnestra in Strauss' "Elektra."
>
> As the applause persisted well past midnight Tuesday, the Met management finally lowered the black fire curtain and turned up the house lights. That prompted a chorus of boos, and, so, out came Rysanek in front of the curtain for one last round of cheers from her diehard fans. They did not want to let her go. (AP, January 3, 1996)

When asked about the unusual length of her career, Rysanek said:

> "I was blessed by nature with a strong, healthy voice, and I worked very hard," she says. "But, most importantly, I knew how to say no. I never oversang; if anything, I undersang. I could have sung Brunnhilde or Isolde, but I never did. I didn't sing Salome until late in my career, and sang Elektra only once, for a film with Karl Bohm." (Leonie Rysanek Of Met, 25 Years of Memories, Tim Page, *The New York Times*, 1984)

Selected Recordings, Commercial and Live

Leonie Rysanek's recording history was odd and disjointed. Compared to many of her contemporaries, and considering her fame, Rysanek made few trips to the recording studio. Although her career spanned over forty years, she made commercial recordings only during the first ten.

Her first recordings were made for EMI in London in April of 1952 (shortly after her sensational debut at Bayreuth in August a year earlier), These recordings were:
Wagner: Three excerpts from *Der Fliegende Holländer* (two years before she first sang the role in Vienna in 1954)
Strauss; Arabella's Final Monologue
D'Albert: Marta's Aria (*Tiefland*)

In 1954 she was asked by Wilhelm Furtwaengler to sing Sieglinde in his complete recording of Wagner's *Die Walküre*.

In May of 1955, again for EMI, she recorded Leonora's act IV aria ("Pace, pace") from La forza del destino. In October of that year, she made LP albums of highlights from *Der Rosenkavalier* (during which she had a cold) and Aïda.

Strauss—*Der Rosenkavalier* (exc)—Berlin EMI with Elisabeth Grummer, Erika Köth, Gustav Neidlinger—conducted by Wilhelm Schüchter.
https://www.youtube.com/watch?v=m5lyO9mke6Q

A number of selections from these recording sessions were collected into a CD album called "Leonie Rysanek Opera Arias" (EMI References 5-65201) released in 1994.

Despite the brevity of her time in the recording studio she did leave some valuable studio recordings. As mentioned, her first complete opera recording was Wilhelm Furtwaengler's *Die Walküre* (EMI, 1954) where she was paired with an equally intense Marta Mödl as Brünnhilde, Ferdinand Frantz as Wotan, Ludwig Suthaus, Margarethe Klose, Gottlob Frick, and with Erika Köth (of all people) as a dynamic Helmwige. This was the first complete recording of the opera. It continues to be revered despite the many recordings that have followed. After this came the important, first recording of Die Frau ohne Schatten with Hans Hopf, Elisabeth Höngen, Christel Goltz, Paul Schöffler, conducted by Karl Böhm (Decca, 1955) and then *Fidelio* (DGG, 1956).

Strauss—*Die Frau ohne Schatten*—Decca 1955 (first recording)
https://www.youtube.com/watch?v=QS-IT7xOLT4

After a switch to RCA Victor in 1958, Rysanek recorded an introductory album of operatic arias, including arias from La forza del destino, Aïda, *Tosca*, Andrea Chenier, Cavalleria rusticana, *Turandot*, and *Otello*. A remarkable album, it offers some invaluable singing from this artist. This album was followed by the making of complete opera sets of Macbeth (with Leonard Warren in 1959), *Otello* (1960), Fliegende Holländer and Ariadne auf Naxos (1961). Except for a single Herodias in *Salome* with conductor Giuseppe Sinopoli for DGG in 1990, she did not record commercially after 1961.

Inexplicably, Rysanek never made complete recordings of some of her most famous roles—*Salome*, Chrysothemis in *Elektra*, *Tosca*, or the Marschallin in *Der Rosenkavalier*. Neither did she record her later triumphs as Ortrude in Lohengrin, Kostelnichka in Jenufa or Santuzza in Cavalleria Rusticana.

Perhaps, in a way, this is not a surprise. Rysanek was a creature of the stage. To be fully appreciated and understood, one needed to experience her in the theater. Fortunately, her career coincided with the era of pirate recording and her great roles were preserved. Today, in addition to her commercial recordings, one can hear (sometimes multiple) performances of Rysanek in *Fidelio, Medea, Jenufa, Cavalleria Rusticana, La Gioconda, Tosca, Dalibor, Die ägyptische Helena, Ariadne auf Naxos, Elektra, Die Frau ohne schatten, Der Rosenkavalier, Salome, Un Ballo in Maschera, Don Carlo, Macbeth, Nabucco, Der fliegende Holländer, Parsifal, Tannhäuser,* and *Die Walküre.*

The earliest Leonie Rysanek live item preserved, is act III from the 1951 broadcast of *Die Walküre* at Bayreuth. It was the first post-war performance and her Bayreuth debut. She sang with Astrid Varnay and Sigurd Bjoerling; conducted by Herbert von Karajan. It is available on EMI References CD.

1953 presented two more live-recorded operas featuring the soprano: Weber's Oberon and Strauss's Electra (Chrysothemis). Each successive decade brought forth more live performances saved for posterity. The reason is not hard to understand—every performance featuring Leonie Rysanek is its own world.

Wagner—*Die Walküre* (EMI CD CHS 7630435 2) with Marta Mödl, Ludwig Suthaus, Ferdinand Frantz, Margarete Klose, Gottlob Frick; Wilhelm Furtwangler conductor. 1954

Recorded only three years after her sensational debut at Bayreuth, Rysanek is fresh-voiced, spirited, and committed. There are unique qualities that Rysanek brings to this, her first recorded role. She sang Sieglinde over 200 times for 37 years in 33 productions. It was a signature role. Along with Chrysothemis in *Elektra* it was probably one of her most-often performed characters. This is a classic Wagner recording and every opera lover should have it in their collection. First, there is a finely drawn Brünnhilde by Marta Mödl, caught in her dramatic soprano heyday. It is a portrayal rich in nuance and color, and contains constant surprises. No matter how familiar one is with her work, additional hearings will prompt some new insight previously overlooked. Ferdinand Frantz is a Wotan of tremendous virility, yet evokes poignant gentleness during the opera's final pages. Klose is wonderful as the hectoring Fricka and, refreshingly, this Fricka sings, rather than barks. Rysanek is a womanly Sieglinde (her "Du bist der Lenz" provides an exquisite, enthralling moment) and she and Suthaus are involved, convincing lovers. You will find this an engrossing listening experience imbued with rich detail by Furtwaengler's leadership. He died just two months after this recording was made.

Across the 37 years that she sang Sieglinde, Rysanek became famous for her interpolated scream in the first act.

> During her long career, Rysanek has been lionized—or criticized—almost as much for her histrionic intensity as for her opulent voice with its gleaming top extension. She invented, for example, Sieglinde's much imitated coital scream when Siegmund pulls the sword from the tree in the first act of Die Walkure. (Chris Pasles, Los Angeles Times, 9/9/94)

Obviously enamored with the effect, Rysanek also supplied similar screams in Die Frau ohne Schatten and *Elektra.*

Wagner—*Die Walküre*—Angel 1954 (originally)
https://www.youtube.com/watch?v=ZaJBcT-Nqt0

1955—Verdi: *Aïda* Vienna 5/10/55 (MYTO MCD 023.267) with Hans Hopf, Jean Madeira, George London, Gottlob Frick; Rafael Kubelik, conductor.

Rysanek's famous Vienna Aida (in German) from May 10, 1955 was originally released on Mr Tape's "Legendary Recordings" LP label back in the early 1980s. Since then, it has been released on MYTO CD. This was an important performance as it occurred during the reopening of the Vienna Staatsoper. Rysanek is incandescent in the title role, partnered by a remarkably volatile Jean Madeira as Amneris, Hans Hopf was Radames and George London sang a strong and pushy Amonasro. All are led sublimely by Rafael Kubelik. Although the performance is sung in German it still manages to convey surprisingly authentic Italianate fire in the singing of the principles. Especially nice is hearing the much under-appreciated Jean Madiera in a role worthy of her art. The scenes between Madiera and Rysanek are unforgettable.

Despite her success in the role, Aïda was a role primarily sung in Rysanek's youth.

> Aida was not a staple of her repertoire (it seems to have been active from about 1954 through 1963): she sang it 19 times in Wien (usually in German or bilingual performances with some colleagues singing in Italian), seven times with the Met (four at the house, three on tour), and three times with San Francisco Opera including one performance in Los Angeles. (leonie on the nile by Jungfer Marianne Leitmetzerin, parterre box, 11-14-16)

Available in somewhat rough-and-ready sound (on Melodram, and now YouTube) is a San Francisco opera performance (1960) taped in-house. The sonics are nowhere near the clarity of the 1955 broadcast from Vienna, but to be able to hear Leonie Rysanek sing the role in Italian with Jon Vickers is a treat.

Verdi—*Aïda*—Vienna 1955 with Hans Hopf, Jean Madeira, George London conducted by Rafael Kubelik.

https://www.youtube.com/watch?v=lIxxs3RLd0U

Verdi—*Aïda*—San Francisco, 1960 with Jon Vickers, Irene Dalis, Robert Weede, Giorgio Tozzi, conducted by Francesco Molinari-Pradelli.

https://www.youtube.com/watch?v=EkpeZpl-dIY

Strauss—*Die Ägyptische Helena* Munich August, 1956 with Annelies Kupper, Bernd Aldenhoff, Hermann Uhde, Ira Malaniuk—conducted by Josef Keilberth.

What an evocative beginning this opera has. This is a lovely, eccentric score and an odd story but, oh my, what a performance! The Orfeo CD release (Orfeo CD C 424 962) is excellent documentation of this important 1956 Munich revival. In spectacular sound it is one of the few recordings I have found that gives an accurate aural picture of the Rysanek instrument. Not only is the sweeping soar of her top register perfectly captured, but her fine range of dynamics as well. Rysanek's voice had one of those top registers that blossomed as it ascended. In this performance one experiences the tremendous impact the effect had in a theater venue.

A surprise is the solidity of her middle register. Although thick and unwieldy in places, it is full of color. High Bs and Cs and even the C-sharp in the famous awakening scene, soar fearlessly into the theater's acoustics. There are a number of high Cs in act II that are some of the most glorious and exciting sounds Rysanek ever sang. The trademark Rysanek sharping is evident but it is counterbalanced by her fascinating tapering of phrases, leaning into tones and her many finely spun pianissimi.

There are actually two performances from this production circulating—this August 10, 1956 performance and a later one from August 27, 1967. Both are recommended.

This performance (as do all Rysanek's Strauss) underlines an incongruity. While there is no doubt that Rysanek was a premiere Strauss specialist of the twentieth century, her singing belies this. Strauss's vocal lines demand an ability to pinpoint pitch and then move rapidly forward. In many ways Rysanek was incapable of doing this. Her voice needed time to settle into a pitch. Actually, I feel that she was an "impressionist" of soprano singers. Her voice and pitch, while in the midst of complex Strauss lines, found itself sketching pitches rather than delineating them. To better understand this, compare Rysanek's final scene from *Salome* with that sung by Ljuba Welitsch (or Behrens, or Nilsson). That said, Rysanek's instinct for the construction and direction of a Straussian phrase was infallible—her freely soaring top register was the real thing.

Kupper's Aithra is not as fresh in timbre as is Barbara Hendricks on Gwyneth Jones' complete recording, but there is something endearing about her portrayal despite its shrewishness. She certainly understands the particular complexities of Strauss phrasing. She manages Aithra's awkward leap to high D during the act I finale with ease and great beauty. Aldenhoff and Uhde provide excellent contributions. Indeed, Aldenhoff's clean, clear timbre contrasts well with Rysanek's more burnished color.

Fortunately, for those who prefer to possess only one version of an opera, they need not worry. The Gwyneth Jones commercial recording is of the original version. However, the Orfeo release is the Strauss-revised version so you can own both without feeling you are overdoing a good thing. They are considerably different, especially in the structure and music of act II. Both have superb "Awakening Scenes" in act 2.

While speaking about the awakening scene it should be noted that there are some wonderful recordings available of this piece: Rysanek, Jones, Rose Pauly, Alessandra Marc, Kiri Te Kanawa, and others. However, Leontyne Price's version, recorded more than fifty years ago for RCA Victor, remains the supreme classic performance. The combination of her smoky, dusky timbre, sensual manner with the music, and easy, soaring, warmly spun voice cannot be bettered. That recording should be a Straussian cornerstone in everyone's record collection.

Strauss: ***Die Aegyptische Helena—Munich 1956***
   https://www.youtube.com/watch?v=p49ZPr_7LeE&t=48s
   Verdi—*Macbeth*—RCA 1959 with Leonard Warren, Carlo Bergonzi, Jerome Hines—conducted by Erich Leinsdorf.

This was the first commercial recording of Verdi's early masterpiece. As most people know, Rysanek replaced Callas for the Met premiere and covered herself with glory (as this recording proves). She may not have had the florid dash or the psychological insight that Maria Callas (or Marta Mödl) brought to the role, but Rysanek's idiosyncratic voice provides an unusually vivid portrait of a woman on the brink of madness.

Rysanek sang three broadcasts of Macbeth at the Met: 1959, 1960, and 1962. All three are available on CD and all are recommended for the exciting singing they contain and the sense of occasion that they exhibit.

Oddly, despite her international notoriety singing this role, she never sang it at her "home" house in Vienna. After 1962, she seems to have laid the role to rest, concentrating on other Italian heroines: Tosca, Desdemona in *Otello*, Amelia in *Un Ballo in Maschera*, and Elisabetta in Don Carlo.

This 1959 studio recording is a classic recording. Rysanek is paired with the Macbeth of

Leonard Warren, whose warm, human character, obviously troubled with insecurities from the start, provides a strong contrast to Rysanek's temperamental Lady coupled to a youthful, copper-voiced Carlo Bergonzi. Dramatically, Rysanek's delineation of Lady Macbeth's mental instability is smooth and inevitable. Vocally, she is up to almost all the florid demands of this difficult score. Her high notes have a glorious sheen, including the interpolation of an excellent top D-flat at the end of act I. In this case, her peculiar middle register works to her credit—providing fascinating colors during the course of the opera and especially in the sleepwalking scene.

Wagner—*Der Fliegende Holländer*—Bayreuth Festival July 1959, with George London, Fritz Uhl, Joseph Greindl, conducted by Wolfgang Sawallisch.

Senta in *Der Fliegende Holländer* was a very important role for Rysanek, especially in the first decade-and-a-half of her career. In addition to the number of times she sang the role at Bayreuth and in Europe during the 1960s, she sang 32 performances of the role at the Metropolitan Opera. No other role in her repertoire at the Metropolitan was repeated as many times, the closest being Elisabeth in *Tannhäuser* (31).

Despite minor flaws, the Bayreuth performance is magical and in excellent sound. It preserves a famous production with the pairing of Rysanek with George London being especially potent. His solid, impenetrable Dutchman is almost frightening in its strength, while Senta's obsessive passion for him is perfectly depicted in Rysanek's (at times wild) vocalism. Conductor Wolfgang Sawallisch provides a propulsive account of the score. He is more dynamic and exciting than Antall Dorati on Decca in 1961. The entire Bayreuth performance is wonderful, but the power of the final scene is remarkable—Rysanek's high Bs blow everyone off the stage. If you choose to have only one Dutchman with Rysanek, this is the one. If you want another, find the 1966 Milan performance with Crass as the Dutchman again with Sawallisch conducting. It is on the budget label, Opera Doro. Further, there are three Metropolitan Opera broadcasts:1960 (just months after the famous Bayreuth performance),1963, and 1968. Because Senta was another signature role of Rysanek's, comparisons between them is a fascinating listen. Below are five links to YouTube.

Wagner—*Der Fliegende Holländer*—Bayreuth 1959
https://www.youtube.com/watch?v=4juFfHrv3E0&t=245s
Wagner—*Der Fliegende Holländer*—Decca Commercial 1961
https://www.youtube.com/watch?v=u5hc9HNPay4
Wagner—*Der Fliegende Holländer*—Metropolitan Opera broadcast 1963
https://www.youtube.com/watch?v=XGXVvaHNrJo
Wagner—*Der Fliegende Holländer*—Milan 1966
https://www.youtube.com/watch?v=KPHICknWHaM
Wagner—*Der Fliegende Holländer*—Metropolitan Opera broadcast 1970
https://www.youtube.com/watch?v=vbu6yrOBH2g

Verdi—*Otello* RCA C *Otello* D 09026-63180-2 with Jon Vickers, Tito Gobbi, Miriam Pirazzini; Tullio Serafin. (The original three-LP release included the ballet which was omitted on the two-CD reissue)

Considering her fame in such Germanic roles as Sieglinde, Senta and Chrysothemis, one might forget that Rysanek first came to the Metropolitan Opera to sing Italian roles.

Like Ariadne auf Naxos, this *Otello* was originally recorded by Decca but "lent" to RCA. It was part of the fabulous Soria RCA LP sets that, when originally released, came with a large, beautiful libretto filled with color photographs, recording sessions shots, and articles about the work and the artists. It was pretty much the last word in sumptuous LP opera albums.

This is in many ways a classic recording. It puts forth a combination of first-rate operatic actors: Vickers, Gobbi, and Rysanek, who are led by a master conductor, Tullio Serafin. The result, while uneven at times, is never less than fascinating and often is transcendental. The sound is superb; typical of the excellent recording work by Decca that took place during that era. Vickers, who had yet to sing *Otello* on stage, but who was to become famous for his portrayal of the Moor, is found here in ringing, virile voice. His interpretation may have broadened and become more subtle by the time of the later Karajan recording, but if I could have only one of his two *Otello* recordings, I would choose this one. At the Metropolitan Opera, Vickers sang at least 3 *Otello* broadcasts during the 1970s, and twelve other live performances of him in that role circulate among collectors. Tito Gobbi's kaleidoscopic timbre creates an Iago not easily forgotten, his slimy insinuations against Desdemona during act II are the stuff of nightmares.

Rysanek, as Alan Blyth candidly comments in his review for Gramophone, is "not ideally steady" in her singing of Desdemona. She does, however, bring a feminine quality to the role along with her considerable musicianship. There are many moments of absolutely beautiful singing. Her voice is caught well by the microphones, as is the idiosyncratic placement of her slippery middle register. Desdemona is perhaps not a showcase role for the particular glories of the Rysanek instrument, but it is an excellent verification of her ability to let loose with some huge, exciting sounds. Not only that, but she is still able to trim her voice down to spin soft piani of great beauty. The act III duet, with *Otello*: "Dio di Giocondi" shows superb interplay between the two singers and prompts beautiful phrasing from Rysanek. As one might expect, the famous "Willow Song" from act IV is one of the highlights of the Rysanek performance.

Verdi—*Otello***—**Rome 1960 with Jon Vickers, Tito Gobbi—Tullio Serafin
https://www.youtube.com/watch?v=NVvQ-kLq5xo

Strauss—*Ariadne auf Naxos* Decca CD 443675-2 with Roberta Peters, Sena Jurinac, Jan Peerce, Walter Berry, Mimi Coertse; Erich Leinsdorf, conductor.

It will take effort to find this CD set as Decca did not feel there was enough of a market to release it in America. It has been available only as an import from Europe. (At the time of this writing, it is not yet on YouTube.) This was another of the famous RCA Soria releases (Like the *Otello* above, it was originally recorded for RCA by Decca). The original LP release is somewhat a collector's item because of the extravagant booklet that accompanied the set. This is very well recorded. It was the first stereophonic recording of this opera. While there are many Ariadnes to choose from today, this recording was released when there was but one other version, the classic EMI set with Elisabeth Schwarzkopf and Rita Streich.

Rysanek is appropriately divatic if not as nuanced as Schwarzkopf. She lets loose with glorious upper register singing that is often missed among other singers who essay the role. Roberta Peters' Zerbinetta is one of the best. The only drawback is that the placement of her top register did not take well to the recording process. However, when it comes to assurance in complex florid work, easy high Ds and Es and elegant humor, you can't beat Peters. Peerce is perfectly acceptable as Bacchus, but maybe not ideal; Jurinac sings a composer to savor. An added bonus in the casting is Mimi Coertse as Najade. Coertse was an under-appreciated artist of which you can hear proof in the classic Solti-conducted Arabella (on London). She is easily the most appealing Fiakermilli on disc. She brings to that thankless and impossibly difficult role superb musicianship, exquisite vocalism, and secure coloratura—plus spectacular high Ds!

If you are interested in a live version of Rysanek in Ariadne, you may be able to find the 1967 Vienna performance (on Melodram) with Rysanek and Jeannette Scovotti singing a charming and bright Zerbinetta. Tatiana Troyanos is one of the best Composers you can hear. This is a wonderful, exciting performance. Both the commercial and the live recordings deserve a space in your collection.

Strauss—*Ariadne auf Naxos*—Vienna November, 1967 with Leonie Rysanek, Jeanette Scovotti, Tatiana Troyanos, James King, Erich Kunz—Karl Böhm
https://www.youtube.com/watch?v=XI9WriU3EPU&t=2s

Strauss—*Die Frau Ohne Schatten* DGG CD 457-678-2 Vienna June, 1964 with Christa Ludwig, Grace Hoffman, Jess Thomas, Walter Berry; Herbert von Karajan, conductor.

Rysanek knew her strengths and was aware of her weaknesses. It is said that when she was to first sing Die Frau ohne schatten in August of 1954 in Munich, (see below) it was planned that she sing the role of the Frau, not the Empress. She looked at the score and noticed that most of the high notes lay within the part of the Empress and immediately went to the theater's intendant. She told him that if she was to sing in this opera, it must be as the Empress. This began a love affair between a soprano and an operatic role that was to last more than thirty years.

> The more coveted and sympathetic role was the dyer's wife, Die Frau of the title, later a favorite of Miss Nilsson's. But Miss Rysanek was attracted to the stony Empress. 'I looked at the score, saw the high D's and thought: I have the best top in the world. I am the Empress! Ach, I was so arrogant.'
> (*A Diva's Farewell: Myriad High C's And Few Regrets*, Anthony Tommasini, The New York Times, 1-1-96)

Rysanek's belief in this opera was matched by Karl Böhm, as well as all of the principals who took part on the first commercial recording made for Decca in 1955. Decca was hesitant to record such an unknown work—especially one of such complexity. In an unprecedented move, and to their credit, all agreed to record the opera without fees.

I learned this opera from the 1963 DGG live recording from Munich. It was presented at the inauguration of the rebuilt Munich Bayerischer Staatsoper on November 21, 1963 with a cast that included Ingrid Bjoener, Jess Thomas, Inge Borkh, Marta Mödl and Dietrich Fischer-Dieskau, with Ingeborg Hallstein and Brigitte Fassbaender singing lesser roles. That live recording remains a favorite of mine despite the fact that its conductor, Josef Keilberth hacked the score to bits. Bjoener may not have the soaring top register of Rysanek, but her voice, based on "float" rather than "spin," has different merits. Where Rysanek had a sumptuous slush in her sound, Bjoerner had a clean, cool edge to her voice that suits the Empress's ethereal character, thus enabling the many thrusting lines of the role to emerge brilliantly. This is especially evident in the quality of her other-world pianissimi and the touching naiveté of her timbre.

Recorded late in her career, Mödl is practically voiceless as the Nurse, but she somehow manages to carve out a characterization that is difficult to forget. Despite her limitations, she manages to triumphantly crown the end of act II with a high B-flat. She is mesmerizing in any scene she appears in and her tone painting of the demonic Nurse is effective and haunting. Inge

Borkh is a committed, shrewish Frau, her timbre contributing much to the success of her interpretation. Her occasional shrillness is tempered by the elegant, soft-toned Fischer-Dieskau. (He is a frightening force of nature in act II.) Their vocal combination works well. Although this 1963 set has had its detractors, I feel that its imperfections help to underline the great humanity of this classic work.

Rysanek's Empress is a masterly portrayal of this character. The role perfectly suited her voice and its abilities. As mentioned before, the singer certainly knew her voice inside and out. Pace Karajan's idiosyncratic trimming and rearrangement of the score in Vienna in 1964. The pairing of Christa Ludwig and Rysanek as the Frau and the Empress in that performances is electric. It took place two years before its famous Metropolitan premiere at the "new house." Here are two artists who can match each other in soaring Straussian lines. Along with her Marschallin in *Der Rosenkavalier*, Ludwig's Frau remains a crowning achievement in her career—the perfect match of voice and temperament to a role. Her intense performance and interplay with her real-life husband Walter Berry as Barak transcends art; it is sublime. Grace Hoffman is one of the finest Nurses one can hear. She sang the role for years. Her familiarity with the role shows the potential variability of its demonic portrayal. She is one of the highlights of this performance. Her dramatic finish to act II is probably the best you can find on disc.

The newly mastered DGG set of this 1964 production offers the best sound I have heard of this performance. I have heard perhaps four different versions. Produced well, with pictures of the production appearing in the libretto, this is a performance to savor. Rysanek was at a high point in her long career and, like the Egyptian Helen above, it is a performance that makes one want to get to one's knees to thank God that pirated live performances exist. (It also contains performances by the young Lucia Popp [still in her Queen of the Night days] and the wonderful Fritz Wunderlich.)

Collectors will undoubtedly want the later DGG release of a live 1977 Vienna performance with Rysanek, Birgit Nilsson as the Frau, James King, Walter Berry, and Ruth Hesse as a splendid Nurse. It is an excellent appendix to the 1964 Karajan. Below are just a few of the choices to be found on YouTube. Although the Metropolitan Opera 1966 or 1968 broadcasts are not yet on YouTube, I am sure they will be in the future.

Strauss—*Die Frau ohne Schatten*—Munich, August 1954—Leonie Rysanke (1st), Marianne Schech, Josef Metternich, Hans Hopf—Rudolf Kempe
https://www.youtube.com/watch?v=D27_A5mT3qQ&t=7709s

Strauss—*Die Frau ohne Schatten*—Decca Commercial 1955—Leonie Rysanek, Christel Goltz, Paul Schöffler, Hans Hopf, Elisabeth Höngen,—Karl Böhm
https://www.youtube.com/watch?v=QS-IT7xOLT4&t=210s

Strauss—*Die Frau ohne Schatten*—Vienna 1964—Leonie Rysanek, Christa Ludwig, Grace Hoffman, Walter Berry, Jess Thomas—Herbert von Karajan
https://www.youtube.com/watch?v=SGm3FsBnPEM&t=5s

Strauss—*Die Frau ohne Schatten*—Salzburg, 1974—Leonie Rysanek, Ursula Schöder-Feainen, James King, Walter Berry, Ruth Hesse—Karl Böhm
https://www.youtube.com/watch?v=iSnGDzV24qM&t=7025s

Strauss—*Die Frau ohne Schatten*—Vienna 1977—Leonie Rysanek, Birgit Nilsson, Walter Berry, Ruth Hesse, Lorenzo Alvary—Karl Böhm

Strauss—*Elektra*—Orfeo C 886 1421—Vienna, 1965 with Birgit Nilsson, Leonie Rysanek, Regina Resnik, Eberhard Waechter, Wolfgang Windgassen conducted by Karl Böhm.

A well-sung performance of *Elektra* is one of the most intense experiences one can have in an opera house. That is what you get with this release from Orfeo.

Standing Room Only (Legato Classics SRO CD7833-2) also released this performance decades ago in almost-comparable sound. As a bonus they included the final scene from *Salome* sung by both Rysanek (1974) and Nilsson (1954) along with fourteen minutes from a 1965 Bayreuth performance of act II of *Die Walküre* featuring both singers.

This is an invaluable documentation of a trio of singers (Nilsson, Rysanek and Resnik) all known for their performances of their roles in this opera. During the 1960s the three were often cast together in this work and this virtuoso performance demonstrates why.

It was recorded at the Vienna Staatsoper on December 16, 1965. The matching of the three voices (and temperaments) is a rare one. They contribute a frightening vividity to the score, an almost Freudian detailing of the psychological motivations of each character that bears up well under scrutiny. Böhm knows the music inside out. This is clear in his detailing of the magnificent, complex score.

The sound is quite acceptable on the Orfeo (and Legato) set with only an occasional overload appearing during the loudest passages. This is of no consequence in hearing the superb work done by the cast. Nilsson was a vocal phenomenon. This performance is a perfect display of her powers. She was an amazingly consistent singer and little difference can be found between her live performance and a studio recording. Caught in her prime, the jagged, often craggy high lines of the role are sung with complete assurance, nuance, and great beauty of tone. Like a force of nature, the Nilsson sound pours out without constriction or impediment and sweeps away all that is before her. Her scenes and the interplay with Rysanek as Chrysothemis and Regina Resnik as Klytemnestra are wonderful to experience. They benefit from multiple hearings. Rysanek is in fabulous voice and is vocally alluring as the gentler sister (who also demonstrates backbone). Her involvement in the music is almost palpable. The veteran, Resnik, famous for her Klytemnestra brings a harrowing realism to her part.

An added bonus is Gundula Janowitz as the fourth serving maid, and Danica Mastilovic (a future *Elektra*) as the domineering Overseer. Do yourself a favor, get this one, then lock all your doors.

(A visit by Vienna to Montreal—a 1967 performance—is included in the 31-CD Sony box set: "Birgit Nilsson the Great Live Recordings.")

One of the most interesting and coveted of *Elektra*s is the December 10, 1966, Metropolitan Opera broadcast with the trio of Nilsson, Rysanek, Resnik—conducted by Thomas Schippers. Fortunately, "Noack Somewhere" uploaded this fantastic broadcast in December of 2023—fifty-seven years later for all to enjoy.

Strauss—*Elektra*—Metropolitan Opera broadcast 1966
https://www.youtube.com/watch?v=NReADJBmdKY

My favorite Nilsson *Elektra* is probably the 1971 Metopolitan Opera broadcast with Jean Medeira—one of the great Klytemnestras and Leonie Rysanek as Chrysothemis. Conducted by Karl Karl Böhm.

This is one of those impossibly impassioned performances of the opera one can hear.

Madiera, near the end of her life gives a harrowing performance of the haunted queen with countless colors and nuances. Rysanek and Nilsson show their supremacy in their roles. This is not easily forgotten.

Strauss—*Elektra*—Metropolitan Opera—February 27, 1971
https://www.youtube.com/watch?v=LILNcHTHM0I&t=2s

Smetana: Dalibor (BMG CD74321 57735 2) Vienna, 1969 with Ludovico Spiess, Lotte Rysanek, Eberhard Waechter, Oscar Czerweka—conducted by Josef Krips.

This is a justly famous Rysanek performance. It was a German-sung revival of Smetana's work at the Vienna Staatsoper. The BMG recording of the archival tape is in superb stereo sound having tremendous dynamic range. It is unfortunate that the conductor, Josef Krips, elected to prune the score, thereby excising some of its finest music. It is also unfortunate that BMG does not include a libretto. (A previous MYTO release included a libretto, but the recording is of less enticing sound.)

The famous act I aria of Milada, "Ist es War" (the original Czech: "Jak je mi") (CD 1, track 15), was once a favorite with Emmy Destinn who recorded it twice (in 1908 and 1909). Destinn's performance is classic with few beating the combination of steely thrusted top notes and solid, chested low tones. Comparatively, Rysanek acquits herself well, if not surpassing her predecessor. The role of Milada is a dramatic tour de force and it suits Rysanek's voice and temperament. The wonderful tenor Ludovico Spiess, so neglected by commercial recording companies, proves what a loss this was for all of us. Waechter and Czerwenka both add immeasurably to the allure of the performance.

But the surprise and the unique aspect of this performance is in the rare pairing of the two Rysanek sisters. Possessing similar timbres, it is a most unusual experience to hear them in the same opera. The lyrical Lotte Rysanek (1924–2016) was an accomplished singer although she was somewhat displaced by the overshadowing fame of her elder sister. She made her debut in 1950 in Klagenfurt as Manon. Lotte was a favorite in Vienna, however, and sang with that company from approximately 1956 to 1987. She was especially admired for lyric roles such as Nedda in Pagliacci, Mimi and Musetta in La Bohéme, Liu in *Turandot*, and Micaela in *Carmen*, but she also sang parts like the Trovatore Leonora and she probably holds the record for singing Helmwige in *Die Walküre* in Vienna—109 or so times.

Hearing their two voices in Dalibor, blending in the magnificent duet that ends act I (CD 1, track 8), is an experience not to miss. This is especially so toward the end of the duet when they unite as a single voice on high B.

The release is a fitting and endearing memento of the two sisters. Smetana's music is as grand as one would expect from the composer of Libuse and, cut or not, this is certainly worth having in your library.

Unfortunately, this performance is not yet on YouTube.

Strauss: *Salome* Opera D'Oro OPD 7004 with Grace Hoffman, Hans Hopf, Eberhard Waechter, Waldemar Kmentt; Karl Böhm, conductor.

As I mentioned before, Leonie Rysanek is an "impressionist" among sopranos. It must be admitted that one could never, in good conscience, recommend her recordings to a student for the purpose of learning the notes or rhythm of a Strauss role. But one could recommend her recordings without reservation to demonstrate the accurate concept of soaring, Straussian style, and that indefinable, elusive something called vocal charisma. Rysanek was a vocal tornado with the concomitant indescribable quality that is inherent to unique performers. Like Maria Callas, Leyla Gencer, and Renata Scotto, Rysanek painted in broad strokes and was no miniaturist. Not surprisingly, she gave few concerts of operatic excerpts.

Rysanek did not undertake *Salome* until 1971, some twenty years into her career. She sang the role for about a decade but never commercially recorded any of *Salome*'s music. (She did, however, record Herodias on the DGG recording of *Salome* with Cheryl Studer and Bryn Terfel conducted by Giuseppe Sinopoli.) Of her Strauss roles, *Salome* less suited her than the Marschallin in *Der Rosenkavalier*, the Empress in Die Frau Ohne Schatten, or Chrysothemis in *Elektra*. Rysanek's voice was warm and fastly spun, capable of tremendous thrust and visceral soaring, but *Salome*'s spiky music did not suit her gifts. That is not meant to imply that her Salome is not of a special level. Although her vibrato was naturally rapid, as Rysanek descended into her middle register it began to decrease in its oscillations as muscles began to interfere with its production. During the 1980s this became evident by the odd, shaking tremolo she acquired as these muscles fought for control during her descents into the middle-register. Rarely obtrusive, this often lent a colorful, sobbing quality to such lines. The particular construction of Salome's music, however, is not compatible with this type of middle-register issue. Also, Rysanek's natural, overly ripe timbre hindered the projection of youthful, petulant teenage innocence.

At least three performances of Rysanek's *Salome* are on CD and others are available on YouTube. Of the 15 performances of *Salome* with Rysanek that I know of, 6 are of her as Herodias. More than any other artist, Rysanek's performances demonstrate the problems in recording this piece. Although there are many touches that she imparts to the role, much is learned from her final scene. Rysanek conjures an oddly attractive but diaphanous concept of the scene's pitch and rhythm. Although not easily submitted to scrutiny, it is a powerful effect that she creates.

My favorite performance of *Salome* with Rysanek is not on CD and has yet to appear on YouTube—although I am sure it will in the future. It is her 1972 Metropolitan Opera broadcast. In the meantime, there are enough on YouTube to satisfy most Rysanek enthusiasts.

The first recording is a Melodram CD of a Munich performance on July 26, 1971, with Ferdinand Leitner. One of her first performances of the role, it has typical Rysanek sharping and the alteration of rhythms portrayed with broad, interpretive strokes. It is an incredibly intense and furious performance having grand, dramatic accents. Her recalcitrant middle register contributes fascinating color that is contrasted by searing, abandoned thrusts to high notes. Rysanek's hollow, sluggish middle register was especially unruly between F at the bottom of the staff and B-flat in the middle. While it was clearly a flaw in her production, she never forced this area and it remained mostly unchanged during forty years of professional singing. Rysanek's mature, sensuous voice is not girlish, but like the character of Salome, its use definitely sounds obsessively motivated.

Another performance on CD is the one listed above. It was released by Austrian Radio on BMG as part of their Vienna State Opera series (69430), but has been out of print for a number of years. It can now be found on Opera D'Oro. Dating from December 22, 1972, it documents the premiere production of the newly opened Staatsoper. It is stunning. It was presented only a few months after Rysanek's performances of the same role at the Metropolitan Opera in March of that year. New to her usual and otherwise consistent interpretation, she presents a shriek of satisfaction as the severed head of John the Baptist is presented. (As mentioned in the 1954 *Die Walküre* recording above, Rysanek often screamed while in performance and her interpretations were similarly peppered with this overt, but effective device.) By this time in her career, *Salome*'s music was securely in her voice and she is able to offer tremendous authority, incorporating even more nuances than earlier. Thanks to Böhm, many sections are smoother in their connection and presentation. Errors occurring in the year before have been corrected, but new ones appear.

Strauss—*Salome*—Vienna December, 1972
https://www.youtube.com/watch?v=o6PTtIcEMOg

Another version of the final scene on CD took place in 1974. It does not appear elsewhere on CD or on YouTube. It originates from a 1974 Vienna Staatsoper tour of Japan. It is filler in the Standing Room CD release of a 1965 Vienna performance of *Elektra* with Nilsson and Rysanek. It is one of the best representations of Rysanek's *Salome*. The dramatic vehemence brought in previous performances is built upon and presented formidably. Special in this accounting is "Und das Geheimnis der Liebe ist grösser als das Geheimnis des Todes" ([and] the mystery of love is greater than the mystery of death) which boasts a tiny high G (almost G-sharp) pianissimo. (This phrase had always been a problem for Rysanek. By this time, however, she had satisfactorily worked it out.) The murmurings that follow the kiss are wonderfully evocative and particularly loathsome. Her wayward pitch and hollow, foggy tone add a psychotic edge to the natural unease of the music. Rysanek finishes with an awesome accent on the final "Mund."

A famous performance of this opera took place that same year at the summer festival of Orange. It was one of the few pairings of Rysanek with Jon Vickers. A cohesive, exciting performance in very good sound, it is rightly held by most as a cherished cult item.

Strauss—*Salome*—d'Orange, July 1974 with Jon Vickers, Thomas Stewart, Ruth Hesse, Horst Laubenthal conducted by Rudolf Kempe
https://www.youtube.com/watch?v=rxMX3pr_-00

A famous revival from San Francisco is now on YouTube. Rysanek was always loyal to the San Francisco Opera and gave some of her finest portrayals at that house. This *Salome* was one of them.

Strauss—*Salome*—San Francisco, 1974 with Sigmund Nimsgern, Hans Hopf, Astrid Varnay, William Neill—conducted by Otmar Suitner
https://www.youtube.com/watch?v=n7ncc3zdwQM

Strauss—*Salome*—Metropolitan Opera broadcast, February, 1977 with Norman Bailey, Ragnar Ulfung, Astrid Varnay Kenneth Riegel—Erich Leinsdorf
https://www.youtube.com/watch?v=es86ooJPWCc

Another performance, presented in Tokyo in 1980, is now on YouTube.

Strauss—*Salome*—Tokyo, October 1980 with Bernd Weikl, Gertrude Jahn, Hans Beier, Josef Hopferweisser -conducted by Heinrich Hollresier. This was probably Rysanek's last *Salome*.
https://www.youtube.com/watch?v=G2VED30EM8g

Cherubini—*Medea* RCA Red Seal (Austrian Radio, 1972) with Bruno Prevedi, Lucia Popp, Nicolai Ghiuselev, Margarita Lilowa, Edita Gruberova; Horst Stein, conductor.

Medea first premiered in March of 1797, more than thirty years before Bellini's Norma. Although it was written for the French public, the work proved to be more popular in German, where the original dialogue was replaced by recitative passages composed by Franz Lachner in 1855. Until about 1980, this was the edition that was used in international performance when the opera was given (which was not often). It was not until the famous 1953 revival in Florence with Maria Callas and Vittorio Gui, that the opera began to appear in the repertory of other opera houses.

Curtailing its performance over the ensuing decades was the challenge of casting the lead character. By the 1980s, however, Medea had become popular enough to draw unusual artists who welcomed the extraordinary challenges of the opera: Magda Olivero, Gwyneth Jones, Montserrat Caballe, Shirley Verrett, Grace Bumbry, Olivia Stapp, Margarita Hallin, Anna Caterina Antonacci, Marisa Galvany, Adelaide Negri, Josephine Barstow, Iano Tamar, Phyllis Treigle, and many others.

Despite its many top notes, Medea does not suit Rysanek's voice well. Although *Medea* has many soaring lines and numerous high B-flats and Bs, much of the important music of the role lies in the middle and lower register. The role needs a voice with a strongly focused and expressive middle register in the recitative work and to ply the music Cherubini sets for the coaxing and manipulation of various characters, which Medea spends much of her time doing. As one might expect, it is in the soaring lines of the role that Rysanek shines. Where she fails to make an impact, for instance, is during the moments of the all-important asides Medea makes during the act II finale. In that spot the role calls for a metallic cutting edge to the lower register that Rysanek simply cannot provide. A comparison between Rysanek and the Callas/Gui (1953, Florence) or the Callas/Rescigno (1958, Dallas) performances shows the problem clearly. Still, there is something satisfying in hearing the Rysanek voice wend its way through the labyrinth of notes and emotions that occur in this role. YouTube has this performance in various clips.

YouTube also has a video of a performance with Rysanek from Arles in 1976. The cast included Costanza Cuccaro, Nadine Denize, Veriano Luchetti, Dimiter Petkov—conducted by Serge Baudo.

https://www.youtube.com/watch?v=Y58Hjylb0t0

Ponchielli—*La Gioconda* (MYTO CD MCD 992.205) Berlin, 1974 w/ Franco Tagliavini, Nicola Paskalis, Eva Randova, Peter Lagger, Vera Little—Conducted by Giuseppe Patane.

There is much of interest in this performance although it is not an important entry in the Rysanek legacy. I have included it here for those curious about Rysanek's undertaking of such a role. To be honest, much of her singing (in act I, at least) is a trial to hear unless you are a hard-core Rysanek fan. Some of the middle-voice singing is almost embarrassing because of the wavering pitch and sluggish vibrato fluctuations as Rysanek tries to get her voice under control. More than any other opera discussed here, *La Gioconda* underlines the placement middle-register problems that Rysanek experienced. Like many spintos, the "ah" vowel in the middle and upper-middle areas posed specific placement problems. Rysanek's solution (and not the best one), was to force the tone back into her throat which (of course) then misaligned her voice for anything that followed. Only when the pitch began to rise could she (by instinct) release the tone and place it closer in the mask, making it ready to soar.

By the end of Act I, Rysanek has warmed up and gained some control over her unruly middle and delivers a powerful and effective finish to the act with fine exclamations appearing over the chorus. Acts II and III have exciting dramatic singing, but despite the thrill of her soaring top register, it is obvious that Gioconda simply lays wrong in her voice to be fully effective (similar to Medea). Both roles require more of a united chest register than Rysanek had at her disposal.

Vera Little is a solid La Cieca, and Eva Randova is a sumptuous, almost veristic, Laura. Randova was a wonderful singer and was not used nearly as much as she should have by commercial recording companies. Her Kostelnička in Jenufa at London's Royal Opera in 1987 was nominated for a Lawrence Olivier Award in the category of "Outstanding Achievement in Opera." What a wonderful singer she was! Paskalis and Tagliavini do excellent work, but cannot achieve the artistic intensity of the two main ladies. The chorus is a bit out of control, but enthusiastic.

Ponchielli—*La Gioconda*—Berlin, 1974
https://www.youtube.com/watch?v=Dt5dkMhHW3Y

Mascagni—*Cavalleria Rusticana* (Legato CD LCD 202-1) Munich, Christmas Day, 1978 with Placido Domingo, Benito Di Bella, Ruth Falcon, Astrid Varnay—conducted by Nello Santi. In 2016 this performance was released in superlative sound by Orfeo CD.

This sizzling performance was obviously a Christmas present from Domingo and Rysanek to their Munich audience that day. And what a present it was! I am grateful that, more than forty years later, we can hear this gift from so long ago. It may not be completely idiomatic—especially when it comes to Rysanek—but it is a unique performance and an aural world cleverly crafted by the singers. During his career Domingo was often paired with Rysanek in productions of *Tosca*, Ballo in maschera, and Cavalleria rusticana; the combination of the two was incendiary. Both singers are known for commitment to their art, and it is more than obvious in the all-out, white-hot heat of this performance.

This was the first of a series of performances of Cavalleria that Rysanek sang throughout Germany from 1978 until 1981. It was the continuation of a sensible (and slow) process that she began of undertaking "lower" roles with Kundry in 1976 (in Frankfurt and Hamburg). She sang Kundry until 1985. Four performances at the Met in April seem to have been her last. It became obvious by that time that the soprano was integrating certain schwischen-fach roles into her repertoire to facilitate a switch to more mezzo-soprano-oriented roles. This process wisely took more than ten years to complete. By 1982, she had added Ortrude in Lohengrin, Mascagni's Santuzza in Cavalleria Rusticana, and, in 1985, Kostelnichka in Jenufa. The process was continued in 1989 when she undertook her first Herodias (*Salome*), and concluded in 1990 with her first Klytemnestra in Elektra in Bordeaux.

Her first thrust into "Mamma Lucia" tells us that she is in superb voice and we are in for a special night. Full of passion and abandon, Rysanek shows what one can do with so varied a role. She sounds a bit mature for the young, innocent Santuzza, but Rysanek's voice sounded ripe and mature even at the onset of her career. One can enjoy the unusual pointing and excellent dramaticism she brings to the part. I especially appreciate the way she keeps herself as part of the ensemble in the beautiful "Easter Hymn" rather than to promote the idea of "Madame diva accompanied by the chorus." Her pleading cries of "Oh Signor" at its conclusion are especially eloquent. She finishes the Easter hymn with a huge and beautiful high B that she thrusts over the chorus. "Voi lo sapete" is rich in nuance and intensely dramatic. Even after all the earlier drama she has undergone, Rysanek sounds fresh at the end of the opera, providing an fine high C.

Domingo is superb as the callous Turridu, his effulgent, dark-hued voice and concentrated intensity match Rysanek note for note. Although this opera did not play a large part in his career, as did, say, either Contes d'Hoffmann or Ballo in maschera, the music and character suit his temperament. His stage confrontation with Rysanek is the stuff of legends and is alone worth almost any price. He offers a fabulous top B at the end of the Brindisi. His farewell to Mamma Lucia is movingly sung and Santi leads the orchestra into a frantic, horrifying conclusion. For once, the listener is truly startled and left breathless!

Cavalleria is an odd opera. So many things must come together to make it work. I have heard performances in which everyone sang well, spending seventy minutes to create almost unbearable tension only to have it completely dissipate during the lame efforts of the "screamer" at the end. Although often slighted, the poor soul who runs in to announce Turridu's death must somehow make her contribution count. Fortunately, the Metropolitan Opera has had a number of excellent (and often unnerving) screamers who not only did their part realistically, but added immeasurably to the tension and excitement of the denouement.

This performance has the advantage of a rich and full-voiced Lola sung by Ruth Falcon, who, during the 1980s, proved to be a remarkable Norma, Empress in Die Frau ohne schatten, Senta, Leonora in Il trovatore, and *Turandot*. Although the role of Lola does not show off her voice or range (Falcon had rock-solid high Ds and E-flats) she sings it beautifully and with character. Astrid Varnay provides cameo glamour as Mamma Lucia while Benito di Bella obviously relishes his confrontation with the mercurial Rysanek. One might wish that he barked a bit less in his squeezed-method of vocal production, but he is intense and involved. Not only is the solo singing excellent, the choral work of the Vienna Staatsoper is excellent.

Mascagni—"Ah lo vedi" *Cavalleria rusticana*—Vienna 1978
https://www.youtube.com/watch?v=C2jnh5-kFG4

Wagner: Lohengrin—Vienna broadcast, January 4, 1985—WH 047 with Placido Domingo, Caterina Ligendza, Hermann Becht, Peter Wimberger—conducted by Peter Schneider.

Although Rysanek sang the role of Elsa in Bayreuth as early as 1958, it is her Ortruden (which she took on much later) that prompts the most vociferous response from listeners.

This performance was one of the great nights at the Vienna Staatsoper in the 1980s. It is so good, that it should have been released by one of the large commercial record companies. One is grateful that WH saw fit to release it. You may have to search a bit to find it on CD now but it is worth the effort. (A YouTube link is below.) By the time of this performance, Rysanek was well situated in the role of Ortrude, having sung it in San Francisco in 1982 and later in Berlin and Marseille. Like Kundry, Ortrude was a great role for her art. She eventually sang eight performances in 1985–86 at the Metropolitan Opera (which seem to have been her farewell to the role). She sang only two performances at the Vienna Staatsoper; this broadcast was one of them. Domingo is a suave Lohengrin of passion. What a treat it is to hear such a smoothly sung, darkly-hued rendition. Ligendza uses her pure, cool voice to great effect as the sweet Elsa. Her "Euch lüften" in act II is beautifully floated. Hers was a wonderful voice capable not only of lyricism but the drama needed in the church scene at the end of the act. She is an excellent foil for Rysanek's darkly lush and decadent Ortrude. Ryanek's performance is a whirlwind of thrust and soaring high lines as she bites into Wagner's tempestuous music with vengeance. Although she has important moments in all three acts, act II is essentially Ortrude's act and Rysanek certainly makes the most of it. The first half of the act, with an excellent, forceful Telramund by Hermann Becht, who sings rather than barks the music, is the stuff of nightmares. The scene that follows, with Elsa, is rife with insinuation and nuance and is audibly mesmerizing. Anyone knowing the Rysanek voice will anticipate that the "Entweite Götter" will be a special moment. It is stunning. No less impressive is her final denunciaiton in the final scene of the opera, "Fahr heim! Fahr heim, du stolzer Helde" in which countless high As ring out with tireless force and power.

Wagner—*Lohengrin*—Vienna broadcast 1985
https://www.youtube.com/watch?v=f404s1eIyII

Wagner—*Lohengrin*—San Francisco 1982
Here is an earlier, 1982 San Francisco performance of *Lohengrin* with Peter Hoffman, Pilar Loranggar, Herman Brecht, David Ward—conducted by Heinrich Hollreiser.
https://www.youtube.com/watch?v=-0kMPXuDo8o

Wagner—*Lohengrin*—Metropolitan Opera 1968
For a taste of Rysanek's Elsa in *Lohengrin*, here is a Metropolitan Opera performance from 1968 with Christa Ludwig, James King, William Dooley, Bonaldo Giaiotti—conducted by Berislav Klobucar.
https://www.youtube.com/watch?v=LkAmlrfW4kM

Janacek: *Jenufa* (BIS CD 449-4- Carnegie Hall, March 30, 1988 with Gabriella Benackova, Wieslaw Ochman, Peter Kazaras—conducted by Eve Queler.

This release by BIS CD is a good example of why live performances must be preserved. It documents one of those special nights when everything and everyone came together with a cohesiveness striven for, but rarely achieved. Dark obsessions, disfigurement, a love triangle, madness, infanticide, forgiveness—how would one not love this opera? Although Jenufa requires work and familiarity on the part of the listener to appreciate its nationalistic musical idiom, the rewards are great. This excellent CD is a souvenir of one of the most distinguished performances given at Carnegie Hall in the 1980s. Sung during Holy Week in 1988, it was a precursor of the phenomenal performances given by Benackova and Rysanek at the Metropolitan Opera in 1992. I had wanted to attend but, I had Church services to sing.

Benackova floats her justly famous and peerless interpretation of the title role over an enthralled audience. Poised, sympathetic, sweet-toned, feminine, and musical to a fault, she turns Jenufa's often craggy vocal lines into bel canto legato. Her singing of the role remains a model for all sopranos who seek insight into the idiosyncratic requirements of Czech vocal music; a way of pointing and emphasizing various notes within musical phrases without losing the sense of legato. This nationalistic style has textual motivation, but is frequently presented purely as a form of musical expression.

Rysanek steals the show with a powerful, almost frighteningly intense performance of the proud, guilt-ridden Kostelnichka. She illuminates the difficult music with striking intuition. The many high B-flats and B-naturals, the hair-line pianissimi of the role soar effortlessly into the acoustics of Carnegie Hall. In this case, her trademark sharping adds to the thrusting excitement of her most dramatic utterances. Ochman and Kazaras are effective foils for the ladies and Eve Queler provides strong support. I would never want to be without this dark, intensely sung performance.

Donald Henahan wrote in the New York Times:

> ...this was Miss Rysanek's night. As Jenufa's stepmother, Kostelnicka, she had by far the more complex and fascinating role, one that can be red meat and heady drink for a superior singing actress of Miss Rysanek's caliber. The rigid older lady, moral arbiter of the village, must dominate Janacek's drama, and certainly did this time. Her Kundry-like screams of guilt and self-reproach hung in the listener's ear and imagination for hours afterward. (*The New York Times*, March, 1988)

Janacek—*Jenufa*—Carnegie Hall, 1988
https://www.youtube.com/watch?v=1Zeq8GnBpCY

In *Jenufa* Rysanek was often paired with Gabriella Benackova. Here is a wonderful broadcast from Brno National Theatre in October of 1988 with Milan Kopacka, Josef Abel, Jan Hladik—conducted by Frantisek Jilek. Jenufa premiered at the Brno Theatre in 1904, eighty-four years before this performance. Thankfully, this legendary performance was uploaded to YouTube by "starman22" so that all can enjoy it in superb sound.

https://www.youtube.com/watch?v=cudg8JY5j_U&t=245s

Another fine performance comes from Innsbruck in June of 1990 with Barbara Daniels, Riccardo Calleo, and Heinrich Wolf. Conducted by Arend Wehrkamp.

https://www.youtube.com/watch?v=u0ugLeGA0Ow&t=146s

Of other recordings, I also recommend the "Karl Böhm" Wagner Ring Cycle on Philips CD. Still popular, you can find it on Amazon. It remains one of the most famous and satisfying of Ring Cycles. Rysanek is Sieglinde in *Die Walküre*. The Böhm Ring is an excellent mid-career document of Rysanek who is caught not only in her element (on stage) but surrounded by such worthy colleagues as Birgit Nilsson, James King, Marta Mödl, Anja Silja, Theo Adam, and others. To give you an idea of the merits of this Ring, below are links to most of the Cycle on YouTube.

Wagner—*Die Walküre*—Bayreuth 1967
https://www.youtube.com/watch?v=B8EwMbGlLGc
Wagner—*Siegfried*—Bayreuth 1967
https://www.youtube.com/watch?v=d046U6DHOMA
Wagner—*Die Gottrdammerung*—Bayreuth 1967
https://www.youtube.com/watch?v=MqV0Y1TXi8c

Leonie Rysanek and Met Broadcasts

Rysanek took part in forty-two broadcasts from the Metropolitan Opera: five of *Elektra* (1961–1992), four of Senta in *Der Fliegende Holländer* (1960–1969) and *Die Frau ohne schatten*, (1966–1978), and three each of *Macbeth* (1959–1962), *Die Walküre* (1965–1988), and *Der Rosenkavalier* (1969–1973). Not to be missed are broadcasts of *Un Ballo in Maschera* (1962), *Don Carlo* (1959, 1964), *Ariadne auf Naxos* (1963, 1970), *Salome* (1972, 1977), *Lohengrin* (as Ortrude) (1985), *Tannhäuser* (1960, 1982), *Nabucco* (1961), *Otello* (1964),

Parsifal (1985, released by the Metropolitan Opera Guild, but act II can be heard on YouTube), and others.

Rysanek sang four Metropolitan premieres—Verdi's Macbeth and Nabucco, and Strauss's Ariadne auf Naxos and Die Frau Ohne Schatten (which premiered two weeks after the opening of Lincoln Center.)

All are recommended without reservation. Most of those listed are available on CDs from Europe and many can be heard on YouTube. Of special note is the April 20, 1985 performance of *Parsifal* with Jon Vickers with James Levine conducting. It seems to have been her farewell to a most special role in her "newer" repertoire.

Wagner—*Die Walküre*—Metropolitan Opera broadcast March 1988, with Hildegard Behrens, Peter Hoffman, Theo Adam, Waltraud Meier, Auge Haugland—conducted by James Levine. This was Rysanek's last Sieglinde in New York and she puts her signature role to rest with triumph.

https://www.youtube.com/watch?v=EWUSsY8ZZVY

Some additional Leonie Rysanek performances on YouTube:

Wagner—*Die Walküre* Act I—Amsterdam, December 1979 with Peter Hoffman, John Macurdy, conducted by Bernard Haitink

https://www.youtube.com/watch?v=j7CLfVzxigA

Wagner—*Die Walküre* Finale of Act I—Metropolitan Opera Gala in honor of Rudolf Bing, 1972 with Jon Vickers—conducted by Max Rudolf. This was not televised in the United States. The source is from German Television.

https://www.youtube.com/watch?v=X8mHOCW7kT8

Strauss—*Ariadne auf Naxos*—Metropolitan Opera broadcast 1970 with James King, Reri Grist, Evelyn Lear, William Dooley, Theodor Uppman—conducted by Karl Böhm.

https://www.youtube.com/watch?v=dF30upvF1dY&t=64s

Strauss—*Ariadne auf Naxos*—Vienna performance, 1980 with James King, Patricia Wise, Eberhard Waechter—conducted by Christoff Perick

https://www.youtube.com/watch?v=WglCw-iIF3w

Strauss—*Der Rosenkavalier*—Metropolitan Opera broadcast, February 1969 with Christa Ludwig, Reri Grist, Walter Berry, Rudolf Knoll, Nicolai Gedda—conducted Karl Böhm

https://www.youtube.com/watch?v=JS6nizFuE1g

Verdi—*Nabucco*—Metropolitan Opera broadcast—December 1960 with Cornell MacNeil, Cesare Siepi—conducted by Thomas Schippers

https://www.youtube.com/watch?v=qqWAlAfgnww

Verdi—*Nabucco*—Metropolitan Opera performance January 7, 1961 with Anselmo Colzani, Cesare Siepi, Eugenio Fernandi, Rosalind Elias—Conducted by Thomas Schippers

https://www.youtube.com/watch?v=qzTMlBKwhpM

Wagner—*Parsifal*—Frankfurt, 1976—This was Rysanek's first assumption of the role of Kundry. She sang her first on April 11, 1976 in this production.

https://www.youtube.com/watch?v=G5xdbUAfKPU

Wagner—*Parsifal*—Paris, October 1982 with Sigfried Jerusalem, Kurt Moll, Bernd Weikl, Kurt Rydl, Hermann Becht, conducted by Marek Janowski

https://www.youtube.com/watch?v=8Q5SQvZwo4k&t=7584s

Wagner—*Parsifal*—Metropolitan Opera broadcast April 1985 with Jon Vickers, Simon Estes, Kurt Moll, Franz Mazura, Gail Robinson—conducted by James Levine—One of the legendary broadcasts of this work from the Metropolitan Opera. Vickers and Rysanek in Act II are outstanding.

https://www.youtube.com/watch?v=IwK7pe-MjB4

In early 1984 there was a Gala Concert in honor of Rysanek's 25th Anniversary with the Metropolitan Opera. With Peter Hoffman, Franz Mazura, Gail Robinson and others Rysanek sang Act II of *Parsifal*, and with Peter Hoffman, John Macurdy Act I of *Die Walküre*. I was there and it was a remarkable evening. During it she gave New York audiences a taste of what her Kundry would be like the next season. I would hazard a guess that there were at least five people there that night taping the event. I know of at least three.

Leonie Rysanek Concert on her 25th Anniversary with the Metropolitan Opera, February 26, 1984

https://www.youtube.com/watch?v=JS-mnvaH0rs

Single Albums

There are a number of fine compilations of this artist. Because Rysanek was a creature of the stage there are comparatively few recordings of set pieces from operas. When she did perform in concert, it was usually in complete acts of operas which gave her a better chance to sink her teeth into the essence of a role. Like others of her kind, she was not a miniaturist and her most powerful impact was found in the total concept of the role she was performing rather than in arias of four-or five-minute segments.

1952, 1955: Opera Arias (EMI CDH 5652012):

Fliegende Hollander (3), Arabella, Rosenkavalier (5), Tiefland, Forza, Aida (2).

If you are a fan of Rysanek you must get these early renditions to compare them to her later American and European efforts. This disc is the only commercial documentation of her output in such roles as Arabella, Tiefland, and Rosenkavalier.

However, look for the Voce Della Luna release of a 1971 Vienna performance with Christa Ludwig and Hilde De Groote, conducted by Josef Krips (VL2001-3). It is a worthy portrayal of her Marschallin and a treat. Also (as filler), the set includes Rysanek in arias from *Elektra, Frau,* and *Leibe der Danae* from the early 1950s.

1958: Operatic Arias (RCA 09026-68920:

Forza, Aida (2), *Chenier, Turandot, Otello, Ballo* (2), *Cavalleria, Tosca,* plus *Macbeth* (2), *Otello*; conducted by Arturo Basile.

This remarkable album was recorded in 1958 in Turin, Italy. It was Rysanek's only commercial aria album, recorded the year before her debut as Lady Macbeth at the Metropolitan Opera (replacing Maria Callas). It is now one of BMG's "Living Stereo" re-releases. It presents the Rysanek voice in all its youthful splendor. Originally, the LP album was to include eleven arias, including two from *Un Ballo in Maschera*. When it was first released on LP, however, those two arias had to be omitted due to time constraints. BMG has now included the *Un Ballo in Maschera* arias as they were meant to be and has sweetened the pot by filling out the CD with two arias from *Macbeth* (from the complete 1959 set) and the act I love duet from Verdi's *Otello* with Jon Vickers (also from the complete recording made in Rome in 1960).

In the liner notes for the BMG re-release, Rysanek confessed dissatisfaction with her commercial recordings:

People who know me are well aware that I have a very strained relationship with my recordings—especially my studio recordings…Certainly, my best recordings are those that were made live, where one can sense the audience's deep silence and their concentration on the stage (and visa versa)…"

She does admit, however, that of all her commercial recordings, it is this recital of which she is "largely satisfied…. Even today I still stand by these recordings…." (1996)

Although her faults are in evidence, her glorious top register is thrillingly projected. These are important mementos of her Aïda, *Tosca*, La forza del destino, and Andrea Chenier.

Although some may object to Rysanek's Germanic approach to Maddalena's aria, no objection can be made about her intensity and commitment to Giordano's music. She offers an appealing vulnerable opening with her erratic middle register providing colorful effects. Although her natural, overly ripe timbre lacks youthful ardor, her interpretation, governed by a controlled, smoldering intensity, is superbly constructed. Her outburst on high B is magnificent.

The disc is worth any price to hear her remarkable rendition of "In questa reggia" from *Turandot*. (Rysanek felt it was one of her best recordings.) Although by the time she came to record this album she had given up *Turandot*, she left us an idea of what it must have been like to hear her in this role in the theater.

(A live performance of this aria from a 1953 concert can be found [see below] that is even more exciting than this studio recording.) Of all the arias on this disc, it is the aria from *Turandot* that most accurately resembles the thrilling intensity of Rysanek's top register as it was heard in the theater. One can understand why, of all of her studio efforts, Rysanek was most proud of this album.

Puccini—*In questa reggia* (*Turandot*)—Munich 1953 conducted by Wolfgang Sawallisch
https://www.youtube.com/watch?v=6pwUA9L3UKs

Leonie Rysanek: The Soprano Queen—10-CD set Membran

This is a fascinating boxed set. No notes, just a track listing on the back of the cardboard sleeves. It is intended for fans of the soprano and it is certainly a good way to obtain and enjoy her special charisma. Most selections are recorded live, although there are some studio recordings as well. The amount of material is impressive: There are substantial excerpts from Lohengrin, Macbeth, Nabucco, Fliegender Holländer, *Die Walküre, Otello*, Aïda, *Don Giovanni, Turandot*, Tosca, Fidelio, *Tannhäuser*, Egyptische Helena, Ariadne auf Naxos, *Der Rosenkavalier*, Arabella, *Elektra*, and more. The 1958 recital discussed above is included in this box set as well.

Leonie Rysanek—Live Recordings 1955–1991—2-CD box set Orfeo

This is an excellent set for experiencing the overall trajectory of the Rysanek career. From Jenufa (Kostelnichka) to *Parsifal* (Kundry) with *Fidelio*, Die Frau ohne Schatten, Dalibor, *Elektra* (Klytemnestra), Lohengrin (Ortrude), Medea, Ariadne, Aïda, Cavalleria Rusticana, and the final scene from *Salome*.

There are some wonderful selections here. The only problem was that I wanted to hear even more of them. Of all the compilations of this artist, it is probably this Orfeo set that covers her art the most completely. Especially welcome are the scenes from *Lohengrin, Jenufa* and *Elektra* (with the wonderful Hildegard Behrens).

Gala CD set
Gala (100.542) offers a 2-CD set of primarily early Rysanek with arias and scenes from *Fidelio*, Oberon, Macbeth, *Otello*, Aïda, *Tosca, Turandot, La Gioconda*, Fliegende Holländer, and Der Rosenkavallier. This is a good selection of basic Rysanek material that offers no surprises. Considering the low cost of Gala issues, you cannot go wrong.

Leonie Rysanek—Orfeo CD C504 991 B) Excerpts from various performances of *Elektra 1953–1996* a remarkable collection in which she performs all three lead roles.

Released in 1999 this CD documents a first in opera annals—a single artist performing all three leading characters in Strauss's masterpiece. For that reason alone, it is invaluable.

It is unfortunate that the complete soundtrack of the Böhm film of Elektra has not been released on CD. It is, however, available on YouTube. For Rysanek's interpretation of *Elektra*, it should not be missed. Although Rysanek did not perform the role on stage, it was fortuitous that she agreed to make the film. Doing so, however, had personal repercussions.

It caused a serious rift in her relationship with her colleague and friend, Birgit Nilsson. Nilsson was rightly offended when Böhm slighted her in favor of Rysanek for the film; the movie should have been Nilsson's as she had owned that role for 2 decades.

I love Nilsson, especially as Elektra, but I confess I am thankful Rysanek accepted the assignment to sing Elektra in the film. To hear the monologue in the Rysanek voice is a dream come true. "Rings um dein Grab" with its triumphant high B-flat has never sounded more sexually climactic. It is a searing, demonic performance with thrilling high notes and intense declamation.

Strauss—*Elektra*—(soundtrack of the 1987 Böhm film) with Caterina Ligendza, Dietrich Fischer-Dieskau, Astrid Vanay

https://www.youtube.com/watch?v=jq1qfG0r4LE

The most astonishing thing about the above Orfeo disc is the vocal consistency that Rysanek demonstrates across the forty-plus years that are represented (1953–1996). Her voice sounds much the same in 1953 as it does in 1996, except for the change of fach, of course. Orfeo's sound is first rate and the music is arranged in a sequence that creates a fascinating aural picture of Rysanek's suitability to the music. Although generous in its timing (more than 73 minutes), I wish it had been possible to include the entire confrontation between Hildegard Behrens (Elektra) and Rysanek (Klytemnestra) from a 1996 Vienna performance. The chemistry between the two singers is such that when the selection ends after eighteen minutes, one is left craving to hear the rest of the scene.

WH 4-CD Memorial Set
If you can find it, one of the most interesting tributes to Rysanek is a 4-disc set issued by the pirate label, WH. It concentrates on the last years of her career. It includes the entire Metropolitan Opera Silver Anniversary concert (mentioned above) that Rysanek gave on February 26, 1984.

John Rockwell of The New York Times noted:

> ... this was no farewell. Hers is an odd voice, hollow at the bottom and opening up to a big, bright, securely supported upper extension. Her top may be a little less sure now, but her lower range is filling out in compensation.
>
> Miss Rysanek has never been a singer who stresses an even vocal line and abstract bel-canto virtues. She is an Expressionistic actress, given to splintering significant words under the stress of

emotion and to wrenching her body and chopping her arms in a way that inevitably distorts her singing. But the result, a few mannerisms aside, is not the disruption of the music but the enhancement of the drama

During the frenzied final ovations Miss Rysanek had to shield herself from a barrage of bouquets." (The New York Times, February 1984)

The WH set also includes: Act II excerpts from Rysanek's final Ortrude in Lohengrin at the Metropolitan Opera on January 16, 1986 with Eva Marton and Peter Hofmann. Act II of Jenufa from a December 19, 1992 Metropolitan Opera performance (in-house). the Elektra/Klytemnestra scene from Elektra in Salzburg in August of 1996 and a 1995 Interview with George Jellinek.

Thanks to recording technology and the era of pirate recordings, we can revisit Leonie Rysanek and the many wonderful performances she left as her legacy any time we choose!

A much-abbreviated version of this text (without links) first appeared in parterre box, #39, 1999

Maria Callas
December 2, 1923—September 16, 1977
(On the 100th Anniversary of her Birth)

Suggested Live Recordings
By Nicholas E. Limansky
November 20, 2023

This article is one of a number of pieces that first appeared in *Liner Notes Magazine*, a quarterly E-Zine devoted to classical music, in their December 2023 issue in honor of the anniversary of Maria Callas's 100th birthday. It is included here with permission from its editor, Joe Moore. The original article has many color photos. I urge you to visit their site
https://liner-notes-magazine.com
to see this and other issues.

Introduction

Millions of words have been written about Maria Callas. After all these decades she still captivates.

I believe it is because of the effect her voice has on listeners. Everyone who has heard her singing has had a unique reaction. Some love it. Some hate it. Because of the trajectory of her career, I believe that how one is introduced to her voice may affect how they appreciate her art.

My discovery of Maria Callas was serendipitous. It was through her early, 1954 LP recital, *Operatic Arias (Coloratura/Lyric)*. The record was sent home to me from a kindly Baltimore book-mobile librarian in 1965 when I was home sick from school. She heard that I had just discovered opera and thought I should hear this soprano. I have remained in her debt ever since.

There is no question that my initial exposure to the Callas voice had everything to do with my love for her singing. Had I been introduced to her singing through one of her later albums like *Carmen* or the second complete *Tosca* (1964) my impressions might have been quite different.

It was *Coloratura/Lyric* that helped form my operatic tastes. To this day I can recall my wonder when I first heard Maria Callas singing the contrasting arias from *Adriana Lecouvreur*, *Andrea Chenier*, *La Wally*, *Mefistofele*, *Il barbiere di Siviglia*, *I Vespri Siciliani*, *Dinorah* and *Lakmé*.

How was such singing possible? In the *Mefistofele* mad scene alone, her interpretation was so intimate I felt I was listening in on someone's private grief.

Maria Callas—Operatic Arias—Angel, EMI, Warner
https://www.youtube.com/watch?v=l-F0fmOFC1M

I was intrigued by Callas' voice and its myriad sounds. It was a voice that could be both coarse and elegant—often within the same piece of music. At that formative time of my musical life, my mind was like a sieve and I absorbed every color, every inflection that Callas brought to her arias and roles. The Angel (EMI—now Warner) commercial opera sets were magical and before long I was borrowing the Callas *Aïda, Rigoletto, La sonnambula, Lucia di Lammermoor, I puritani*, and various aria albums from the Baltimore library.

The Voice

So, what was so special about this voice? First of all, it was easily identifiable—no one had the Callas "sound." For a voice of its size, it also had an exceptional range—from F# below the staff (heard in *I Vespri Siciliani*), to the high E (heard in *Armida*)—just under three octaves. Then there was the bold, yet elegant use of her instrument. Her studies in Greece with Elvira de Hildago, the famed coloratura soprano of the early twentieth century, were intense and comprehensive. Through de Hidalgo Callas discovered a life-long love of bel canto and the florid repertoire. She also developed an outstanding coloratura technique. Her innate knowledge of ornamental patterns and the structure of cadenzas was second to none.

Few singers have matched the diaphanous beauty of her downward portamenti, chromatic scales, or her sense of structure and the tapering of a phrase. Other factors that set her apart from colleagues were her attention to rhythmic movement, crisp diction, and attention to *agogic* accents.

But this was not a perfect voice. There were problems—even in its youth. To be honest, it was never a "pretty" voice. Callas' voice resembled a painter's palate in that she used her voice as a foundation to create her imaginative colors and nuances. It was expressive and capable of fascinating shades and hues, that, combined with her musicality, illuminated any music she sang.

There were always "registration" problems around the area of F#, G and A at the top of the staff—especially during soft (piano) singing. High C could be a battle depending on how it appeared in the score and notes above that often had a knife-like edge. What was so amazing was that Callas was able to take those problems and make them work within her interpretations.

Anyone who knows the Callas voice has their own idea about the cause of her early decline.

I believe there were actually a number of factors contributing to her decline. I do not feel that her (occasionally dangerous) wide-ranging repertoire was solely responsible.

I do believe, however, that her decision to sing through her weight loss of 80 pounds between 1953 and 1954, did much to contribute to her eventual vocal crisis. If one compares her singing on live recordings from 1952 and 1953, while Callas was heavy, with her singing on the Lyric/Coloraura or Puccini albums recorded in September 1954, it is clear that something severe has altered in her voice—a "slimming down" of her vocal core and timbre.

Ironically, these changes allowed Callas to adopt more feminine and affecting timbres for many of her characterizations.

Then there were the problems in her personal life. Make no mistake, one's personal life plays a huge part in any singer's art. Singing is 90% cerebral and anything that adversely affects the singer is going to affect their voice.

According to what she said in articles during her last year of life, Callas, herself, felt that her vocal problems stemmed from a loss of confidence due to a loss of breath control.

There was also muscular manipulation in her vocal technique. This manipulation had to do with the "squeezing" of the voice into a narrow space in the back of the throat during upper-register piano singing.

All the above played a part in her decline.

What is intriguing about all this is that even during her decline, Callas always had first-rate coloratura flexibility. (For example, listen to the intricate Polonaise from *Mignon*—recorded in April of 1961—a time when one might have questioned whether Callas could handle such intricate fioriture. Despite some obtrusive wobbles, she glides through Thomas' scales and difficult triplet figures with remarkable refinement and poise.)

Other examples can be heard in the many times Callas scheduled the florid final aria in Rossini's *Cenerentola* for concerts in the mid 1960s. No matter what condition her voice was in, it was never sluggish in movement between notes. Callas' voice was always responsive to rhythm.

To get a sense of the all-embracing views of the causes for Maria Callas' decline, I urge the reader to check out the Wikipedia page on Maria Callas. Their section on Callas' vocal decline is surprisingly good and thorough. As Wikipedia rightly observes:

Whether Callas's vocal decline was due to ill health, early menopause, over-use and abuse of her voice, loss of breath-support, loss of confidence, or weight loss will continue to be debated. Whatever the cause may have been, her singing career was effectively over by age 40, and even at the time of her death at age 53, according to Walter Legge, 'she ought still to have been singing magnificently'".[1]

Callas and the Pirates

Maria Callas' career was well documented by the "pirates," though often with varying sonic results. Her best years were 1949 to 1959. There was, however, fine work done after that. For instance, I would never want to be without her January 24, 1964, London *Tosca* with Renato Cioni and Tito Gobbi. Or her Paris *Norma* from the next year. Fortunately, all but a few of her great roles were captured live.

Most surviving Callas performances originate from radio broadcasts thoughtfully captured by faceless pirates and aficionados during the 1950s and 1960s. A few originated "in-house"—though that was a rare occurrence. One of the first was a Callas concert in London on September 23, 1959. This was an in-house recording made by Michael Scott (1935-2019)—author of the indispensable *The Record of Singing*, and Biographies of *Enrico Caruso* and *Maria Callas*. Only the sleepwalking scene from *Macbeth* and a few fragments of the mad scene from *Il Pirata* exist.

I took a large, cumbersome tape recorder into the auditorium and managed to get it to work uninterruptedly in the sleepwalking scene, one of the first pirate live recordings made in Europe..." (Nicholas E. Limansky *Pirates of the High Cs,* YBK publishers, New York 2020—page 10)

There are sixty-plus live performances of Maria Callas on CD—all worth investigating—despite questionable sonics on some of them. Considering their importance, one is grateful they exist at all. Maria Callas (along with Leyla Gencer—dubbed "the Queen of the Pirates," and Magda Olivero) was one of the main reasons for the rapidly-growing world of operatic pirating during the 1950s and 1960s.

Space prohibits me discussing all Callas' live recordings of importance. I urge you to look for her performances of *Andrea Chenier, Iphigenia en Tauride, La traviata, Tosca, Un Ballo in Maschera, Il barbiere di Sivigia, Il Pirata, Poliuto*, not to mention all her commercial recordings as well.

I have decided to discuss the live recordings of Maria Callas that resonate most with me. Some I will just mention, others I will go into detail. *ALL* are indispensable. My choices might not be everyone's but then, that is the glory of all this. We all have our preferences.

From all reports Callas appreciated the work of the "pirates" and was actually delighted (if not tickled) by their attention. She even had a number of the recordings herself.

So why do Maria Callas' live recordings remain significant even after seventy years? The main reason, which is often overlooked, is that as documents of a singer's art, the Callas pirates prove exactly why such recordings should exist in the first place.

We have all heard commercial recordings that are beautifully made but that left us emotionally unmoved. Live opera recordings do the opposite. They may not have perfect sonics, or presentations, we might not agree with the interpretation, or some of the singing, but there is an honesty to them. Live opera recordings represent what the singer can do at that moment in time—blemishes and all. They are moments that have been captured—without editing—for posterity.

When I started collecting live recordings in 1971, they were very much "under-the-counter" and could only be found in specific stores in bigger cities and on mail-order catalogues. They were quite costly—usually about $20.00 an LP. And this at a time when an LP could cost as little as $1.98. The famous 1951 Mexico City *Aida* cost about $60.00 (which translates today to over $400). Because of that, purchases of pirate recordings were few and far between—especially for a poor music student at West Virginia University.

Today, some fifty-two years later, you can buy a CD of that 1951 *Aïda* for a fraction of the original LP cost, or even listen to it for free on YouTube.

During its hey-day in America, pirated opera recordings were available on such labels as BJR (which specialized in Maria Callas and Montserrat Caballe), MRF (which offered not only Callas pirates but also those of Leyla Gencer and Magda Olivero), and Penzance. Then there were the 900 or so performances released on the Eddie Smith labels: Unique Opera Records Corporation (UORC), A.N.N.A. Record Company, and Golden Age of Opera.

BJR and MRF releases were class acts and often included beautiful booklets with glossy photographs and/or liner notes and artist biographies. Indeed, their presentation often put to shame commercial releases.

BJR was known for their pressings on good vinyl and for excellent sound quality. BJR LPs released in 1975 still sound good fifty years later.

BJR quickly became known as the "Callas label." Their fine sound quality was because they owned many of the original transcription discs of Callas' performances. Charles Johnson and Santiago Rodriguez (the "J" and "R" of BJR) were also the owners of the label, Robin Hood Records—a "budget" label of BJR. In those releases no booklets or librettos were offered.

I met Santiago in the late 1970s when I visited him at his home on West End Avenue in Manhattan to pick up a couple LP sets of Callas. Many standing-room patrons of the Metropolitan Opera in the 1970s remember him passing out recording lists during performances, inviting buyers back to his apartment to buy the most recent sets.

After his death in 2009, the Callas collection went to Pablo D. Berruti of Divina Records. The first half of the collection was given to him directly by Rodriguez and Johnson during a visit to New York in October of 2008. Unfortunately, Santiago died the following year so Jon

C. Harding of Philadelphia saw to it that the rest of the important BJR catalogue of original acetates and master tapes were safely put into Divina's hands. Thankfully, to this day, Divina Records continues to honor the fine legacy of BJR by releasing these important documents on CD and as downloads on their website: divinarecords.com." (Nicholas E. Limansky, *Pirates of the High Cs*, YBK publishers, NY, 2020)

Suggested Live Recordings of Maria Callas

For the most part in the following discussions, I will focus on Callas' contributions rather than those of her colleagues.

Although Maria Callas was a colorist and a detailer, she was not a miniaturist. To get the full impact of her power as an interpreter, one must experience her singing through her interaction with other characters. For instance, as marvelous as her two solo arias are in Verdi's *Aïda*, it is her scenes with Amneris, Amonasro or Radames that highlight Callas' special interpretive abilities.

Verdi—*Nabucco*—Naples, December 20, 1949

Although Maria Callas originally made her operatic debut in Greece in 1941, this *Nabucco* is the first complete surviving Callas performance. Even though the sound leaves much to be desired—being boxy with occasional overload and distortion, Callas' singing of the fierce Abigaile is spectacular. Exceptional moments include a dynamic, forceful entrance and trio in Act I, and the famous Act 2 scena with its infamous 2-octave leap from high C to middle C, and the concluding cabaletta, "Salgo gia," This 10-minute scena highlights Callas' remarkable downward runs and secure top register as well as her elegant concept of Verdi's music despite its dramaticism.

The massive Act 3 duet with Nabucco (Gino Bechi) is the climax of the performance. After some furious declamation and drama, Callas caps the scene with a penultimate, sustained high Eb. The audience goes insane. This was a shocking feat at the time, and did much to advance Callas' fame. All is conducted with fire by Vittorio Gui.

Like many important Callas live performances, this *Nabucco* is available on YouTube with a piano/vocal score embedded into the video. This is invaluable for anyone interested in studying the Callas art. It was an obvious labor of love by YouTube contributor—BaroneVitellioScarpia1.

Verdi—*Nabucco*—Naples, 1949

https://www.youtube.com/watch?v=fcKjD1duakM

Verdi—*Il trovatore*—Mexico City, June 20, 1950

This was Callas's first assumption of the *Il trovatore* Leonora. This is an important document if only for the fact that it shows how Callas prepared a role on her own. Tullio Serafin, her musical mentor, was not able to work with Callas on this Leonora and so she made her own artistic choices. Overall, it is a remarkable success. Perhaps, because she is on her own, and without restraint, the Mexico City performances emphasize her youthful trait of interpolating high notes. These include two spectacular high E-flats in Leonora's Act I aria, "Tacea la notte placida." The first is in the cadenza of the aria proper, and the second is a huge, penultimate high E-flat that Callas hurled into the end of the "Di tale amor" cabaletta. This was once a Luisa Tetrazzini interpolation (as heard on her 1911 recording). The improvisational triplets Callas introduces into the aria can also be heard on Tetrazzini's recording. The next Mexico City performance (June 23) and others that followed over the years, found her revising her interpolations. Most can be heard on YouTube.

Another *Il trovatore* performance not to be missed is the 1953 La Scala broadcast with Gino Penno, Carlo Tagliabue, and Ebe Stignani—conducted by Antonino Votto. (Callas also sang a broadcast of the opera in 1951, with the legendary tenor, Giacomo Lauri-Volpi.)

By 1953, Callas had refined her interpretation, and her singing reflects the elegance of that conception—especially the Act IV "D'amor sull'ali rosee." The highlight of the performance, however, remains Ebe Stignani's searing portrait of Azucena. Her volcanic singing of "Condotta all era ceppi" in act two, borders on alarming realism—especially her heart-rending cries of "Il figlio mio!" The audience bursts into spontaneous applause. (This was originally released on BJR's "Robin Hood" label. It is now on MYTO CD and YouTube.)

Verdi—*Il trovatore*—Mexico City, 1950
https://www.youtube.com/watch?v=jc_gEtB6gls&t=583s

Verdi—*Il trovatore*—Milan, 1953
https://www.youtube.com/watch?v=lDGMchTQiT8&t=1588s

Wagner—*Parsifal*—RAI Rome, November, 1950

This is an important radio broadcast in the Callas annals and is preserved in very good monaural sound. It is a rare document of Callas' Wagner singing (there are only a few, and no other complete performances). Her intriguing interpretation perfectly blends the merits of elegant bel canto with dramatic Wagnerian singing. It is an intoxicating mixture. Despite its Italian text and various cuts to Wagner's score, this is a captivating recording and worth serious study. It also features Lina Pagliughi as the First Flower Maiden. This is the only time two famous singers of *Lucia di Lammermoor*—one former and one soon to be—can be heard in the same performance of *Parsifal*. Callas is a formidable, darkly-hued Kundry, while Pagliughi is a sweet, limpid Flower Maiden. Even though Africo Baldelli is a cypher as Parsifal, Boris Christoff, Rolando Panerai and Giuseppe Modesti are real treats in this music—conducted by Vittorio Gui. This performance is easily found on CD (and on YouTube with vocal score). It should be in every personal library.

Wagner—*Parsifal*—Rome, 1950
https://www.youtube.com/watch?v=Nits7NyD0hI&t=27s

Verdi—*I Vespri Siciliani*—Florence, May 26, 1951

My nostalgic favorite remains the Florence *I Vespri Siciliani* with Callas and the bass, Boris Christoff ripping the scenery apart with delightful determination. Back in 1971, this was my first live recording with Maria Callas (on LP) and it has always been a favorite.

Verdi—*I Vespri Siciliani*—Florence, 1951
https://www.youtube.com/watch?v=-jODLketXwA&t=13s

I remember the label was Penzance Records (#6)—its title being a clever allusion to pirating! There was no libretto or booklet in the black box with its red label stuck on the front, just three, red-labeled LP records, in protective paper sleeves. Despite the barebones presentation and somewhat primitive sound quality, the performance was unlike anything I had heard on recordings up to that time. I was captivated. It had a spark of creativity, electricity and passion that were enthralling and that I had never experienced on any recordings before. I immediately began to miss those qualities in commercial recordings.

Callas' opening scene in Act I highlights her remarkable intensity and fire. Not to mention her musical "face" so important in opera recordings. It was on this recording that I first discovered those peculiar (almost mystical) vocal sounds (mouth resonance) that, over the decades, Callas sporadically offered to listeners. "In vostro man" has a smoldering passion that burns itself into the listener's brain. Her subsequent scenes with Boris Christoff are all magnificent. An added bonus was conductor Erich Kleiber's decision to include the full, 30-minute ballet in Act 3. Although some object to this practice, I love the vigorous, imaginative music and orchestration.

The 1951 *I Vespri* proves, however, that Callas was not an infallible singer. Most opera lovers know of her infamous high E miscalculation during the final measures of the Act V Bolero. Although shocking, Callas immediately fixes the "crack" and finished the aria with poise.

(Author's Note: After CDs arrival in the 1980s, this performance was released by Melodram. A new version was then unearthed by Elisabeth Schwarzkopf. She found it in her husband, Walter Legge's archives after his death. In much-improved sound, it was released by Testament CD in 2008 minus the Overture).

Verdi—*Aïda*—Mexico City, July 3, 1951

This is the legendary 1951 Mexico City *Aïda* with Callas' interpolation of a massive high E-flat at the end of the act II triumphal scene. In acceptable sound, it underlines what Callas was able to bring to the role of Aïda. Icing on the cake are the Radames of Mario Del Monaco—stentorian and masculine and a sympathetic, dramatically vivid Amneris by Oralia Dominguez (the finish of the judgement scene is extraordinary). This *Aïda* is available on a number of CD labels. It is also available on YouTube with a piano/vocal score as part of the video. Although Aïda was not her most congenial role, Callas' interpretation should be heard and studied for the many felicities of nuance that she brings to it. There are a couple of live performances of Callas in this role including another (1950) performance from Mexico City (also with a top Eb), another from London, in 1953, conducted by Barbirolli, as well as her commercial recording.

Verdi—*Aïda*—Mexico City, 1951
https://www.youtube.com/watch?v=1wLSF9lyTeE

Rossini—*Armida*—Florence, April 10, 1952

Despite sonic flaws, the celebrated revival of Rossini's *Armida* is one of the most electrifying of the Callas performances. It is an absolute must for anyone interested in this artist. When this performance took place, it caused an international sensation—dramatic coloratura singing like this had never been heard in the 20th century. Despite its murky sound, the tape exhibits Callas's genius in phrasing florid music from the otto cento repertoire. It is a caressing and phrasing of legato lines and melismatic patterns that speaks of a remarkable degree of understanding and musicality. It is hard to believe that Callas learned the role in only five days—in between performances of Norma and I *puritani*.

Armida also shows Callas' daring penchant, during her youth, for interpolating extreme high notes. The high note count in *Armida* is staggering. Without taking into account the dozens of high Cs peppered throughout the score, there are high Ds and a sustained high E interpolated into the ensemble during her Act I entrance, a high E-flat at the end of the Act I love duet, numerous high Ds in the famous Act II Aria with Variations: "D'Amore al dolce impero" (which is nothing short of magnificent), and a final high E-flat at the end of the 10-minute, dramatic, final scene.

I first heard this opera on FWR (#657) and loved every minute of those two LPs. If you are interested, I suggest you get the Divina Records version. Despite the sonic imperfections present in all existing sources, the Divina edition is the most complete and has the best sound of them all. They also offer a first-rate presentation.

Rossini—*Armida*—Florence, 1952
https://www.youtube.com/watch?v=l0s7zLThW7w

Bellini—*Norma*—London, November 18, 1952

There are a number of *Normas* with Callas. Most listeners prefer the 1955 Milan broadcast. I prefer, however, the November 18, 1952 London performance. I like the solid dramaticism of Callas' singing in 1952. There is a fierce, steely determination and an abandoned use of a strong, cutting chest-voice that I find intoxicating. There is also a "classy" Clothilde sung by a young Joan Sutherland. Ebe Stignani is a sympathetic Adalgisa who blends well with Callas during their important duets, and bass Giacomo Vaghi and tenor Mirto Picchi who both work their way through the opera with success.

Callas is in remarkable voice during this broadcast. One fun moment is her early "leaping" to a penultimate high C at the end of the "Casta diva" cabaletta.

During the finale of act one the difficult "No, non tremare" finds Callas easily winding her way through Bellini's intricate coloratura and wide leaps. She then offers a special high note—a long, penultimate high D that she inserts at the end. For some reason, this was an interpolation Callas only sang live—it is not on either of her commercial recordings.

Later, in Act 2, there is an exquisite "Teneri figli" and a heart-breaking "Deh non voleri vittime" in the finale of the opera with beautiful portamenti. All is sensitively conducted by Vittorio Gui. This is a very special performance. At this time Act I can be found on YouTube.

Bellini—*Norma*—London, 1952—only Act I
https://www.youtube.com/watch?v=ahqxeLUY1ow

Verdi—*Macbeth*—Milan, December 7, 1952

I originally bought this BJR LP set during a visit home to Baltimore in 1971 and it has remained a beloved recording ever since. This is an important Callas pirate. Although Enzo Mascherini is not an ideal Macbeth, during the performance his work with Callas is solid.

Callas is unforgettable—a powerhouse of passion and dramatic coloratura exuberance. Her three set arias are masterfully sung as is the banquet scene's Brindisi full of trills and coloratura. The second verse of the Brindisi, especially, Callas uses subtle nuances to underline Lady Macbeth's determination to keep Macbeth under her control.

There are too many lines to single-out, but I must mention one. It is during the Act 3 duet with Macbeth: "Menzogna! Morte e sterminio sull'iniqua razza!" Nowhere else on record can one hear such vicious singing of that line. Callas manages—in that one line of text—to completely illuminate the character of Lady Macbeth. This duet with Macbeth is one of the finest moments during the performance. Despite all the fury and chest voice she uses during the scene, Callas crowns the duet with an electrifying, penultimate high C. (It is also nice that the ballet was included in this performance.)

Despite some conflicts with the conductor, Victor de Sabata, (he wants to go faster, she wants to go slower) Callas' Sleepwalking scene is a vocal triumph with a sweet, piano high Db at its conclusion.

Verdi—Macbeth—Milan, 1952
https://www.youtube.com/watch?v=UUNinTk6msc&t=36s

Cherubini—*Medea* Florence, May 7, 1953, Milan, December 10, 1953, Dallas, November 8, 1958

Callas sang the role of Cherubini's *Medea* some thirty times during the course of her career. I am partial to the fiery singing of her first, Florence performance conducted by Vittorio Gui. In this performance Callas uses her chest voice with shocking abandon and provides an unforgettable, harrowing finish to act II. Gui also opens cuts in Cherubini's music that other conductors omit. Here Callas' voice has a suitable cutting edge in the top register. Taken as a whole, in terms of vocal shadings and hues, this is an incredibly ornate interpretation—Medea's relentless conniving fury being brought vividly to life.

(It is interesting that it was during these Florence *Medeas* that Callas decided she needed to lose weight. She felt she needed a leaner face and body to help sharpen her interpretation of this and other roles to follow.)

The Bernstein-led performance from Milan on December 10, 1953, is also held in high regard. I find it similar to the Gui-led performance. Both are shockingly strong with various lines of recitative jumping out at the listener. None the less, I prefer the Gui. Not only does the Gui performance include an uncut final scene, but the finale to Act II is better recorded—Callas' asides over the chorus frighteningly clear in their daemonic intensity. In the Milan broadcast Callas' important asides are often covered and not audible. Gui's also has a stunning, interpolated penultimate high C at the end of Act II that soars over the orchestra. From the wealth of inflection and detail Callas imparts to this music it is obvious she felt a particular affinity for the character. The score drew from Callas some of her most fervent singing.

The November 1958, Dallas *Medea* is legendary—and rightly so. If possible, it is even better than the Gui-led performance of 1953. It is the stuff of nightmares and is arguably the finest rendition of this opera you can find.

It is a performance full of individual, startlingly vivid phrases throughout. Where else can you find such an array of vocal colors? Cherubini's Medea was originally sung in French, then, in 1855, after Cherubini's death the conductor/composer Franz Lachner translated the work into German and presented the opera in Frankfurt.

In the early twentieth century, Lachner's version was translated back into Italian for its premiere at La Scala. It was this Italian-language hybrid *Medea*, in its shortened version and with Lachner's recitatives, that was revived for Maria Callas in 1953 and that is heard in most productions and recordings since that time. Only since the mid-1980s have a few productions attempted to go back to Cherubini's original French *opéra-comique*." (Conductor Martin Pearlman program notes for 2010 Boston Baroque performance of *Medea*.)

Although many complain about the use of the Lachner additions, in the case of Callas' performances of the role, I would not want to be without them. That would deprive the listener of the kalaidoscopic colors Callas brought to these links of musical text.

Medea is a long, arduous role. Yet during this 1958 performance the countless high Bbs are nothing short of a visceral experience for listeners and the excellent combination of Callas with Jon Vickers, Teresa Berganza, Elisabeth Carron and Nicola Zaccaria is potent. Callas responds with some of the most electrifying and abandoned singing of her career. (Oddly, the 1957 commercial recording on Mercury, has little of this intensity.)

In Dallas, the ending of Act II and the beginning of Act III are testaments to Callas' dramatic instincts. If possible, Callas' furious singing of "Questa promessa un di, tu l'avesti per me" at the end of Act 2 surpasses the 1953 Gui-led reading.

Act III in Dallas, is a study in contrasts with the use of every vocal trick in the book to promote a living character. This includes clean vocal attacks, coarse glottal strokes, a clever use of breath for dramatic effect, and various shades and hues to illuminate the text. "Del fiero duol che il cor mi frange" is four minutes of startling imagery. It is sung on a solid legato with an inventive use of chest and top registers and vacillating moods that perfectly delineates the character.

Callas' concept of *Medea* changed little over the 8 years she performed the role. Her voice did, however, undergo changes.

Although the December 1961 La Scala performance is not held in as fine a regard as earlier performances, it is just about as impressive as the Florence and Dallas performances. Sure, some of the finer dramatic points may be better highlighted in the two earlier performances—but the voice is still capable of riveting dramaticism. Vocal concession was made to avoid her usual high C at the end of Act II, but it hardly matters in such a remarkably vibrant portrait. The third act remains malevolently powerful and haunting. This one, by the way, partners Callas with Jon Vickers, Giulietta Simionato and Nicolai Ghiaurov as protagonists.

Cherubini—*Medea*—Florence, 1953—Gui
https://www.youtube.com/watch?v=lX5duz_Ds5U&t=6211s
Cherubini—*Medea*—Milan, 1953—Bernstein
https://www.youtube.com/watch?v=HSh3FTs4sQI&t=5950s
Cherubini—*Medea*—Dallas, 1958
https://www.youtube.com/watch?v=eHOOVo4Tf5s&t=5877s
Cherubini—*Medea*—Milan, 1961
https://www.youtube.com/watch?v=jLcnMJokq9U
Bellini—*La sonnambula*—Milan, 1955; Edinburgh, 1957

Callas' performances of *La sonnambulas* are definitely worth investigating. These include the 1955, Milan performance (her first) with Leonard Bernstein conducting; the July 4, 1957 Köln performance; and the August 21, 1957 Edinburgh performance conducted by Antonino Votto.

La sonnambula was an important Callas revival because it demonstrated her remarkable ability to lighten her voice to underscore the delicacy of Amina. None of her other roles show such gentle sweetness. All surviving performances (including the commercial 1957 recording) are of interest. The 1955, Bernstein-led performance still finds an occasional edgy quality creeping into some high notes. By 1957, though, this had disappeared.

By that time, Callas had polished the final scene's "Ah non credea" into a striking piece of singing that could stop time.

For a voice of this type, the ornamentation Callas used during the act one "Come per me sereno" and the final scene are inventive and novel in their freshness.

The now traditional ascent to a sustained high Eb between the two verses of "Ah non giunge" was first sung by Callas. It seems to have originated sometime after the 1955 Bernstein performances in Milan (since she did not sing it at that time). This ornamental passage is now used by practically anyone who sings the aria. During 1957 performances (and on her commercial recording) Callas stunned listeners by offering a gorgeous diminuendo on the top Eb.

Bellini—*La Sonnambula*—Milan, 1955—Bernstein
https://www.youtube.com/watch?v=ok6VX9A9lt8&t=20s
Bellini—*La Sonnambula*—Edinburgh, 1957
https://www.youtube.com/watch?v=bEUSQTsFVCM&t=737s

Other Important Callas Performances

Whatever you do, do not miss the eleven rough-and-ready Mexico City performances (in variable sound) from 1950-1952. These important aural documents include *Il trovatore* (1 ½), *Lucia di Lammermoor* (revelatory when first heard), *La Traviata (2), Aïda (2), I puritani, Tosca (2), Rigoletto* (her only live performance of the role) and *Norma*. These provincial performances are sometimes maddening—at times coarse, at times elegance personified. But I would never want to be without them. They are available in two Melodram box sets as well as individual CD sets and on YouTube for the most part.

Despite scrappy orchestral playing and occasional, sloppy singing from others in the cast, these performances explain much about Callas' growth as an artist. A few like *Lucia di Lammermoor, I puritani, La traviata* and *Rigoletto* are priceless. In the 1952 *La Traviata,* there is a special treat for high note enthusiasts. Callas interpolates a huge high Eb at the end of the act II gambling scene. (Also, when it comes to examples of Callas' ability to shade her voice, listeners should check out any of her *La traviatas*. Her "sick" voice is unearthly and startlingly realistic.

One note of interest. In the Mexico City *Rigoletto*, Callas sang "Caro nome" down a half step from the original so that she could honor an old tradition (since at least 1918) of interpolating a final high note (in this case an Eb) at the end of the aria. Along the same lines, she takes a spectacular high Eb at the end of the act III "Vendetta" duet and a high Db at the end of the act IV Quartet.

Donizetti—*Lucia di Lammermoor*—Mexico City, 1952
https://www.youtube.com/watch?v=ujQ0I0hjmoI&t=5491s
Verdi—*Rigoletto*—Mexico City, 1952
https://www.youtube.com/watch?v=svMW6LskxSI&t=49s
Verdi—*La traviata*—Mexico City, 1952
https://www.youtube.com/watch?v=JZCH8oW6dAE&t=5943s

Another classic is the 1955 Berlin *Lucia di Lammermoor* with Karajan conducting (Divina Records). This is, of course, the typically cut version of the opera used at that time. Callas is at her most elegant—spinning many lines of gossamer delicacy and sweetness. She is partnered with Giuseppe di Stefano and Rolando Panerai. In exceptional sound, Callas gave one of the greatest performances of her career. The mad scene alone is a treasure—full of sweet shadings, high pianissimi, and a wonderful, otherworldly cadenza with flute. Different from earlier performances, she eschews the first Eb at the end of the cadenza—saving that climactic high note (and a good one) for the end of the scene.

Donizetti—*Lucia di Lammermoor*—Berlin, 1955
https://www.youtube.com/watch?v=_maNJkybAwI

Also extraordinary is the Milan *Anna Bolena* in April of 1957, conducted by Gianandrea Gavazzeni. This was one of her most important revivals. Although cut to shreds, what remains is a fantastic tapestry of singing and colorations from Callas. Not hurting matters, she is partnered with the wonderful mezzo-soprano Giulietta Simionato. Their act II duet is a highlight of the performance. Tenor Gianni Raimondi and bass Nicola Rossi-Lemeni round out the cast. The famous 20-minute Mad Scene at the end of the opera was an eye-opener for original audiences. Callas gives a master class in the art of bel canto singing. Special mention must be made, though, of the La Scala women's chorus who perfectly establish the mood for Callas' grand Mad Scene with their beautiful and sympathetic singing of the preceding chorus.

Donizetti—*Anna Bolena*—Milan, 1957
https://www.youtube.com/watch?v=GG2aH3MS2kg

Not to be missed is an important revival concert—the 1959 *Il pirata* from Carnegie Hall in New York. Callas was very fond of the Mad Scene at the end of this opera. She frequently programmed it on concerts during the late 1950s. In addition to the commercial recording, I believe there are at least four other surviving performances. All are worth studying. There is a fascinating video from Hamburg of the Mad Scene from a May 15 1959 concert. It finds Callas acting through the long prelude—which is something to behold. Even though she omits the penultimate high C, the video is a prize—don't miss it. (You can see it on YouTube.) Her commercial recording of this scene (found on "Mad Scenes") is one of the finest things she ever recorded.

Bellini—*Il Pirata*—Carnegie Hall, New York 1959
https://www.youtube.com/watch?v=OwhwY6olOc0

Callas Concerts

During the early 1950s Callas gave three remarkable concerts that were broadcast over Italian radio and have survived in excellent sound. In relation to Maria Callas' art, they are indispensable. Although she often gave concerts during her career, these three strikingly showcased her versatility.

Rome, February 18, 1952 (*Macbeth, Lucia di Lammermoor, Nabucco, Lakmé*—conducted by De Fabritiis)

This must have been shocking for that first audience. Never before had a soprano offered such varied arias during a single concert.

For Callas it was typical. She had already sung *Nabucco* on stage, *Lakmé* was an important part of her early studies with de Hidalgo, she was scheduled to sing her first *Lucia di Lammermoor* in Mexico City in four months, and Lady Macbeth was to follow for Milan in December. All par for the course. Luckily it was preserved in very good monaural sound.

All the arias are well-sung by Callas—though one wishes she had included the "Salgo gia" cabaletta of the Nabucco aria. The act I aria of Lady Macbeth is a tantalizing taste of what would come in December. The Lucia Mad Scene is a remarkable display from beginning to end. Already apparent are Callas' strikingly individual thoughts on this character. The cadenza with flute is (as it would be throughout her career) the traditional Estelle Liebling cadenza. It is beautifully sung with nuance, and is nicely synchronized with the flute. Callas crowns the aria with a long, high Eb.

Considering the color and size of Maria Callas' voice, the real curiosity of this concert was the difficult Bell Song from Delibes' *Lakmé*. This aria was usually sung by light-voiced sopranos such as Lily Pons. For 1952 audiences, the idea of Callas singing such music was incomprehensible.

It is obvious, however, from the care with which she approached this music, that Callas had worked on it extensively with her teacher, the Spanish virtuosa, Elvira de Hidalgo. It is in the Bell Song from *Lakmé* that one notices a most unusual combination (or contradiction).

Here was an instinctive dramatic interpreter with a voice and temperament suited to the histrionics of the dramatic repertoire, but one thoroughly schooled in bel canto elegance. de Hidalgo passed on to her student the strict training of a coloratura specialist as well as a love for the artistic challenges of florid work.

This is the only live performance of Callas singing this aria. It has been available in various LP and CD incarnations for decades.

It is a big-voiced, overtly Italian-sung performance. The original 1952 audience must have been bewildered at hearing such delicate music coming from the throat of such a huge-voiced soprano. Yet, interpretively, Callas succeeds in suggesting Lakmé's unfortunate situation.

Her naturally aggressive manner of singing, however, and the cutting edge of her upper register are not entirely fitting for the gossamer French music. The final bell refrain, though, is extremely agile with superb shadings, accents, agile runs, good trills and high staccati. Callas finishes with an excellent high B trill (with a decrescendo) and a massive high E that is heroically sustained to the end. The amazed audience goes berserk.

Two years later (1954) Callas brought the aria down from the shelf one last time and commercially recorded it (again in Italian) for the *Coloratura/Lyric* LP recital. She left posterity one of the great performances.

Due to a rapid weight loss, her voice had undergone some significant changes. Like her body, Callas's voice had thinned down and lost much of its former cutting edge and dramatic soprano fullness; the bright bite in the top register was replaced with a softer, more pliant quality; lyrically floated rather than dramatically punched.

Because of this, Callas gives a remarkable performance, full of musical insight, restraint, and floated head voice; the aggressiveness of two years earlier having been diluted.

Not surprisingly, her gentle effects demonstrate an extensive palette of colors that better suit Delibes's music. Callas' finish of the first bell refrain is notable for the sweet sweep over the high E. The last bell refrain is extraordinary: light staccati, echo effects and an unaccompanied passage of high staccati that ping effortlessly. Delibes's scales are note-perfect and build in intensity to the coda (one of the cleanest on disc) not one tone of the arpeggiated figure is out of place.

(Callas's secret was not putting any pressure on the ascending arpeggiated notes, letting her voice easily slip into the head register, instinctively realizing their height would be their emphasis.) The final high E is less sustained than in 1952, but rich with overtones. I find this final high E more satisfying; pure and less bright than the longer one found at the end of the 1952 live RAI concert."

Rome, February 18, 1952
  https://www.youtube.com/watch?v=s37itqU9L-U

San Remo, December 12, 1954 (Entführung, Dinorah, Louise, Armida—conducted by Simonetto)

Two years later, Callas displayed similar versatility, singing arias from *Die Entführung aus dem Serial*, *Dinorah*, *Louise*, and *Armida*. "Martern aller arten" (sung in Italian) from *Entführung* is a remnant of her rare singing of Mozart. It is given a dramatic, focused performance of glittering coloratura, solid low notes and full high notes. Dinorah's gentle waltz with her shadow is sung with grace, delicacy, superb, shaded scale work, and a remarkable blending with the flute during the final cadenza. One would never have anticipated that the Callas voice could blend so sweetly with a single flute—but it does. The famous aria from *Louise* (in Italian) is a breath of lyrical air in this most demanding concert. The concert closes with the difficult aria with coloratura variations from Rossini's *Armida*. Although not as formidable as the 1952 Florence reading, it is just as impressive.

San Remo, December 12, 1954

https://www.youtube.com/watch?v=gInlCY4bSps&t=15s

Milan, September 27, 1956 (La Vestale, Semiramide, Hamlet, I puritani—conducted by Simonetto)

This 1956 RAI concert mimics the previous two with arias from *La Vestale*, *I Puritani*, *Semiramide*, and *Hamlet*. Just as varied as the other two concerts, this has the benefit of a dramatic *La Vestale* aria with a fine high C, a fluent "Bel raggio" from *Semiramide* (rarely heard at that time), and an unusual programming choice—the Act I finale of *I puritani* (with chorus). A final aria, a colorful Mad Scene from *Hamlet* is given in a generous, Italian-sung performance. Callas would sing this aria often at concerts during the next couple of years.

Milan, September 27, 1956

https://www.youtube.com/watch?v=TJ_t2dROpk4&t=1570s

Dallas—1957 Rehearsal

Just as important as the above concerts is the 1957 Dallas rehearsal. For this concert Callas sang major scenes from *Entführung aus dem Serail* (in Italian) *La traviata*, *Macbeth*, and mad scenes from *I puritani* and *Anna Bolena*. (Unfortunately, only the rehearsal exists—though in very good sound.) This too, is available on YouTube.

This is a very important aural document since it provides an interesting glimpse into Callas at work while singing some of her most demanding arias. There is little "marking" here (when a singer takes things down an octave to rest the voice). Most are thrillingly sung full-voice.

Dallas Rehearsal 1957

https://www.youtube.com/watch?v=T9csyNVWgCE&t=2395s

The Los Angeles Concert November 29, 1958

In 2000, VAI CD released a newly-unearthed in-house tape of a Callas concert. The repertoire included arias from *La Vestale, Macbeth, Il barbiere di Siviglia, Mefistofele, La Bohème* and *Hamlet*. Like the Dallas rehearsal, it resembled the wide-ranging programs of earlier years.

Although one misses the close miking of a broadcast, the tape does show the size and penetrative power of the Callas voice. The *Vestale* (a rather long 10-minute warm up aria) may not be as steady as her commercial version, but I would not want to be without this—with its fine legato sweep and build to a dramatic finish with a thrust to a final high C. Although I enjoyed the whole concert, I did miss the cabaletta to the act I Macbeth aria (though I understand why she left it out—to save her voice for the rest of the demanding concert)

There are two special performances here and both are mad scenes. One is the Mad Scene from Boito's *Mefistofele* (the last great, Italian-written mad scene). What a desolate, atmospheric piece this is. Callas' voice and timbre seem tailor-made for this music. Her "Laura è fredda" perfectly depicts Margherita's pathetic condition. The flights of coloratura and birdlike trills are masterfully phrased. This is especially obvious in the second verse with its rise to a sustained high B (to which Callas adds a lovely diminuendo).

Callas is one of the few artists whose sense of timing is perfectly judged during the last two measures of this aria. This was one of her greatest gifts—an instinctive knowledge of how long high climactic notes should be sustained. A release a second earlier or later could lessen the impact of the music. One notices this time and again on her recordings of both live and commercial.

The other standout is the *Hamlet* Mad Scene. Sung in French, (a recent practice for Callas at the time) this was always a good aria for Callas. She showers it with countless colors and nuance that help create a tangible portrait of the mad Ophelia. Especially lovely are the descending chromatic scales which glisten like pearls and all the coloratura which is phrased with fluidity and grace. Callas even interpolates trills that Thomas did not ask for. The difficult chromatic run to high E is successful and all is brought to a rousing finish.

In reviewing this CD online, Milan Petkovic of Toronto Canada noted that, in actuality, the arias on this concert have been well documented throughout Callas' career. This would include:

Il barbiere di Siviglia—7
La Vestale—6
La Bohème—5
Macbeth—4
Hamlet—3 1/2
(*Author's Note*: Mefistofele—also at least 3).
Los Angeles Concert 1958
https://www.youtube.com/watch?v=RHEIM3MzRQw

(*Author's Note:* There was also a famous Turin concert on March 12, 1951 with Sesto Bruscantini that was preserved. This was one of the earliest times Italian audiences experienced Callas' virtuosity. It was two months before the famous Florence revival of *I Vespri Siciliani*. A surviving tape of three of her selections exists: an aria from *Un Ballo in Maschera*, the *Mignon* Polonaise, and the difficult Theme and Variations by Proch (which Callas was fond of and had wanted to commercially record). The Proch Variations especially, is a remarkable demonstration of her coloratura abilities. Callas even included the challenging section of trills and wide leaps that other singers usually omit because of its difficulty. Inserting a difficult cadenza with flute at the end, she caps the concert piece with a leap to high Eb resolving to a final Db. Extraordinary.

Unfortunately, the sonics are the worst of any of the surviving Callas tapes (even worse than *Nabucco*). It is available on CD and on YouTube but it is only recommended for die-hard Callas fans.

Turin Concert 1951
https://www.youtube.com/watch?v=1SjJS4C8zlo

John Ardoin once said to Callas "It must be very enviable to be Maria Callas." And she said,

'No, it's a very terrible thing to be Maria Callas, because it's a question of trying to understand something you can never really understand.' Because she couldn't explain what she did—it was all done by instinct; it was something, incredibly, embedded deep within her" (Wikipedia)

Callas' legacy of live performances are available as various single CD box sets, as well as the large Warner—45 CDs—box set. Fortunately, for today's listeners, almost everything is available on YouTube.

In regards to the Callas concerts do yourself a favor and go to the Divina Records website: https://divinarecords.com.

On the Home Page you can download for free the original BJR 3 LP set: *Maria Callas Soprano Assoluta.* You can also download the superb, informative booklet that originally came with the set. According to the Divina web site, the 20 selections from 1949-1959, are courtesy of Charles Johnson, Santiago Rodríguez and Dagoberto Jorge of BJR Enterprises.

Originally released in 1977, the year of her death, this is a fantastic compilation of Callas' most important concert material. Restored and remastered in 2018, by Pablo Berutti, this is a most generous gift to listeners from Divina Records. It is a treasure not to be missed.

EIGHT COMMERCIALLY NEGLECTED (BUT FORTUNATELY PIRATED) U.S. SOPRANOS OF THE 1980S

The era of opera pirating was very different from now. At that time, despite the illegality of pirating, most singers were grateful their work was being documented and circulating to the public—that they were not being ignored. Most feared that they would be forgotten because they were not recording for major record labels. There was no Internet; no uploading of performances to YouTube; no personal blogs, no Tik-Tok. Many of America's greatest singers were either under-recorded or were not recorded at all. Even when recordings exist, it is only through their live recordings (pirating) that one can experience the variability of their art and be able to compare their artistic accomplishments.

Following are eight sopranos (alphabetically) who frequently performed at the New York City Opera and around the New York City area. While they may not have made many commercial recordings (some not at all), their work is highly sought after on pirated recordings and collectors. None, except Ruth Welting and Beverly Hoch, commercially recorded their specialty. Fortunately, today, due to the convenience of technology and the kindness of up-loaders to YouTube, these artists can be heard in their métier.

Below are a few of the sopranos who I feel have been neglected. There are many other singers of all voice fachs who are equally neglected.

Faith Esham (1948–) Although she recorded Micaela in a respectable 1984 Erato film/recording of *Carmen* (with Placido Domingo and Julia Migenes Johnson), that won a 1985 Grammy award, and Cherubino in an EMI recording of *Le nozze di Figaro* in 1987. She also took part in the Studio Cast recording of Villa-Lobos' *Magdalena* in 1989 with Judy Kaye and Jerry Hadley. Magdalena is an obscure work that is rarely revived. It premiered at the Los Angeles Civic Light Opera Association in 1948.

Villa-Lobos—*Magdalena*—Studio Recording, New York 1989
https://www.youtube.com/watch?v=dPOyAtFT98g

For the most part, however, Esham's extraordinary lyrical talents have gone completely unexploited on commercial disc. Thankfully, more than twenty pirated live performances exist of her work on international stages.

Born in Ohio, and presently an adjunct assistant professor of voice at Westminster Choir College, this remarkable singer began her career in the late 1970s as a light mezzo-soprano, singing such roles as Cherubino in Nozze di Figaro (her New York City Opera debut was in 1977 while she was still at Juilliard) and Isolier in New City Opera's 1979 revival of Rossini's Le Comte Ory. (See link under Ashley Putnam.)

In the mid-1980s she miraculously (but carefully) metamorphosed into one of America's finest Gildas in Rigoletto. (She sang during a Live from Lincoln Center telecast of the New York City Opera's production of Rigoletto in 1988.) Esham also sang an exquisite Pamina in the 1987 televised NYCO [New York City Opera] performance of Die Zauberflöte.) When she made her Metropolitan Opera debut in December of 1986, as Marzelline in *Fidelio*, the Metropolitan seemed not to know what to do with this gifted artist and no further contracts were offered.

Verdi—"Caro nome" and Vendetta duet *Rigoletto*—NYCO 1988
https://www.youtube.com/watch?v=jswBSrOc7Uw

Esham was a very versatile singer, singing such diverse roles as Melisande (Pelleas et Melisande) a delicious Cendrillon in the Massenet opera, Susannah in Floyd's Susannah, (a now much-neglected American operatic masterpiece), Marguerite in Faust, the four heroines in Les Contes d'Hofmann, a sweetly gentle Leila in Les pêcheurs de perles, and a superb Manon. Her sweetly spun soprano voice reached an easy high E-natural.

Of her Manon, Donal Henahan wrote in The New York Times:

> Miss Esham, you may remember, caught the fancy of New York audiences two seasons ago in the title role of Massenet's Cendrillon, and her work this time in the composer's most popular opera made, if anything, a stronger case for her as an internationally important soprano…Miss Esham's pure, unspoiled soprano is a chameleon instrument, capable of creamy head tones, dizzying coloratura flights and lyrico-spinto power of the sort that soars easily over large ensembles. One can think of a dozen roles in which her voice and style would show to advantage. (*The New York Times*, August 20, 1985)

Massenet—Excerpts *Manon*—NYCO 1985, with Richard Leech
https://www.youtube.com/watch?v=I6gwUh6Hjb8&t=11s

Massenet—"Enfin je suis ici" *Cendrillon*—NYCO 1983
https://www.youtube.com/watch?v=m9_BPudumv0

Despite consistently fine reviews throughout her career, major recording labels never chose to spotlight Esham in repertoire that had become her specialty. She was a fine Desdemona (in Wales in 1990), and a devastatingly moving Baby Doe (at NYCO in 1988).

Many fans of this soprano have individual personal favorites among her roles. For me it is her deeply moving Baby Doe. I saw her sing that opera a number of times at NYCO (and taped them) and have always felt that it was an artistic crime she never got to record it commercially. She was sublime—natural and unaffected in her portrayal of the tragic character of Baby, her voice as alluring in Moore's music as was her acting on stage. Baby has a number of arias and all of them were true highlights of her performance. Her singing of the final aria (often called the "Leadville Liebestodt") with its gently suspended, F-sharp over the orchestral postlude, found few dry eyes in NYCO audiences.

Both Esham and Ruth Welting (who sang the telecast of the opera from NYCO in 1976) were able to tap into the specific emotionality and the gentle dignity of the role of Baby Doe.

Esham was an elegant singer who was consistent as well as musical; anything that she appeared in was enriched by her artistic presence. Welting and Esham learned much about the role's interpretive intricacies from its most famous interpreter, Beverly Sills. Perhaps, not surprisingly, Esham's view of the role, and of the last aria in particular, shows her great affinity for the music and understanding of the character.

> If you play (Baby Doe) as premeditated, you're going to have problems…That's why the idea of her having this fantasy is so important to me, I may be naïve, but I don't think she was out to land

Horace, I think she was absolutely smitten with him....

'No one ever accepted her,' maintains Esham. 'Even her two daughters by Horace left her. She had a very unhappy life after he died, and knowing that colors the last aria for me. It's her most poetic piece of music, and it also possesses a kind of strength that her other arias don't have, which reflects the strength she developed during the course of her marriage. Her undying love and devotion for Horace make her bigger than life in the end. It's a complex and fascinating role.' (Interview with Sheryl Flatow—*A New Baby Doe*—NYCO Program, October 18, 1988)

Moore—Four Arias of Baby Doe *The Ballad of Baby Doe*—NYCO in-house 1988
https://www.youtube.com/watch?v=GBOYQ33ilW4

Beverly Hoch was born in Kansas in 1951, and is currently one of the voice faculty at Texas Woman's University. Hoch's is a special case. In many ways her voice harks back to the old-fashioned coloratura soprano voice; light, delicate, extremely flexible by nature, with a sweetly floated high register not easily forgotten. She has always been a lovely artist who was concerned about her art and who specialized in concert work. She was also one of the few artists of her time to successfully exhibit extreme high notes—before Natalie Dessay (and others) made this popular.

Her coloratura technique was practically flawless, her trill real and beautifully supple, and she is one of the few singers I have ever met who "thought" like a coloratura. By that I mean, by instinct, her mind knew exactly how to spontaneously construct cadenzas and flourishes that underlined what she wanted to say musically. A remarkable talent.

After winning a number of difficult competitions in 1977 and 1979, she arrived on the New York music scene in January of 1980 with a radio recital from the 92nd Street Y and never looked back.

The New York Times music critic Donal Henahan wrote:

> Miss. Hoch's voice is pure and agile, which satisfies the basic requirements of a coloratura soprano, but it also has an attractive vibrato that lends itself to warmth and color. Like many coloraturas, she can use it in a precise instrumental style, and did so dazzlingly.

Although Hoch sang with a number of opera companies (Hawaii, Royal Swedish Opera, Glyndebourne, Wexford, Opéra National de Lyon, Paris, Strasbourg), as well as regional opera houses in the United States including Washington D.C.—The Merry Wives of Windsor, and Arizona Opera—*La Sonnambula* (1991), and Lakmé (1989), she was best known for her international concert programs.

During a 1986 concert in Marmö, Sweden, Hoch shocked listeners with her singing of Mozart's difficult concert aria, "Popoli di Tessaglia" (with its two written Gs above high C), by throwing in a third sustained, penultimate G at its conclusion. During the same concert she sang Proch's intricate "Theme and Variations" with a penultimate high A-flat. Many divas have recorded these notes in the safety of a studio but Hoch sang them live, all the time, with no fear. A tape of a 1986 Detmold performance of Hoch singing the original 1912 version of Zerbinetta's aria (Ariadne auf Naxos) has been a cult item for years. It was uploaded to YouTube in 2009.

Strauss—Zerbinetta's Aria 1912 version of *Ariadne auf Naxos*— Beverly Hoch Detmold 1986

https://www.youtube.com/watch?v=OmYmy0Fo_fM

She recorded Carmina Burana for Decca, Mozart's Queen of the Night in Die Zauberflöte for EMI (1990), and the first recording of Handel's Imeneo for Vox (1985). She also recorded a solo recital album in 1987 (The Art of the Coloratura) that is now considered a classic of its type. On that album she sings one of the finest performances of the infamously difficult Gliere Concerto for Coloratura Soprano and Orchestra with its spectacular pyrotechnics, all of which were musically framed and expressive. Afte a beautiful rolled trill on high C, Hoch takes a perfectly sustained high F. The solo album also has one of her signature tunes, Theme and Variations by Proch. During the 1980s she habitually ended this complex concert aria with a stunning, penultimate A-flat above high C.

Reviewing the album when it was first released, Gramophone noted:

> The Queen of Night's staccatos and triplets have an almost clockwork accuracy; Milhaud's charming Ronsard songs enjoy an ease of execution that belies their difficulty; Mozart's *Vorrei spiegarvi* shows a refined musical taste at work; Proch's *Variations* find time for tenderness and sensitive rubato in-between the trapeze stunts, flying ever higher above the top C eventually to hit (and hold) the A flat *in alt*... Marvelously, the young American award-winner disarms criticisms at once: she is extremely proficient and a great pleasure to listen to.

Despite her success, Hoch remained quite humble. I saw and heard her many times in concert and in recital in New York, including a brilliantly sung Gliere Concerto for Coloratura Soprano and Orchestra at Alice Tully Hall in February of 1991. The next month there was a wonderful Avery Fisher Hall (David Geffen Hall) concert for children where Hoch sang a stunning "Der holle rache" from Die Zauberflöte at 10:00 am and again at noon. All her high Fs' were intact as well as was a gracious, Marcella Sembrich-like high D that Hoch threw in for fun at the end of the aria. The kids loved it, and so did I.

Beverly Hoch—Great Coloratura Solos (1987)—Arne, Handel, Mozart, Proch, Benedict, Milhaud, Alabiev, Gliere—conducted by Kenneth Schermerhorn

https://www.youtube.com/watch?v=tMCK8IHQhCU

Beverly Hoch & Stuart Burrows in Hong Kong, 1987—Proch, Delibes, Mozart, Gounod—conducted by Barry Wordsworth

https://www.youtube.com/watch?v=WwTJbXrD58Y&t=310s

Beverly Hoch—Mozart—"No, no, che non sei capace" (Concert Aria)—Connecticut 1985

https://www.youtube.com/watch?v=LVCGt2j1Vrw

Beverly Hoch—Vivaldi, Holst, Bach—1983 broadcast

https://www.youtube.com/watch?v=KpcYmSDqeuQ

Beverly Hoch—Thomas—*Mignon* (exc)—Wexford 1986 with Cynthia Clarey, Curtis Rauam

https://www.youtube.com/watch?v=igy5vpeTzXA

Ashley Putnam (1952–) Ashley Putnam first studied the flute. In 1976, however, she won first place in the Metropolitan Opera National Council auditions and shortly thereafter became one of the most important young singers at NYCO. She went on to sing at the Metropolitan Opera (as did other NYCO alumnae, Gianna Rolandi and Faith Esham) as well as at many other international houses.

Putnam won the National Council auditions with her singing of the mad scene from *I puritani* and "Bel raggio" from *Semiramide* (containing a number of brilliant high Es). She did not make her formal debut with the company until seven years later while on tour in April of 1983, as *Lucia di Lammermoor*. After seven tour performances of that role, she did not return to the house until 1990, as Marguerite in *Faust* and Elvira in *Don Giovanni*. Her last appearance there was in April of 1990.

Putnam sang all over the world. For many of her younger years I feel that she was mismanaged; pigeon-holed into roles from the coloratura literature that did not really suit her. One of her first New York concerts (December of 1978) included mad scenes from Hamlet and I puritani as well as arias from La bohème and Pagliacci. (These can now be heard on YouTube.) Although Putnam possessed a good high E-flat and even E, these were not notes that she should have been exploiting time and time again. She was a full-bodied, beautifully expressive lyric soprano, not a coloratura. Even so, she was regularly hired for *Lucia di Lammermoor*, La fille du regiment (including a NYCO broadcast on April 1, 1979), I puritani, Hamlet, I Lombardi, and other roles that stretched her top register dangerously.

Of her performance of *Lucia di Lammermoor* at the Kennedy Center, however, The Washington Post, had this to say:

> Her voice is sweet, accurate, flexible and beautifully expressive, and she uses it in the service of a considerable acting talent—though Lucia is hardly the ideal opera to judge dramatic ability. Her work in the opening scenes, was melodramatically stylized—as this script almost requires. She played it like a rather fragile and downtrodden Victorian young lady who has suffered more than her share of abuse. The portrayal grew gradually credible until the mad scene, when it blazed forth—repression released in a performance that blended bravura singing with bravura acting. (Joseph Mclellan, 2/23/80)

Bellini—Mad Scene *I puritani* Ashley Putnam NY Philharmonic Concert 1978
https://www.youtube.com/watch?v=ZmqauLj-6Jo

Thomas—Mad Scene *Hamlet*—Ashley Putnam NY Philharmonic Concert 1978
https://www.youtube.com/watch?v=WS13rnvaJQI

Rossini—*Le Comte Ory*—NYCO September 1979 with Rockwell Blake, Faith Esham, Samuel Ramey—conducted by Imre Pallo
https://www.youtube.com/watch?v=uIJ1gE6cZc0&t=2s

Mozart—"Se viver" *Mitridate*— Ahley Putnam Aix en Provence 1986 w/ Yvonne Kenny
https://www.youtube.com/watch?v=_lyh3v8-dg0

Dvorak—Rusalka (Act I)—Philadelphia, November, 1988 with Ben Heppner, Moignon Dunn—Steven Mercurio conducting
https://www.youtube.com/watch?v=PVz6nti4sTU

the latter part of the 1970s she recorded Musetta in Puccini's La bohème, with Sir Colin Davis for Phillips (1979), and Mary in Thea Musgrave's Mary, Queen of Scots, for Moss Music.

A fine musician during her prime, Putnam had a luscious lyric sound and excellent musicianship as well as a beautiful grace on stage. Her coloratura facility was excellent and she was a daring performer, one of the brightest of stars at NYCO in its heyday. During the 1980s her Arabella was something to see and to hear. A wonderful video is available of a 1984 Glyndebourne performance of the opera with Putnam as Arabella and with Gianna Rolandi as

Zdenka. Putnam is now a member of the voice faculty at the Manhattan School of Music and adjudicates for the Metropolitan Opera National Council Auditions. I cannot think of anyone more qualified.

Gianna Rolandi (1952–2021) was one of the most gifted coloratura sopranos ever to come out of the United States. You might not know that unless you had seen her in the theater, or are familiar with her live pirate recordings. These include a 1982 NYCO telecast of *Lucia di Lammermoor* and a 1980 NYCO *La cenerentola* telecast during which she stole the show with her dynamic, virtuoso singing of a whacky Clorinda.

Offenbach—Doll's Song *Contes d'Hoffman*—Gianna Rolandi NYCO 1975 (debut)
https://www.youtube.com/watch?v=gF_Wr4mR-Tw

Rossini—Clorinda's Aria *La Cenerentola*— Gianna Rolandi NYCO , 1980
https://www.youtube.com/watch?v=dcldIEfQKXA

Delibes—Bell Song *Lakmé*— Gianna Rolandi NYCO, 1984
https://www.youtube.com/watch?v=KZsEwCFDJdI

Argento—1810 Wedding Scene *Miss Havisham's Fire*— Gianna Rolandi NYCO 1979
https://www.youtube.com/watch?v=0abMfSrvDVI

And for context, here is the final Mad Scene from Argento's wonderful opera with Rita Shane (same performance).
https://www.youtube.com/watch?v=24f_cs4HYN4&t=19s

Gianna Rolandi Collection—Arias by Mozart, Adam, Berdi, Bellini, Bernstein, Puccini, Strauss
https://www.youtube.com/watch?v=G8FdeGlGnLE

Rolandi's timbre showed remarkable similarity to that of Beverly Sills (who was still active at NYCO when Rolandi made her debut as Olympia in 1975). She was a Met Opera Auditions finalist in 1974 and debuted at NYCO the next year. The first time I heard Rolandi was during a NYCO radio broadcast of Il barbiere di Siviglia. I thought I was hearing an early recording of Beverly Sills, so uncanny was the resemblance.

Like her colleague, Gianna Rolandi could sing faster than practically anyone else in the world, and managed to do so with remarkable musicianship and a beautiful, crystalline sheen to her voice. It is said that she was hired by New York City Opera while still at the Curtis Institute. She was immensely popular with NYCO audiences. Her performances in the late 1970s and early 1980s of *Lucia di Lammermoor*, I puritani, La fille du regiment, Rigoletto, The Cunning Little Vixen, Lakmé, Coq D'Or, Mignon, Naughty Marietta, and Giulio Cesare were some of the finest to be heard during that decade. Of her Zerbinetta in Ariadne auf Naxos on April 25, 1982, Donal Henahan wrote:

> In Gianna Rolandi, the City Opera had a Zerbinetta capable of creating pandemonium in any opera house anywhere. Her deft and virtually unflawed handling of her big, florid aria, one of opera's most feared obstacle courses for coloratura soprano, brought the performance to a halt for as extended an ovation as this reviewer has heard at either of our opera houses this season. Besides shooting the eyes out of that showpiece, however, Miss Rolandi danced and otherwise cavorted with amazing grace and buoyant humor. Zerbinetta often steals the show in "Ariadne," but seldom with such justification. (*The New York Times*, April 26, 1982)

Gianna Rolandi—Strauss—Zerbinetta's Aria *Ariadne auf Naxos*—NYCO, 1975 (first)
https://www.youtube.com/watch?v=K4XyK9GD7cg

Rolandi made her Metropolitan Opera debut in 1979. In four seasons ('79, '83, '84, and '85) she sang 17 performances. Also in 1979, Rolandi gave a stellar broadcast performance (Avery Fisher Hall) of the difficult Concerto for Coloratura Soprano and Orchestra by Gliere (with a wonderful final top F) that she performed with Lily Pons's former husband, Andre Kostalanetz, conducting.

Rolandi married Sir Andrew Davis in 1989 and retired from the stage in 1994. Davis became the music director and principal conductor of the Lyric Opera of Chicago. In 2002, Rolandi became the Director of Vocal Studies for the Lyric Opera of Chicago's Ryan Opera Center and its Lyric Opera Center for American Artists until the 2012–2013 season.

Because of her own career, Rolandi was in a position to give invaluable guidance and advice to young students:

> Everything they go through, I have been through. The first thing I want to pass on to them is *how* to do it. I was fortunate to have a solid technique and could sing standing on my head if I had to, and that's what I want for them—an easy production.... Kids this age have to be careful; they all want to sound like Brunnhildes. Having been a coloratura, I know it is possible to be heard in big houses without screaming your guts out. I want them to develop patience and a real sense of self-confidence, so they can stand up for what they believe in musically and not be pushed around. That's so important in this field; you can have four sessions with four different coaches and they will all tell you something different. You have to learn how to make something your own, and how to tell somebody that's the way you do it. I want them to be unique. (Gianna Rolandi, Wikipedia)

Diana Soviero (1946–) One of the great American spintos, she made her debut as Nedda (*Pagliacci*) with NYCO in 1973, and went on to sing internationally. Soviero has often been considered an artist in the line of Magda Olivero, Rosanna Carteri, and Virginia Zeani, and with good reason. Like them, her art hinges on the exhibition of musical and character realism. Her portrayal of such heroines as Angelica in Puccini's *Suor Angelica*, Mimi in *La boheme*, Butterfly in *Madama Butterfly*, and Liu in *Turandot* have garnered praise throughout the world. She is also known for her delicate Leila in *Pecheurs de Perles*, Manon, Violetta in *La traviata*, Adriana in *Adriana Lecouvreur*, Fedora, and Juliette in *Roméo et Juliette*. With excellent technique and stagecraft, Soviero has been one of America's great musical treasures. Her art is of such quality that one questions why she was so ridiculously ignored by the major recording companies. In 1995, Analekta released an album of verismo arias that perfectly displayed her artistic talents, conducted by Joseph Rescigno. Her voice was suited to many types of roles and her performances were always memorable. I saw her a number of times at the Metropolitan Opera, especially as *Suor Angelica*. Soviero was the alternate cast for Teresa Stratas (who was also excellent.) At the end of the opera much of the audience was in tears, so touching was Soviero's acting during the final moments. You can see a scene from act II of her signature role, *Madama Butterfly*, on YouTube. It is an intense, emotional experience.

Of her single aria disc, Neil Kurtzman wrote:

> Soviero inhabited her roles. If you were lucky enough to see her as *Madama Butterfly* or Suor Angelica (just two of the roles that she excelled at) you were in the presence of genius. One of the great moments in my 60 years of opera going was her 1989 performance of the title role of Puccini's

Suor Angelica at the Met. She was a last minute replacement for Teresa Stratas. It was a Saturday matinee, so a recording of the broadcast is doubtless floating around someplace, but I don't have a copy of it.

She also did not record very much. This disc is the only studio recording that I can find by Ms Soviero. As fine an artist as she was and despite much recognition by connoisseurs of opera, her career is an all too common example of how recognition and reputation are often dispensed with a tenuous connection to merit. Why this happens is difficult to dissect. The professional life of a performer is brief. If, for whatever reason(s), the public isn't instructed whom it should prefer it oftentimes fails to realize the worth of some performers while overestimating the capacity of others. Or, life is just unfair. (http://medicine-opera.com/2015/06/recording-of-the-week-verismo-diana-soviero/)

Bizet—***Pearl Fishers*** (exc) Diana Soviero NYCO, 1980 with Barry McCauley, Dominic Cossa—Calvin Simmons
https://www.youtube.com/watch?v=RIIAz7pkHYg

Puccini—***Suor Angelica***— Diana Soviero Madrid, 1987
https://www.youtube.com/watch?v=nHpbOfnTX-Y

Puccini—***La Rondine***— Diana Soviero Catania October, 1991 with Fabio Armililato, Penelope Luisi—conducted Joseph Rescignoby
https://www.youtube.com/watch?v=-lAOp5ROD8o

Verismo Opera Arias— Diana Soviero Adriana, Butterfly, Rizurrezione, Iris, Chenier etc. conducted by Joseph Rescigno. (Playlist on the right)
https://www.youtube.com/watch?v=nK3oj06qSa4&list=PLdV4REIvR-E6z0X0oYkfE1-TSpDkMTm70

Olivia Stapp (1940–) made the difficult move from mezzo-soprano to soprano and was also a NYCO alumnae. She began as *Carmen* and as Eboli in *Don Carlo* (a late 1970s concert performance during which I sang in the chorus) and ended up a Norma, Elektra, and as Abigaile in *Nabucco*. Despite such a dramatic change in repertoire during the 1980s, she was one of the finest of international singers of such roles as Lady Macbeth in *Macbeth*, Abigaile in *Nabucco*, Tosca, Medea, Norma, and Elektra.

Born in Brooklyn, Stapp's career centered in Europe until about 1983 (except for three seasons at NYCO). She originally wanted to be a poet! Unlike many singers, she never went to a music conservatory, studying only with private teachers.

> …someone suggested I apply for a Fulbright Scholarship to study singing in Europe,' she recalled, 'I took it as a dare, and I got a scholarship for Rome. I wanted to study for concert work, but in Rome you study for opera.' (Frederick M Winship, UPI Senior Editor, January 4, 1983

http://www.upi.com/Archives/1983/01/04/An-American-sopranos-dilemma-Olivia-Stapp-has-no-time-for-Met/9049410504400/)

While in Italy she met and married Henry Stapp, an American theoretical physicist who was vacationing there. By that time she had sung some opera performances in Italy and Germany. She moved with her husband to Berkeley, California where he is a member of the University of California faculty.

> I dropped out of opera to have my son, Henry, who is now 16,' she said. 'I tried to keep busy—cooking, schools, faculty wives, but nothing worked. My husband said why not sing? So I went back to Europe and started at the Vienna Folksoper in 1971, singing mezzo roles because I was a mezzo then. I must have sung hundreds of *Carmen*s.

Homesickness for her family forced Mrs. Stapp into a second retirement in Berkeley, although her husband warned her she'd be unhappy again.

> Well, I wasn't unhappy but I was restless,' she admitted. 'I'm a real homebody but very gregarious and I had no one to talk to. My husband told me to go to New York and get an agent, and I did. I made my debut at the City Opera in 1972. (ibid)

Her initial plan was to work six months in New York and spend six months at home in California. Due to an international upsurge in her career when she began undertaking dramatic soprano roles, that schedule did not work. She was soon in demand as Tosca, *Turandot*, Norma, Iris, Elektra, Medea, Minnie in La fanciulla del West, Abigaille in Nabucco, and Lady Macbeth in Macbeth (probably her most famous role.) Often during the course of her career she was compared to Maria Callas, which Stapp felt to be a gross exaggeration.

After she retired from the stage, Stapp was the general director of Festival Opera in Walnut Creek, Ca. from 1995 to 2001.

A daring singer, Stapp was known to push the vocal envelope. She even adopted Maria Callas's Nabucco "interpolation" of an (excellent) high E-flat at the conclusion of the act III grand duet with Nabucco (Zurich, 1979). A YouTube audio in which she sings the 1847 cabaletta, "Triomphai" from Macbeth should be considered mandatory listening for any aspiring spinto or dramatic soprano. She was a remarkable Minnie in La fanciulla del West, Iris, Medea, Tosca, La Straniera, Anna Bolena, Roberto Devereux, and many other roles.

She was a stunningly fearless Elektra. She first sang the role in Syracuse in 1977. Under the headline, "Strauss Epic Astonishing," Frank Macomber of The Post-Standard of Syracuse wrote:

> As Elektra, Olivia Stapp was equal to every horrendous demand which Strauss places upon the character. Her voice is enormous, her range very large, and her capacity for cutting through the full orchestral ensemble unflagging. Just getting through the role is a formidable task, and Miss Stapp hurtled herself through it unstintingly. (April 22, 1977)

Stapp also sang *Elektra* in Toronto in 1983 (a most frighteningly dramatic performance). Both were preserved on tape and her mastery of Strauss's difficult music is impressive. I had the pleasure of seeing her only performance of Elektra at the Metropolitan Opera on December 8, 1984 and will never forget that experience. (And, yes, I taped it. . . .ssshhh.)

Somewhat agreeing with The New York Times review, I suspect that Stapp would have been more effective in this killer role in a smaller opera house than the cavern that is the Met. No matter. I loved her wild abandon in the role and her visceral thrust to high notes. She was like a caged animal on stage, an unforgettable performer.

Stapp was also adventuresome when it came to repertoire. In November of 1984 in New Jersey, she gave a concert of mad scenes (Lucia di Lammermoor, Anna Bolena, Macbeth, and Mefistofele). It was a remarkable night for those lucky enough to be in attendance. The pirate tape is now a revered cult item.

Although at least forty of Stapp's performances are circulating privately, I know of only two commercial recordings—an LP of Opera Arias from a 1978 Recital released by Bon Giovanni. There was also an LP/CD of Bellini and Donizetti works with mezzo-soprano Ida Kirilova. It was recorded in Czechoslovakia in 1988 and released the following year. It has selections from Norma, Anna Bolena, and I Capuletti.

Opera Arias by Mozart, Verdi, Puccini, Mascagni, Olivia Stapp
https://www.youtube.com/watch?v=WTD6IZx-u5w
There are many clips on YouTube. Below are just a few that I particularly enjoy.
Mascagni—Act II Love Duet *Iris*—Naples 1978 with Flaviano Labo—conducted by Olivero de Fabritis
https://www.youtube.com/watch?v=zx2wgZLdOCk
Verdi—*Nabucco* (exc)—San Francisco, 1982—with Olivia Stapp (w/D), Matteo Manuguerra, Gordon Greer, Paul Plishka—Kurt Herbert Adler
https://www.youtube.com/watch?v=W6IoEIIckM8
Mascagni—*Cavalleria rusticana*—Chicago, 1978 With Olivia Stapp, Giorgio Merighi, Mayyeo Manuguerra, Brenda Boozer—conducted by Riccardo Chailly
https://www.youtube.com/watch?v=2SpHe-wco60
Verdi—*Macbeth* (exc)—Berlin, 1980 with Olivia Stapp, Renato Bruson, Veriano Luchetti,—Giuseppe Sinopoli
https://www.youtube.com/watch?v=ZdWOFPKCxTk&t=3s
Donizetti—*Anna Bolena*—NYCO 1973 with Beverly Sills, Olivia Stapp, Robert Hale, Vittorio Terranova—conducted by Julius Rudel
https://www.youtube.com/watch?v=N6-7NdvoO_w
Donizetti—*Anna Bolena* (exc)—NYCO in Los Angeles 1980 with Olivia Stapp, Sanuel Ramey, Susanne marsee, Rockwell Blake—conducted by Charles Wendelken-Wilson
https://www.youtube.com/watch?v=wHcEWaDyR1Q
Donizetti—Mad Scene *Anna Bolena*—Treviso, 1984 with Olivia Stapp—Evelino Pido
https://www.youtube.com/watch?v=FffJCpV1wOY
Strauss—*Elektra*—Toronto, 1983—Olivia Stapp, Viviane Thomas, Maureen Forrester, Tom Fox, Phil Stark—conducted by Gabor Ötvös
https://www.youtube.com/watch?v=yfaDinh_KEs&t=1544s

Ruth Welting (1948–1999), a Memphis-born soprano, is represented by only a few commercial recordings, including Mozart's *Impressario*, Massenet's *Cendrillon*, and Thomas's *Mignon*. I saw Ruth in performance a number of times, mainly in concert in New York. On one memorable program in May of 1975, she sang the extended mad scene from *Hamlet*, the bell song from *Lakmé,* as well as Linda's bubbly "O luce di quest anima" (*Linda di Chamonix*). I had just come to New York and it was the first New York concert I attended.

The high point of Ruth's career came early. It was her unforgettable portrayal of Baby in Douglas Moore's *The Ballad of Baby Doe* in a NYCO telecast in April of 1976. (It was the first complete opera to be broadcast live over PBS.) What an exquisite opera this is. Welting was surrounded by such colleagues as Richard Fredricks, Frances Bible, and the conductor, Judith Somogi. Welting gave one of the finest performances of her career. By virtue of her inherent timbre and refined musicianship, she captured the complex essence of the character with disarming simplicity, yet great emotive power. It is unfortunate that the telecast has yet to be commercially released. Only pirated copies are available. Apart from being a superb demonstration of belcanto, Welting's singing of Baby Doe's final aria ("The Leadville Liebestodt") transcended art to become a cathartic experience for listeners. It was one of the most moving moments during that entire decade of American operatic performances.

Moore—Final Duet *Ballad of Baby Doe*—NYCO Telecast April, 1976
https://www.youtube.com/watch?v=NWZHO3DP-18

Because of my own performing schedule during the 1980s, I rarely traveled to hear other singers, but I made an exception in February of 1986, when I returned to my hometown of Baltimore to catch two performances of Ruth Welting in *Lucia di Lammermoor* on February 13 and 17. She sang her first Lucia in May of 1974, in Washington DC, following it with NYCO performances in the following September. both of which exist on pirate tapes. Her Lucia has always been of interest to me due to her own clever ornamentation for the role, including a pyrotechnical cadenza in the mad scene performed in its original key of F major. During her inventive mellismas she threw out arpeggios, trilled on high E, and reached high F four times, crowning both halves of the scene with brilliantly sustained high Fs.

She was magnificent in Baltimore, her voice rang out with authority, putting forth solid high notes as well as hair-line pianissimi. (Of course, I taped both performances—again, ssshhh.) By the time I arrived in Baltimore for the first performance, I had come down with a bad flu and barely remember any of it—but the tape is there to remind me how wonderful the performance was. I was in much better shape for the next performance I attended. I am not positive, but I believe that that February 17th performance was her last of that role. The middle performance on the 15th (I believe) has been uplated to YouTube. The links are below.

Donizetti—"Regnava nel silenzio" *Lucia di Lammermoor*—Baltimore Opera, 1986
https://www.youtube.com/watch?v=gcrDeYiggIE

Donizetti—Mad Scene *Lucia di Lammermoor*—Baltimore Opera, 1986
https://www.youtube.com/watch?v=3KjV_TU4Y1s

YouTube also has a complete video performance of a *Lucia di Lammermoor* with Welting from Hamilton, Ontario in 1985. I also saw a couple of her final Met performances as the Queen of the Night in Die Zauberflöte in 1991—as well as a wonderful Impresario in August of 1992, when Welting also sang the concert aria, "Sol nacente."

Mozart—"Sol nacente" (Concert Aria)— Ruth Welting New York concert, 1992, conducted by Julius Rudel
https://www.youtube.com/watch?v=A_oWnuqKa94

Her death at the age of fifty-one from cancer was a great loss to the musical world.

Enzo Bordello" of Opera L Archives, related a tragic story about Ruth's sister, Patricia (1938–1986):

> In the1970's, I spent my summers as an apprentice with a repertory company on the Tulane University campus. One afternoon, Ruth's sister Patricia came to the theater box office with her children and requested tickets for one of the plays I was working on. Patricia Welting had enjoyed a respectable career as a soprano and even sang roles like Papagena and Oscar at the Met during the Bing years. I recognized her face immediately--she looked almost exactly like Ruth—and struck up a conversation with her. She related that she would soon be joining the faculty of the music department at Tulane. Imagine my horror when I was watching the local news a few years later and it was reported that Patricia Welting and her children were brutally murdered by Welting's husband, who then killed himself…I sent my condolences to the surviving family. What a terrible tragedy! (Opera L Archives, Sun, 14 Sep 1997)

Below are some links to Ruth Welting:
Offenbach—"Doll's Song and Exit" *Contes d'Hoffman*— Ruth Welting Florida, 1973
https://www.youtube.com/watch?v=HM-5lbtVipk
Donizetti—"O luce di quest anima" *Linda di Chamonix*— Ruth Welting London, 1975
https://www.youtube.com/watch?v=VafnVts5pIg
Strauss—*Ariadne auf Naxos*—Chicago, 1978 with Leonie Rysanek, Ruth Welting, Yvonne Minton, William Johns Conducted by Marek Janowski
https://www.youtube.com/watch?v=xhFRGsqxuwE
Delibes—*Lakmé*—Dallas, 1980 with Alfredo Kraus, Paul Plishka, Maria Spacagna—Nicola Rescigno
https://www.youtube.com/watch?v=_yh9CKl5UHw&t=4935s
Massenet—*Cendrillon*—Ottowa, 1979 with Federicka von Stade, Maureen Forrester, Delia Wallis, Louis Quilico—Mario Bernardi
https://www.youtube.com/watch?v=cpNVGe_uC0s&t=7037s

With a voice of good size and a first-rate technique, no one—not even Dame Joan Sutherland—could match the perfect high E-flats that Welting crowned "Salut a la France" and the finale of La fille du regiment. Part of the reason was her impeccable timing in placing the note. Some singers wait too long; some not long enough. Ruth timed it perfectly; always maximizing the effect that this note would have within the framework of the music and its climax.

Donizetti—"Chacun le sait" *Fille du regiment*—Parma, 1988 (This is the famous production that used a cadenza for trumpet and soprano at the end of this aria. Unfortunately, on this night, for whatever reason, the trumpet did not show and so Welting sang the entire cadenza acapella.—still finishing on a brilliant high F.
https://www.youtube.com/watch?v=5uIOw2Z1Vjo
Donizetti—"Par la range…Salut a la France" *Fille du regiment*—Parma, 1988
https://www.youtube.com/watch?v=jWjiShqlJDs
Donizetti—Finale of Opera *Fille du regiment*—Parma, 1988
https://www.youtube.com/watch?v=mE3oYBaSWe8&t=27s

Sheryl Woods was beautiful of voice and elegant in demeanor. As a lyric coloratura, she made her operatic debut with the Santa Fe Opera while she was still an apprentice, filling in for an ailing colleague as Adele in Rossini's *Le Comte Ory*. She went on to perform with the New York City Opera, Lyric Opera of Chicago, Houston Grand Opera, San Diego Opera, Dallas Opera, and the Washington Opera, as well as in Baltimore, New Orleans, Pittsburgh, Atlanta, and Central City. During the late 1980s she excelled in NYCO's productions of *Lucia di Lammermoor, La traviata, Ariadne auf Naxos* and was an unforgettable Birdie in Blitzstein's *Regina*. I saw Sheryl Woods many times at NYCO, especially *in Ariadne auf Naxos*, *La traviata*, *Martha*, and *Lucia di Lammermoor*. She was never less than wonderful in everything I saw her in. In 2002 she took part in the Chandos recording of Tobias Picker's *Térèse Requin*. (Some clips from this can be found on YouTube.)
Donizetti—*Lucia di Lammermoor*—Montreal 1993 with John Fowler, Gaetan Laperriere, Joseph Rouleau—conducted by Joseph Rescigno
https://www.youtube.com/watch?v=vtKeJumRLy0&t=6456s

Bitzstein—*Regina*—Miami 2002—with Lauren Flanigan, Sheryl Woods, Kristine Winkler, Andrew Wentzel; conducted by Steven Robertson
https://www.youtube.com/watch?v=zoviO5x1jfw&t=233s
In New York Magazine (8/20/90) Peter G Davis commented:
> Many sopranos have gone mad in Lucia di Lammermoor since the (NYCO) production was first staged for Beverly Sills in 1969, but I can think of none who have done it better lately than Sheryl Woods. Like Sills, she accomplishes much with a voice that is best described as pleasantly utilitarian rather than remarkably beautiful or strikingly individual…Even at that, her soprano is solidly structured, finely schooled, health-sounding and firmly projected, better still, she puts these assets to use with unusual musical intelligence and expressive imagination…She paced the role as a slow crescendo, building surely to a mad scene that, for once was both a tour de force and the opera's dramatic climax.

WHAT DOES A NOVICE OPERA PIRATE DO WHEN NOT PIRATING?

To better understand the musical climate of opera piracy in New York City during the period 0f the 1970s-1980s, it is important that the reader have an idea of what it took to make one's living as a freelance musician and be aware of the many changes occurring in musical circles at that time. Although presented from an autobiographical perspective, it also describes the unusually busy concert seasons in New York at that time.

New York City is an amazing place, and so too are the people who choose to live there. One thing is almost a given, the average musician often takes on a second or even a third job to make ends meet. Voice and music lessons, coaching, formal clothes for concerts, these are not cheap. As you will see, at one time I had not only an office job, but a church job along with various choral gigs enabling me to survive comfortably in the city,

I was fortunate to be involved in the music scene during the decades of the 1980s and '90s. Looking back, it was an era of job opportunities for freelance professional classical (choral) singers. During some of those years there was generous government funding available—enough that producers were able to mount more complicated and specialized television events, concerts, recordings, and, overall, were able to hire a greater number of professional singers.

Significant change came about that benefitted the contractors who supplied such jobs. Tom Pyle (Choral Associates) was a dynamic pioneer who hired professional choral singers in New York. Anne Bynam handled the church work. When Tom died in the mid-1970s his work passed on to soprano Betty Baisch, once a member of the Roger Wagner Chorale.

When my wife Gale and I first arrived in New York City in January of 1975, there was a musicians' strike. There was no work for freelance singers; not even auditions! We did what is called "temping"—secretarial-type jobs at companies that hired you for short periods. The temporary agency we worked with was called "Kelly Girls." I enjoyed telling new employers that I was their new Kelly Girl!

Gale and I were told by music friends in the city that the way to become successful in New York City as a singer was to secure professional choral work because there was very little solo work for non-managed singers. That sounded good to us we just wanted to be professional (i.e., PAID!) singers. Together, we got church jobs at Metropolitan Duane Methodist Church at 13th Street and Seventh Avenue (in Greenwich Village), along with a friend of ours from West Virginia University, Anna Schumate. I moved to Saint Michael's Church on 99th and Amsterdam a few years later where I was the tenor soloist for nearly eighteen years. Gale followed me to St. Michael's shortly after. Saint Michael's choir was the starting place for the well-known early music quartet, Anonymous 4.

Our first professional choral work audition was for Betty Baisch at the Nola Studios in the Steinway Building on West 57th Street on September 28, 1977. I know that date so well because immediately after the audition we went to Patelson's on West 56th Street and I bought John Steane's, tome, The Grand Tradition (about historical singers). It is a book that has become very important to me since that time.

Because of the fallout from the musician's strike, it took a while to get other auditions. It also took a couple of more years to work ourselves onto Betty's large roster of singers. She explained that she wanted to use us, but, of course, owed her primary allegiance to singers she had used before. Our first job was two years later, in 1979, singing with the Bach Aria Group and, later, other jobs that she arranged.

This was well before the Internet, email, and YouTube. All hiring for jobs was conducted through postal mail, on the telephone, or by word of mouth learned while you were employed at other jobs.

In 1979, Joseph Flummerfelt (1937–2019), then the director of choral activities at Westminster Choir College, in conjunction with the New York Philharmonic, founded the New York Choral Artists. Auditions were held that fall. Cynthia Richards Hewes (now Wallace) and Jacqueline Pierce presided at the auditions along with Flummerfelt. Before then, Cynthia (Cindy) had handled all of the contracting for the New York Philharmonic. However, when Flummerfelt was brought on by the Philharmonic to prepare professional choruses, he hired Jacqueline Pierce as his contractor because he had known and worked with her before. Pierce was known for her solo work in the 1960s. She sang in the legendary performance of Les Huguenots at Carnegie Hall in 1969 with Beverly Sills. She also sang with Joan Sutherland in Lakmé in Philadelphia in 1968. She continues to do choral contracting for New York Choral Artists, Concert Chorale of New York, and Melodius Accord.

For this series of auditions Cindy participated as well. This made sense as she also contracted for the premiere professional choral group in New York City at the time, Musica Sacra (conducted by Richard Westenburg), as well as contracting all musical events at the Cathedral of Saint John Divine.

When Jacqueline Pierce took over the contracting for the New York Choral Artists, she brought in a tenor friend of mine from West Virginia University, Martin Doner, who handled the contracting of church and synagogue work in the five boroughs. Because of my friendship with Martin, at times Jacquie invited me to sit in on auditions and provide feedback.

Within a year or so, although other names began to pop up as contractors, the most prestigious professional choral work contractors in New York City remained Cynthia Richards Hewes, Jacqueline Pierce, and Martin Doner. The three together hired singers for many organizations, holding regular auditions throughout the year to hear new singers.

Because of the creation and formalization of the New York Choral Artists anyone interested in being considered for the group had to audition. This was whether you had worked with any of the contractors before or not.

I remember my audition in late fall of 1979 very well. It was held in a large room on the main floor of Manhattan Plaza. I was very, very nervous because it was an important audition. It was one that would have tremendous impact going forward on my success as a professional singer in New York City.

I was asked to sing an aria (I think I sang "Le Reve" from Manon, or it might have been the "Sicilienne" from Meyerbeer's Robert le Diable—so I could show off my coloratura ability and trills.)

I was then asked to sight-read a really difficult tenor-line from one of Bach's Cantatas without accompaniment. It was not an easy audition and when it was finished, I was exhausted. I remember thanking them for hearing me, and walking out of the audition room in a fog. I had been so tuned into what I was doing during the audition that I had no idea whether I had done well or not.

By January 1980, I was singing with the New York Choral Artists and I had been hired by Cindy Richards Hewes and was singing with Musica Sacra in a performance of the Brahm's Requiem with Leona Mitchell and Samuel Ramey at Avery Fisher Hall.

Despite an influx of classical singers in New York City at that time, there remained a core group of about 60 of us who sang virtually all the professional choral work in and around New York City—as long as our schedules permitted.

In was also in 1979–80 that I began working part time as an audio technician for Ralph Ferrandina, also known as "Mr. Tape," one of the leading opera piraters in New York City (discussed in Chapter one).

As a general rule, the singers who sang in Musica Sacra also regularly sang in the New York Choral Artists (the New York Philharmonic)—although not necessarily the reverse as Musica Sacra was a considerably smaller group. So, too, did these singers also sing with the Opera Orchestra of New York, Schola Cantorum, and many of the other choral jobs in the city. Often, when we left a performance at Carnegie Hall, audience members would be outside waiting for the "famous people". They would see us in our tuxes and gowns and often asked how many times during the year the chorus members rehearsed, where were we from, and questions of that nature.

"They never understood that, in actuality, although we had just finished a concert at Avery Fisher Hall, we were the same singers that they had heard the week before singing a concert at Carnegie Hall and before that at Alice Tully. Because of this, as singers, we were like an extended family and, because we all saw each other at the same jobs throughout the year, there was more socializing among the group, more camaraderie and more friendships." (Private conversation with Martin Doner, June 10, 2017)

A perfect example of this camaraderie between singers at that time was during the aftermath from a building fire at the brownstone where Gale and I lived on 95th Street off Central Park West.

On Christmas Day 1992, Gale had hosted a big Christmas dinner in our apartment for singer friends. Our good friend Anne-Lynn Gross (see Early 20th Century Opera Singers. YBK Publishers) was visiting from Maryland and I had taken her to see a performance of Janacek's Jenufa at the Met a few days earlier. On the day after Christmas (Saturday) while Anne-Lynn and I listened to the Metropolitan Opera broadcast of Jenufa with Gabriella Benackova and Leonie Rysanek, at about two that afternoon, our building burned down due to faulty wiring in the basement. It was Gale, who was in the kitchen, who alerted us to what was happening.

At the time, Gale and I were soloists at St. Michael's Episcopal Church. Fortunately, for us, the rector had recently retired. Robert Barrows (1943–2014), the organist and choir director of

Saint Michael's, immediately arranged for us to move into the empty rector's apartment for a couple of weeks while we sought to regain our bearings. Betsy Watson, a soprano friend of ours from Musica Sacra, took us to a drug store and made sure we had the immediate necessities needed for that first night away from home. I remember standing out on the curb, looking up at our building and thinking as it burned, "Okay, I can let it all go—all of the things we had. We can start over. We'll figure it out." I remember, too, that one thing that upset me greatly was that I would have to figure out how to rewrite my book on Yma Sumac. Back then, back-ups were carbon copies, and they and all my notes and work were there—in a burning building!

We got Anne-Lynn on a train back to Maryland and then began to concentrate on what we were going to do. Amazingly, although we lost many things, everything we lost was replaceable. By some miracle, all of our music—CDs, records, scores, programs, even Gale's expensive concert gowns, *and* the draft of my book on Yma Sumac survived. We couldn't believe how lucky we were. The congregation of Saint Michael's kindly took up a collection and also gave us many wonderful things that helped replace what we had lost, including clothes, bedding, and kitchen utensils. Afterward Gale joked that their kindness provided nicer clothing than we had before the fire!

In the week between Christmas and New Year, Gale and I trudged back to the burnt-out apartment every day to pack up what was left of our belongings. There was hardly any roof left and the building was freezing. Seeing our breath in the frigid air, we had to wear gloves. Our baritone friend, James Bingham, simply showed up one day to help us pack and help us smile.

The most gratifying experience about that horrific fire was what happened behind the scenes.

Nancy Wertsch, a fellow singer and composer was involved in establishing her own choral contracting business around 1990. She was soon a major player contracting New York singers' work. Nancy arranged for thirty-six of our singer colleague/friends to come to our apartment building on the morning of January 2. Forming a fire brigade-style line to the top floor, everything remaining there was passed down the line to the street, packed into cars and trucks, and brought to the undercroft of Saint Michael's Church for safe keeping. Witnessing that many friends who came to help us when we so needed it, was one of the most humbling things I have ever experienced. We have never forgotten Nancy's kindness, nor the kindness of our friends.

By the end of January, 1993 we had moved into our new home at the intersection of Cabrini and 187th Streets in Washington Heights. On that intersection's corner was a building filled with performers and singers, many of whom we sang with.

We remained there until 1998, when we bought a house in Yonkers with the help of our parents. (Betty Baisch told me during a service at Temple Emmanuel on Fifth Avenue in Manhattan that the house next door to hers was for sale. We went to see it with our friend Judy Cope—a wonderful soprano—and eventually became the neighbors of the woman who had given us our first professional singing jobs in New York!)

The camaraderie of choral singers was especially important during the Kurt Masur/Philharmonic years (1991–2002). Before that time, during the wonderful Zubin Mehta years (1978–1991), the New York Philharmonic usually contracted the New York Choral Artists several times each year. There were usually between four and six jobs each season with multiple performances of each job. When Masur took over, however, he made no bones about the fact that he did not like working with professional choral singers and the opportunities, and our income, began to dry up.

Not surprisingly, Masur was not an easy conductor to work with. During rehearsals of "his" Philharmonic, it was obvious to us singers that Masur had big issues with us. He was a rude and disagreeable man to work with. Zubin Mehta, Charles Mackerras, Rafael Kubelik, Karl Richter, and James Levine were a pleasure, but Masur was not.

There also seemed to be a serious communication problem between Masur and Joseph Flummerfelt of the Westminster Choir College, the conductor who prepared us. Sometimes I felt badly for Flummerfelt, who carefully and diligently prepared us (supposedly the way Masur wanted us prepared) but when we got with Masur for final rehearsals we would have to change everything we had previously modified and marked in our scores. It was frustrating to say the least. During one rehearsal Masur was so rude to the chorus that the orchestra members demanded he publicly apologize to us.

During the period 1979 to 1989 there were many organizations that used choruses, providing almost constant work. If you had a Church or Temple job, or some other time-flexible job, you could survive comfortably as a professional musician. Your days became busy singing for such groups as The Bach Aria Group, Gregg Smith Singers, Schola Cantorum, Choral Associates, NY Choral Artists, Musica Sacra, Opera Orchestra of New York, the Alvin Ailey Dance Company, the Mark Morris Dance Group (at Brooklyn Academy of Music), Virtuoso Singers, and Music in a Great Space. Almost all of the available work was funneled through Richards Hewes, Pierce, Wertsch, and Doner

For many years Gale and I were hired by Betty Baisch to sing in the chorus of the "Revelations" ballet (originally choreographed by Alvin Ailey in 1960) and the "Rainbow" ballet. This was before they began using a pre-recorded soundtrack (admittedly saving the company quite a bit of money). The chorus for that gig was small, maybe sixteen singers and the instrumental ensemble, also was small, but it was a great job. At that time Alvin Ailey performed at the old New York City Opera home: the New York City Center theater on West 55th Street.

For over a decade Gale was the soprano soloist. I considered this to be one of the best jobs in the city because the chorus would be fitted out in tuxedos and gowns and "get down" with the score of spirituals arranged by Sister Ella Jenkins, Brother John Sellers, Howard Roberts, and Hall Johnson. It was about forty minutes of musical heaven for the singers. Performances often took place around Christmas time or other important tourist seasons and there were usually a minimum of ten performances, providing financial security during the holiday season. (It didn't hurt that we could watch the incredible Alvin Ailey dancers as well.) One perk to the job once we moved to Yonkers was being able to ride into the city with Betty and her husband, Fred, who was the percussionist for the group. Even better, we got to ride home!

Although many singers accepted summer tour jobs after the musical season was over, there was almost as much work in the city during the summer months. There were the Martin Josman Concerts in the Parks, (held throughout the five boroughs), the New York Park Concert Series, the newly inaugurated Bard College Music Festival (begun in 1990), the Mostly Mozart festival at Avery Fisher Hall (now David Geffen Hall) and Alice Tully Hall (during the directorship of Gerard Schwarz from 1984 to 2001), and various visiting ballet companies that performed at the Metropolitan Opera House and the New York City Opera House during the summer. Dance companies often used a professional chorus for choral works that were adapted into new ballets.

This doesn't take into account the various Verdi Requiems at Carnegie Hall (I sang in three or four of them), specialized concerts of Bach Passions, French opera, Strauss operas, Rossini operas, televised concerts, and recordings. There were TV concerts with Luciano Pavarotti, Kathleen Battle, Frederica von Stade, Marilyn Horne, and others. At all of these, one saw and worked with the same singers and, when someone was absent, you missed them.

There are two Musica Sacra recordings I sang in that I remember especially well. One was the still popular album of Christmas carols recorded at Saint Barnabas Episcopal Church in Greenwich, Connecticut in 1989 for Deutsche Grammophon during the height of the summer. We had a great time those couple of days but it was very hot and the church was not air-conditioned. It seemed very strange to perspire while singing Christmas carols!

The second was the wonderful "Songs and Psalms of the Divine." Recorded in 1992 for RCA Victor, it contains the wonderful Strauss "Deutsche Motet" (one of our specialties) as well as a number of other pyrotechnical choral pieces that included the impossible forty-voice Thomas Tallis, "Spem in alium." I remember it quite well because it was done very late at night near the high altar in the Cathedral of Saint John the Divine. There was very little ambient light and the cathedral loomed over us, huge, and frighteningly dark. It was also eerily quiet. Maybe that ambiance contributed something to the wonderful recording that it became. I was not able to take part in the famous Messiah recording made some years earlier, but I sang in many Messiahs with Musica Sacra.

At times I was even able to incorporate my pirating abilities. As I mentioned, one of Musica Sacra's specialties was Richard Strauss's difficult accapella Deutsche Motet which we sang and recorded a number of times.

> A concerto for choir by any other name, Richard Strauss's *Deutsche Motette* has a good claim to being the hardest piece of tonal music in the choral repertoire. Splitting its singers into 20 parts, stretching them across a four-octave range and climaxing in a fugue of monumental complexity, it's a work not often recorded and still less frequently heard in concert) Alexandra Coghlan, Gramophone, 2013)

While rehearsing this piece for concerts at Avery Fisher Hall and the Cathedral of Saint John the Divine, I was able to tape both rehearsals and performances. Although the resultant contraband is not of great sound quality, it occupies a revered place in my library nonetheless.

In reviewing the RCA recording Gramophone noted:

> ...Randall Thompson's prayerful Alleluia and Schoenberg's emotionally charged Friede auf Erden exert a powerful force on the heartstrings, with Westenburg firmly treading the fine line between delicate sensitivity and emotional abandon. It's especially good to have such a confident and self-assured account of Richard Strauss's all-too-rarely heard Deutsche Motette with its remarkable similarities with Rachmaninov's The Bells (both works were written in the same year). The almost operatic quality of the voices as well as Westenburg's spacious reading would yield these compelling results regardless of acoustic environment. — Marc Rochester, Gramophone [1/1993]

I also taped the dress rehearsal of the concert performance (in English) of Janacek's From the House of the Dead when the New York Philharmonic and New Choral Artists performed it in March of 1983. Such a fascinating work! (See Chapter one)

As happens, the times change, and by the 1990s the world of professional choral musicians had begun to shift again.

New and excellent groups were formed, like Voices of Ascension. (It was originally called Ascension Music before it became formally founded as Voices of Ascension in 1990.) Housed at the Church of the Ascension on Fifth Avenue and 10th Street in Greenwich Village, conductor Dennis Keene led a group of singers who came mostly from the church's choir, but also from Musica Sacra and other groups. They made numerous recordings and became a Grammy-nominated group.

All of this does not include other jobs one might squeeze into one's schedule. This included jobs like High Holy Day services. For ten years I was tenor soloist at Brown's Hotel in the Catskills for their High Holy Day services (and once for Passover). The cantor was Abraham Wolkin (1918–2014). He was well known in the New York area and a remarkable musician. Our quartet humorously called ourselves "Cantor Wolkin and the Wolkinetts." Gale joined me only once at Browns, for Passover services. Most of the time she had her own High Holy Day services in Manhattan. I loved going to Browns as it was one of the few times I left the city. We got to use the many facilities at the hotel and, although the services were long and could be exhausting, the food was great!

During 1987, I sang at Church of the Ascension as a choir member and soloist under the direction of Dennis Keene. Because of physical issues attributable to a mugging on 34th Street in 1988, I moved on to another church solo position slowly making a change from tenor to bass.

Ironically, after retiring from singing in 2000, I took a job as parish administrator at the Church of the Ascension, remaining there in that position until 2014. During my years there, Dennis Keene and I had many conversations about singers and opera in general. Once he mentioned a memorable performance he had seen of Donizetti's La fille du régiment with Joan Sutherland and Luciano Pavarotti at the Metropolitan Opera. His surprise was genuine when I went to the music office the next day and presented him with a gift—a recording of that very performance. In 2023, Voices of Ascension is still going strong (https://www.voicesofascension.org).

Reverend Shelley D. McDade came to Ascension in 2010 while I was administrator. She had a remarkable resume for a priest. Before she was called into ministry, she spent 24 years working in the corporate world managing regional marketing and advertising programs for clients such as Exxon Mobil, McDonalds and Pepsico in North America and the Pacific. Mother Shelley earned her Masters of Divinity in 2010 from The General Theological Seminary.

Church of the Ascension was her first job after seminary amd one of my jobs was to help ease her into Ascension's way of doing things. She eventually became interim rector there in March of 2013, when Father Andrew Foster retired. After I left Ascension in 2014, she moved on as well the next year. She took an interim-rector position at St. John's Episcopal Church in Brooklyn. Shortly after that, she brought me in to work with her as her part-time administrator. She eventually became rector. I remained at St. John's until the end of January 2019. We worked together for nine years and she, Gale, and I had become best friends. By 2019-2020 she had accepted a Rectorship in Rehoboth Beach, Delaware. She presides over not only All Saint's Church, but also St. George's Chapel in Harbeson, Delaware. In June of 2023, Gale and I travelled to Rehoboth Beach to visit Mother Shelley and to have her preside over our renewal of vows for our fiftieth wedding anniversary.

By 1988, the music situation was becoming financially too precarious for Gale and me and so I took a full-time office job in order to make ends meet. It wasn't until that year (1988) that we finally got some medical insurance. I was 37 years old. Within a year or two, because of a decrease in governmental funding, fewer jobs were available. Special concerts at Carnegie Hall disappeared, as did virtually all television and recording work. A number of our colleagues moved from the city as jobs were obviously thinning out and musicians' priorities had begun to shift.

As if in reaction to the severe funding cuts in the 1990s, new choral contractors began to pop up. Many fizzled out, but among them, Nancy Wertsch continues with Virtuoso singers, Bard Music Festival, and Music in a Great Space (the last two were originally contracted by Cynthia Richards Hewes). Conductors, as well as singers, began to dabble at professional choral contracting, seeking with varying degrees of success to edge others out of the business. Desperate for work, some singers went so far as to attempt to sabotage colleagues, indulging in extremely unethical behavior. It became an unfortunate time of change in both priorities and behavior.

I was able to carefully juggle a 9 to 5 office job, a church job, and assorted professional choral gigs for about ten more years. But it took its toll. I slowly had to let each of the choral jobs go as I became more and more exhausted and frustrated with constantly switching working hats. I was fortunate that my office job permitted me time-off to go to daytime rehearsals, but I had to make up that time. As I began to make more money at my office job, my responsibilities increased as well.

Gale had been singing many choral jobs with me—Musica Sacra, New York Philharmonic and so on, but in the mid-1980s she began to concentrate on a solo career that took her throughout the United States and Europe—appearing especially in a fine performance of the Verdi Requiem with Klaus Weise and the Opera de Nice.

In the early 1990s she worked on a CD of folk music with Gil Robbins (1931-2011), the father of the actor and screen director, Tim Robbins. Gil was a famous folk singer and musician and was a member of the folk group The Highwaymen from 1962 until they disbanded in 1964. When Tim was preparing to produce the film, Dead Man Walking (it won four Oscar nominations), he wanted to create a particular emotional effect during the scene of the prison execution. He had decided to use a recording of a Russian song called "Sacred Love," by the composer Sviridov. His father, Gil, urged Tim to hear Gale sing it, since he had heard Gale sing the piece in Manhattan with a visiting Russian chorus and was very moved by her performance. Gil felt it would have much more impact if the piece were sung live. Tim hired Gale immediately on hearing her and, in appreciation for her work, provided her with a full-screen credit at the end of the movie.

Sviridov "Sacred Love"—Gale Limansky (*Dead Man Walking*, movie)
https://www.youtube.com/watch?v=ih8z1jMnPbc

Around this same time, Gale was chosen to record the final "Libera me" from the Verdi Requiem on a 1996 Vox recording, "A Tribute to Diana."

By 1998, I had to let the last of my choral jobs go—Musica Sacra. Richard Westenburg had created the group in 1964, at Central Presbyterian Church. It was "…the first all-professional, paid admission choral series ever undertaken by a church. By the early '70s, the popularity of its concerts caused it to become independent and move to larger venues, including Carnegie Hall..." (Musica Sacra website, accessed, Jun. 10, 2017)

For more than thirty-five years the group reigned above all other professional groups of its kind in New York City. Even after Westenburg's death in 2008, it remaind a viable chorus. After Westenburg, leadership went to Kent Tritle who had been Westenburg's talented conducting protégé at Juilliard. Tritle is also director of music at the Cathedral of Saint John the Divine, and the Oratorio Society of New York.

For a group of such excellence, it was not surprising that every singer in Musica Sacra also performed solo work in the New York tri-state area. Although not generally known, one of the reasons for Musica Sacra's success was the remarkable tonal palette that contractor Cynthia Richards Hewes created for Westenburg by her choice of singers. Westenburg took no part in the auditioning process—that was Cindy's job. She put together the sound that Dick wanted to work with and it became enormously successful and famous as the "Musica Sacra Sound." To be part of that group was not only an honor—and a reflection of your accepted excellence as a singer—it was a privilege. I am not ashamed to confess that when I called Cindy to tell her that I couldn't sing with Musica Sacra any longer, I cried. Of all my music involvement in New York, it was Musica Sacra that I was most proud of—that I loved the most.

I had been a core member for almost twenty years, from January of 1980—1998, and had made many close friends through Sacra. As an example, Cindy and I gave a joint recital at the Recital Hall of St. Michael's Church in Manhattan on May 13, 1985 with pianists Michael Collier and Janet Montgomery. We sang a varied program of arias, songs, and duets by Schumann, Dvorak, Beach, Niles, Wolf, Brahms, Debussy, Mozart, Wertsch, Massenet, Hahn, Meyerbeer, and Kodaly.

I kept my church job since it involved only Sundays, but by 2000 I had decided to retire from singing. Singing only once a week had become a chore trying to keep the voice warmed up and ready. Getting to the Catholic church on the upper-east side of Manhattan from Yonkers, where we lived at that time, was equally tiresome. Further, my job as the registrar for brokers at Marsh & McLennan on the 99th floor in Tower One of the World Trade Center took up a lot of my time and energy. The company had given me a significant raise equaling what I was earning at the church job, so in 2000, I decided the time had come to let it all go. (I wasn't that concerned since I still had a creative outlet with my writing.)

I had begun singing professionally at the age of ten when I was hired as a boy soprano soloist for the Cathedral of the Incarnation in Baltimore City. On reflection, I felt that forty years was not a bad career in professional singing. It was time to move into a new chapter of my life and concentrate on a regular job and my writing. (I had first started a book back in the 1970s which eventually evolved into my book on Yma Sumac.)

I had originally begun as a temporary administrative assistant in the Professional Development department of Marsh & McLennan, but after a couple of months I was hired permanently for a new position that they created for me—Registrar. When I began with the company, they were in temporary offices on Bank Street while new offices on 3 floors in One World Trade Center were being created. Within a year, my office moved to the 99th floor of Tower One. After a couple of years, Professional Development was relocated from One World Trade Center to the main Marsh & McLennan offices on West 46th Street. That was three days before the September 11, 2001 attacks on the World Trade Center!

I was supposed to be on the 99th floor of Tower One for a meeting on that morning of the 11th, but it was decided to do the meeting via conference call so that I could finish setting up my office at 46th Street. The conference call never happened. From the windows of my new office, I watched in horror as Tower One was destroyed by a plane that entered through my floor. As can occur in large companies, it had not been expected that my department's move would happen in a timely manner. Because of that, I was on the inter-office list of the dead until notification was sent that I was indeed alive at the new 46th Street office. I lost many colleagues that day. Marsh & McLennan set up a center for the families of victims in a mid-town hotel in Manhattan and all of us from professional development worked there helping families and survivors deal with their horror. As with so many other people, that day signaled a big shift in my life priorities.

Changes continued to occur in the professional choral scene in New York. Although I lost touch with much of it because of my new life trajectory, while reminiscing with Martin Doner for this book, it appears that major changes began to occur in 2012 in the placing of church and temple jobs. It was around that time that a Facebook group called NYC Choral Freelancers was created. Charles Sprawls and Brian Dougherty started the page as an informational forum to help singers with social networking. It was not originally meant to be a platform for hiring, but over the years that is exactly what happened. Apart from the absence of vetting, this is not a bad thing. Beyond knowing exactly the type or quality of singer you will be getting, there are other drawbacks for the singers themselves. Because things tend to be offered last minute and everything is done through the digital system, there is less time to socialize or have the feeling that you are a participant in a human group. You go. You do a job. You go home. In 2016, Martin, too, decided it was time to retire.

THE EFFECT OF THE RICHTER CD-ROMS AND LOOKING FORWARD

(This chapter was originally written in March of 2005. Changes in technology are reflected here that bring the article current to 2024. Also, many of the performances that I discuss in this chapter are now on YouTube.)

Mike Richter was a pioneer of the live operatic digital age. These writings are presented so that his pioneering work is suitably documented.

Operatic pirating began in the 1960s, but Mike's work more than forty years later marked the transition of pirating into a different level and importance. Although Mike died in October of 2013, his famous CD ROMs continue to be available online. See

https://www.premiereoperaintl.com/cd-rom.aspx
and
https://www.operapassion.com/cd-roms.html

An idea came to Richter in 1995. He wanted to create encyclopedic coverage of recorded opera history through audio selections enhanced by HTML, the language of the World Wide Web. Thus, in late 1995, his Audio Encyclopedia was born. His first release, in 1996, was a CD of all of Caruso's recordings. As he noted then on his site (no longer active):

> A prototype was distributed early in 1996 with the complete recordings of Enrico Caruso. It was well received in very limited distribution and both its comprehensive coverage and its sound quality were particularly noted by the recipients. Several lessons were learned in the process which are incorporated in later releases. Among them, we now include a simple Windows browser as an alternative to the commercial products; and we have upgraded the sound quality so that in most cases it now approaches that of monaural FM radio. Our hope is to use the broad coverage of each volume to inspire publication of at least selected materials in higher quality from better sources using modern processing. Ideally, the Encyclopedia will become a reference work, summarizing in sound a portion of our history otherwise preserved only in text and pictures. As with any reference, the Encyclopedia is intended to support research and education while pointing to the best materials for further investigation.
>
> (http://www.mrichter.com/ae/ae.htm)

Richter worked for many years as an aerospace systems engineer. An avid opera fan, his remarkable encyclopedia (containing mostly mono MP3 sound files) combined aspects of both his vocation and his avocation. Although his idea was refined over the years, the basic concept remained the same—and was definitely ahead of its time.

As Mike explained on his personal site (now defunct):

> (The) discs run on a computer CD, not on a conventional CD player. They have been tested on many platforms, including PC's with various Windows implementations, Macintosh systems with OS 7 and above, and Unix boxes. On the most common configuration (a PC with a 486/100 or above and Windows 95 or above), the discs will operate without requiring any installation. On a Mac, you should download Quick Time 4 from Apple and install it into your preferred browser. You then simply browse WELCOME.HTM on the disc—no Internet connection is required. Earlier discs in

this series contained instructions and files to support the Mac; they are no longer required. (http://www.mrichter.com/ae/replace.htm)

So what does this mean?

Working the same way in 2020 as it did in the early 2000s, depending on the computer's operating system, when you insert one of his CDs into the computer, a "welcome" screen comes up (or a set of icons, in which case one double-clicks on the welcome icon). Links are clicked just as they would be on a web page to be taken to various places within the disc. For instance, if you click on the welcome page of the Munich Opera CD, you are taken to a title page that lists the contents (operas) offered on the disc. When you click on each opera, you are taken to another page with pictures, the cast list, markers to take you to the music by act, and a generous outline of the story and action of the opera. On other discs there will be singer biographies and other information.

In the January 28, 2003 issue of New York Magazine, Peter G. Davis wrote:

> Want Wagner's complete operas on one small CD-ROM for $10? Yes, that's right, more than 40 hours of hard-to-find live performances, featuring singers and conductors you won't hear anywhere else. But wait, there's more. Another disc, for the same low price, offers all of Strauss's operas. Then there's an anthology of French opera, mostly rarities recorded between the early forties and the seventies, starring native artists still in touch with a fading vocal tradition. Callas widows, rejoice—there's a disc that holds all 46 hours of Maria Callas's 1971–72 master classes at Juilliard. There are collections of golden-age voices from the Bolshoi; of British singers born before 1900; and more, much more.
>
> I've been addicted to Mike Richter's CD-ROMs for years, and the time seems right to pass the word on. Each disc, playable on a PC or Mac, is assembled by Richter, a retired engineer in California whose knowledge of opera and singers rivals his technology expertise. These little discs constitute The Audio Encyclopedia, a modest title considering the riches they offer and how thoroughly they provide access to the history of recorded singing. The audio is compressed, but it's tolerable through desktop speakers and better on earphones. It's not a profit-making enterprise; the $10-per-disc price allows Richter to just clear his costs and postage.

The audio encyclopedia includes almost thirty discs. A few of the earlier discs have gone out of print. Most missed are the three superb volumes covering performances given at the San Francisco Opera during the 1960s to the 80s. These were withdrawn at the request of the opera company. Sixty-one performances were documented on those three discs ranging from in-house, pirate taping (the earliest during 1960), through many broadcasts, some of which have become legendary. These include Magda Olivero's soul-wrenching Voix Humaine, Beverly Sills's Manon and Lucia, Jon Vickers's Peter Grimes (as well as an unforgettable Aida with Leonie Rysanek), Anja Silja's Salome, Geraint Evans's Falstaff, a Dialogues of the Carmelites with Leontyne Price, Regine Crespin, Virginia Zeani and Carol Vaness, Leyla Gencer in *La Gioconda*, and tons of others, including one-of-a-kind documents like Nancy Tatum's Forza del Destino (during the 1970s she was one of the most promising of American sopranos), Amy Shuard in *Turandot* and Siegfried, and Colette Boky as Zerbinetta. There is also Birgit Nilsson in an in-house-taped *Tristan und Isolde* which, although missing part of act III, is in excellent sound and perfectly demonstrates her "force of nature" voice. To hear her soar easily through the dense Wagnerian orchestral fabric is to have a lesson in correct singing. Fortunately, some of the performances featured on the San Francisco Opera CDs have been commercially released by such labels as Gala, MYTO, and Living Stage. Most, however, will never see commercial publication.

When I asked Mike Richter how much time it took to create each volume he said:
> The answers vary tremendously with the different volumes. For example, if someone comes up with an idea from which the material is on hand, or if a colleague has a full draft needing only technical corrections, it can take only a month or so. For example, the Callas master classes disc took about three weeks to produce, but I worked on the audio a lot more than 40 hours each of those weeks. At the other extreme, it took more than three years to produce the first disc of Bulgarian opera, including several trips to Sofia by my colleague and lots of political maneuvering. (private conversation)

No matter the time necessary to create them, each of the Richter CDs showed great care in regard to presentation and individuality. One can spend many fun weeks with these discs and not come up for air. Conservatively, it could take one months, if not years, of non-stop listening to get through (and digest) all the material found on the Richter CD discs. Considering the amount of time the discs cover, the few errors that occur are inconsequential.

The audio encyclopedia CDs can be divided into groups, such as discs featuring works by a single composer (Richard Strauss, Richard Wagner, and Giacomo Meyerbeer); discs featuring operas given at a single house: Munich, Bayreuth, and Teatro Colón; and discs featuring broadcast performances from various countries (Paris, Germany, Russia, Bulgaria).

One disc contains all twenty-three of Maria Callas's master classes that were given at Julliard between 1971 and 1972. Ten other discs are more informal, simply called "WWW Site on a Disc." They are a history of audio pages from Richter's web site covering 1995 to 2012 containing countless surprises and treasures. Another category is "Replacement Discs." These are CDs meant to replace once-prominent LP collections that would now be too costly to acquire. Anyone who has owned such LP sets as the mammoth EMI "Record of Singers" understands what the consequences would be were even one record to warp or become otherwise compromised. It would mean the loss of between twelve and twenty selections per LP. Richter's discs are meant to solve that problem.

There are three CD Replacement discs:
1) "Singers on Record" which includes all of the music from the huge, four-volume EMI set with "an integral index in the sequence of issue and a cross-index by all named singers." With Richter's CD, finding a singer and the selection is simply a click away due to his superb indexing.
2) "Mapleson and Wagner" is a specialist item, but of great importance. As Richter explains:
> The invaluable LP issue of the Mapleson cylinders from the New York Public Library at Lincoln Center is supplemented by three LPs from IRCC. The IRCC (International Record Collectors Club) transfers duplicate those of the Library but were made at earlier playing of the cylinders and with significant technical differences.
>
> Even if one already owns these original LPs, Richter's versions make for much easier reference.
>
> The Wagner segment of this disc has all the selections from four different compilation LP sets and three individual LPs: the EMI sets of *Wagner on Record* and *Sänger auf dem grünen Hügel* supplemented with Acanta's *Richard Wagner—Sein Werk in dokumentarischen Aufnahmen*. A total of thirty-six LPs are indexed as in the original releases, as well as by title and by singer.

3) 1950s/60s *The Metropolitan Opera Record Club* releases. As Mike noted on a tray card created for this CD:

In the late 1950's, the Metropolitan offered a series of recordings at reasonable prices. Most were abridged, some nearly enough to defy recognition. I choose not to comment on the translations used in some cases. We present here all the titles offered by the MORC to fill in a lamentable hole in the available record of our audio heritage.

Long collector's items, these releases offered fine performances from singers that, at the time, were considered second-string artists at the Metropolitan Opera. One of my favorites is the abridged Tales of Hoffmann (sung in English) with Jon Crain as a dynamic Hoffmann, Laurel Hurley as an icily pure (and fleet) Olympia, and Lucine Amara as a sweet and affecting Antonia. Presented with narrative, there is a coziness to the recording that I find appealing; kind of like a story accompanied by musical selections.

Another fascinating abridgement is the Aïda with Lucine Amara successfully graduating from the lyrical Antonia to the dramatic Aïda. She was known for her performances of this role at the Metropolitan Opera during the 1960s. There are quite a few other notable renditions including Andrea Chenier with Richard Tucker, and *Madama Butterfly* and Tosca, both with the wonderful Dorothy Kirsten.

Although not live recordings, these LPs were extremely important in the history of the Metropolitan Opera's releasing recordings under its own auspices. These recordings eventually led to the release of Metropolitan Opera live recordings. The series was comprised of nineteen operas recorded in the mid-1950s that were released by the Book of the Month Club. They were of great importance as a set of auxiliary recordings related to the Metropolitan Opera.

In the 1950s, the Metropolitan Opera

> ...entered into an agreement to record and distribute operas through the Book of the Month Club. As they were advertised, all of the nineteen operas were 'Abridged for Home Listening'—some slightly and others greatly. The first ones were recorded at the Metropolitan Opera House but the technical quality of the recording (v)aried between very good and less so.
>
> (After numerous letters of complaint), Columbia was hired for their expertise to record the remaining operas, but no mention was ever made on the discs or elsewhere that Columbia was doing the actual recording. (*The Metropolitan Opera on Record: A Discography of the Commercial Recordings.* by Frederick P. Fellers, Scarecrow Press; 2 edition (June 11, 2010)

On the Internet forum, "Opera L," Frank Drake provided information to compliment information given by Gene Lavergne in his original post in July 1995.

To Gene's list, I have added some recording dates and casts for the operas not included in his list.

MO113—*Carmen* (Elias, Baum, Amara, Cassel, Krall, Roggero; Rudolf) 4, 5, & 6 Jan 1956

MO214—Rigoletto (McFerrin, Barioni, Hurley, Votipka, Warfield, Sgarro; Cleva)

MO315—*Le nozze di Figaro* (Singher, Amara, Conner, Tozzi, Miller, Glaz, Baccaloni, De Paolis, Carelli, Cundari; Rudolf) 15 November 1955

MO417—Boris Godunov (Tozzi, Rankin, Kullman, da Costa, Scott, Franke, Valentino, Roggero, Hurley, Warfield, Budney; Mitropoulos) 5.6. & 7 March 1956

MO518—Die Fledermaus (Hurley, Krall (Rosalinda), Haywood (Alfred), Sullivan (Eisenstein), Miller, Brownlee, Harvuot; Kozma)

MO610—La Boheme (Amara, Barioni, Krall, Valentino, Moscona, Harvuot, de Paolis; Cleva)

MO711 (and MO7021)—Aida (Amara, da Costa, Elias, Guarrera, Tozzi, Sgarro, McCracken, Vartenissian; Cleva)

MO710—*Les Comtes d'Hoffmann* (Crain, Hurley, Elias, Amara, Singher, Vanni, Franke, Harvuot, Scott, Warfield, Anthony; Morel) 22 October 1956

MO713—*La Perichole* (Munsel, Uppman, Ritchard, Herbert, Franke, Krall, Chambers, Elias, de Paolis, Anthony, Marsh; Morel) January 1957

MO715—*Don Pasquale* (Baccaloni, Anthony, WIlson, Guarrera; Kozma)

MO717—*Hansel and Gretel* (Hurley, Miller, Resnik, Votipka, Cundari, Marsh; Rudolf) 7 & 8 February 1957.

MO722—*Madama Butterfly* (Kirsten, Barioni, Harvuot, Miller, Chambers, de Paolis, Hawkins, Marsh, de Cesare; Mitropoulos) 10, 11, &13 December 1956

MO724—*Tosca* (Kirsten, Barioni, Guarrera, Harvuot, Baccaloni, de Paolis, Cehanovsky, Sgarro; Mitropoulos)

MO726—*Il Trovatore* (Curtis-Verna, Elias, Baum, Guarrera, Scott, Vanni, McCracken; Rudolf) 18, 25 & 26 March 1957

MO728—*Die Walkuere* (Schech, Vinay, Scott, Harshaw, Thebom, Uhde, Lind, Ordassy, Krall, Warfield, Lipton, Moll, Elias, Amparan; Mitropoulos) 11 & 14 February 1957

MO811—*I Pagliacci* (Da Costa, Amara, Guarrera, Anthony, Marsh; Adler)

MO823—*The Magic Flute* (Amara, Hurley, Allen, Sullivan, Uppman, Sarastro; Kozma) 4, 15 & 16 April 1957

MO824—*Eugene Onegin* (Amara, Elias, Lipton, Amparan, Tucker, Guarrera, Tozzi, Cehanovsky; Mitropoulos)

MO826—*Andrea Chenier* (Curtis-Verna, Sereni, Tucker, Elias, Lipton, Amparan, Carelli, de Paolis, Cehanovsky, Hawkins, Valentino, Pechner, Scott, Sgarro; Cleva)

The following operas were issued on two LPS:

Andrea Chenier, Die Zauberflöte, Boris Godunov, Madama Butterfly, Tosca, Eugene Onegin, Aida, Il Trovatore, Die Walküre. All others were excerpted on one LP. RCA issued the following titles commercially: *Don Pasquale, Hansel and Gretel, Die Zauberflöte, Boris Godunov, Les Contes d'Hoffmann,* and *La Perichole*.

> The dates I have supplied come from a book called The Metropolitan Opera On Record: A Discography of the Commercial Recordings, complied by Frederick P. Fellers. Greenwood Press, 1984...
> I would say that each album is definitely worth seeking out, as there is always something of interest to be found on each recording. The Boris, for example, is essential for Boris mavens, as it is the only commercial recording of the Rathaus version used by the Met in the early 50s. (Note, that the Met—that great bastion of conservatism—has not used the Rimsky version of Boris since the late 40s!)
> (Frank Drake, Opera L—Thursday, November 9, 2000,

The Book of the Month releases were of tremendous importance because they highlighted the "other casts" singers who often sang on nights when star performers were not available. Also, the records were ideal for bringing in new listeners and making opera more accessible to newcomers since most of these albums included a translated libretto as well as an additional booklet with pictures and information about the operas and productions.

In 2006, a 3-CD set was released of various excerpts from the releases, An Era Recaptured: Highlights from the Metropolitan Opera Record Club. The excellent transfers were done by Dan Hladic. The set included two booklets of almost 140 pages containing the texts and English translations, as well as brief singer biographies.

It was a well-produced set and gave a taste of what the original issues were like. Typical of such releases, it leaves you wanting more.

I mentioned earlier that Mike Richter's concept for the audio encyclopedia was ahead of its time. This was because the idea centered on accessing music through one's computer. That immediately, however, limited the audio encyclopedia's accessibility to those listeners having computers. Further, the incorporation of a hosting web-like page and the necessity of using a mouse, restricted its use in other possible listening schemes. As time passed, however, MP3 music files found acceptance beyond computers alone. The Walkman, the iPod, and similar devices opened up listening possibilities on many other platforms. Today you can hear Mike's sound files on every kind of computer as well as portable CD/ DVD players, and audio devices on every platform. When presented on other than a computer, one will not see the wonderful screens, graphics, photos, pages, and other background information that Richter created for each CD, but you will be able to hear the music! These new alternatives no longer chain one to a computer to listen to these priceless performances.

How is the Sound on the Richter CD-ROMS?

I find the sound more than acceptable. In some cases it is amazing! Some time ago I listened to one of the three *Elektra* performances on the Richard Strauss disc using a portable Panasonic DVD player (L-550). The in-house, taped sound was clean and clear. It is not as perfectly balanced as a commercially recorded CD, but that is not the point of Richter's work. His discs are reference points for the listener, not definitive sound documents. One must be realistic. Do not expect modern-day digital sound. These are almost all *monaural* files. Considering the sources, the variability of the sound quality one experiences is not surprising, but I must emphasize that I have never found the sound to be less than acceptable and enjoyable. The recordings come out of private libraries (mostly) and they can be victim of the vagaries of the opera pirater: there are occasional musical lapses when tapes had to be turned over, the under-balancing of audio, poor quality recording equipment, and the mufflings and spurious glitches caused by having to hide the equipment. However, these intermittent problems are inconsequential when compared to the merits (even glories) and the usefulness of these discs.

The packaging and presentation of the CDs is basic. There are no frills; no jewel-cases or inserts. The discs come in simple white sleeves. Not to worry; Margo Briessinck has prepared tasteful inserts for the encyclopedia's volumes at http://www.gopera.com/opera/ae/index.html. They are excellent and can be printed at no cost from her PDF files, cut out with scissors, and inserted into your own jewel-case.

Each recorded disc costs about $10.00. Containing more than twenty hours per disc, the cost is less than fifty cents per hour of music! And because of Richter's great instinct in choosing the performances that appear on each disc, you will want to hear them more than once.

It is important to note that Richter considered himself primarily an editor and publisher of the CD material. As he wrote to me in an email:

None of the discs would have been possible without the work of others. Some are well known and acknowledged, such as John Ardoin for the Callas master classes. Others chose not to be identified. But all are essential; no volume of the encyclopedia would have been what it is without them."

The Discs

Richard Strauss

All of the Strauss operas are represented (some more than once) in live performances dating from 1977 to 1994. All but one take place at Munich and include such presentations as a 1988 *Schwiegsame Frau* with Julie Kauffmann as Aminta, and a 1988 performance of *Die Frau Ohne Schatten* with Cheryl Studer, Ingrid Bjoner, James King and Theo Adam. The late Sabine Hass can be heard in no fewer than eight of the twenty-plus performances, from a dynamic *Friedenstag,* to an incandescent *Liebe der Danae*. Some of the singers heard on this disc were famous for their roles and recorded them commercially, but others were not so fortunate. Luckily, documents such as these exist to show the work of such singers as Ingrid Bjoener and Janice Martin as Elektra, and the delicious Lillian Sukis as Daphne (Sukis was one of those singers who rarely got more than a comprimario role at the Metropolitan Opera, yet in Europe showed her worth by singing superb performances of such diverse operas as Dvorak's *Rusalka,* Verdi's *Luisa Miller,* and the 1977 *Daphne* presented here). Lucia Popp is heard as Arabella and in *Capriccio,* while Edita Gruberova is heard in her signature role of Zerbinetta in 1984. Gwyneth Jones is heard in a surprising 1987 outing as the Egyptian Helen and Hildegard Behrens shows her prowess in a 1987 *Salome* and an almost-over-the-top 1994 *Elektra* with Hass and Christa Ludwig.

I have returned to this disc time and again and, if you love Strauss, so will you. It should be stressed, however, that most of these performances were taped in-house. Considering the denseness of Strauss's orchestration, it should be listened to in conjunction with one's other recordings of the Strauss operas. Used that way, it will enrich your knowledge of the Strauss canon and performing practices.

Wagner

This disc is as impressive as the Strauss and, amazingly, contains all of the Wagner operas. The selections are excellent and include a few landmark performances including the famous 1970s English BBC revivals of his early works: *Die Feen, Das Liebesverbot* and *Rienzi*. These broadcasts were very important at the time and hearing them today proves that they have withstood the test of time. What I enjoy most about the Wagner CD is that Richter's choices of performances are often unusual. For instance, for the *Fliegende Hollander,* instead of offering a more common performance, Richter chose the sound track of the more obscure, 1975 English TV production with Gwyneth Jones and Norman Bailey.

For Lohengrin, Richter chose an October 6, 1964 Teatro Colón performance providing the note:

The sound of this recording is not what one would wish; in particular, portions of Act III are quite poor. Given the historical value of the recording, we hope you will be tolerant of those failings."

No matter the sound problems, it is a glorious performance starring Victoria de los Angeles, Christa Ludwig, and Fritz Uhl, conducted by Lovro von Matacic. There is also the Ring Cycle from the 1970s RAI cycle conducted by Sawallisch. The Die Meistersinger featured on this CD is in English sung by the Sadler Wells Opera company with Norman Bailey as Hans Sachs, and Reginald Goodall conducting.

More than any other, the Wagner CD makes the study of such complicated and often overwhelming music easier than ever before. For listeners who tend to be lazy (and I include myself in that category) the disc eliminates the necessity for getting up to change the LP or CD. It allows the listener to concentrate on the music. Further, Richter has included the German libretti for each of the works as well.

Another CD: "Opera from Bayreuth" includes Ring Cycle performances taken from the famous 1976 Boulez cycle that encourages the hard-core Wagnerian to compare available commercial CD (and video releases) of that 1976 Ring with these alternate performances from the same cycle—potentially an invaluable learning tool. Not only that, but you get two renditions of Tristan: a less-known 1970 performance with Nilsson and Windgassen, and a more recent 1999 performance conducted by Daniel Barenboim with Siegfried Jerusalem and Waltraude Meier.

Meyerbeer
For lovers of "florid song" the Meyerbeer disc offers some real stunners. There are classic revivals here as well as some rarities. One of the Meyerbeer classics that everyone should own is the heavily cut, but still indispensable, 1968 Italian revival of *Robert le Diable* with Renata Scotto, Giorgio Merighi, and Boris Christoff. For those who do not know this performance, it was one of Scotto's great nights. Her voice was in spectacular shape—from a rich lower register throughout a top that included a sustained E above high C. Coloratura flights (and there are many) were dispatched with the fluency of a true mistress of that art and interpretively, she cannot be faulted. Add to her contribution the creativity and darkly resinous voice of Boris Christoff and you have an unforgettable night at the opera. Not only that, but the sound of the surviving recording is excellent. (At one time it appeared on the famous MRF LP Records.) For those interested in this opera and its performance history, you can compare the merits of the 1968 Florence performance with a more recent 2001 performance featuring Nelly Miricioiou, that is also on the Meyerbeer disc.

There are two performances of Le Prophete: one a classic 1970 revival with Nicolai Gedda and Marilyn Horne; and a newer rendition with Placido Domingo and Agnes Baltsa. There are two contrasting performances of the epic L'Africaine: one with Jessye Norman; and another (that is almost note-complete) with Martina Arroyo. Included is the classic 1975 Opera Rara revival of L'Etoile du Nord with the remarkable Janet Price and the underrated Deborah Cook. There are three Les Huguenots. One is recorded in Germany with Karl Terkal, Gottlob Frick, Maud Cunitz and Valerie Bak (as Marguerite) that is quite rare and should prove of interest to collectors of curiosities. Complimenting that is the now-classic 1971 Vienna performance with a suave Nicolai Gedda, a brilliant Rita Shane as Marguerite, a virile Justino Diaz, and perky Jeanette Scovotti (as Urbain). Even more, there is the famous twentieth-century revival in 1962 from La Scala with Franco Corelli, Joan Sutherland, Fiorenza Cossotto, and Giulietta Simionato (as Valentine). You also get Il Crociato in Egitto, two modern performances of the composer's surprisingly effective Dinorah, and much more.

The disc also contains a wealth of additional historical solo recordings from Meyerbeer operas that were recorded during the first three decades of recording. For the opera novice, this disc is a great way to hear and learn about some of the great artists from the early years of the twentieth century.

Italian Opera from Teatro Colón
Another must-have CD for any collector. Since Richter's creation of this disc, a few of these performances have been released by commercial companies, MYTO and Living Stage for example. However, having fifteen complete performances from this magnificent theatre on Richter's disc is a real treat. It helps demonstrate the extremely high level of artistry that has paraded across the stage of the Teatro Colón. *I Puritani, Simon Boccanegra,* and *Rigoletto* with Leyla Gencer, *Lucia* with Beverly Sills and Alfredo Kraus, a not-to-be-missed, white hot *La Gioconda* with Elena Suliotis, *Aïda* with Martina Arroyo and Carlo Bergonzi, *Otello* with Jon Vickers and Raina Kabaivanska, *Tosca* with Regine Crespin, *Turandot,* with Birgit Nilsson and Montserrat Caballe, and many others.

From Which We Came
This is a fascinating CD that presents the earliest opera sets (1907–1930). These include the not-to-be-missed 1908 *Carmen* and *Faust* with Emmy Destinn, as well as sets of *Aïda, Rigoletto, Il trovatore, Il barbiere di Siviglia, Cavalleria Rusticana, Pagliacci, Madama Butterfly, Die Walküre, Tristan und Isolde, The Ring Cycle,* etc. Many of these sets are, understandably, abridged since they were originally released on 78 rpm discs with all the limitations of that medium. But, in many regards, that is irrelevant; as a part of our operatic and recorded heritage these sets are invaluable. And do not think for a moment that just because they are old they lack verve. In matters of intensity and commitment some of these ancient sets surpass more modern attempts. The CD also offers the first sets (1917–1924) of four Gilbert & Sullivan operettas: *HMS Pinafore, Mikado, Princess Ida,* and *Ruddigore.* The inclusion of these sets was an excellent decision since they round out a lot of opera with some lighter fare. As if not enough, there is also a good sampling of the German–sung Kurzoper (highlight) recordings made in the early electrical days. The operas represented are *La bohème, Carmen, Der Freischütz, Lohengrin,* and *Martha.*

Fanget An
This CD is a systematic survey of Germanic tenors of the twentieth century. As Mike explains on his site: "We included in this collection singers from Germany and from other countries singing largely in the German language, in German style and the German fach…tenors are heard in a total of 648 complete selections." The 200 tenors range from Bernd Aldenhoff to Heinz Zednik. It is a true feast of voice and repertoire.

Stars of David
Originally, this was the second CD of the Richter series and is probably one of his most stunning discs, an unbelievable feast of over six hundred selections sung by two hundred singers, both familiar and unfamiliar. The premise is simple: to document opera and song (and some liturgical fare) as sung by Jewish artists. It is an amazingly rich array of talent.

As Richter notes on his web site:
> All artists are listed with biographical information and pictures where they could be found. In many cases, additional pictures are provided if you click on the one in the title line. Much of the material is exceptionally rare, and a great many of the recordings have never been reissued or even published.

From what I have listened to on this disc so far, Richter is absolutely right. His choices of representative pieces are often inspired and surprising. For instance, for Beverly Sills, instead of more typical material, he offers a live performance of the 1912 version of Zerbinetta's aria, the infamous "Sillsiana" potpourri, and "Myself I Shall Adore" from the now cult-classic 1968 performance of Semele. All three highlight perfectly the Sills voice and talents. For Roberta Peters, one of the selections is a sparkling 1963 "Glitter and Be Gay" from Candide, (sung at a time when the aria was still a novelty). Another is the doll's song (Hoffmann) from a 1956 TV appearance.

Marisa Galvany, Beverly Sills's nemesis in the 1970s New York City Opera's Three Queen productions, has her talents highlighted (among other arias) by a spectacular rendition of Odabella's difficult "Santo di Patria" (Attila) taken from a piano-accompanied recital. Readers who have followed this singer's career know that Attila was a Galvany specialty. She sang in a number of productions and revivals of the work. Galvany chooses to end the aria with a final high E-flat that defies the clock. The early mezzo Margarete Matzenauer's versatility is underlined not just by mezzo arias, but also a 1907 recording of the Stryienne from Mignon (with a final high D). Hermine Bosetti is represented by her early and still rather rare recording of the 1912 version (somewhat cut) of Zerbinetta's aria. As one can imagine, the wealth of operatic singers is mind-boggling. Then there are the cantors—from the earliest recorded, Gershon Sirota to more recent exponents of cantorial art. This disc proves just how enjoyable a learning experience can be while sampling the myriad singers found here.

Opera Russe
The opera Russe (Western opera sung in Russian) disc includes an important first complete recording (1946) of a coloratura favorite: Delibes's *Lakmé* with Nadezhda Kazantseva and Sergey Lemeshev. Although this is not one of the better versions on record, it is still fascinating to hear the first complete recorded attempt of this work. (It has been released commercially by Gala CD) The disc also contains a number of complete recordings featuring the famous Russian tenor Ivan Kozlovsky (1900–1993) who has always been a favorite of collectors. In all, twenty-two operas are presented, covering composers from Gluck (*Orfee*) to Wagner (*Lohengrin*). Richter has managed to cover most of the operatic styles as well: from coloratura to verismo, Wagner to Mozart, French, German, and Italian, all are represented here. Although listening to Western opera sung in Russian can occasionally be an unnerving experience, once one adjusts and accepts the recordings for what they are (nationalistic documents of then-current interpretations of Western operas) the benefits and rewards are many.

Sir Thomas Beecham
This is a wonderful tribute disc and the only one in the series that honors an individual conductor. There are a number of unique performances that include one of my favorites, an intense 1958 *Carmen* from the Teatro Colón, sung by the underrated American mezzo/contralto, Jean Madeira. What a wonderful artist she was.

There is a famous 1939 Bartered Bride sung at Covent Garden with Richard Tauber. The exquisite Gwen Catley is heard in an English revival of Bizet's Jolie Fille du Perth (with a beautifully sung mad scene), and Aïda is represented by the justly famous 1939 Covent Garden performance with Maria Caniglia, Ebe Stignani, and Beniamino Gigli. Just as famous (or legendary) is the 1937 London broadcast of *Tristan und Isolde* with Kirsten Flagstad and Lauritz Melchior. The almost-forgotten coloratura soprano, Ilse Hollweg, is featured in a famous 1950

Edinburgh revival of the 1912 version of Ariadne auf Naxos. Hollweg's high, airy voice suited Zerbinetta's extravagant vocal lines and she is a success despite the use of a disturbing conglomeration of the 1912 and 1916 versions superimposed one on top of the other. (One suspects a rather eccentric decision on Beecham's part.)

There is a Teatro Colón performance of Die Zauberflöte with Rita Streich as the Queen of the Night and Pilar Lorengar as her daughter—and a rarity: a 1948 broadcast of Delius's A Village Romeo & Juliet. There is more, including a complete 1947 Messiah performance, as well as a Sibelius symphony, three Mozart symphonies, and the Delius Piano Concerto, plus highlights from various operas.

The remarkable thing about Richter's CDs is that no matter how specific your reason might be for getting one of them, what inevitably happens is that you start listening to other works (just to idly check them out) and you get caught up in them. Be prepared to postpone the spring cleaning for a week, or delay that chore you had promised yourself you would do.

Opera From Paris
This is a favorite. It features French radio broadcasts of mostly French works that took place between 1942 and 1976. The casts are, for the most part, superb. *Herodiade, Les Huguenots, Mignon, Mireille, Otello, Roi D'Ys, Sigurd,* and *Thaïs* are among the list of nineteen works. When one considers that this disc holds more than thirty hours of music, the magnitude of the project becomes even more apparent and impressive.

Some of the performances are abridged since that is the way they were originally broadcast. While I like everything on this disc, one of my favorites is a 1963 performance of Massenet's Herodiade with Suzanne Sarroca, Lucienne Delvaux, Paul Finel, Robert Massard, and Jacques Mars. It is dynamic, idiomatic, passionately sung, and strongly conducted by Pierre Dervaux. There is so much to savor on the disc including a French Don Carlos as well as a lesser-known 1976 performance of Les Huguenots with Alain Vanzo, Louise Lebrun, Jules Bastin, and Della Jones. Even the most accomplished collector will probably find something of interest. In addition to Aïda, Thaïs, Samson et Dalia, Mignon and La traviata, you will find the French version of Mozart's Idomeneo as well as radio revivals of obscure operas such as Massenet's La Navarraise and Lalo's Le Roi D'Ys, and the wonderful Wagnerian-like epic Sigurd by Reyer (once released by MRF on LP). As if all this were not enough, there are also selections from various French radio concerts showcasing such distinctly different singers as Geori Boué, Regine Crespin, and Teresa Stitch-Randal.

Opera from Germany
Another disc full of surprises! Everything from *Martha* to *Elektra,* a total of twenty-one recordings presented in more-than-acceptable sound. Some are early classics such as Erna Berger's *Hänsel und Gretel.* Many date from the late 1930s and early 1940s, and some of you will recognize that a number of them had been available in the U.S. on the Urania label. As I have found with all of Richter's CDs, whether or not you enjoy all of the performances, all are worth hearing, and some might surprise you. On this disc, for instance, one of the surprises was a delightful recording of Pfitzner's *Christ-Eflein* recorded in Hamburg in 1950 with the wonderful Anneliese Rothenberger. Although complete libretti are not provided with this CD (like some other CDs in the series), a decent synopsis of the opera is, and it is presented in a way that is useful to the listener.

Another recording familiar to some is the 1942 *Der Rosenkavalier* with Viorica Ursuleac and the sweet Adele Kern. While it is not one of the best renditions of the opera (at least not in regard to the role of the Marschallin) I have always had a soft spot in my heart for this recording. Ursuleac may sound like someone's grandmother, but her concept of the role, and her way with the text, is appealing and certainly her commitment cannot be questioned. Adele Kern floats her way through Sophie with grace, and Georgine von Milinkovic (Octavian) and Ludwig Weber (Ochs) are wonderful. Clemens Krauss's conducting shows his obvious affection for the score. Here also, is Marianne Schech in Lohengrin, Marta Fuchs in the rarely recorded Wolf opera, Der Corregidor, Lea Piltti, the Finnish version of Adele Kern and a delightful singer in Entführung aus dem Serail and Die Zauberflöte, and much, much more.

Opera auf Deutsch
Twenty-four broadcast operas are presented and there are some wonderful things here. The broadcast dates range from 1936 to 1952 and many are now classics. Many performances were considered important revivals at the time and a few have been commercially released by labels such as MYTO and Preiser. The operas include *Fra Diavolo, Cavalleria Rusticana, Pagliacci, La bohème, Tosca, Aïda, Ernani, I Vespri Siciliani* (the famous German-sung revival of the work with Helge Roswaenge and Maud Cunitz), *Manon, Le nozze di Figaro, Bartered Bride, Otello* with Torsten Ralf and Hilde Konetzni (one of my favorite, non-Italian performances of this work), and others.

An all-time love of mine is the 1948 recording of Dvorak's exquisite Rusalka that once appeared on a Urania LP. It was, if I am not mistaken, the first complete recording of the work highlighting the wonderful singing of Elfriede Trötschel as Rusalka with Gottlob Frick and Ruth Lange, Josef Keilberth conducts. Although riddled with cuts and sung in German, it can be an excellent introduction to the opera. A reason I am so fond of this recording is that it was my own introduction to Dvorak's musical world. Like Lillian Sukis in the 1970s, Trötschel's lovely timbre suited the role and she presented a memorable portrait of the tragic water nymph.

Then there is the charming Erna Berger in Don Pasquale, Contes d'Hoffmann, and Orfee which includes a young Rita Streich. Indeed, the comprehensiveness of this disc is one of its main attractions. Various operatic styles are well represented: Verdi, Wagner, Auber, Mascagni, Smetana, Tchaikovsky; there is something here for everyone, and Richter has thoughtfully provided biographies of most of the singers.

Opera from Munich
This is another wonderful array of performances and an excellent example of the glorious singing at this opera house. Twenty-one operas are offered, including such contrasting works as *Die Fledermaus, Fidelio, Clemenza di Tito, Faust, Pique Dame, La traviata, Werther, Die Zauberflöte, L'Incoronazione di Poppea,* and *Die lustigen Weiber von Windsor*. Again, the material presented to the listener holds some unforgettable renditions. There are some real rarities, such as Edita Gruberova as Massenet's *Manon*. This performance is from an in-house tape and quite different from the broadcast that circulated a number of years ago. She is also featured in a wonderful performance of *La traviata* with Carlos Kleiber. There is also one of those "special nights at the opera" featuring Montserrat Caballe as *Maria Stuarda* with a scenery-chewing Brigitte Fassbaender as Elisabeth. Caballe was in such fine form that night that she decided to interpolate a fine high D at the end of act II (a rarity for this artist who rarely

went above high C). There is much to savor here, performances by Julia Varady (*Pique Dame*), Mirella Freni (*La bohème, Manon Lescaut, Faust*), Lucia Aliberti (*Rigoletto*), Kurt Moll (*Die Zauberflöte, Lustigen Weiber*), Lucia Popp (*Lustigen Weiber, Die Zauberflöte, Gianni Schicchi*), Hildegard Behrens (*Fidelio*), Giacomo Aragall (*Tosca*), Luciano Pavarotti (*La bohème*), Matteo Manuguerra (*Rigoletto*), Raina Kabaivanska (*Tosca*), and many more.

Opera from Bulgaria, Bulgarian National Radio, and Russian Opera from Bulgaria

The most fascinating and involved of the Richter CDs are the three-volume Bulgarian series. These volumes took years to produce. It must be clear that I love these CDs, but don't take my word for it. If you are interested you can see for yourself. The University of Pittsburgh hosts the three Bulgarian volumes on line at http://www.ucis.pitt.edu/opera/ (At this time it is undergoing some reimagining and hopes to re-open sometime in 2023-24.

Once it re-opens, you can go there and experience for yourself the marvels that Mike created. It will give you an opportunity to see how the audio encyclopedia works. You will adapt immediately, but I warn you that it is addictive! The University of Pittsburgh is to be applauded for hosting the pages, as should be Mike's colleague, Frank Fischer, who was responsible for the concept and assembling this remarkable set of discs.

My favorite of the group is the Bulgarian National Radio presentation of ten operas that include such works as Bizet's Les pêcheurs de perles, Mefistofele, Der fliegende Holländer, as well as *La Gioconda, Turandot*, and Verdi's Macbeth, Nabucco, and Don Carlo. The sound quality of the broadcasts is excellent. It is clear, clean, and upfront and spacious; the performances are stylistically well sung, although the soprano who sings Gilda is more a lyric than a lyric coloratura, while Julia Wiener is excellent as Lady Macbeth, and young Ghena Dimitrova proves why Abigaille in Nabucco was a signature role of hers; the chorus may not be as good as the Metropolitan Opera, but they appear to be well trained and enthusiastic. Intriguing for the Western listener is to see how Bulgaria presents these operas in its own language. Although hearing familiar works in that language takes a bit of getting used to, don't dismiss the experience. This disc is wonderful and I think you will be pleasantly surprised.

The disc has a number of sections. One of the most astounding is its collection of singers (most of whom recorded for the Balkaton label). Like the Stars of David disc, the listener is presented with a large array of artists with a generous sampling of their work. There is a section of Bulgarian-composed opera as well as a complete Lohengrin, an abridged *Un Ballo in Maschera*, and excerpts from such diverse works as Norma, acts I and IV of *La Gioconda* (what I heard of these made me sorry more of the performances do not exist), *Turandot*, Aïda, Attla, and Il trovatore. Not only is there the opportunity to hear how Bulgarian opera houses present opera, you get the opportunity to hear and learn about the types of operas being composed in that country.

Russian opera from Bulgaria

This is exactly what it states. There are some stunners here. The 1977 performance of *Prince Igor* is live, with an excellent cast that includes young Ghena Dimitrova as Yaroslovna (performing a wonderful lament). *Boris Godunov* is a 1957 Sofia performance with Nicolai Ghiaurov singing a wonderful Pimen. Ghiaurov also appears in a 1975 performance of *Khovanschina*. There are performances of Petrov's *Peter I*, Rimsky Korsakov's *The Golden Cockrel*,

The Snow Maiden, Boyarinya vera Sheloga, and five other works. If you sample these volumes online you will need a comfortable chair since they contain an unbelievable amount of information and music that you will want to hear.

WWW Site on a Disc

These are some of the most intriguing of Richter's discs. Although I prefer his thematic discs, these are wonderfully casual catch-alls that present the listener with a huge amount of material. Before his death, Richter created ten of these CDs. There is so much material on each CD that it would be impossible for me to more than hint at what will be found.

One of the most important is on disc #3, a La traviata from Lisbon that starred Maria Callas and Alfredo Kraus. It is not the tacky, horrible-sounding version heard on the EMI commercial release.

For those not familiar with the story, in December of 2000 the Lisbon opera released a courtesy CD (available to financial supporters of the Lisbon opera) of a digital, newly mastered broadcast of *La Traviata* that had been given in March of 1958. This caused quite a stir in the opera world because the master tape was of spectacular sound quality. Two thousand discs were produced and were gone within a month. It has never been re-pressed. It matters little that the master tape for Richter's disc is an MP3 file format. The quality of the sound runs rings around what EMI offers. While it is true that MP3s are compressed files and usually not thought well of as full-range recordings, the original was of such high quality that the sound quality on Richter's CD well outshines the EMI release You can hear the Callas voice up front and close, as if she were singing in your living room. Because of the improved sonics and close-miking, I could hear felicities of Callas's interpretation that are missing on other versions of this performance.

While discussing Maria Callas, another disc (#5) includes an alternate performance that she gave of Bellini's *La sonnambula* in Edinburgh on August 26, 1957. Although not markedly different from the more accessible performance of August 21, I prefer this rendition. Callas's voice appears to be in slightly better shape, the legato singing is sweet and lush, all top E-flats (three of them) are sustained without a hint of strain, and coloratura is fleet, accurate, and phrased to perfection. Perhaps the most interesting aspect of this performance is the manner in which Callas traps upper-register pianissimi in her mouth cavities, almost humming the notes. This is especially evident during the sleepwalking scenes where that sound gives the aural impression that Amina is talking to herself; that the listener is eavesdropping on private thoughts. Fascinating.

There is still more on these discs! There are tributes to Mado Robin, Jussi Bjoerling, John Alexander, Claudia Muzio, Marisa Galvany, Joan Sutherland (early recordings), Alain Vanzo, Beverly Sills (Christmas record), Rosa Ponselle (Christmas songs from Villa Pace), Russell Oberlin, Jan Peerce, Lucia Popp, Anna Moffo, Ewa Podles, Susan Dunn, Nelson Eddy, Irene Jordan, Aureliano Pertile, Galina Vishnevskaya, Thelma Votipka, Gottlob Frick, Julia Culp, Licia Albanese, Sarah Walker, Rose Ader, Janet Price, Franco Corelli (a 1968 recital), and too many more to list.

There are special treats. They include four versions of Berlioz's *Les Nuits d'ete* with Suzanne Danco, Eleanor Steber, Nicolai Gedda, and Victoria de los Angeles, Mahler lieder with Rita Gorr and Vera Soukupova, Schumann's *Dichterliebe* with Suzanne Danco, another with

Dietrich Fischer-Dieskau accompanied by Vladimir Horowitz, another with Pierre Bernac, yet another with Rudolf Schock, and so on. There are excerpts and complete works that cover almost the entire vocal repertoire of Monteverdi's *Il combattimento di Tancredi e Clorinda*, Bellini's *Il Pirata*, Schönberg's *Ertwartung*, Max Kowalski's *Pierrot lunaire*, as well as the more familiar Meyerbeer's *Les Huguenots*, Donizetti's *Lucrezia Borgia*, Bellini's *Norma*, Halevy's *La Juive*, Giordano's *Andrea Chenier*, Verdi's *Luisa Miller*, Wagner's *Lohengrin*, Donizetti's *Lucia di Lammermoor*, Puccini's *La bohème*, Wagner's *Die Walküre*, and many others.

There are fascinating and educational comparison pages that present various singers interpreting the same piece: Mozart's "Alleluia," Wagner's "Ho Yo To Ho" Zerbinetta's aria (1912 version), Wotan's *Abschied*, Edgardo's aria from *Lucia*, and more. There is even more: Poulenc songs with Rose Dercourt, lyric tenor reference recordings, excerpts from Goldmark's monumental and beautiful *Kőnigin von Saba*, songs from *Alice in Wonderland* by Duke, and excerpts from the legendary Stokowski concert with Birgit Nilsson and George London. I wish I could list everything on these discs to show the huge diversity of material, but if you visit Margo Briessinck's website showing the liner sleeves, you can get a better idea of the comprehensiveness of the material. She has created sleeves for the first four WWW discs.

There are priceless live performances here as well as commercial recordings that have been out of print for decades. (At one time Richter spotlighted the American soprano, Margaret Tynes on his website, presenting her only aria album on Qualiton. Tynes was an important exponent of the role of Salome during the 1960s. I saw her remarkable performance of that role at the Baltimore Opera during the late 1960s. It was that performance that helped to solidify my love of opera. A particular memory is especially vivid—when Jochanaan rejects Salome and returns into the cistern. Tynes fell to the floor like a spoiled child in a fit of rage and frustration, beating the floor with her hands and feet. To an impressionable 15-year-old this was remarkably shocking and powerful. I have never forgotten it.

On another of the WWW discs Mike Richter spotlights the only aria album by the dynamic mezzo soprano of the 1950s, Oralia Dominguez. She was known for her Amneris in the famous 1951 Mexico City production of *Aïda* with Maria Callas and Mario del Monaco. Many may not know that Dominguez was a quite versatile singer who performed everything from Monteverdi to Rossini, with Verdi, Wagner, and Massenet between. Her album underlines that versatility. Thanks to Richter, many who may not have known that a DGG LP existed, can now hear the wonderful work of this singer. (Since the Richter release, DGG has commercially released that album on CD.) There is Patrice Munsel's 10" RCA LP of Strauss waltzes. There is a tremendous amount of information accompanying the selections.

These discs are kept in a special place in my library where I can grab them in a moment, so often do I refer to them. For some years they were among the few discs in my library for which I made sure I had more than one copy should anything happen to one of them.

John W. Lambert, in an article "Opera on CD: An Encyclopedic View" for the Internet site: Classical Voice of North Carolina wrote:

> Opera is often viewed as the entertainment of dilettantes and the well-heeled. These outstanding CD-ROMs now place the genre within reach of even impoverished students, not to mention other struggling collectors.

(https://cvnc.org/reviews/2001/features/OperaCDRom.html)

The Emergence of YouTube

YouTube first began to offer videos in November of 2005. Since then, it has become one of the most popular websites on the Internet. Millions of videos have been up-loaded to it.

Over the last few years YouTube has evolved into a mighty storehouse for many of the most important historical opera performances that were sedulously pirated in the 1960s and 70s—performances that at one time (not too long ago) could cost close to one hundred dollars each to buy on privately pressed LPs. This does not include the thousands of 78 rpm recordings of historical classical singers that have been uploaded to YouTube as well. These priceless recordings are now available for everyone on the Internet to enjoy. New videos and concerts are added daily. Newly found historical concerts and operas are regularly uploaded to further enrich these archives.

As YouTube has come to the fore as a serious repository of historical operatic and concert performances, I am reminded of my years working with Mr. Tape and the ideals that Ralph Ferrandina expressed. Despite the morass of legal issues, live operatic performances should be made available to be heard by anyone who is interested. In many ways, with the availability of YouTube, Ralph's dream for the easy availability of important historical performances has come true. I think Ralph would be pleased.

ASTRAFIAMANTE:
**ROBERTA PETERS
LAST MEMBER OF A GREAT TRADITION**

(An unpublished interview from August 29, 1985. I include this interview in this book because Roberta Peters is featured in fifty-six Metropolitan Opera broadcasts, many of which have been pirated and are discussed in this chapter. In places where information is inserted at this writing in 2020 I precede that information with the term "author update" and indent any such following information.)

I met Roberta Peters (1930–2017) at her home in Scarsdale, New York, on an August afternoon in 1985 with her accompanist, Lawrence Skrobacs. They were rehearsing for an AIDS Gala, "A Gala Night for Singing," that was held in East Hampton on August 31, 1985. It was co-produced by Robert Jacobson, the editor of *Opera News* at the time, and Matthew Epstein, a vice president of Columbia Artists. The proceeds would go to AIDS research. Peters was among the opera stars appearing that night including Carol Vaness, Aprile Millo, Evelyn Lear, Susan Quittmeyer, Catherine Malfitano, Erie Mills, Jerry Hadley, Brent Ellis, James Morris, Alan Titus, Paul Plishka, and others. Peters was singing music by Handel and Lehar. The event raised $200,000.

Larry, my wife Gale, and I had attended West Virginia University together, and by this time Larry had been working with Roberta Peters for a number of years as her recital accompanist. When I heard that he was going to rehearse with her at her home, I asked if I might come along in order to interview the soprano. Larry checked with her, and since I was a fellow musician, she kindly offered an invitation to not only meet with her, but also to listen to them rehearse.

Larry and I were picked up at the train station in Scarsdale by her husband, Bertram Fields. It was a beautiful, sunny August day and for a while we sat by the pool and chatted before she was to rehearse. She brought out a tray of fruit, mints, and orange juice. Later, she showed me her many music scores that included original opera scores having belonged to the historic coloratura soprano, Frieda Hempel (1885–1955). Bert went off to play tennis. He returned after rehearsal, and because Roberta had a meeting at Carnegie Hall, he drove us all back to Manhattan. He reflected his wife's charm, making it a pleasure to speak with him for this short time.

I was treated to a forty-five-minute recital/rehearsal of songs and arias by Handel, Lehar, Mozart, and Ravel. After listening to this artist in so intimate and relaxed an atmosphere, the one word that comes to my mind to describe Ms. Peters is elegant. This was not a forced or learned quality, but one that was natural and instinctive. It was a trait that permeated her singing as well.

You can learn much about a musician by observing them in rehearsal and many questions were answered as I sat and listened. Ms. Peters was relaxed and secure, and knew exactly what she wanted to achieve during the rehearsal. Authoritative, yet cooperative, she worked with Larry to achieve the best artistic results rather than to dictate the way "she" was going to sing that piece of music. When rehearsing a new aria, and problems arose, they stopped, isolated and analyzed the problem, and, whether it was rhythmical or tonal, vocal or pianistic, they worked together until it was fixed. Although no time was wasted, the atmosphere was relaxed and comfortable. Open to suggestion, she would modify, add, or discard artistic concepts in order to best serve the composer, rather than herself.

That season was Peters's thirty-fifth with the Metropolitan Opera and although it would be her last, it saw no diminishment of this remarkable quality. Not only were her physical gestures gracious and balletic, but so also her vocal gestures. For thirty-five years, no matter what pyrotechnics were taking place, there was always her vocal calm and poise that was as tasteful as it is uncommon. Her list of performances at the Met is impressive—515 performances in 24 roles, with 88 performances of Rigoletto's Gilda leading the list. (And the 56 broadcasts already mentioned!)

When we talked after the rehearsal, I found her to be genial, personable, quick of smile, and charming without being artificial or manipulative. Her longevity as an artist at the Metropolitan Opera is due to factors that she carefully nurtured since her debut in 1950. These included solid, rigorous, and systematic early vocal training, and sensible guidance from her teacher, William Pierce Herman, that included judicious repertoire decisions and, most importantly, common sense. I found it fascinating that despite the many years they worked together, even that day in August, when referring to her teacher, it was with the formal "Mr. Herman," in respectful deference.

By now the story of Roberta Peters' debut at the Metropolitan Opera on November 17, 1950, is well known. How a young girl of twenty stepped onto the stage in the role of Zerlina in Mozart's *Don Giovanni* with only a few hours' notice and without previous stage experience, to capture the attention and the hearts of America. Writing of her debut, Louis Biancolli said in the New York World-Telegram:

> The delightful surprise of last night's performance of "Don Giovanni" at the Metropolitan was the emergency debut of little Roberta Peters in the part of Zerlina. Without having appeared anywhere in public before, and with just a short rehearsal a few hours before curtain time, the 20-year old girl made a brilliant showing in a very tricky role....
>
> The voice came through the big house as clear as a bell, the notes equally bright and focused and the phrasing that of a true musician. And the girl—she is all of five feet-two—turned in a very smooth job of acting, too. She will bear watching—and listening." (Metropolitan Opera Archives, accessed 5-20-16)

What is not so widely known is the immense artistic preparation that enabled this young soprano to accomplish such a feat. It is a unique story of a different era of vocal training in America and of priorities that, in many ways, are no longer available to young singers.

When I started at the age of thirteen, I knew nothing about music or opera. I was just a little girl from the Bronx who liked music and sang. After the tenor Jan Peerce heard me sing (he was a family friend) he recommended that I study with Mr. Herman. Mr. Herman felt I had the possibility for a career in music and he suggested to my parents that I drop out of school in order to concentrate completely on my musical studies—so I did! It really was an amazing thing, I brought the letter into the school and the Principal just let me walk out!"

Roberta soon began an intensive period of study that would last for six years and which included not only voice, but languages, dramatics, ballet, and fencing.

When I was about fourteen or fifteen, Mr. Herman outlined a program of study for me and sent me to French, German, and Italian coaches. Vocally, he started me with Bach and Handel and then, as time went on, we began to delve into Lieder—Schubert, Schumann, and Wolf—all of which I coached with Leo Roseneck, the famous coach of Elisabeth Schumann. I had at least two different lessons a day. You can imagine how much I was absorbing without even realizing it.

The relationship and rapport I had with Mr. Herman was really quite unusual. He was a singer himself—not a very good singer, but he was a good teacher and loved to search for new music. Even if I saw him six days a week (which I usually did) on Sundays we would go walking on the lower East Side to the old book and music stores and search for new music. That was the kind of person he was. He really was a mentor and a friend to me in addition to being my teacher, and he was an influence I had never had before in my life.

As a matter of fact, he even paid for some of my lessons because even with both my parents working, it wasn't enough to pay for all the lessons I took. Every day, from 10 am to 6 pm I was taking lessons. For example, in addition to lessons in music, voice, ballet, language, drama, and the rest, I was studying Dante in the original Italian, with Antoinetta Stabile. To have all this available to me at that time was invaluable and so exciting. I didn't miss school or the proms. I was so involved with my music I couldn't wait to get to Mr. Herman's studio at 10 in the morning.

This kind of involvement, however, can be detrimental for a singer. I've seen singers become too attached to the wrong teacher. In other words, when they're singing and they know something is wrong, they are afraid to say anything to the teacher and are afraid to leave the teacher because where are they going to go? So for some people the kind of involvement I experienced would not be good. I was fortunate to have a teacher who was right for me."

Immersing herself in her music, one of young Peters' favorite pastimes was to sit in William Herman's record library on the third floor of his 94th Street brownstone and listen to the recordings of famous coloraturas of previous eras. It was during such time that she, almost unconsciously, soaked up many of the fine, but elusive points of florid style, phrasing, and tradition.

Whenever I could, I went to the "library" and listened to Amelita Galli-Curci, Maria Barrientos, Luisa Tetrazzini, Frieda Hempel, and Marcella Sembrich. They were my idols. But, you see, I had all that time when I was young to absorb. When I think that now students in colleges get one lesson a week—a half hour, even an hour—it is so sad. You cannot possibly absorb everything in that short amount of time."

Roberta's vocal training with William Herman was intense and very physical. Not only was she expected to sing Rossini's "Una voce poco fa" from Il barbiere di Siviglia with perfect runs, staccati, messa-di-voci, and high Fs, she was expected to do this while bouncing a medicine ball around the studio. Vocal exercises centered on a number of diverse methods: Garcia's "Art of Singing," Duprez's "L'Art du Chant," Damoreau's "Metodo di Canto," Bordogni's "Vocalizes," and even instrumental studies for flute and clarinet (Klose's "Method for Clarinet").

Despite the expected work on agility, emphasis in Mr. Herman's studio was on legato and it was only when Roberta could sing a simple song perfectly with a fluid legato, or execute a perfect mesa-di-voce on a high A or C that he was satisfied.

Ornaments, cadenzas, and interpolations, the special province of the florid soprano, were chosen for Roberta with care. "When I worked with Herman, we went through many books of ornaments pulling a little from the Ricci, a little from the Liebling, whatever he and I felt suited and rode nicely in my voice."

At least one cadenza was specifically written for her voice. It was for voice and flute for Handel's aria "Sweet Bird" from L'Allegro ed il Pensieroso.

That was Samuel Pratt. He was a wonderful flautist who used to play many of my recitals earlier in my career. We were working on the aria one day and I asked him if he could think of a new cadenza for the end of the aria. I have sung his cadenza ever since—I like it very much."

(Author update: Peters used this cadenza until the end of her performing career and recorded it on her third LP for RCA Victor in 1958.)

Handel—"Sweet Bird" *L'Allegro ed il Pensieroso*—Roberta Peters RCA, 1958

https://www.youtube.com/watch?v=T6XZWZxQ5hc&list=OLAK5uy_lYR4cCBCWcQtQkfw-iSPdqEHdqJux7DHM&index=3

As one might expect, because of the exhibitionistic nature of a coloratura soprano's art, there were occasional disagreements with conductors over ornaments and interpolated high notes, whether they be traditional or not. One such instance was the alternate ending to the coda of Gilda's aria "Caro nome" (Rigoletto) which rises in arpeggiated trills to a sustained high E. During the 1950s and '60s, Peters was known for her singing of this interpolation, invariably floating the high E with violin-like purity and ease. A number of singers used this ending, including Frieda Hempel, Maria Ivagùn, Gianna D'Angelo, Lina Pagliughi, Mercedes Capsir, Lily Pons, Rita Streich, Hilde Gueden, and even Maria Callas. Its tradition reached back at least as far as Ines Maria Ferraris's Gilda on the first complete recording of the opera on 78 r.p.m records in 1916. By the 1960s the "tradition" was waning in popularity (at least at the Metropolitan Opera) and the last singer to use this altitudinous variant was Mady Mesple in her house debut in September of 1973.

Concerning this variant, Peters remembers:

The conductor I sang that particular interpolation with the most was Fausto Cleva at the Metropolitan Opera. In the beginning, he did not want me to do it, but" Ms. Peters said, smiling mischievously, "after he heard me sing it in rehearsal a few times, he agreed. At that time I could sing it easily, and if you can do it that way I don't see any reason why it shouldn't be done."

Verdi—"Caro nome" *Rigoletto*— Roberta Peters RCA 1956 Commercial recording
https://www.youtube.com/watch?v=dCX_1kZ1Vss

Shortly after Ms. Peters' debut in 1950, artistic and vocal priorities shifted in her fach due to the arrival of such singers as Maria Callas and Dame Joan Sutherland. Their vocal weight, combined with superb agility, signaled the beginning of a new era in modern coloratura singing. Although there were inherent advantages to this movement, it slowly pushed the "traditional" coloratura soprano (the voice most noted for its lightness, purity and delicacy) into extinction over some decades.

Did this change in audience expectations affect Roberta Peters; she who personified the traditional coloratura singer?

Oh yes!" she said grinning. "It affected me. After the 1950s, everything had to be big and loud. Because of that I had a tendency to give a bit too much and so I had to be very careful and pull back. Lighter voices have to be very careful of this. You see, when you are on stage and are getting emotional there is a tendency to press too much on the lower part of the voice because you are excited and you want to give more sound. We all have a tendency to do this. But that kind of vocal pressure can inhibit one's ability to easily float a high note or a pianissimo. I had to be very careful not to give too much so I could maintain that upper floating."

It was at this point that Roberta Peters' common sense came into play. Her emphasis on the use of head voice and floated high notes worked for her in two important ways. It eliminated unnecessary vocal pressure, enabling her voice to retain its freshness for an unusually long period of time. In addition, careful repertoire choices were made and the more lyrical or dramatic roles such as Mimi in La bohème and Violetta in La traviata were not undertaken until much later in her career. Instead, she sang roles that suited her voice and temperament best: *Lucia di Lammermoor*, Lakmé, Norina in *Don Pasquale*, Adina in *L'Elisir d'amore*, Adele in *Die Fledermaus*, Oscar in *Un Ballo in Maschera*, Rosina in *Il barbiere di Siviglia* and Gilda in *Rigoletto*.

I have always tried, over the years, to maintain the correct repertoire for my voice. Just recently, for example, I was asked to sing Rosalinda in Strauss's Die Fledermaus and I looked at it, but it is just not for me. One has to be so careful—especially when young. I had always wanted to sing Bellini's Elvira in I puritani. When I first began singing at the Met they were not doing that opera. Later they mounted it for Joan Sutherland. But, by then times and tastes had changed and people wanted a bigger sound in that role."

Peters did, however sing Elvira's main arias in concert, and recorded them in 1954 on her first solo album, Roberta Peters—Youngest Member of a Great Tradition—RCA Victor—LPM-1786.

Manon is another role I love. I worked on it about five or six years ago and I was supposed to sing it, but I became ill and was not able to do it."

The year before this interview, Roberta Peters told the Los Angeles Times "I would love to sing *Tosca*…..and *Salome*. Those are my dream roles. But I won't do them, at least not in this life. They would kill me, vocally."

In addition to operatic performances and numerous recordings, Roberta Peters is renowned for her recital and orchestral concerts as well as radio and television appearances. The latter includes a record sixty-five appearances on the Ed Sullivan TV show, twenty-five on *Voice of Firestone*, various television commercials (especially a famous 1981 commerical for American Express where she caroled "Taxi!," and, in 1975, a dramatic guest appearance on the television show *Medical Center*, in which she portrayed an opera singer who was dying of cancer of the adrenal glands.

When asked about various roles, Ms. Peters replied:

Lakmé? I'm sorry I didn't do more performances of that opera. I love the character and studied it in great detail. Actually, the thing I like least about Lakmé is the bell song. Oh, I like the aria and sang it for many years, but there is so much more to Lakmé and I like the rest of the music so much better. There are many wonderful duets and ensembles, and her arias in the last act are so lyrical and beautiful."

Zerbinetta in Ariadne auf Naxos was such a fun role. I didn't sing too many performances of that opera either, although I did sing the aria often in concert. The recording I made of the complete opera was unusual because I recorded the role before I had ever sung it on stage. Many years ago, shortly after I was hired by the Met, I sang the original, 1912 version of the aria which goes up to the high F-sharp, with Dimitri Mitropolous, who accompanied me. Mr Herman had given me the music years before."

When asked if she had ever sung higher than F-sharp in public, Ms Peters grinned and said: "Yes, as a matter of fact I have. When I was in Salzburg, in 1964, I sang the Mozart concert aria 'Popoli di Tessaglia' with its two Gs above high C."

Author update: A tape exists of this performance, showing Peters giving a remarkable performance of the difficult, dramatic 12-minute showpiece.)

Mozart—"Io non chiedo" (Concert Aria)—missing opening recitative— Roberta Peters Salzburg 1964

https://www.youtube.com/watch?v=I08iDo9kMAk

But," she added, "as a general rule I usually never sang above high F."

Lucia? I have many fond memories of working on Lucia. It was the first opera score my teacher gave to me when I was fourteen. I still have that score with his inscription ('To Roberta, my very dear pupil, with all my love—her first opera score.—Maestro.') It was a dream of mine to sing Lucia at the Met. I didn't sing it until 1956."

Author update: Peters sang the role many times over the next few decades. Her final Lucia di Lammermoor was in Utah in October of 1988.

"Gilda in *Rigoletto* was a favorite role of mine. I always find something new in that role. When I was young I thought of Gilda as a coloratura role, but now I find it very lyrical. I really do think a lighter voice is better suited to the music. Gilda needs a youthful sound. Even in act three, not much time has actually passed in her life, and it shouldn't be too heavy or dramatic."

Author update: In December of 2016, joining with Warner Records, the Metropolitan Opera released a box set of live broadcast performances from the inaugural season at the Lincoln Center Met. A 1967 *Rigoletto* with Nicolai Gedda and Cornell MacNeil conducted by Lamberto Gardelli is one of the featured recordings.

During the period I was interviewing Ms. Peters in 1985, she was preparing for recitals she would give with Larry Skrobacs as well as for a new role for the Metropolitan Opera—the Princess in Ravel's L'Enfant et les Sortileges.

Unfortunately, this did not happen. Ms. Peters' final appearance at the Metropolitan Opera House was on April 12, 1985, as Gilda in *Rigoletto* (which included the debut of baritone, Aldo Protti) with tenor Dano Raffanti; Nello Santi conducting. She performed a final Gilda a few days later on tour in Boston (April 25, 1985), also with Protti, Raffanti, and Santi.

Speaking of Roberta Peters on his website, Edmund St. Austell comments:

> … (Peters) knew her repertoire, and she mastered it. More importantly, she stayed within it. Like her friend Jan Peerce, she was extremely sensible and knew how to take care of her gift so that it would last and last.
>
> (http://greatoperasingers.blogspot.com/2011/02/roberta-peters-american-nightingale.html)

When I asked her about the many recitals that she gave annually, she said: "It's strange, some years I have more recital than orchestral dates and some years it's the opposite. This year (1985), its orchestra. All in all I have about forty dates from September to May."

For a brief time in 1952, she was married to baritone Robert Merrill, but they divorced amicably, and in 1955 she married Bertram Fields (Author update: who died in 2010). She has two sons, Paul and Bruce. "I wanted a fuller life than an automation. I did not want to be married to my music and I am very happy with my life." (Although Mr. Fields had always been supportive of his wife's career in music, he maintained his own career as a real estate investor, allowing the couple to, perhaps, strike a balance.)

When asked about the possibility of becoming a teacher she laughingly commented:

I knew that was coming! At the moment I really have no plans regarding teaching. To be honest, I don't like master classes because you really cannot get into a person's vocal life in one session. I believe in a one-to-one teaching relationship, and in going slowly. If I was to find someone whom I felt showed great promise, then I think I might take that person in hand and work with her. I say "her" because I know that repertoire best and have so much music and so much of my own experience to share. I might be a very bad teacher, but all I can offer a person is the benefit of my own experience."

Roberta Peters never found that student. And, as it turns out, her first album for RCA Victor was prophetic. Not only was she the "youngest member of a great tradition," she was the last. The last in a long line of florid singers who offered in their singing not only pyrotechnical brilliance. but beauty and elegance as well.

I saw and spoke with Roberta Peters one last time when she sang for Larry Skrobacs' memorial service at Christ's Chapel in the famous Riverside Church in Manhattan. When I contacted her about his untimely death on March 10, 1987, I asked if she would want to sing at his memorial. There was no hesitation in her response.

And so on May 22, 1987, she sang Rachmaninov's "Here Beauty Dwells" in honor of her colleague and friend. It was a piece they had performed together for many years. Under the direction of conductor Leo Warbington, Gale and I and other friends and colleagues sang "How Lovely Is Thy Dwelling Place" from the Brahms Requiem.

In 1992 and 2006, The New York Library for the Performing Arts bought the "Roberta Peters Collection" (172 boxes of memorabilia)

Touring was always an important part of her work. A highlight was a 1979 tour to the People's Republic of China. Tours of Japan, Korea, Hong Kong, and Taiwan followed in 1987, 1988, and 1990.

She served on a number of foundations. For a number of years she was chairwoman of the National Cystic Fibrosis Foundation. She also served on the boards of the Metropolitan Opera Guild and the Carnegie Hall Corporation. She was an artistic advisor on the boards of the Kravis Center for the Performing Arts and the Jupiter Theatre in Florida.

The soprano received a number of awards: she was the first American-born artist to receive the coveted Bolshoi Medal. In 1992 she received Bnai Brith's Dor L'Dor Award, the organization's highest honor, and in 1997, the National Foundation of Jewish Culture awarded her its Jewish Cultural Achievement Award in Performing Arts for "her talent, her charm, and her commitment to the arts as well as to the Jewish people."

In 1991 she was appointed by President Bush to a five-year term on the National Council on the Arts. President Clinton awarded Peters the 1998 National Medal of Arts, and two years later, New York City Mayor Giuliani awarded her the Handel Medallion, a tribute to individuals who have enriched the city's cultural life.

She has been a prominent spokesperson for many Jewish causes, including the Hebrew University, where she established the Roberta Peters Scholarship Fund, and Israel Bonds, and has served on the board of the Anti-Defamation League. Peters has appeared often in Israel, performing to benefit her endowed scholarship, and for soldiers in 1967, when she and her colleague Richard Tucker were caught in Israel during the Six-Day War.

Roberta Peters died of Parkinson's Disease on January 18, 2017, in Rye, New York.

On October 15, 2017, I got the following email from Ron Pollard, who had been a fan and friend of Roberta's for years:

The Met Opera Guild presented a lovely tribute to Roberta today at the Bruno Walter auditorium. Her sons Bruce & Paul hosted the afternoon. There were several artists from the Met: Rosalind Elias/Elinor Ross (VERY touching)/George Shirley/Sherrill Milnes, Arroyo/Stratas/Plishka/Casei were also there. They had quite a few clips from the Sullivan Show which have never been seen since they were first aired and also from the Bell Telephone Hour. Lots of pictures of her family and early life. The biggest surprise was the appearance of James Levine and all the nice things he had to say about her. It was a lovely afternoon and very well attended." (Private email, October 15, 2017)

As Clyde T. McCants noted in his book: American Opera Singers and Their Recordings (McFarland & Company Inc, 2004)

For many…years, opera house managers, critics, and perhaps even audiences tended to take Roberta Peters for granted. She was always there. She was always dependable, and she always sounded good."

Recommended Albums from Roberta Peters' Commercial Discography:

Like many operatic albums and recitals, over the decades these recordings have gone in and out of print.

Complete Operas (alphabetical by composer)
Donizetti—Lucia di Lammermoor—RCA Victor 1957
Gluck—Orfeo ed Euridice—RCA Victor 1957
Mozart—Cosi fan tutte—Columbia 1952
Mozart—*Le nozze di Figaro*—RCA Victor 1958
Mozart—Die Zauberflöte—Deutsche Grammophon 1964
Rossini—Il barbiere di Siviglia—RCA Victor 1958
Strauss—Ariadne auf Naxos—RCA Victor/Decca 1961
Verdi—*Rigoletto*—RCA Victor 1956

Aria Albums for RCA Victor:
Youngest Member of a Great Tradition—1954
(*Lucia di Lammermoor, I puritani, La sonnambula, Linda di Chamonix*)
Famous Operatic Arias—1956
(*Il barbiere di Siviglia, Lucia di Lammermoor, Rigoletto, Fra Diavolo, Lakmé, Don Pasquale*)
Roberta Peters in Recital—1958
(*Bach, Handel, Scarlatti, Schumann, Strauss, Debussy, Ravel*)

Considering her excellence as a musician I have always found it unfortunate that her uppermost register was not flattered by the recording process. This was an acoustical phenomenon that plagued a number of high sopranos, depending on the structure of their larynx. Peters had a range just under three octaves, encompassing low A to the G above high C. It was a well-focused instrument with a lovely, rich lower register and a head-voice that, in the opera house, floated to the back of the hall, rich in overtones.

A heady voice, that because of its natural placement, when recorded, emerged as back-produced, narrow, and wiry. (This was a problem that plagued other fine sopranos such as Maria Galvany, Elvira De Hidalgo, Renata Scotto, and Ruth Welting. I heard Peters many times at the Metropolitan Opera and at both Carnegie Hall and Alice Tully Hall and never found her voice to be imbalanced; nor did it sound tiny. Of medium size, it floated beautifully in the house. The up-close recording process often underlined an odd, back-produced gargle that could sound distinctly odd when she was in the midst of coloratura flights.

It is interesting that after listening to the fabled divas of the past, Peters found that, vocally, she identified most with Amelita Galli-Curci. It was Galli-Curci who became her model in terms of smooth coloratura and pure vocalization. Undoubtedly, it was that concept that led to her remarkable longevity on the performing stage. She also adopted a number of Galli-Curci's ornaments and cadenzas.

Different from many singers, the earlier portion of Roberta Peters's career (1950–1958) was well documented by commercial recordings. For her mature years however, one must turn to pirated (i.e., live) recordings, of which there are many.

Recital Album—Youngest Member of a Great Tradition—1954

Preceding this aria album, Peters recorded a charming Despina on Columbia Record's 1952 English-language recording of Mozart's *Cosi fan tutte* conducted by Fritz Stiedry, sung with Eleanor Steber, Richard Tucker, and Rosalind Elias. The album was recorded in good mono sound in June, 1952 at the Columbia 30th Street Studio in New York City. (The recording is still in print on CD.)

The all-American cast accurately represented the famous 1952 revival of the opera at the Metropolitan Opera. Despite the stilted (and dated) Ruth and Thomas Martin English translation, and some regrettable cuts in the score, this recording has proven to be very popular over the decades. Its merits center on the conducting of Stiedry and the powerhouse Fiordiligi of Eleanor Steber. Blanche Thebom acquits herself well and although Richard Tucker might not necessarily be one's first choice for a Mozart stylist, he is lyrical and, typical of his overall art, musically sensitive to the requisite style. Peters's Despina was found to be:

> a sympathetic portrayal, earthy rather than prim in style, light but not irritating in voice as so many Despinas tend to be. (Graham Sheffield, *Opera on Record*, pg 89, Hutchinson & Co 1979.)

Shortly after this, Peters signed with RCA Victor. Only a few years into her career, the soprano was already considered by the industry to be a rare professional and a remarkable technician. In order to properly introduce and highlight her talent, RCA settled on an adventurous concept, an homage album. It was one of the first of other "homage" albums that appeared during the ensuing decades. These were albums meant to show a new artist as compared to previous artists who were famous for the same repertoire.

Peters and her conductor, Renato Cellini, took this idea even further by including original 78 r.p.m. recordings of her most illustrious predecessors: Luisa Tetrazzini, Amelita Galli-Curci, and Lily Pons. It was a daring concept for 1954 and one that could have completely backfired had it been anyone else but Roberta Peters. Her remarkably advanced musicianship, technical assurance, and rock-solid preparation made for one of the most interesting homage albums produced during the era of LP recordings.

Ably conducted by Renato Cellini, Peters sang arias from I puritani, *La Sonnambula*, Linda di Chamonix, and Lucia di Lammermoor. The other three singers were highlighted in additional florid arias: Luisa Tetrazzini in Mignon, Amelita Galli-Curci in Il barbiere di Siviglia, and Lily Pons in Lakmé. At the time of the album's release, criticism appeared concerning the wisdom of including highly famous past artists on the same record promoting the young Peters (she was only twenty-four). It was thought to possibly be an unfair comparison given the inexperience of the singer. Although it was a dangerous stance for RCA and Peters to take, she proved that she could surmount any technical challenge. Listening to the album today, one recognizes a first-rate talent. Her singing is practically flawless with perfectly executed messa di voci, easily and immediately taken high notes (up to high F), brilliant staccati and roulades, and throughout the entire range, an effortless, remarkably elegant legato lyricism.

I was most impressed with the arias from operas that she never performed on stage such as I puritani. This includes a sprightly polonaise sung with much verve, excitement, and excellent ornamentation. Peters also sings the celebrated mad scene. It highlights her warm, sweet and solid legato line as well as her unique, perfectly-graded messa di voci, not to mention wonderfully dense ornamentation in the cabaletta, (complete with numerous high D-flats, E-flats, and even a top F!). Of the various versions recorded by "lighter" florid singers, Peters's recording is, hands down, the finest. The music suits her temperament and abilities, and she offers one of the great renditions. Unlike many other singers, during her legato singing she allows the music to speak for itself, not indulging in any overt personality or vocal traits that might obscure the music's intent. It is this simplicity of execution that is so admirable and memorable.

Bellini—"Vien diletto from I puritani" and "Ah non giunge" *La sonnambula*— Roberta Peters RCA 1954

https://www.youtube.com/watch?v=TVFsrqETjCk

Linda di Chamonix was another role she never sang on stage. This is a fine rendition of Linda's act I aria giving a thoughtful, gracefully sung recitative with a strong legato line. Through the use of agogic accents, subtle ritardandi, and clear diction, Peters makes this long recitative a thing of great beauty and interest. The main aria is sung with dexterity and smooth fluidity, including a final cadenza full of arpeggios and scales that run up to high F that was later adopted by Ruth Welting. The tempo is sprightly, yet the diction is always clear and clean. At no time does Peters cross the line to try to make the aria more than it is—a joyous exhibition piece.

Donizetti—"O luce di quest anima" *Linda di Chamonix*— Roberta Peters RCA 1954

https://www.youtube.com/watch?v=BjxCx-l06wc

After the mad scene from I puritani, it is the final scene from *La Sonnambula* that is the best offering on this album. Thankfully, it was decided to record a large chunk of the final scene, almost ten minutes. It is a lovely display of Peters's sweetly floated legato line as well as her remarkable dexterity within complicated fioriture. To her credit, she adopted Luisa Tetrazzini's octave jump to a pianissimo high C during "Potria novel vigore," a beautiful effect. The ending of "Ah non credea" is beautifully shaped. Peters suitably ornaments the second verse of "Ah non giunge!" with ornaments that had been traditional for decades.

Modern listeners might be surprised at the lack of a roulade to high E-flat that is now usually inserted between the two verses of the cabaletta. That variant seems to have originated a year after, in 1955, when Maria Callas first undertook the role of Amina with Leonard Bernstein at La Scala. (The cadenza was probably written by Bernstein himself.) Since that Milan production, virtually every soprano who has sung Amina has incorporated Callas's flourish to high E-flat at that spot in the score.

One thing that sets Peters' recording of this aria apart from others is the refined manner in which she sings her ornamentation. It is definitely brilliant singing, but there is an underlying elegance in her attack and phrasing. As one might expect from a singer of such acuto accomplishments, Peters ends the scene with a brilliant, sustained penultimate high F.

Rather than distracting, the inclusion of Tetrazzini, Galli-Curci, and Pons is instructive; a lesson in the art of fine coloratura singing that underlines the fact that Peters belongs among their group. Peters's selections from this album were released on CD in 2007 by Flare. The CD also includes a few selections from the 1953 film Tonight We Sing: an outrageous "Jewel Song" from Faust with Peters finishing on a long, perfect high E, "Sempre libera" from La traviata, and the love duet from act I of *Madama Butterfly* with Jan Peerce.

In January of 1955, Peters made a small contribution to an RCA Victor highlights album of *Un Ballo in Maschera* (now available on Preiser CD). The recording was intended to commemorate the Met's revival of the opera and to honor the first black American singer to be hired by the house, Marian Anderson. Peters's contribution is a sprightly "Saper vorreste." Zinka Milanov, Jan Peerce, and Leonard Warren also starred on this recording conducted by Dimitri Mitropoulos. The selection was recorded at the Manhattan Center.

Verdi—Rigoletto—1956

1956 found Peters recording her beloved Gilda with tenor Jussi Bjorling and baritone Robert Merrill in an RCA Victor recording conducted by Jonel Perlea. Although it has the typical cuts favored at the time, it is still considered a classic in many operatic circles. Merrill is in spectacular voice as Rigoletto and his characterization, although rather broad, is easy to comprehend and enjoy.

Bjoerling is such an elegant-voiced Duke that one understands Gilda's impetuous fascination with him. His phrasing is magisterial and of great beauty. In addition, the combination of his timbre with that of Peters is a real delight. They complement each other's musicianship.

Peters is lovely and lyrical, and proves that she has an unusually adept grasp of the character of Gilda. I found it interesting that, for the most part, reviews of this set (and of Peters in particular) varied depending on the decade in which they were written. Generally, her performance is found to have merit, although no reviewer commented on her excellent legato singing, her solid lower register, or the sweet float of her upper register. Because Maria Callas had recorded *Rigoletto* the year before (with Tito Gobbi) all sets that came after were subject to comparison to hers. Peters is one of the few sopranos who could easily float the high E alternate-ending of "Caro nome" softly and with elan. Because of the fullness of her lower register, she is able to portray Gilda's rapid maturity in the last two acts. A lovely recording, it is only enhanced by Perlea's conducting.

(An excellent live version from the Met in 1964, was released by Sony around 2001 with Robert Merrill and Richard Tucker. There is also the famous 1967 broadcast with Peters, Nicolai Gedda and Cornell MacNeil, conducted by Lamberto Gardelli which was released in 2016 in the Inaugural Season box set.)

Recital Album—Famous Operatic Arias (only on LP)—1956

1956 also saw the release of her second solo album, arias from *Il barbiere di Siviglia, Lucia di Lammermoor, Rigoletto, Fra Diavolo, Lakmé,* and *Don Pasquale.* At the age of twenty-six, Peters was already six years into her career as a first-string artist at the Metropolitan Opera. Despite its excellence, this album has yet to be released on CD. It is an outstanding demonstration of Peters's gifts and technical resources while in her prime.

The opening aria on the disk is "Una voce poco fa" from Il barbiere di Siviglia. One of her most often performed roles, this is an aria that the soprano knew inside out. Her ornamentation was quite difficult and, different from many other singers, it included a number of high Fs sung with uncommon ease. Peters demonstrates a poised, easy florid technique and is obviously enjoying herself in this aria. She is a lively, coy Rosina, showing an unusual fullness in the lower register and superb musicianship.

Rossini—"Una voce poco fa" *Il barbiere di Siviglia*— Roberta Peters RCA 1956
https://www.youtube.com/watch?v=Ck7PK4uhqKU

Especially lovely is the mad scene from Lucia di Lammermoor, a version recorded the year before the 1957 complete set with Jan Peerce that Erich Leinsdorf conducted. Both versions include the huge cut in the middle of the scene that was common at the time. Of the two commercial versions, this 1956 version, made when the soprano was but twenty-six, is generally considered to be the better of the two. Interestingly, it is almost a minute longer due to Bellezza's spacious conducting (16:39 as against Leinsdorf's 15:55.) The most obvious thing about this recording is Peters's complete mastery of her voice and technique, most notably the superb legato she offers throughout the scene. Everything is linked with expressivity and phrased with the sensitivity of a master of the art. Although some might argue that the scene lacks the extreme drama of Callas's voice and manner, there is an appealing sweetness and innocence to Peters's version that holds up well to repeated hearings. There are some exquisite messa di voci during the scene and Peters includes an unusual ornament, rising in a slow staccato arpeggio to a sustained top D at "Qui ricovriamo, Edgardo, a piè dell'ara." She used this ornament in all performances of the mad scene right up to her last Lucia di Lammermoor in Utah in October of 1988.

The virtuostic duet with flute, almost always the centerpiece of the aria, is presented within an unusually quiet, slow mood. Rather than concentrating on the bravura aspect of the duet, Peters takes her time and opts for a dreamy atmosphere; singing the cadenzas as though Lucia were already on a different plane of existence. Peters sings the roulades with ease and prepares her trills with an elegance rarely heard nowadays. Both high E-flats are intense and are easily sustained (the last through the entire postlude!).

Another impressive aria is the rarely-recorded "Or son sola" from Auber's Fra Diavolo, a true bravura aria.

This aria is actually Marie's act II aria borrowed by Auber from his own opera, "Le Serment" and inserted into Fra Diavolo for Zerlina somewhere around 1858. About the original aria in Le Serment, Robert Letellier wrote:

> The most famous piece in the opera is Marie's *grand air à vocalises* for the soprano ('Dès enfance les mêmes chaînes') in which all the most arduous difficulties of the art of singing are displayed. It was a triumph for Madame Damoreau, and served for a long time as a test piece, *le morceau de concours,* dreaded by young aspirant virtuosi. It was later introduced into the beginning of act two of the Italian version of *Fra Diavolo* as a more substantial and challenging alternative to Zerline's aria as she prepares the room for Lord and Lady Cockburn. (*Daniel-François-Esprit Auber: Le Serment*, edited and introduced by Robert Ignatius Letellier, 2011 Cambridge Scholars Publishing 12 Back Chapman Street, Newcastle upon Tyne, NE6 2XX, UK http://www.cambridgescholars.com/download/sample/58478)

Despite the fact that this is a wonderful and inventive aria, it has never been part of the standard repertoire for the coloratura soprano. It is a difficult, complex aria and it rarely appears on recordings or on concert programs.

> The few who have recorded their versions or sung the aria in concert (or in a staged production) would include Maria Barrientos, Lina Pagliughi, Roberta Peters, Mary Costa, Dame Joan Sutherland, Isobel Buchanan, Angela Denning, Luciana Serra, and Sumi Jo. Generally, however, it is neglected, no doubt due to its excessive technical demands, a number of the passages are extremely difficult to navigate accurately. (N. Limansky, *Early 20th Century Singers, Their Voices and Recordings*, YBK Publishers 2016)

Peters had known this unusual aria for years, having used it for her "aria" in the lesson scene of Il barbiere di Siviglia. A 1952 broadcast performance from the New Orleans Opera has surfaced on which Peters gives a remarkably fleet rendition. The 1956 recording is even better. There is an attractive relaxation to the tempo of the cantabile section that allows Peters to provide some stunning legato singing in the upper register. A misjudgment in pitch during the unaccompanied cadenza between the cantabile and the allegro sections results in the singer finishing a half-step flat. Even so, this remains one of the best performances of this aria ever recorded; the interpolated octave-jumps to high D and E and the messa di voce on high A, absolutely perfect. The roulades and coloratura in the allegro section are smooth and her ornaments, except for a triplet or two, are cleanly sung. Despite the aria's extensive difficulty there is much charm and humor in Peters's recording and the flourish at the end with its long, penultimate high E is brilliantly done.

Auber—"Or son sola" Fra Diavolo— Roberta Peters RCA 1956
https://www.youtube.com/watch?v=3l-CsW1tUuQ

Peters sang the bell song from Lakmé for almost twenty years and it was one of her most popular concert items. (She also sang it in a stage production in Pittsburgh in 1968.) Overall, her account is excellent. The vocalise is beautifully phrased. Oddly, Peters begins the roulades over the high B a half-tone flat so that the rest of the vocalise is a half-step low. The central aria (now back in key) is beautifully phrased and artistically tapered. The "legend" finds Peters coloring her voice with a darker, meaty timbre that excellently depicts the fear and pride of the Pariah maiden. She copes well with the breath-taking speed chosen for the bell refrains (even then such a rapid tempo was an anachronistic touch) and the arpeggiated staccato coda has an elegant descent from a sustained D-sharp. The final E is a focused tone that sits on the high side and is held triumphantly to the end.

Delibes—Bell Song *Lakmé*— Roberta Peters RCA 1956
https://www.youtube.com/watch?v=apVTSov8eII

Ironically, I found the famous aria from Don Pasquale to be the weakest selection on the record. Peters sings it with great care and grace but overall (especially when compared to older recordings of the aria) shows little imagination. I felt that she could have done so much more with the music than she does.

Donizetti—*Lucia di Lammermoor* (Complete Recording)—1957

Recorded in Rome, this *Lucia di Lammermoor* with Jan Peerce finds Peters building on the basic interpretive concepts that she put forth in the mad scene on the 1956 aria album. Unfortunately, conductor Erich Leindsdorf is not a bel canto specialist and, perhaps because of this, the set has always sat on the sidelines. Another strike against this version was the timing of its release which came shortly after Maria Callas's stunning first version on Angel.

Because Peters first began studying the role when she was fourteen, when William Herman gave her a score of the opera, her knowledge of Donizetti's music was complete. One nice side occurrence is that she was able to record the role with her friend and mentor, Jan Peerce. Peters's Lucia is a lovely, sweetly gentle, lyrical character who is driven to madness by her brother's insensitive cruelty. Peters's finest moments are underlined through her lyric pathos rather than in any overt dramatic vocal gestures.

Although her singing of Lucia di Lammermoor can be taken on its own as a valid, historic interpretation of the opera during that era of singing, at the time of its release it was unfavorably compared to the famous 1953 Angel recording of Maria Callas that had been released four years earlier. The Callas version signaled a new introspection of the role of Lucia and because of the tragic stature of Callas's interpretation, any recording that came after was compared to hers.

> The Lucy that Miss Peters re-creates is more the handiwork of Nellie Melba, Marcella Sembrich, Amelita Galli-Curci, and, above all, Lily Pons than of Gaetano Donizetti….(Peters) sings with an efficiency that leaves one, finally, indifferent. Her high Ds and E flats come with clocklike regularity, are held the proper number of seconds, then are dropped….to play Peters and Angel's Callas one after the other is almost to have the impression that one is hearing two different operas. The one Callas sings, though not quite Donizetti's, is infinitely the finer… (D. J. *High Fidelity*, 1957)

In Opera on Record (Volume I) edited by Alan Blyth, Charles Osborne noted:

> I remember hearing this Lucia for the first time in 1959, a few months after experiencing Joan Sutherland's first assumption of the role at Covent Garden. I thought (and still think) Sutherland's dramatic coloratura the right kind of voice for Lucia. I probably dismissed Roberta Peters too quickly as being in the Lily Pons tradition. Listening to her again now, I find her highly attractive when not being rushed along by her conductor. (Hutchinson and Co., 1979, p. 186)

Another thing that did not help the Peters's version was the release in 1961 of Joan Sutherland's first recording.

There is much to enjoy in the Peters/Peerce recording. There are many passages of interest, especially the act I love duet. Most fascinating is an ornamental cadenza (suggested or written by Leinsdorf?) during the "Il pallor funesto orrendo" entrance of Lucia in act II. At the end of the sequence, Peters rides a roulade up to a sustained high E. It is an unusual ornament and not used by anyone else. It nicely suggests Lucia's desperate emotional situation (when confronting her brother) at that moment in the opera. The highlight of Peters's performance is, of course, the mad scene, which she sings with consummate ease and elegance. The legato is pure and smoothly linked, high notes are approached with grace and eloquence, and not once does the listener fear that something will go amiss. Although this set has been disparaged as being in the Lily Pons "mold," this is not really accurate since Peters had a voice of more body and firm strength in the lower registers than did Lily Pons, and her approach to the role was much more in the modern vein. Actually, Peters is an excellent bridge between the two "schools" of artistic interpretation of this role.

Donizetti—"Regnava nel silenzio" *Lucia di Lammermoor* Roberta Peters RCA 1957
https://www.youtube.com/watch?v=riMwz-YromM&list=RDriMwz-YromM&start_radio=1
Donizetti—Mad Scene *Lucia di Lammermoor*— Roberta Peters RCA 1957
https://www.youtube.com/watch?v=C_t1YxtQukU

Also created in 1957 was a Rome-made recording of Gluck's Orfeo ed Euridice with Rise Stevens, Lisa Della Casa, and Peters as Amor. Unfortunately, Stevens should have recorded the role earlier in her career and Della Casa seems miscast. Peters does lovely work in the role of Amor, but considering her specific talents, it seems a waste of her energies. The set never sold well for various reasons and is now long out of print. It was a curiosity of the CD catalogue.

Gluck—*Orfeo ed Euridice*—RCA 1957
https://www.youtube.com/watch?v=QB0aGpSB0tY

1958 found Peters taking part in two recordings of operas highly identified with the soprano: *Le nozze di Figaro* and Il barbiere di Siviglia.

Mozart: *Le nozze di Figaro*

This was actually recorded for RCA by Decca (as was the 1961 *Ariadne auf Naxos*). And, like the *Ariadne*, the rights eventually reverted back to Decca after a decided-upon period of time. Even after the ensuing decades and many other recordings, this version still is one to be treasured. Recorded in Vienna with Erich Leinsdorf, in addition to Peters as Susanna, the cast includes many Metropolitan Opera stalwarts: Lisa Della Casa, George London, Rosalind Elias, and Giorgio Tozzi. Although it was released on CD, the recording is now very hard to find. Hopefully it will return to the catalogue soon. Peters sings a wonderful Susannah (one of her best interpretations).

Adrian Jack of BBC Music Magazine wrote:

> Though this 1958 recording is a studio production, the characters sometimes seem so mobile it makes you dizzy and Figaro, in particular, gets around enough for several people. The Vienna Philharmonic makes a lovely sound, but again its contribution is tinkered with. If you want this set, it will be for the excellently sung Susanna of Peters and Figaro of Tozzi, hardly bettered. Nor was the Countess ever more appealing than when incarnated by the matchless della Casa.

Rossini: *Il barbiere di Siviglia*

If one prefers a soprano Rosina, this RCA Victor set is recommended. This 1958 recording duplicates the leads who sang the March 6, 1954 broadcast of the opera at the Metropolitan. Peters sang no fewer than fifty-two Rosinas with the Metropolitan Opera, and by the time of this recording she had already sung in a number of productions. Her singing is fresh, cultured, and full of wonderful variants. Interestingly, she decides not to take a final high F at the end of "Una voce poco fa" although that was her practice until that time.

Unfortunately, the harpsichord-accompanied cadenza used in the act II "Contro il cor" (composed by Leinsdorf) is wayward in the extreme with an un-stylistic use of chromaticism. Although it brings back the major theme of the aria and shows Peters's ability to float a sweet high E-natural, the construction of the cadenza is too modern for Rossini. The final high D is strong and excellent but the fireworks before it are just odd. A plus for the set is the elegant singing of Cesare Valettti, who sings the final rondo for Almaviva for the first time on a recording. The other main character, Figaro, is beautifully and masterfully sung by Robert Merrill. At times the humor of the opera is overdone, but it still remains a potent listening experience many times over. Antony Bye of classical-music.com (the BBC website) summed it up well:

> The first on record to contain almost all of Rossini's score, this Met-based Barber from 1958 is of more than historic interest, though on its initial release it faced stiff competition from the classic but heavily abridged Callas/Alva/Gobbi account of the year before. It still holds its own well despite recent appearances of more musicologically sound alternatives which are often strong on rectitude but short on joie de vivre. Purists will no doubt baulk at Roberta Peters's sopranino Rosina, but her perky delivery and dazzling virtuosity should silence all but the hardest of hearts; and the lower voices—Merrill's robust Figaro, Tozzi's solid Basilio and Corena's witty Bartolo—make up a close-knit, stylish team, ably supported by Leinsdorf's alert if not always sparkling direction. The real star of the show, however, is Cesare Valletti, as mellifluous and aristocratic an Almaviva as one could hope for, whose effortless vocal fioriture seem a natural extension of his personality and are well captured on this no-nonsense recording.

In 1959 the soprano recorded an unusual album of recital pieces for RCA Victor. Typical of this singer, it included some truly obscure works.

The reasons for such an album are not surprising when one considers that by 1959 the soprano had given over 200 concerts in the United States alone. Recital and concert work had always played a large part in her career. She continued to give recitals long after she had left the operatic stage in 1988, and they proved to be some of the most satisfying evenings one could experience.

This LP highlights her versatility with arias by Bach (e.g., *Cantata 21* and *St. John Passion*), the rarely heard sparkling Scarlatti cantata: "Io vi miro ancor vestite," was recorded only once before by Amelita Galli-Curci. (In this aria there is a remarkable passage where Peters travels from a sustained high E to a low C-sharp.)

Handel's "Sweet Bird" from L'Allegro ed Il Penseroso was always a popular concert and recital piece for Peters. She programmed it for over thirty years. On this LP it is remarkably poised and presented (with its preceding recitative) with tightly knit trills and gossamer high notes all framed in a charming delivery. (Since this was recorded before the early music scholarship of the 1980s, it is sung in the "corrupted" Mathilde Marchesi edition.) There are also songs by Robert Schuman, Richard Strauss (including the difficult "Amor"), Claude Debussy, and a brilliant performance of the aria of the Fire from Maurice Ravel's L'Enfant et les Sortileges. This last is probably the first time this unusual piece had ever been programmed on a recording as part of a recital. Peters was accompanied by George Trovillo on piano and Harold Bennet on flute. Taken as a whole it is a very satisfying recital of interesting and contrasting music.

This album was never pressed onto silver (commercial) CD, but it is available on YouTube.

Although an excellent album with much diversity in its content, it has never been quite as popular as other of her aria albums. Peters's singing on the album is superb and whether she is in the midst of Handelian pyrotechnics or the pathos of a Schumann lied, everything is performed and presented artistically. The liner notes for the album were written by no less a prestigious authority than Francis Robinson, the Assistant Manager of the Metropolitan Opera.

Roberta Peters in Recital—RCA 1958 (playlist on the right side of the page)
https://www.youtube.com/watch?v=4kfu_iXvYvo&list=OLAK5uy_lYR4cCBCWcQtQkfw-iSPdqEHdqJux7DHM
Strauss: *Ariadne auf Naxos* (RCA by Decca)—1961

This recording was originally released as a deluxe Dario Soria LP Set on RCA Victor. (It was actually recorded by Decca.) It came in a beautifully crafted box set with a huge, all-color booklet.

Although she had yet to sing the role on stage, the young Roberta Peters was chosen to sing Zerbinetta for this second studio recording (the first in stereo) of the opera. By this time she was a seasoned artist of the Metropolitan Opera. Even though this set was recorded before she sang Zerbinetta on stage, Peters offers the listener a classic performance, carefully thought out, perfectly paced, and polished with more than an appropriate hint of the soubrette. Her phrasing of the difficult pyrotechnics up to the high E in her main aria is exemplary. It is a bravura performance, rather than one of unusual psychological insight (as Gruberova might deliver), but just as valid since her handling of the aria goes back to the tradition of Maria Ivogün.

Not everyone was as taken with this recording as I was. When discussing the various recordings of Ariadne auf Naxos, Gramophone noted:

> The main interest in Erich Leinsdorf's muddily recorded 1958 studio account with the VPO (currently unavailable) resides in the opportunity it affords to hear Jurinac's Composer again—a little less fresh-sounding and urgent but still richly committed. There's also Leonie Rysanek's generously heartfelt but hardly immaculate Ariadne, as well as Roberta Peters's pinpoint but one-dimensionally soubrettish Zerbinetta. (Gramophone, May 2014)

Peters's Zerbinetta is a fine, spirited, and finished soubrette character study that stands up well against all the other fine Zerbinettas of modern times: Kathleen Battle, Edita Gruberova, Natalie Dessay, and others. When the set was originally released, the 1954 Karajan album was its only competition and so the choice came down to whether one wanted the "cool," sophisticated, and Germanic voices of Elisabeth Schwarzkopf, Rudolf Schock, Imgard Seefried, and Rita Streich on a monophonic recording, or the more intense, flaming singing of Leonie Rysanek, Jan Peerce, Sena Jurinac, and Roberta Peters on a stereo recording. Time has shown that for this opera, the listeners' preference has settled on the Karajan set. With the release of later recordings over the decades, the Leinsdorf has been completely eclipsed. This is unfortunate since Leinsdorf's ensemble was excellent and representative of the finest artists of that time. Both sets (and their casts) have much to offer and belong in both personal and public libraries. Interestingly, Rysanek and Peters were both featured in the first Metropolitan Opera broadcast of the opera on February 2, 1963, with Jess Thomas as Bacchus and Kerstin Meyer as the Composer as conducted by Karl Böhm.

After RCA

By 1962 Peters had left RCA Victor and become a free agent in regard to recording. Returning to her first label in 1963, Columbia, she made an album of highlights from Romberg's *The Stu-*

dent Prince with Jan Peerce and Giorgio Tozzi. It is a delight from start to finish and includes a wonderfully ornate and high-flying rendition of Kathy's famous "Come Boys" with an excellent final high F. Also in 1962 she took part in an album of selections from the Rodgers and Hammerstein musical *Carousel* with Claramae Turner, Alfred Drake, Lee Venora, Jon Crain, and Norman Treigle, conducted by Jay Blackton, recorded in stereo (Command RS 843 SD). It has been out of print for many years and is yet to be released on CD.

Peters also made a contribution to a Command LP of the music of Leonard Bernstein, a fine, bravura performance of "Glitter and be Gay" from Candide. At that time the aria was a rarity, having only been recorded by the original Cunegunde, Barbara Cook, in 1956. This, too, has not been released on CD (although it can be heard on YouTube).

In 1964 (and 1967) Peters took part in a few of the now famous Firestone Christmas LP albums produced by Forell and Thomas. There were at least seven volumes and Peters took part on two of them (#3 and #6) alongside other luminaries such as Jack Jones, Franco Corelli, Dorothy Kirsten, Leontyne Price, Nicolai Gedda, Vikki Carr, Julie Andrews, James McCracken, and the Vienna Boys Choir. The albums were wonderful and presented medleys and seasonal favorites recorded with great energy by the artists and in excellent arrangements. The albums successfully combined both popular and classical artists in rousing and thoughtful performances. Always popular, today there are a number of sites where one can even purchase either the original LPs or CD-Rom versions. Even better, the Firestone LP volumes are now available to hear on YouTube. Peters's contributions included "Ave Maria," "Gesu Bambino," "The First Noel," Hark! The Herald Angels Sing," and the Mozart "Alleluia!"

Firestone Presents Your Favorite Christmas Volume 3
https://www.youtube.com/watch?v=o_V_br4i-yo
Firestone Presents Your Favorite Christmas Volume 6
https://www.youtube.com/watch?v=4cMq7Xmhu5g

Those who grew up in the 1960s will remember these albums with great affection. One of the most beautiful (and popular) was the fifth volume which featured Julie Andrews in Andre Previn's arrangements. Her beautiful, heady voice was superbly supported by Previn's elegant and sumptuous string arrangements. The album was originally released in 1966 and issued by Firestone. It was picked up by RCA Victor (Julie Andrews and Andre Previn's home-base label) and re-released in 1967. It was remastered in 1990 and is now available on CD as: A Christmas Treasure (3829-2-R).

Mozart: *Die Zauberflöte* (Deutsche Gramophone)—1964

In 1964, Peters moved to Deutsche Gramophone for her final complete opera recording. It is appropriate that she would leave posterity her interpretation of the Queen of the Night, since she sang the famous second act aria no less than four times during her Metropolitan Opera audition fourteen years earlier in 1950 and by the time that she made this recording she had sung it in a number of international productions.

Conducted by Karl Böhm and sung by Fritz Wunderlich, Evelyn Lear, Franz Crass, and Dietrich Fischer-Dieskau, this is a special recording, still regarded by many as one of the best versions. Mainly this has to do with the casting of sweet-voiced Fritz Wunderlich as Tamino and the warmth of Franz Crass's voice as Sarastro, as well as the treat to hear Fischer-Dieskau's Papageno.

The timing of this album's release was problematic since the famous Klemperer recording was made in the same year. The Klemperer issue features Nicolai Gedda, Gundula Janowitz, Gottlob Frick, Walter Berry, and introduced the icy staccato spikings of a young Lucia Popp as the Queen of the Night. Popp signaled the beginning of a new type of Queen of the Night that would quickly begin to appear as epitomized by the dramatic fury of Edda Moser in the 1972 Sawallisch recording. Since that time lighter-voiced Queens like Erika Köth and Roberta Peters have become a rarity, audiences and home listeners preferring the ferocity of heavier, darker voices.

Over the years the Klemperer recording has overshadowed the Böhm. But Böhm is still available on CD and remains popular. Criticism of the set centers on the maturity of Lear's voice as the innocent Pamina and the lightness of Peters' Queen of the Night. But, as recordings have proven throughout the decades, when it comes to the Queen of the Night at least, the role can be successfully sung by all degrees of vocal heaviness.

Interestingly, Peter Branscombe found Peters' Queen of the Night only so-so:

> Roberta Peters's (sic) Queen is uneven—at her best very good indeed, but rather limp in her slow music. (*Opera on Record*, pg. 111, Hutchinson & Co, 1979)

On the Archivemusic.com website, Patrick Carnegy, of the BBC Music Magazine noted:

Böhm's 1964 Zauberflöte has long been a strong recommendation. This reissue does not dethrone its position, nor is it diminished by later versions concerned with "correct" performing practice... Böhm's speeds do lock into a powerful, if sacerdotal, view of the whole. The principal jewel is Fritz Wunderlich's Tamino, incomparable in its lyric ardour, musicality and tangible characterization. There is a rock-like Sarastro from Franz Crass and fine Sprecher from Hans Hotter. Evelyn Lear is a radiant Pamina, and Roberta Peters has the stratospheric measure of Queen of the Night."

Mozart—*Die Zauberflöte* (excerpts)—DGG 1964 with Fritz Wunderlich, Evelyn Lear, Dietrich Fischer-Dieskau—Karl Böhm

https://www.youtube.com/watch?v=0xzgZU4_xM4

Other recordings

In 1972 Peters recorded a song recital for a BASF LP: seven songs of Strauss and six of Debussy, including his rarely heard, melismatic "Rondel Chinoise." Today, this is only available on a hard-to-locate LP.

Debussy—"Rondel Chinoise" Roberta Peters
https://www.youtube.com/watch?v=MT3oPP30f-o

In 1975 she made an unusual album for AFE (AFSD 6270) called "Raisons and Almonds" which was subtitled: "Roberta Peters Sings Folk" which included songs from her childhood and heritage.

Raisins and Almonds — Roberta Peters 1975
https://www.youtube.com/watch?v=EethBabG_44

In 1998 the Metropolitan Opera released a CD of Roberta Peters as part of their Met Legends series pressed by BMG. The selections included music from Orfeo, I puritani, Lucia di Lammermoor, Faust, and others.

Live Recordings

Fortunately, one can experience Peters' artistry and remarkable consistency throughout the decades of her career on numbers of live recordings. All her major roles are available on pirated CD, a number of them in multiple versions. Below is a partial listing of the pirated recordings available with the labels on which they appear. Most originate from broadcasts.

Alphabetical (by composer and role)
Donizetti
Adina *(L'Elisir d'amore)*
1966—broadcast w/Carlo Bergonzi (Sony)
1968—broadcast w/Alfredo Kraus (G.O.P)
Lucia (*Lucia di Lammermoor*)
1966—broadcast (Gala)
1971—excerpts (in-house) with Franco Corelli (Golden Age of Opera),
Norina (*Don Pasquale*)
1956—broadcast (Gala)
Mozart
Queen of the Night (*Die Zauberflöte*)
1956—broadcast (Walhall)
1967—broadcast (Warner)
Susannah (*Nozze di Figaro*)
1961—broadcast (Sony)
Zerlina (*Don Giovanni*)
1957—broadcast (Adromeda)
Offenbach
Olympia (*Contes d'Hoffmann*)
1955—broadcast (Sony)
Rossini
Rosina (*Il barbiere di Sivigllia*)
1954—broadcast (BonGiovanni)
1957—broadcast (Walhall)
Strauss
Fiakermilli (*Arabella*)
1955—broadcast (Andromeda)
Verdi
Gilda (*Rigoletto*)
1956—broadcast w/Richard Tucker (Andromeda)
1959—broadcast w/Eugenio Fernandi and Leonard Warren (Walhall)
1964—broadcast (Sony)
1966—in-house w/Alfredo Kraus (Living Stage)
1967—broadcast w/ Nicolai Gedda, Cornell MacNeil (Warner)
Oscar (*Un Ballo in Maschera*)
1955—broadcast (Sony)
1966—broadcast w/Leontyne Price and Carlo Bergonzi (Myto)

Most recently, in conjunction with the Metropolitan Opera, Warner CD released a 22-disc box set of performances from the inaugural season (1966–1967) of the Metropolitan Opera at

Lincoln Center. The set includes not only a 1967 *Rigoletto* with Peters but also a Die Zauberflöte from the same year.

Of her Gilda in the 1967 matinee broadcast of *Rigoletto* with Nicolai Gedda and Cornel MacNeil, Paul Jackson wrote:

To her credit, on this afternoon, the soprano often acts with the voice, that is, she applies realistic touches to notes and phrases, intending thereby (and, for the most part, succeeding) to make audible ecstasy, anguish, remorse, and other emotions. (*Start Up At The New Met*, Amadeus Press, 2006 pg. 34)

Her song repertoire was quite vast and encompassed music of Schubert, Schumann, Strauss, Wolf, Debussy, Chausson, Rachmaninov, Tchaikovsky, Rossini, and many other composers. One fascinating item was a C-Major "Vocalise" written for Peters in 1978, by the famous soviet composer, Aram Khachaturian. She sang it numerous times on tour and most notably at Carnegie Hall on January 17, 1985. Unfortunately, aside from live tapes that are circulating of her many recitals, very little of her song literature is available.

Roberta Peters and YouTube

Much has changed with the coming of the Internet and especially YouTube. The easy access to the site and the uploading of clips has made it a remarkable repository for great music and performances. YouTube has many clips of Peters in full throttle, everything from a 1951 Bravura aria from *The Bohemian Girl*, a 1952 Queen of the Night, many versions of "Caro nome" from *Rigoletto*, the bell song from *Lakmé* and, "Una voce poco fa" from *Il barbiere di Siviglia*.

Delibes—Bell Song (*Lakmé*)— Roberta Peters TV September, 1952
https://www.youtube.com/watch?v=quzDfqx5mgg

There are also a number of tribute compilations:
Roberta Peters Legend—Volume 1
https://www.youtube.com/watch?v=73Mls1K_I4s
Roberta Peters Legend—Volume 2
https://www.youtube.com/watch?v=OaZK1Vv-lMA
Roberta Peters Legend—Volume 3
https://www.youtube.com/watch?v=RAG8hYUYr_Y

There is a stunning "Lo Here the Gentle Lark" by Bishop from an early 1950s television program as well as a shadow song from *Dinorah* from a 1953 television appearance when she was only three years into her career.

Bishop—"Lo Here the Gentle Lark"— Roberta Peters TV c. 1952
https://www.youtube.com/watch?v=UN3cBNG8SAA
Meyerbeer—Shadow Song *Dinorah*— Roberta Peters TV c. 1953
https://www.youtube.com/watch?v=vE6vWLMIrTk

There is a video of a complete dress rehearsal of *L'Elisir d'Amore* with Carlo Bergonzi in 1989.
https://www.youtube.com/watch?v=Xk0oit3C3bk

Perhaps one of the most precious is a rare recording (on a static video) of her single performance of the great Mozart concert aria, "Popoli di Tessaglia" with its two infamous Gs above high C from a Salzburg performance in 1964.
https://www.youtube.com/watch?v=I08iDo9kMAk

Norwegian Television Recital—Roberta Peters 1962. Verdi, Rossini, Mozart—Despite some technical "blips" this is a fascinating video glimpse of the soprano during her prime.

https://www.youtube.com/watch?v=rWOsu0bQjMk

An unusual item is private footage from a 1991 recital Peters gave with Warren Jones at the piano. (Jones became her accompanist after the death of Larry Skrobacs.) She sings a remarkably pure "Caro nome" from *Rigoletto*, complete with a top E-flat in the cadenza, as well as Rachmaninov's "Here Beauty Dwells" and "Spring Waters." The voice is remarkably intact, with a beautiful, heady float. She was seventy-one.

https://www.youtube.com/watch?v=KC0qvUJvuPw

Live Aria Compilation—Roberta Peters—Operatic Arias

At the time this list was compiled (April, 2018), there was only one "aria" album of live material available: *Roberta Peters—Operatic Arias* on Legato CD. Although it was casually produced in regards to location and date information, it is, at least in terms of repertoire, an important release within Roberta Peters's discography. It is the only opportunity to hear her in repertoire she never recorded commercially.

Balfe—"I Dreamt I Dwelt in Marble Halls" *The Bohemian Girl* 1951—Peters sang in the important revival of this opera in London, in 1951. A complete live recording of the event does exist. Below is a link to excerpts from this performance.

https://www.youtube.com/watch?v=2sn4weX3BXw

Mozart—"Der hölle rache" *Die Zauberflöte*—1952

https://www.youtube.com/watch?v=LLJR_0dqYmA

David—"Charmant Oiseau" *La perle du Brésil*—1960 This includes an exquisite voice/flute cadenza. This was an aria that was a popular recital item and one that remained in her repertoire until at least the 1980s.

https://www.youtube.com/watch?v=BpBuVzNB9yc

Eckert—"Swiss Echo Song" 1960

https://www.youtube.com/watch?v=ThU0LBC5UCU

Flotow: "The Last Rose of Summer" (*Martha*) 1960

Meyerbeer—"Prayer and Barcarolle" *L'etoile du Nord* 1960

https://www.youtube.com/watch?v=lYgI2ZLYTjE

Offenbach—"Les Oiseau dans la charmille" *Contes d'Hoffmann* 1955

https://www.youtube.com/watch?v=gYqTNvnIIhg

Thomas—Mad Scene from *Hamlet* (a rarity) 1960

https://www.youtube.com/watch?v=BOL7Z2ALQiY

Verdi: Ah fors e lui (*La traviata*)—1972

There are also rare live performances of:

Auber's "Or son sola" from *Fra Diavolo* 1952

Bellini's final Scene from *La sonnambula*, 1953 and the polonaise from *I puritani*, 1953

www.ingramcontent.com/pod-product-compliance
Lightning Source LLC
Chambersburg PA
CBHW082115230426
43671CB00015B/2705